"Robeson . . . lives, overwhelmingly, in the hearts and minds of the people whom he touched, the people for whom he was an example, the people who gained from him the power to perceive and the courage to resist. It is not a sentimental question. He lived in our times, we live in his. . . . It is a matter of bearing witness to that force which moved among us."
—*James Baldwin*

Paul Robeson was inarguably one of the most important figures of the twentieth century. As this unprecedented biography makes clear, the essential facts of his public life are near legendary. Actor, singer, scholar, and activist—Robeson dominated his era. His father was an escaped slave; his mother, a descendent of distinguished freedmen. With a law degree from Columbia University, a professional football career, title roles in Eugene O'Neill's plays and in Shakespeare's *Othello*, and a concert and film career in America and Europe, Robeson redefined the black male image.

But an intensely private side to Robeson is now revealed in these pages. At last, we can know the whole man. Here is the intimate story of how the preacher's son emerged as a force of breathtaking courage, principle, and compassion. Haunted by childhood trauma and pitted against brutal racists, he battled against his enemies and his demons with a warrior's heart. Although his youth spanned the Harlem Renaissance and the rise of the Ku Klux Klan, he resisted politics for years. Flowering as an artist in Europe, he emerged as a fierce symbol of anticolonial and antifascist struggles around the world. This was the Paul Robeson who returned to New York as a pioneering superstar, ready to challenge America to keep its promise to his people.

The Undiscovered Paul Robeson sets out to explore the connection between the artist's soul and the passions that ruled it. Layering decades of personal conversations, extensive research, and rich insights with previously unpublished excerpts from the private diaries and letters of Paul and Eslanda Robeson, Paul Robeson, Jr., gives us a deeply felt and brilliantly conceived portrait of his father's defining struggles, triumphs, and humanity.

PAUL ROBESON, JR., is a freelance journalist, translator, and highly regarded lecturer on American and Russian history. He served as a personal aide to his father for over twenty years and has been a civil rights activist since the 1940s. He is the owner and archivist of the Paul Robeson and Eslanda Robeson Collection, which consists of over 50,000 items, including thousands of photographs and hundreds of audio recordings.

Jacket Design: Susan Olinsky
Jacket Photos: Courtesy of the Author

THE UNDISCOVERED
PAUL ROBESON

THE UNDISCOVERED PAUL ROBESON

An Artist's Journey, 1898–1939

Paul Robeson, Jr.

John Wiley & Sons, Inc.

New York • Chichester • Weinheim • Brisbane • Singapore • Toronto

Published by John Wiley & Sons, Inc.
Published simultaneously in Canada

ISBN 0-471-24265-9 (hc.)

ISBN 978-1-68442-230-2 (pbk.)

To my wife, Marilyn,
for her wise words,
and for her gift of innumerable moments
of inspiration and solace

Who shall let this world be beautiful? Who shall restore to men the glory of sunsets and the peace of quiet sleep? . . . It is the bounden duty of black America to begin this great work of the creation of beauty, of the preservation of beauty, of the realization of beauty.

W. E. B. DuBois, 1926

CONTENTS

Preface: Paul Robeson: "I Am Myself"   xiii

I.   MOTHERLESS CHILD (1898–1919)
  1   The Preacher's Son (1898–1915)   3
  2   In His Glory: Robeson of Rutgers (1915–1919)   20

II.   DESTINY AND DECISION (1919–1926)
  3   Essie (1919–1921)   43
  4   A Taste of Theater (1922)   55
  5   The Performer Triumphs (1923–1924)   71
  6   Seeker of Grace (1925–1926)   85

III. FROM PERFORMER TO ARTIST (1926–1932)
  7   "Ol' Man River" (1926–1928)   137
  8   "The Power to Create Beauty" (1928–1929)   153
  9   To Feed His Soul (1930)   165
 10   Troubled Spirit (1930–1931)   178
 11   Giver of Grace (1931–1932)   189

IV.   TRIBUNE OF A CULTURE (1933–1936)
 12   Film and the Politics of Culture (1933–1934)   203
 13   Test Run: London–Moscow–Hollywood (1934–1935)   218
 14   White Film, Black Culture (1936)   235

V.   To Be a Prophet (1936–1939)

15   Russia's Sun; Stalin's Shadow (1936–1937)   279
16   Spain's Ramparts: "The Artist Must Elect" (1938)   297
17   A Home in That Rock (1938–1939)   314

     Notes   337
     Index   367

Photo sections begin on pages 102 and 247

ACKNOWLEDGMENTS

For both insights and material, I am grateful to many sources. My most important source has been my father himself. Through many conversations over a period of forty-two years, he shared with me a significant part of his inner life and his world outlook. My collection of tape recordings of him speaking in both public and private settings was also of great help in defining his personal style.

My most comprehensive source consisted of the Paul Robeson and Eslanda Robeson Collections—some thirty thousand letters, diaries, notes, interviews, writings, speeches, photographs, programs, notebooks, books with marginalia, annotated music sheets, and news clippings—accumulated over five decades. Diaries written by my mother for the years 1924–1926, 1928, 1930–1934, 1938, and 1939 were especially helpful, providing not only unique insights but also background and color. My father's own 1934–1936 notes on culture, combined with his 1929 diary and extensive unpublished writings, offered important examples of his thinking during the critical years of his artistic, intellectual, and political growth.

This book could not have been written, nor could his legacy have been preserved, without the unwavering dedication of my mother, who meticulously saved the items that now constitute the Robeson Collections.

My father paid a fitting tribute both to her accomplishments and to her loyalty. On the dedication page of his autobiography, *Here I Stand*, he wrote:

> *To Eslanda Goode Robeson*, distinguished writer and anthropologist:
>
> thanks for many things—
>
> For your untiring labors in the interests of the African peoples;

For your devotion to the struggle of our folk here in America for full freedom;

For your constructive analyses of the momentous events at the United Nations;

For your deeply shared belief in and labors for the attainment of a lasting peace for all the peoples of the earth;

And deepest gratitude for your help and guidance over many years of struggle, aspiration, achievement, and the constant awareness of a better future for our children and grandchildren.

The many conversations I had over the years with my mother and with my parents' closest friends provided me with additional perceptions and nuances of my father's character.

I am especially grateful to the Paul Robeson Archives and its two directors: Roberta Yancy and Marilyn Robeson. For a decade, from 1973 through 1983, the Archives organized, preserved, duplicated, transcribed, and catalogued the materials that are now known as the Paul Robeson and Eslanda Robeson Collections. In addition, the Archives acquired and continues to administer an extensive collection of Robeson documentary film, feature film, and videotape from both domestic and foreign sources. This visual archive, combined with the Archives Collection of duplicates of the Robeson Collections, eased my research burden immensely.

Many thanks also to Harry Belafonte, who in 1973 produced the historic Seventy-fifth Birthday Salute to Paul Robeson at Carnegie Hall. This gala event marked the beginning of my father's return to America's cultural mainstream and financed the creation of the Paul Robeson Archives.

Many people helped with the conceptualization and writing of this book. I am indebted to them all, but I can mention only a few. Janet Hulstrand edited my first and most disorganized draft with loving care, helping me to pare it down and to focus on the essentials. Carole Hall, my editor at John Wiley & Sons, guided me through two difficult drafts, helping me to make critical decisions. Her skillful, considerate, and dedicated support allowed me to extend myself far beyond my expectations. Mary Dorian did an excellent job of copyediting the final manuscript, as did Lisa Vaia, associate managing editor.

My wife, Marilyn, has served as an invaluable reader-critic-consultant throughout this project, often providing me with new insights and unforeseen options.

My literary agent and friend, Lawrence Jordan, has patiently and tenaciously shepherded this project through good and bad times for five years with unflagging energy. He never lost faith in its ultimate success. For this and for his staunch moral support, my deepest thanks.

PREFACE

PAUL ROBESON: "I AM MYSELF"

There is a vast contradiction between Paul Robeson's current relative obscurity and the majesty of his achievements over a fifty-year career. Although he is the only African-American charter member of the National Theater Hall of Fame, his name does not appear in the index of *Notable Names in the American Theater,* and he has no entry of his own in *Famous Actors of the American Stage.* In 1944, at the peak of his career, *American Magazine* called him "America's number one Negro," yet five years later, in 1949, he was the nation's most vilified black man. For the next twenty-seven years, until his death in 1976, he was blacklisted as an artist in the United States.

The reason for his banishment from the nation's public life lies in his relentless challenge not only to anti-black stereotypes but also to the cultural foundations of American racism. Touted in the 1940s as the ultimate black role model and the "proof" that the American system worked for blacks, he nevertheless condemned the system for failing to provide the same opportunities for all African-Americans.

The media-nurtured myth that his political persecution stemmed from a "love affair" with communism, or that he was "duped" by Russian or American communists, has always been aimed at obfuscating his dedication to the goal of immediate and full freedom for his people. The truth is that my father was never a communist, nor did he ever seriously contemplate joining the Communist Party. His defense of the Soviet Union and his refusal to abandon his communist friends did not stem from a fascination with left-wing ideology or from personal pride. Rather, these decisions were based on his love of Russian culture and his conviction that the Soviet Union and communists in general were the most reliable opponents of Nazism, colonialism, and racism.

Another false but persistent image of my father is that he was a bitter, disillusioned recluse during his years of retirement. This myth, too, has been deliberately manufactured by the mass media. After illness had robbed him of his artistic and prophetic gifts, he felt no obligation, even to his admirers, to appear in public or to see anyone outside of his select personal circle. In retirement, he declared his personal life off-limits to all but those of his personal choice. At the same time, he basked in the glow of the massive civil rights victories of the sixties. Fully aware of his singular contribution, he needed no medals or acknowledgments.

I hope to tell his story as it was, and with no attempt at political, racial, or any other kind of "correctness." Since in life he despised sycophants, it would be an insult to his memory if I were to make the slightest attempt to satisfy those who crave a Robeson icon, those who wish to worship at a shrine, or those who are beguiled by his political persona. Driven for different reasons, they pose as staunch defenders of the Robeson image against all manner of real and imagined detractors. But Paul Robeson has nothing to fear from history, from the public, or from any critic; his true image speaks for itself and needs no polishing or protection. It is time simply to bear witness to history. As the late James Baldwin so aptly wrote:

> Robeson . . . lives, overwhelmingly, in the hearts and minds of the people whom he touched, the people for whom he was an example, the people who gained from him the power to perceive and the courage to exist. It is not a sentimental question. He lived in our times, we live in his. . . . It is a matter of bearing witness to that force which moved among us.[1]

Paul Robeson was an original. He had no counterpart. During his formative years, he cultivated the image of a free spirit who came and went, belonging to multitudes but owned by no one. Like a gentle summer breeze, or the moonlight shimmering on the surface of a still lake, he would not be confined. While he learned from and respected many outstanding people, he had no "role model," and did not aspire to be one. He worshiped "wisdom and knowledge of the ways of men," not heroes.[2] "To be as good as someone else is no high ideal," he said. "I am myself."[3]

In a 1934 essay titled "My Brother Paul," Rev. Benjamin C. Robeson, Paul's older brother and pastor of Harlem's Mother A.M.E. Zion Church, wrote:

> To understand Paul, one must know this. He moves by his inner revelations. Experience has taught him to do this. He never fails, is never disappointed or perplexed when he follows his flash. He is at perfect ease moving this way. In a moment he senses everything; he asks every question that comes to the normal mind, and answer or no answer, he obeys his flash.

In these pages, I have sought to recreate the development of the character he personally revealed to me. I have ventured an exploration of his vulnerabilities and his inner struggles, with a focus on the revelations that accompanied his growth as an artist. I have sought to portray the connection between his sense of himself and the preoccupations that dominated his life. It is my hope that those who do not know the essential facts of his career will discern its historic significance, and that those who already do, will discover more about the man behind it and learn about his motivation and reasoning. Robeson scholars and those who knew him personally will discover that there were pivotal aspects of his personality that he kept mainly to himself.

As I was writing this book, striving to ensure the accuracy of its contents, I realized that it would be naive of anyone who had experienced my father's aura, much less his son, to claim to be entirely objective about him. Therefore, I have not attempted to write a memoir or an exhaustively detailed life story, but rather an intimate, informal biography. In shaping it, my opinions and personal experiences with him are inevitably an element within the story.

It divides naturally into two main parts. The first, which I tell in this book, extends from his birth on April 9, 1898, through October 12, 1939. It is the story of the preacher's son, an emerging artist who departs for Europe to become a citizen of the world and returns as a prophetic superstar. In a second book, I will explore his life as a prophet in search of full freedom for his people.

There is much to be learned from and about this great artist who combined courage and gentleness, militancy, activism, and scholarship, and who functioned on the cutting edge of the social and political issues of his time. In 1944, on the occasion of his forty-sixth birthday, Mary McLeod Bethune, the well-respected educator, described him as "the tallest tree in our forest." Today, as I travel the world lecturing and talking about my father, I see that a veritable renaissance of interest has followed the 1998 celebration of the centennial of his birth. I hope this book introduces an ever-widening audience to his spirit and humanity.

I
MOTHERLESS
CHILD

(1898–1919)

(*Above*) Paul Robeson at age twelve (reclining in the bottom foreground), shortstop of the Westfield High School baseball team, although he was still in the seventh grade at Westfield Junior High. *From the personal collection of Paul Robeson, Jr.*

(*Below*) At Rutgers College, 1917. *Courtesy of Rutgers University.*

I

THE PREACHER'S SON

(1898–1915)

Paul Leroy Robeson's soul as an artist was formed in a journey through life that began on April 9, 1898. His father, the Reverend William Drew Robeson, vigorous at fifty-four, had been pastor of the Witherspoon Street Presbyterian Church in Princeton, New Jersey, for nineteen years. Paul's mother, Maria Louisa Bustill Robeson, was forty-five, partially blind from cataracts and suffering from disabling asthma.

Paul was the last of the seven Robeson children, two of whom had died in infancy.[1] His oldest surviving sibling, William Drew Jr. ("Bill"), born in 1881, was seventeen and attending high school; John Bunyan Reeve ("Reed") was twelve; Benjamin ("Ben") was six; and Marian was four. Now that Maria Louisa could no longer teach and tutor, the family lived more frugally than they had before. Paul's late arrival, though welcomed unreservedly, must have added to William Drew's burdens. But he believed that God would provide.

A dark-skinned man descended from the Ibo tribe of Nigeria, Reverend Robeson was of medium height with broad shoulders, and had an air of surpassing dignity. His calm manner was reinforced by a straight bearing and a penetrating look. Early on, Paul developed a complex bond with this devout paragon of personal discipline.

My father was always extremely reluctant to talk to me about his father's personality, as if some painful memories were associated with such recollections. Reverend Robeson was often silent and remote at home, rarely dispensing praise and unlikely to demonstrate affection. Though he was a devoted family man who was respected and loved by all the Robeson children, he was also feared. Quick to anger and short on humor, he could not have failed to demand excellence from each of them.

Distant and determinedly private, Reverend Robeson rarely talked to his children about his early years as a slave, or about his parents, Benjamin and Sabra. He expected his children to rise in the world.

Freedom was life's blood to Reverend Robeson. In 1858, as a fifteen-year-old field slave on the Roberson Plantation in Roberson-ville in eastern North Carolina, he had escaped with his older brother, Ezekiel, on the Underground Railroad to Pennsylvania.[2] There William Drew, as he was known, worked as a farmhand, earning enough money to aid his parents, whom he returned to visit twice during the next two years despite extreme hazards. When the Civil War began in April 1861, William Drew and Ezekiel joined a Union Army labor battalion that ultimately accompanied the advancing Union troops in 1864. According to family legend, the two brothers took up arms, along with others in the battalion, to repel a surprise attack by the Confederate general George Pickett on the Union-occupied city of New Bern, North Carolina.[3] At the end of the war, Ezekiel returned to North Carolina to work as a farmhand with his parents.

William Drew remained in Pennsylvania, went to a Freedmen's School, and in 1867 managed to enter the one-year preparatory class of Lincoln University, a pioneer black college. He eventually completed Lincoln's four-year bachelor of arts program. In 1876, he was awarded the degrees of master of arts and bachelor of sacred theology.[4]

During his studies at Lincoln, William Drew met Maria Louisa Bustill, a young Philadelphia teacher, who frequently visited her uncle's house in the nearby town of Lincoln. On July 11, 1878, she married the earnest divinity student who excelled in ancient languages. Maria Louisa was tall and handsome. She was known for her gentle, compassionate, sunny disposition. One day she would serve as William Drew's intellectual companion, help him compose his sermons, and act as his right hand in his community work.

The social gulf between the runaway son of North Carolina field slaves and the elder daughter of the Bustills of Philadelphia was enormous. The Bustills, a family of mixed African, English Quaker, and Leni-Lenape Indian stock, could trace their American ancestry as far back as 1608 and had produced many outstanding men and women. Cyrus Bustill, Maria Louisa's great-grandfather, who was born a slave in Burlington, New Jersey, in 1732, became apprenticed to a local baker, learned the trade, and soon bought his freedom. He went on to become a baker with a thriving business that extended far beyond his local customers. During the Revolutionary War, he baked bread for George Washington's troops, and in 1787 he was one of the founders of the Free African Society, the first mutual aid organization of African-Americans.

Through the years, the Bustills became teachers, artists, businesspeople, and pioneers in many professions. Prior to the Civil War, members of the family played key roles in running and maintaining the Underground Railroad. Maria Louisa's uncle Joseph had been one of the organizers of the Underground Railroad terminal in Harrisburg, Pennsylvania. After the war, the Bustills helped lead the fight for black rights.[5] Paul would grow up to be both proud and conflicted about his mother's distinguished family, who looked down on his father's kin living nearby in Princeton.

By the time of Paul's birth, the Robesons had become pillars of Princeton's sizable, tightly knit black community. As pastor, William Drew had developed Witherspoon Church into a center of civic and social activity. He had also become an effective defender of the community's interests, and was universally respected. However, his occasional outspokenness provoked certain high-ranking members of Princeton's white elite.

When Paul was two, his brother Bill tried to enroll at Princeton University, but he was rebuffed. Refusing as usual to compromise on matters of principle, William Drew appealed in person to Woodrow Wilson, then president of Princeton, for Bill's enrollment. Reverend Robeson refused to accept any of Wilson's repeated and forceful attempts to avoid a direct response, compelling the future president of the United States to declare angrily that Princeton did not accept "colored."[6] It was long rumored in Princeton's black community that this defiance cost William Drew his pastorate.

A wealthy white Presbyterian church had built Witherspoon for its black members after having accommodated them in balcony seats for decades. But ultimate control remained with the white authorities, and one day they took William Drew's pastorate from him on a spurious pretext. Despite his well-argued statement of defense at his hearing and the near-unanimous support of his congregation, the decision to remove him from his pastorate (which he had appealed) was announced as final on November 17, 1900.

Paul was probably in the audience sitting with his mother, brothers, and sister when Reverend Robeson preached his last sermon at Witherspoon Church on January 27, 1901. Well known throughout the region for his dramatic power and inspiring messages, the reverend filled the sanctuary with his deep, melodious bass voice. Paul would always recall it as the greatest speaking voice he ever heard. On that day, William Drew made no direct mention of his dismissal. But he did intimate that his departure stemmed from his refusal to curtail his determined criticism of social injustice.[7]

On January 29, 1901, two days after William Drew had preached his farewell sermon at Witherspoon Church, George C. White, of William Drew's home state of North Carolina and the nation's sole remaining black congressman, defiantly addressed the U.S. House of Representatives. His term was coming to an end, he said, and the electoral rigging legitimized by the U.S. Supreme Court in the service of white rule had denied him any hope of reelection. His departure, he noted, was "perhaps the Negroes' temporary farewell to the American Congress; but we say, Phoenix-like he will rise up some day to come again."[8] So too would William Drew rise again.

The Robeson family had to leave the comfortable Witherspoon Street parsonage and move to a smaller house on Green Street around the corner. Bill boarded at Lincoln University and two years later enrolled in the University of Pennsylvania Medical School. William Drew gave himself to making a living. Paul would write about this period later in his autobiography:

> He was still the dignified Reverend Robeson to the community, and no man carried himself with greater pride. Not once did I hear him complain of the poverty and misfortune of those years. Serene and undaunted, he struggled to earn a livelihood and see to our education. He got a horse and wagon, and began to earn his living hauling ashes. This was his work at the time I first remember him, and I recall the growing mound of ashes dumped in our backyard. A fond memory remains of our horse, a mare named Bess, whom I grew to love and who loved me. My father also went into the hack

business and as a coachman drove students around town and on trips to the seashore.

Mostly I played. There were the vacant lots for ball games, and the wonderful moments when Bill [then in his mid-twenties], vacationing from college where he played on the team, would teach me how to play football. He was my first coach, and over and over again on a weed-grown lot he would put me through the paces— how to tackle a man so he stayed tackled, how to run with the ball.[9]

Paul chose not to mention that the meager rations of the Robesons in Princeton had to be supplemented by relatives in North Carolina who sent up "cornmeal, greens, yams, peanuts and other goodies in bags." From that time on, he relished a good meal in a way that those who have always been well fed do not.[10]

On the morning of January 19, 1904, Reverend Robeson went to Trenton on business. He told twelve-year-old Ben to stay home from school to help Maria Louisa, by now nearly blind, to clean the living room. All the other children except Paul, who was still at home, were away at school. According to Ben and Marian:

[Maria Louisa] decided first to take up the carpet, but the stove was in the way; she and Ben conferred about it, and decided she would lift the stove while he pulled away the carpet underneath. The stove had a sliding front door which opened as she raised the front legs, and a hot coal fell out. It set fire to her dress, but neither of them saw it until the blaze had caught on well and she felt it burn her feet and legs. She tried to beat it out with her hands which were terribly burned. Ben tried frantically to help her, but her full skirts were a dreadful hindrance. When he realized the task was beyond him, he rushed out of the house terrified, screaming for help. A neighbor who was passing came to his mother's aid, put out the flames, tore off her hot clothing, sent Ben for a doctor, and did what he could to ease her pain. The doctor found that her skirts had partially smothered the flames close to her body and that her feet, legs and hands were horribly burned; part of her hair was burned off, and she had even swallowed some of the flame. He used quarts and quarts of linseed oil to try to alleviate her suffering, but she lay in dreadful agony. "This is the way I am to go," she said courageously, "and because God intended it I am content."[11]

She survived long enough to say farewell to her heartbroken husband that evening. Then the doctors gave her a heavy dose of opiates, she lapsed into unconsciousness, and she died.

This tragedy engulfed Paul, leaving an emotional wound that may have never healed fully. So thoroughly would he block the events of that day out of his memory that he would never recall where he was at the time. Long afterward Paul wrote that he could not remember her, or the accident, though his recollection of other things went back to times before it. He remembered only "her lying in her coffin, the funeral, and the relatives who came."[12]

Ben recalled that Paul might well have been in the house: "Paul just suddenly showed up in the midst of all the confusion. I hadn't seen him earlier, and no one, including Paul himself, could remember where he had been. If he'd been out playing or at a neighbor's house, someone would have remembered it. It's something he never talked about, and we didn't bring it up." Contrary to myth, Paul may have been present, seen his mother burning, and been so terrified that he ran and hid.[13]

A residue of fear, guilt, self-doubt, and discomfort with intimacy would have burdened a sensitive child for a lifetime. Reverend Robeson tried to ease his six-year-old son's trauma. "Pop," as Paul came to call him, was reliable, predictable, and available—a secure home base.

The affluent and light-skinned Bustills distanced themselves from the dark-skinned and poor William Drew. Only the Robeson relatives helped him through the hard days ahead with whatever they could spare. In Paul's autobiography, he wrote with tenderness about his feelings of deep attachment to the people who provided nourishment and comfort to his father. And significantly, those feelings are inextricably interwoven with his first awareness of music. Infused virtually from the cradle with African-American culture, he recognized its powerful emotional expression in diverse types of music.

> Hard-working people, and poor, most of them, in worldly goods— but how rich in compassion! There was the honest joy of laughter in these homes, folk-wit and story, hearty appetites for life as for the nourishing greens and black-eyed peas and cornmeal bread they shared with me. Here in this little hemmed-in world where home must be theater and concert hall and social center, there was a

warmth of song. Songs of love and longing, songs of trials and triumphs, deep-flowing rivers and rollicking brooks, hymn-song and
ragtime ballad, gospels and blues, and the healing comfort to be
found in the illimitable sorrow of the spirituals.

Yes, I heard my people singing!—in the glow of the parlor
coal-stove and on summer porches sweet with lilac air, from choir
loft and Sunday morning pews—and my soul was filled with their
harmonies.[14]

At the time and for years to come, the spirituals were a source of
consolation and self-expression for Paul. In his mature years, he
would say that singing them released a flood of deep feelings and, on
occasion, a transcendence that could be called a state of grace.

Photographs of Paul as late as 1913 reveal a haunting sadness
in his eyes.[15] There was no denying it—Paul was often alone, left to
his thoughts. Nevertheless, in later years he underplayed this loneliness. "There must have been moments when I felt the sorrows of a
motherless child," he wrote in his autobiography.

Paul's older brothers and sister were back and forth from school:
Reed and Bill were at universities, and Marian was at the Scotia
boarding school in North Carolina. Only Ben, who was six years
older than Paul, stayed behind until 1906 to look after him, and then
Ben left for prep school in North Carolina.

William Drew, now sixty-two, remained a friend and companion
to his eight-year-old son, taking him along on visits to his former
parishioners and drawing him into church life in the hope that ultimately he might enter the ministry. "How proudly, as a boy, I walked
at his side, my hand in his," Paul recalled. The two of them also
shared a love for checkers, and they spent many a winter evening in
the parlor engrossed in play. They didn't speak much but were "wonderfully happy together." The terrible memory of Maria Louisa's death
dimmed. Paul grew accustomed to his father supervising his schoolwork on a day-to-day basis as a stern, uncompromising taskmaster.

To satisfy William Drew, high grades were not enough: the goal
was always *perfect* grades. At the Princeton elementary school that
Paul attended—for black students only, in accordance with the
town's rigid segregation—the principal, Abraham Denny, a classmate

of Reverend Robeson's at Lincoln University, loved his students and created a lively learning environment. Paul flourished academically as William Drew tested him on his lessons, oversaw his reading, and trained him to recite lines of classic poetry and prose. It was to this intensive guidance that Paul would later credit his phenomenal powers of concentration.[16]

Through daily interaction with his father, Paul began to absorb, mostly by example, the credo that was to last a lifetime. First was the importance of living up to his individual potential, rather than worrying about winning for its own sake. Next came the strong belief in his ability to achieve. Then there was the concept that all people must be respected and that the entire human race is a single, though diverse, family of equals. Paul also noticed that William Drew was a model of compassion for others. Paul observed his dedication and accountability to the community, not merely to the pursuit of wealth and influence, but to his commitment to principle as well, even at the cost of personal sacrifice.[17]

With the experience of slavery deep in his bones, William Drew began explicitly to teach Paul the techniques of survival in a viciously racist climate. He insisted that Paul must never appear to be challenging the claim of white superiority. "Climb up if you can," he would say, "but always show that you are grateful. . . . Above all, do nothing to give them cause to fear you." However, while he counseled the show of humility, Reverend Robeson manifested not even a hint of servility. Somehow, he managed to convey this dignity without any overt show of anger or resistance. Paul learned this lesson well and added his own twist—he had an affable, smiling demeanor, combined with an irresistible empathy for his peers.[18]

Paul was insulated from white Princeton by his almost exclusive confinement to the fairly large local black community and his attendance at an all-black school. He was not old enough to work for white people and had very little connection with them. There were some white children among his playmates, including a boy about his age, whose father owned a grocery a few doors from the Robeson house.[19] But Paul belonged to a cohesive community where his identity was both powerful and strongly reinforced.

Many members of Witherspoon recognized something extraordinary in their former preacher's motherless son. They regarded him as a child of destiny. He wrote in his autobiography:

I early became conscious—I don't quite know how—of a special feeling of the Negro community for me. I was no different from the other kids of the neighborhood, and yet the people claimed to see something special about me. Whatever it was, and no one really said, they felt I was destined for great things to come. Somehow they were sure of it. I wondered at times about this notion that my future would be linked with the longed-for better days to come, but I didn't worry about it. Being grown up was a million years ahead. Now was the time for play.[20]

The Robeson family moved away from Princeton in 1907, when Paul was nine. Reverend Robeson had finally given up on the Presbyterian Church and switched to the African Methodist Episcopal Zion denomination. Assigned a minor pastorate in Westfield, New Jersey, with no church building, he had a small potential congregation. Though far fewer African-Americans lived in Westfield than in Princeton, the predominantly working-class white population was more accepting of blacks than Princeton's elite.

William Drew started building a small church from the ground up. Paul helped his father carry bricks to the bricklayers. Meanwhile, they lived in the attic over a grocery store where William Drew worked, and they washed up in a shacklike extension at the rear of the store. It was a difficult transition for Paul. His close relatives, who had lived just around the corner from him in Princeton, were now thirty miles away; the black community was far smaller than Princeton's; and his closest brother, Ben, had gone away to prep school. Visiting Princeton's black community still meant "being at home."[21] Nevertheless, Paul gradually adjusted, and William Drew achieved a near miracle by finishing his construction of the small St. Luke African Methodist Episcopal Zion Church on Downer Street, complete with a parsonage, in a little more than a year.

In the three years he lived in Westfield, Paul expanded his horizons in a seamless progression of busy days. He came to know more white people, frequently visiting the homes of his working-class schoolmates and always receiving a friendly welcome. Still, he felt the subtle difference between his unquestioned belonging to the black community and his qualified acceptance by whites. Fifty years later, he would comment, "I wasn't conscious of it at the time, but now I realize that my easy moving between the two racial communities was rather exceptional. For one thing, I was the respected preacher's son, and then, too, I was popular with the other boys and girls because of my skill at sports and studies."[22]

Paul's popularity with his peers was probably due far more to his athletic skills than to his proficiency at his studies. Practicing sports and playing games stood him in good stead in escaping his grief over his mother's death. Some days he would finish his homework early, practice by himself, and then play with his schoolmates until darkness fell.

Since Westfield had too few black children for a segregated school system—unlike Princeton—Paul attended fifth and sixth grades in Westfield's integrated elementary school and then entered seventh grade in the integrated junior high school. Tall and gangly at twelve, but wiry strong, fast, and exceedingly agile, he was already capable of competing at the high school level. Ben, who by this time was attending Biddle University,[23] had taken over from Bill as Paul's baseball and football coach with stellar results: when Paul was still in seventh grade, the Westfield High School baseball team recruited him to play shortstop as a regular.[24]

At about the time of William Drew's move to Westfield, Paul's brother Reed—hotheaded and aggressively independent at twenty-one—suddenly turned up as a dropout from Lincoln University at the start of his senior year. Paul was overjoyed by his older brother's return, but Reverend Robeson was deeply aggrieved by Reed's failure to complete his college education and by his cavalier refusal to offer any explanation or apology for such an affront to Robeson family values. Nevertheless, despite the sacrifices he had made to send Reed to college, William Drew swallowed his anger. He even helped Reed to acquire a horse and carriage so that he could go into the hack business.

It was an uneasy peace. Many years later, Paul described its unraveling:

My father was sorely disappointed in this son and disapproved of his carefree and undisciplined ways. Yet I admired this rough older brother, and I learned from him a quick militancy against racial insults and abuse. Many was the time that Reed, resenting some remark by a Southern gentleman-student, would leap down from his coachman's seat, drag out the offender and punish him with his fists. He always carried for protection a bag of small, jagged rocks—a weapon he used with reckless abandon whenever the occasion called for action.

Inevitably there were brushes with the Law, and then my father, troubled in heart, would don his grave [formal] frock-coat and go to get Reed out of trouble again. But this happened once too often, and one day I stood sadly and silently as Pop told Reed he would have to leave—he must live his life elsewhere because his example was a dangerous one for his young brother Paul.

I remember Reed with love. "Don't ever take low," was the lesson he taught me. "Stand up and hit them harder than they hit you!" When the many have learned that lesson, everything will be different.[25]

Paul could not help feeling responsible when Reed left around 1909, ultimately settling down in Detroit, where he had a minor career in the hotel business.

In 1910, William Drew posed for a formal photographic portrait. Looking heavier but composed, his thoughts seemed to be elsewhere. He had, rather abruptly, regained much of his former high status. The church hierarchy assigned Reverend Robeson to pastor the St. Thomas A.M.E. Zion Church in Somerville, New Jersey, about halfway between Westfield and Princeton. Once again, the black community of Somerville was not nearly as large as Princeton's, but the church was a substantial one serving a fairly large parish in the surrounding area. The Robesons were again "somebodies" by the time Paul graduated from eighth grade at Somerville's small "colored school." At the closing ceremonies in June 1911, he gave a rousing oration that included Patrick Henry's cry, "Give me liberty, or give me death," undoubtedly thinking of Reed.

Arriving at Somerville High School, Paul had to stand tall to carry the day. There were only a dozen blacks in a student body of two hundred. And the principal, Dr. Ackerman, was consistently hostile, relishing any opportunity to demean him. When Paul joined the glee club, Miss Vosseler, the music teacher, had to overcome the principal's angry opposition to having Paul as the soloist.[26] But Paul was already aware that he had an unusual singing voice and a natural talent for using it. One day, he and brothers Bill and Ben had been hanging out together, and Bill had suggested they sing a few tunes. As Ben told the story more than twenty years later:

> We started off with gusto. We were making one of those minors known only to home-loving groups; Paul was bearing down on it with boyish glee; in fact, all of us were. Out of all the discord, Bill yelled: "Wait a minute, hit that note again, Paul." Paul hit out of the lot, and Bill said: "Paul, you can sing, but just to be sure that we have no accident, I want you to sing 'Annie Laurie.' If you satisfy me, the Robeson manse will issue its first musical diploma." Paul had to satisfy him to have any peace. Bill listened as he warbled, and concluded: "Paul, you *can* sing."

For years, Paul had been singing mainly for himself. Blessed with perfect relative pitch, he could comfortably sing a capella, readily shifting keys to suit his adolescent voice. But after his experience with Bill and Ben, Paul became more conscious of his voice as an instrument for entertaining others; when called upon to perform, he sang rather than recited. The emerging self-awareness of his singing talent—as well as of his other abilities—became a source of comfort and assurance in a difficult social climate. In his autobiography he remembered wryly:

> Miss Vosseler, the music teacher who directed our glee club, took a special interest in training my voice. Anna Milner, English teacher, paid close attention to my development as a speaker and debater; and it was she who first introduced me to Shakespeare's works. Miss Vandeveer, who taught Latin, seemed to have no taint of racial prejudice; and Miss Bagg, instructor in chemistry and physics, made every effort to make me feel at ease in the school's social life of which she was in charge. Miss Bagg urged me to attend the various parties and dances, and when I did so, it was she who was the first to dance with me. But despite her encouragement, I shied away from most of these social affairs. There was always the feeling that—well, something unpleasant might happen; for the two worlds of white and Negro were nowhere more separate than in social life.[27]

William Drew kept close track of Paul's studies, placing special emphasis on Latin and classic literature, but it was Bill who took charge of cultivating Paul's lively mind during frequent visits home. The perpetual student, Bill had been nicknamed "Deep Stuff" by those with whom he worked. Years later, Paul would recall that Bill was the smartest member of the family:

> For me Bill was the principal source of learning how to study. During my high school years in Somerville, Bill was often at home, between colleges and railroad runs, and he spent much time directing my studies. He was never satisfied when I came up with a correct answer. "Yes, but *why?*" he would insist sharply. What was the relation of one fact to another? What was the system, the framework, of a given study? When I couldn't explain, Bill would quickly and clearly demonstrate the mystery to me; and to my constant amazement, he could do that, after a very short inquiry, even in subjects he had not previously studied.

Paul admired Bill's analytical mind and dogged ambition. When Bill dropped out of the University of Pennsylvania Medical School for lack of funds, he supported himself for years afterward by working on the railroads as a Pullman porter and as a redcap at train stations. Some years later, he enrolled in another medical college (Paul recalled that it was in Boston), from which he graduated only to find out that the college was not properly accredited. Ultimately, he would obtain his M.D. degree in 1921 from Howard University College of Medicine in Washington, D.C., at the age of forty.[28]

Sister Marian also remained close to Paul, taking care of him even though she was not at home as much as Ben or Bill. She brought to the Robeson household "the blessing of laughter," and although she did the cooking when she was home, she left the dishes for him.[29]

Self-esteem and mutual respect were cornerstones of Paul's relationship with his family. All of the internal tensions he felt at school and at home, he learned to curb. So it was rarely apparent to anyone that he suppressed a violent temper.

Playing pool in the local pool hall one afternoon with some black friends, Paul encountered an older black youth who picked a fight with him and hit him with a pool cue. Paul grabbed one of the solid ivory pool balls, backed away, and shot it at his assailant's head with all his might. The ball barely missed its target, but the force behind it was so great that it blasted a hole through a paneled wood wall. On the spot, Paul resolved never again to let the disturbing power of his anger spin out of control: he knew he would probably kill some-one if he did.

From then on, when he felt emotional pressures that were too great to redirect, he withdrew into his inner world in solitude for a respite. This became a lifetime pattern that he used with consistent success. Now he adopted an exceedingly quiet, nonresentful posture.

He preferred to avoid confrontation, but he seldom ran from it. If cornered, he made clear to would-be assailants that he would not submit willingly. Almost always, potential opponents sensed the resolve behind his placid manner, and as they hesitated, he would politely and graciously move past them—winning the conflict with-out actually having to engage in it. This discipline was self-imposed. His father had relentlessly demanded courtesy and restraint, and Paul had internalized the lessons.

However, things were different on the athletic field, where he could legitimately respond in a physical manner. By his senior year in high school, Paul was over six feet tall and weighed 190 pounds. He achieved such dominance in football that state officials changed the rules to neutralize him. Double-team and triple-team blocking were legalized, but still he couldn't be stopped. On offense, he played fullback. But it was on defense, where he backed up the line, that he truly found an outlet. He gained a statewide reputation as a deadly tackler who could hit with unparalleled ferocity.

Paul paid a heavy price for his aggressiveness. In a late-season 1914 game against Phillipsburg, rated the best team in New Jersey at the time, the officials looked the other way as the entire Phillips-burg team constantly piled up on him every time he carried the ball. Even so, he scored three touchdowns in a 24–18 loss that many called the greatest high school football game ever played in New Jer-sey. Finally, he was forced to the sidelines with a broken nose and a broken collarbone. The lack of intervention by the officials, and even by his teammates and coaches, left him deeply embittered. It became linked in his mind with mob violence against blacks. William Drew, who attended almost all of Paul's games, had undoubtedly watched in horror and prayed for his son's survival.[30]

True, the young Paul was a gifted athlete. In baseball he also played the position of catcher, and in basketball he played guard.[31] Ben continued to be his coach, and, since the professional level of the Somerville High School coaches was relatively low, Ben's instruction, based on actual play at the college level, was invaluable to Paul's development. But that day in Phillipsburg, it was the depth of Paul's fiery spirit that was tested more profoundly than his physical prowess. He passed the test, but his rage at the brutalization to which he was subjected with such impunity never dissipated.

The A.M.E. Zion religious faith ran deep, connecting the Robeson men. Paul sang solo in the senior choir at this point and often taught Sunday school classes. Occasionally he even preached a sermon from the pulpit when his father was called away. Ben had decided to follow his father into the ministry, and William Drew hoped that Paul would ultimately do the same. He didn't push his son in this direction, but he continued to guide him toward oratory, giving him suggestions for classic pieces to recite and maintaining close supervision of his diction. Even in those years, there were many who remarked about the perfection of Paul's enunciation and his mellifluous speaking voice. On occasion, Paul continued to accompany his father on his rounds visiting parishioners. To William Drew, it seemed that Paul was ideally suited to be a minister. But Paul had no vocation in mind, and he wrestled with the decision, hoping it could wait until he was in college.[32]

As ambivalent as Paul was about being groomed to succeed Reverend Robeson in the ministry, he had always assumed he would follow his father and brother Bill to Lincoln University, where he would be free from the necessity of coping daily with the racial prejudice at a white college. However, in his senior year, he heard about a competitive examination open to all New Jersey high school students. The prize was a four-year scholarship to Rutgers College, then an exclusive private school with a student body of 500 white males. A full scholarship would relieve Reverend Robeson of the burden of paying tuition.

William Drew liked the idea. In truth, he had wanted one of his sons to attend an esteemed white university ever since Bill had been refused entry to Princeton. He felt strongly that at least one of his sons should have such a broadening experience—one to which he himself could never have aspired. Besides, Rutgers was only fifteen miles away in New Brunswick, so Paul could remain close to family and friends.

William Drew convinced Paul to enter the scholarship contest, and together they threw themselves into preparing for it. They soon realized that the high school principal, Dr. Ackerman, had deliberately failed to notify Paul about a preliminary test covering the subjects studied in the first three years of high school that he could have taken at the end of his junior year. Consequently, Paul was faced with an examination that embraced the entire four-year course in the same three-hour period in which the other competitors would be tested only on the senior year's work. However, this handicap served only to intensify his resolve to win.

He worked intensively but also systematically. Bill's academic coaching had trained him well in applying his critical reasoning skills and in sorting out the essential from the superfluous detail. It was, according to Paul, "a decisive point" in his life—it was not just that he won the scholarship to Rutgers; he had proven to himself beyond any doubt that he was not inferior to anyone.[33]

In the late spring of 1915, Paul also entered a statewide oratorical contest. His text was Wendell Phillips's famous abolitionist oration on the great black liberator of Haiti, Toussaint L'Ouverture:

> My children, France comes to make us slaves. God gave us liberty; France has no right to take it away. Burn the cities, destroy the harvests, tear up the roads with cannon, poison the wells, show the white man the hell he comes to make!

The audience apparently suspended its wariness. Despite the symbolism involved in the black youth's passionate recital of these incendiary lines, they gave Paul an unreserved ovation. The judges only awarded him third place, but Paul would long remember the sound of the audience affirming his victory.[34]

Soon after, Paul packed his suitcase and headed for the Imperial resort hotel in Narragansett Pier, Rhode Island, where he joined Ben for the second year. The first year he had worked there as a lowly kitchen boy, but now he advanced to dining room busboy, while Ben returned to his waiter's job. Many other young blacks, including a number of star football players from black colleges, were employed at that hotel and at others in town. Forty-three years later, Paul wrote about his relationship with Ben as if it were almost magical, despite the demeaning drudgery that was associated with it:

Closer to me in age than my other brothers, Ben was my favorite.
It was he who first took me out into the world beyond our small-
town life. When I was in high school, Ben got a job for the summer in Narragansett Pier, in Rhode Island, where many Negro
students found vacation-time employment in the resorts of the rich.
I went along with Ben to serve as kitchen boy. My work—and I'm
sure I have never again in all my life worked quite so hard—began
at 4:00 A.M., and it was late evening before I emerged from the
mountains of pots and pans I scrubbed, the potatoes I peeled, [and]
the endless tasks ordered by the chef, the second cooks and helpers.
But always there was the comforting presence of brother Ben,
around somewhere, keeping [an] eye out for the kid brother.

This year, Paul and Ben devoted their free time at Narragansett
to playing touch football on the beaches and playing baseball for the
hotel team. Under Ben's watchful eye, Paul ran through special workouts to prepare for the Rutgers football team tryouts, determined to
be ready, both physically and mentally.[35]

2

IN HIS GLORY: ROBESON OF RUTGERS

(1915–1919)

Founded in 1766, Rutgers College was one of America's oldest. On its picturesque campus on the banks of the Raritan River in New Brunswick, New Jersey, generations of white men had been steeped in the finest educational and athletic traditions. Paul, only the third black student in the history of Rutgers, cut a solitary figure when he arrived on campus in September 1915.

His freshman interview with the dean of students was brief and impersonal. Barely looking up from the papers on his desk, the dean made a few cursory remarks as he handed up Paul's freshman orientation packet. He concluded by crisply announcing that Paul could not live in the student dormitory because there was no other black student on campus for him to room with. Paul soon found a warm and welcoming haven at the home of the Cummings family on Morell Street in the nearby New Brunswick black community, but in that moment his sense of dislocation must have been acute.

Although Paul continued to radiate confidence, he experienced severe culture shock. Most of the students stared at him either condescendingly or with open contempt; he sat entirely alone in the cafeteria, where the white female servers avoided eye contact with him, and most of his professors ignored the open hostility often expressed toward him by the other students in the classroom. Only his English professor would reach out that week, making Paul feel welcome in his class.

Paul hid whatever anxiety he felt. Years later, all of his white professors and classmates remembered him as a handsome and imposing six-feet-two, 200-pound seventeen-year-old who was quietly genial and pleasantly accommodating, with a polite and friendly manner and an irresistible smile. They remembered his deep, musical bass voice and large, penetrating eyes that appeared to change texture with changes in his moods. He was referred to as an entertaining conversationalist who enjoyed listening to others and a natural singer who loved to share his musical talent. Above all, they recalled that he was an easy mixer and an uncomplaining good fellow who never expressed anger.[1]

A few people, however, immediately grasped that Paul concealed a high level of anger. One was football coach Foster Sanford, who had watched Paul play for nearby Somerville High School. "Coach Sandy" was considered by the football world to be one of the greatest coaches in the nation and was preparing a strong team of veteran players for what he hoped would be a championship season. He called Paul in for a chat his first day on campus. A graying, powerfully built man of medium height with a square jaw and a benevolent look, Sanford matter-of-factly offered Paul his hand and put him at ease. However, his laconic message was not reassuring.

The veterans on the team had rebelled against even the idea of a black player trying out for "their" team, and it had taken some time for Sanford to suppress threats of a strike. This was why Paul had not been invited to preseason practice. However, Sanford was determined to give Paul a fair chance to make the team, but he would have to start out at the bottom with the nonvarsity "scrubs" and without training table privileges. It would be a tough task to make the varsity under the best of circumstances but next to impossible after missing preseason practice, so Sanford said he would understand if Paul preferred to wait until next season.

Paul replied unhesitatingly: "I'd like to make a try at it, Mr. Sanford."

"Call me Coach," Sanford replied gruffly. "Report to the equipment room tomorrow before practice. Here are some instructions you should study beforehand."[2]

The next day, disconcerted but excited and hopeful, Paul trotted onto the practice field. The warm-up exercises, and even the one-on-one blocking and tackling routines, proceeded in the standard way, except for the fact that no one but the coaches spoke to him. He shrugged off this silent treatment, concentrating intently on what was happening on the field. Then the scrimmage began, with Sanford positioning Paul at left defensive end.

The first varsity play was run to the right side, but Paul, having diagnosed it immediately, crossed over from the left side and tackled the runner after a short gain. The next play went up the middle; again Paul was in on the tackle. The next three plays were run directly at Paul's position. The first two gained only a yard each, and the third was thrown for a loss. Then the varsity team ganged up on Paul continuously for more than a dozen plays, battering him so unmercifully that he was finally forced to limp off the field. His fellow scrubs said nothing; Sanford and his assistant coaches said nothing.

Battered and despondent, Paul went home. He had no broken bones—only bruises and a sprained shoulder. But his resolve was shaken. He was reminded of the championship high school game the previous year, when the opposing team had ganged up on him to break his nose and collarbone in full view of the crowd, the officials, and the coaches. The cold brutality suggested a lynching.

Paul told Ben that he intended to quit and attend Lincoln University the next semester. He was sick of being brutalized by white people. But he just didn't know how to tell their father. Ben, although not much of a talker, knew his younger brother's psychology well and delivered an inspired, impromptu sermon to dissuade him. Paul wasn't just representing himself or the family; his was a mission on behalf of all the black boys who wanted the chance to play major college football. He owed it to his race; he couldn't just quit. "Besides," Ben concluded, "you know you can make it if you decide to."

Paul recovered his strength, bolstered his resolve, and went back out to practice. Then holding his own in a tough scrimmage, he was subjected to a sneak attack. He had made a clean, hard tackle and momentarily lay facedown with his arms outstretched to catch his breath. Just then, passing by on his way back to the huddle, a varsity halfback named Frank Kelly deliberately stomped on the fingers of Paul's right hand. The bones didn't break, but the pain was excruciating. Enraged even more by the insult than by his pain, Paul leaped to his feet. But he did not attack Kelly. Instead, he harnessed the immense energy of his anger and coiled his body in preparation for the next play. In his mind he focused on avenging an insult not just to himself but to the entire black race.

The next play was run directly at him, with Kelly carrying the ball. Paul uncoiled, hurling aside the blockers, and drove his shoulder into the onrushing Kelly with a thump heard across the practice field. Then, in a single coordinated motion, he planted his feet widely, wrapped his arms tightly around Kelly, and with an explosive effort heaved Kelly over his head. He was in full control of his rage, but only he knew that; his murderous body language and facial expression frightened all the onlookers, who feared he might kill Kelly.

Coach Sanford screamed the first thing that came into his mind: "Robeson! You're on the varsity!" Paul silently dropped the terrified halfback to the ground and stalked off the field, holding his injured fingers.

He recalled this incident as a symbol of the savagery of America's popular culture. At the time, he experienced a liberating revelation. It was as if he had used the energy of his rage to convince a group of hostile white men that he might kill at least one of them in self-defense if they attacked him. For the first time in his life, he had cast off his father's cautionary strictures about never angering white people. At last he had been able to savor the heady feeling of siding with his rebellious brother, Reed.

Twenty-nine years later, Paul was still deeply concerned with his assertion of this point. On January 16, 1944, in an interview with Robert Van Gelder of the *New York Times*, he recalled how he made the Rutgers football team: "The ball carrier was a first class back named Kelly. I wanted to kill him, and I meant to kill him. . . . I was going to smash him so hard to the ground that I'd break him right in two."

I was puzzled when I read this passage, since my father had previously told me that his real objective had been only to frighten the onlookers into *thinking* he might kill Kelly. His intention had not been to harm him. I asked my father why he deliberately gave such a false impression of his intentions. His reply was memorable. In a quiet, measured tone that belied the emotional intensity behind it, he said: "It's good and healthy in *today's* America for white people who view me as their favorite Negro to understand that I might *deliberately* kill a lyncher."[3]

Only rarely, in early childhood, as Paul would write three decades later, had he so assertively defied his father's rules in any consequential way. The results had been disastrous:

> My father told me to do something and I didn't do it. "Come here," he said; but I ran away. He ran after me. I darted across the road. He followed, stumbled and fell. I was horrified. I hurried back, helped Pop to his feet. He had knocked out one of his teeth. Never did he have to admonish me again.[4]

Losing his temper in the pool hall had been equally appalling to him. But on that Rutgers football practice field, driven to defend himself, Paul was prepared to individuate himself from his father. As much as he wanted to follow his father's code, his natural bent was to stand up against a frontal assault during one of the most racist periods in modern U.S. history.

Scores of blacks were being lynched regularly not only in the South but also in the Midwest, and D. W. Griffith's film, *Birth of a Nation*, was playing to turn-away audiences all across the country. This dramatization of the Civil War from the Southern point of view portrayed blacks as evil subhumans and marketed the notion of Aryan superiority with a fervor that would have been envied by Hitler's Nazis. The film became so popular among whites that it incited widespread attacks against black communities. Reverend Robeson preached a sermon condemning the film and the NAACP protested it. President Woodrow Wilson, by contrast, featured it at a special showing in the White House.[5]

With growing respect, his white teammates gradually accepted him. They nicknamed him "Robey" and even protected him from attempted fouls by opponents who were especially hostile to the first black player they had ever faced. Since traveling to games away from home was dangerous for Paul, the swimming coach, who also served as an assistant football coach, was assigned to room with him. A quiet, unassuming, friendly man, he became one of Paul's protectors on the Rutgers campus.[6]

Coach Sanford, a perceptive judge of individual character and athletic talent, took Paul under his wing. He taught Paul how to make the most of his phenomenal emotional discipline, and helped him to concentrate, calculate his moves, and respond with explosive action. Sanford's advice was to play a smart game, rather than an emotional one. Moreover, he taught Paul how to protect himself.

Sensitivity to its black freshman was in the college's best interest. Rutgers fielded a formidable team in 1915, winning all but one of its games. Paul played in four games out of the eight-game schedule. In his Memory Book he confided that he was a "promising" tackle, and at the Thanksgiving Day team banquet he was one of the players singled out by Coach Sanford for special praise.

William Drew, however, was less pleased. Paul had worked hard at trying to meet his father's expectations during that term. His grades were good by normal standards but not up to the elder Robeson's expectations: He earned all As and Bs, except in English composition, where he got a C. That grade upset William Drew so much that he made Paul forgo tryouts for the basketball team. Forced to concentrate fully on his studies, Paul achieved stellar second-term grades. William Drew, his judgment vindicated, allowed Paul to play varsity baseball in the spring.

Meanwhile, Paul cultivated friendships in the familiar black communities of the nearby New Jersey towns. They were worlds apart from the all-white Rutgers campus—worlds where he fully belonged. In these places he was immensely popular. His status as a Rutgers varsity football player and his singing voice added luster to his reputation as the life of the party. Harlem's St. Christopher basketball team, a popular black club, recruited him to play. Black businessmen and pretty girls sought his company. Despite his modest finances, he moved easily and with full acceptance at the top of black society.

In the spring of 1916 he met Geraldine Mamie Neale ("Gerry"), a beautiful, petite, olive-skinned high school senior from a middle-class black family. That day at the Freehold, New Jersey, YMCA, he most likely recited some poetry, gave a dramatic reading, and sang a mixture of popular ballads and Negro spirituals. But it was Gerry who lingered in his mind, and she would become his steady girlfriend by the end of the following year. This enigmatic reference to her appears in a July 1918 entry in his Memory Book: "Princeton. Six young ladies—in particular, *one*. First, the trials of rowing; second, the lunch; third, the aftermath—the most beautiful part."[7]

Like most of the women he dated in his college years, Gerry was eager to be seen with this strikingly handsome youth. Few dark-skinned men, and even fewer dark-skinned women, had the chance to go to college in those days, so Paul stood out in any crowd. He could not have missed the irony in his identification with dark-skinned working people, whom he associated with his father, and his high-toned reputation as the darling of the light-skinned elite.

That summer he worked again at the Imperial Hotel in Narragan-sett, but now as a waiter on a black staff that included other college athletic stars. Fritz Pollard, college football's first black All-American at Brown University that fall, was also working there. He spent some of his off hours with Paul, coaching him on the fine points of play-ing end and catching passes. Pollard was also a fairly good pianist, and he often accompanied Paul when he sang at social gatherings. The two became good friends, even though Pollard was several years older.[8]

As the only black football player besides Pollard at a major college in the eastern United States, Paul was keenly aware of his pioneer role and was determined to make the most of his talent. His self-evaluation of his freshman season on a first-rate team was that he was "promising" but had a long way to go. He trained intensively during the entire summer, reporting for preseason football practice weighing 210 pounds and standing six feet two and three-quarter inches tall.

Meanwhile, a second black student, Robert Davenport, arrived. Like Paul, he was a native of New Jersey. "Davvy," as his friends called him, was a slim, dark-skinned, studious young man of medium height with an infectious sense of humor. Paul invited Davvy to room with him in Winants Hall, the student dormitory conveniently located at the center of the campus. Sociable and well connected in the sur-rounding towns, Davvy became a good friend to Paul both on and off campus. In Paul's college Memory Book, he wrote: "In you I see more and more the qualities of my ideal."

In 1916, Rutgers faced a tough schedule with a young, relatively un-tried team. Coach Sanford built his line around Paul's ability to play several different positions—tackle, guard, and end. He even designed a special "tackle-back" play for him to carry the ball.

Playing mostly at left tackle, Paul became a mainstay. Several sportswriters heralded him as a player of All-American stature, and many of them placed him on their 1916 football honor roll. In the game against Washington and Jefferson, which Rutgers lost by the close score of 12 to 9, he was called Rutgers's strongest player. In the other game lost by the Rutgers team—to Brown University—the Brown captain and star lineman, Fauvam, was so thoroughly dominated by Paul that he had to be taken out of the lineup. Rutgers outplayed Brown for most of the game but wound up on the short end of a 21-to-3 score due to the heroics of Fritz Pollard, who eluded Paul on three long touchdown runs for Brown. Paul, one of the surest tacklers in football, would later say that Pollard was the greatest running back he had ever faced and that he had been given a lesson in tackling a runner when he missed him three times in the open field that day.

On trips Paul continued to room with the swimming coach, and his locker stood separate from the rest at games played both at home and away. He dismissed these slights as minor, but he deeply resented being benched for the homecoming game against Washington and Lee, a Southern college that formally requested Rutgers not to play its black star.

The game marked the celebration of Rutgers's 150th anniversary, and the university administration, anxious to avoid controversy, ordered Coach Sanford to field his team without Paul. When the Rutgers team heard this news, a large majority favored refusing to play, but Sanford ultimately convinced them to go along with the administration's decision. Paul was angry but held his peace and kept his silence; he knew All-American status would almost surely be his the next year, so it didn't make sense to challenge his coach and benefactor over this one game. Without his participation, the team barely struggled to a tie. The incident prompted a stern rebuke to Rutgers president William Demarest from James Carr, the college's first black graduate, who decried Demarest's willingness to permit "men whose progenitors tried to destroy this Union to make a mockery of our democratic ideals."[9]

Paul's grades, especially in Latin and Greek, held up that fall despite the distractions. He got a C again in English composition, but this time William Drew bit his tongue when Paul decided to try out for the varsity basketball team. William Drew may have regretted his forbearance. During the following spring term, Paul participated in both varsity baseball and varsity track, and his grades continued to show the strain of his schedule. However, he took pride in an impressive B-plus average overall for his first two years.

His rising reputation as a scholar-athlete brought him invitations to prestigious events, such as a banquet for Manhattan's black assistant district attorney, F. Q. Morton. "A real host of celebrities," he noted in his Memory Book. "Attorney Sims; Matthews of football fame; [Dr. W. E. B.] DuBois; [James D.] Carr [Rutgers's first black graduate and the man who had protested Paul's exclusion from the homecoming football game]; Stewart; Mal Queen; Wheaton, et al. Fine speeches. A real insight into political life of New York City."

He had few complaints, although the racial slights rankled. He encountered no overt hostility in the Winants Hall dormitory. Excluded from most Rutgers social activities or accepted only at the periphery, Paul was invariably popular at the songfests that took place on the steps of the various fraternity houses he was not allowed to enter. When he received an invitation to appear at the prom as a singer, he stationed himself on the balcony above the dance floor. From this vantage point he sang a medley of the most popular current ballads to enthusiastic applause, but he never descended from the balcony. And the Rutgers Glee Club eagerly recruited him to sing with them, but Paul performed at home engagements only; they decided that it would be impossible to have a black member traveling with them. Nor was he welcome at the social events after the Glee Club performances at home.

With seemingly great humor and tact, Paul graciously declined well-meaning but unwitting invitations that would violate these tacit exclusions. Always, no matter how spectacular his achievement might be, he quickly retreated, still in dutiful obeisance to his father's instructions, into an excessive modesty.

After another summer of waiting tables at Narragansett Pier's Imperial Hotel and workouts on the beach several times a day, Paul reported to football practice in the fall of 1917 towering six feet three and a half inches tall, weighing 220 pounds, and having lost none of his speed and agility. When Coach Sanford looked Paul over at the first team practice, he realized he had perhaps one of the greatest players of all time, and he decided to build the entire team around Paul.

For Paul, that 1917 football season would harbor an almost mystical significance; in a 1917 Memory Book entry he confided: "Robeson—In His Glory." At a time when prejudice barred black players from the vast majority of college football teams, and Southern universities adamantly refused to play against the few teams that did include them, he had the potential to become the first black athlete to dominate the premier national sport. "Robeson of Rutgers" became a household name across the nation. He was hailed by the entire college football world as everybody's All-American: the number one player in the country. His sense of the impact of his powerful black male image on the popular culture of the times was palpable, though not explicit. The public response to his playing roused his enthusiasm, but "superblack" was a label that he would continue to reject throughout his life.[10]

As the mainstay of his team's offensive and defensive strategy in every game, Paul needed to remain cool and level-headed. He was not only under constant pressure but also subject to relentless scrutiny and often the target of vicious play by the opposing team. Thus, he had to be sharp and lucid to protect himself from injury and to control his temper regardless of provocation. With the dedicated help of Coach Sanford, he practiced ceaselessly, remaining uninjured, and was never penalized for unsportsmanlike conduct.

Paul developed canny techniques to protect himself from dirty play. Remembering the painful lesson he had learned during his tryouts for the team, his first rule was to start getting up forcefully as soon as he hit the ground. Coach Sanford also taught him to use both the inside and the outside of his huge forearms as clubs wielded close to his body in short, lightning-fast chops. He practiced this technique until he could smash wooden barrels or packing boxes with either forearm from almost any position, with blows delivered so fast they could barely be seen.

That season, according to the *New York Times*, Paul "stood head and shoulders above his teammates for all around playing. He was a tower of strength on the Scarlet defense, and . . . he pulled down forward passes that an ordinary player would have to use a stepladder to reach."[11]

When Rutgers was to play the powerful visiting West Virginia eleven, the coach, the legendary Earl ("Greasy") Neale, approached Coach Sanford before the game with the request that Paul be benched because his team objected to competing against a black player. San-ford flatly refused, and Neale threatened that Paul would risk getting badly hurt. Sanford replied with an enigmatic smile: "I think Robe-son will be able to take care of himself." Apparently Neale took the hint, because the West Virginia team played tough but clean. At the end of the game, the West Virginia players showed their respect for Paul by lining up to shake his hand.[12]

In the season's final game, played in New York's Ebbets Field against the favored Newport Naval Reserves, Paul led Rutgers to a decisive 14–0 victory with a spectacular performance. According to the *New York American*, "Robeson . . . was a mighty man in the game . . . he was as destructive as a hunk of shrapnel on offense."[13] On defense, Paul spearheaded an effort that held Newport to a mere two first downs for the entire game.

The Rutgers team did not achieve an unbeaten, untied season record. However, playing a tough nine-game schedule against strong college teams and armed services teams studded with former college All-Americans, they won seven, lost one, and tied one. Paul was named first-team All-American by every major selector in the coun-try, beginning with Walter Camp, the nation's leading football expert, who declared: "There never was a more serviceable end, both in attack and defense, than Robeson. . . . He is the most powerful defensive end that ever trod a gridiron, a veritable superman."[14] Tom Thorp, another leading expert, called him "a football genius . . . the fastest thinking football player I have ever seen."[15]

When Paul also won the unusual distinction of being elected to the national Phi Beta Kappa Honor Society in his junior year, it seemed that being a football hero and honor student might change his status as social outsider. But no fraternity asked him to join, and it was still understood that he would not participate in campus social events. When the football team elected its captain for the 1918 sea-son—his senior year—his name was never even mentioned from the floor during the nominations. The best football player in America could not serve as captain of his team. But Paul expressed neither surprise nor anger: by now he knew this was the way the white world operated, and he was able to shrug it off.

In an era of rising protest and simmering anger among the masses, he avoided partisan political activities and social protests. On campus he echoed the patriotic rhetoric of the day. When the United States entered into World War I, he served proudly in the Reserve Officers Training Corps program at Rutgers. Only in private meetings with black students from other colleges did he plunge into discussions of controversial issues. According to Gerry Neale, he defended the radical views of leading black educator and writer W. E. B. DuBois over the conservative positions of Booker T. Washington, who was black America's dominant leader until his death in 1915.[16]

No doubt Paul's caution among whites was doubled by the knowledge that political dissent on campus was punished with extreme harshness. In April 1918, a white freshman "refused to advocate the sale of Liberty Bonds in a public-speaking class. He was seized by an irate group of students, held for several hours in a room in Ford Hall, and in the evening turned over to a mob to be stripped, covered with molasses and feathers, and paraded through town."[17]

Paul reveled in his celebrity, nonetheless. Ignoring a minor decline in his grades, he spent more time than ever during the winter and spring of 1918 enjoying himself on the local courts and playing fields. He starred at center on the Rutgers basketball team and became its leading scorer. He also played center for Harlem's St. Christopher club basketball team as captain alongside the Jenkins brothers, who later starred on the great Harlem Renaissance club. In April, he was playing catcher on the varsity baseball team and winning a varsity track letter in the pentathlon.

Paul's college Memory Book entries for 1917 also included a note about the annual football banquet at the Hotel Klein, where his remarks "gave inspiration" to an audience that included Rutgers President Demarest. He spoke and sang at the freshman banquet held at the Hotel Hollingwood in New York City.

His Memory Book entries under the heading "Favorites" reveal the range of his pursuits during this period: from mathematics to psychology, and from Browning, Hardy, Shakespeare, and classical opera to Paul Lawrence Dunbar and the current mainstream hit tunes. He used singing and reciting not only to draw others to him as the life of any party but also to earn spending money:

> There were the inevitable times when cash was scarce. I used to hustle around, fix up a concert, and bill myself as the star attraction. . . . I would go on the stage, sing a group of songs, orate and flourish for twenty minutes, and then sing again. Usually this

brought about fifty dollars [a large sum in those days], and apparently everyone was satisfied. These one-man shows were splendid practice.[18]

As Paul's performances grew stronger and more popular, a vision of his future began to form in the back of his mind. Finally, he dared to speak plainly to his father about his intentions. William Drew had counted on Paul following him into the ministry, and he was bitterly disappointed when Paul told him he "did not wish to enter the church." According to Paul, his father "made no attempt to upbraid me . . . , and it was decided that . . . I should take up the law as a profession."[19]

Paul obviously yearned for his father's approval and took pride in pleasing him, but the emotional drain and stringent accountability demanded of a minister were not for him. All his life, he had been cared for rather than being a caregiver himself. Still, he was certain that he had a destiny to fulfill. Whatever it might be—and it was not yet clear to him what it was—he felt certain that his father had already assiduously, rigorously, and lovingly prepared him for it. He had often felt moved when he listened to his father's sermons, or when he sang certain spirituals. In later life, he would recognize the import of these early intimations.

Having sought and received absolution from his father for rejecting a career in the ministry, Paul felt a strong obligation to obtain a law degree. In fact, he showed little substantive interest in the law. From a practical point of view, as long as he showed progress toward achieving a prestigious way of earning a living, he could count on his father's approval. The pressures to find a deeper, more satisfying calling were internal.

Speaking of his future to his father, he revealed a keener sense of independence than William Drew had seen in him before. Reverend Robeson, who had shown similar independence from authority throughout his life, calmly acknowledged the fact that his son was becoming his own master.

In the middle of May, Paul's budding sense of independence was put to trial. Scrawled across the top of an unidentified article from a local newspaper pasted into his Memory Book, he wrote a terse but poignant note: "My dear Dad. Departed this life May 17, 1918." The article, titled "Death of Rev. William D. Robeson," read, in part:

> The death of Rev. W. D. Robeson takes from this community one who has done a quiet but successful work among his own people for the past eight years. Rev. Robeson was a man of strong character. He was very familiar with the characteristics of his race and was always interested in their welfare. He quickly resented any attempt to belittle them or to interfere with their rights. He had the temperament which has produced so many orators in the South, and he held his people together in the church here with a fine discernment of their needs. He has left his impress on the colored race throughout the State, and he will be greatly missed here.

William Drew had been ill for some time but in characteristic fashion had suffered stoically in silence.[20] When he was certain he had little time left, he summoned Paul to help him for a few days to put his affairs in order. Then he dispatched him back to Rutgers, having decided to die alone at home. His final request was for Paul to participate in the upcoming Junior Oratorical Contest at Rutgers; he died three days before that event.[21]

Paul summoned the control to win the contest, as he had the freshman and sophomore contests the two previous years. He gave an eloquent presentation titled "Loyalty and the American Negro," in which he discussed "the place of the Negro in American society, American democracy, and the hopes for the future."[22] The speech underscored the compelling record of African-American loyalty during America's wars despite the injustice of pervasive discrimination in both military and civilian life. And it echoed the profound bitterness of thousands of black war veterans when they returned to the United States to increasingly virulent racial oppression.

Soon afterward, Paul made contact with his siblings at the eighth annual Bustill family reunion in Philadelphia on June 21, 1918. He could not have known it would be the last time all the Robeson siblings were together and the last time he would see Reed and Bill. Ben arrived from the U.S. Army's chaplain training school at a Kentucky military camp. Bill traveled from Washington, D.C., where, as he neared the age of thirty-eight, he was still more than two years away from finally obtaining his M.D. degree from Howard University. Reed, who had been completely out of touch, arrived from Detroit, and Marian came in from West Chester Training School for Teachers in Pennsylvania.

For Paul, the gathering of his extended family at that critical time was a great comfort. The organizers of this gathering of over 150 people included a committee of ten people and the six officers of the Bustill Family Association. The program consisted of eight speakers and several musical selections. Paul gave an address, titled "Loyalty to Convictions," and all four Robeson brothers were members of the twenty-eight-person Reception Committee.

Reverend Robeson's death deprived Paul of his only mooring, and his feeling of abandonment was not assuaged by the knowledge that he had helped make his father's last days happy ones. After the Bustill reunion, Paul was left on his own. Dependable older brother Ben departed, Reed vanished, Marian went to summer school, and Bill headed down to Washington, D.C.

Uncharacteristically, Bill, who was usually too detached from everyday life to provide much emotional support, offered Paul practical advice: "Always behave the way Pop would have wanted you to behave. Strive for excellence and you will rise above mediocrity." This November 8, 1918, note inscribed in Paul's Memory Book helped to rekindle Paul's emotional dependence on his father. In the years to come he would try again to break free of his need to seek his father's approval. But now he clung to it for emotional survival.

In the summer of 1918, Paul worked as a laborer in a shipyard. He hadn't returned to wait tables in the Narragansett Pier hotel because he had become fed up with the insults and racial slurs of the white hotel guests. Coping with his grief, he feared he might lose his temper and throw a tray at one of them.[23] That fall, he arrived on the Rutgers campus a few pounds heavier and a bit more muscular than he had been the previous year. He found comfort by driving himself to excel. His senior year became a string of great performances.

Coach Sanford, a sensitive man despite his gruff manner, filled in as a surrogate father for Paul. Sanford kept him focused on his studies and on his quest for football fame, reminding him often of his debt to William Drew and of his responsibility to be a role model to his race.

For the second year in a row, he was the top college football player, chosen as a first-team All-American end by all the major selectors.[24] Not only had Paul won the phenomenal total of fourteen varsity letters—four each in football and baseball; three each in basketball and track—but for the fourth year in a row he led the Rutgers debating team and won the class oratorical prize. He preserved his Phi Beta Kappa rank and had been inducted into the Cap and Skull Society, which honored the four seniors who best represented the ideals of Rutgers.

On Commencement Day, June 18, 1919, Paul walked to the speaker's platform. In an extraordinary tribute, the audience rose as one to applaud him and remained standing until he had reached the podium. He had given his valedictory address the innocuous title "The New Idealism." But actually the speech was about race. Fully aware of the wave of lynching and violent attacks being unleashed against blacks in many cities across America, Paul could hardly have picked a more ironic theme. In some places the African-American community, often led by an alliance of black war veterans and black gangsters, fought back fiercely against invading white mobs, sometimes routing the attackers and inflicting high casualties. The bloody "Red Summer of 1919"—a time when invading white mobs burned entire black communities and killed hundreds of blacks—was beginning.

From June to December, twenty-five cities erupted in race violence, with white mobs launching pogroms in an attempt to drive the newly migrated blacks from the South beyond the city limits. However, black resistance was fierce enough not only to prevent a forced exodus but also to put a permanent end to general mass violence against black communities. Lynchings continued, but the era of the antiblack pogrom was essentially over by 1920.[25]

In the 1940s, when I was a teenager, I asked my father about what had happened during that time. He replied that his brother Bill, a resident of Washington, D.C., had told him how a well-armed alliance of black war veterans and black gangsters ferociously defended Washington's black community against a large invading white mob. I recall my father's eyes flashing and his voice rising as he spat out his words: "They killed those sons of bitches without mercy—more than a hundred—and lost only four men. There's never been a race riot in Washington since."

Nationwide, white public opinion swung strongly toward open support of enforced segregation. The membership of the Ku Klux Klan soared well beyond 100,000, North and South, with hundreds of thousands of sympathizers. Both political parties supported segregation and the civil rights movement was at an all-time low. Liberals abandoned the fight for desegregation, and the entire left, including the Communist Party U.S.A., segregated its social events.[26]

Responding to the incendiary political and social environment of 1919, Paul evoked William Drew's indomitable sermons and the tradition of the Southern African-American preacher. He wrote his text and committed it to memory. His wholly positive theme; his soaring rhetoric and deep bass voice; his pace, modulation, and timing; and his distinctive style would have met William Drew's highest standards.

Paul had discussed his commencement oration thoroughly with President William Demarest of Rutgers and submitted his text to him in advance. Eleven years later, Demarest recalled that "It was one of the outstanding things of the twenty commencements over which I presided." He went on to say that the inspiration for the title—"The New Idealism"—came from Paul's vision of a renaissance for the Negro, the dawn of an era when the richness of the Negro contribution to art and music would win just recognition from the rest of the human race.[27]

To an audience that overwhelmingly shared the racist stereotypes of the time and believed strongly in segregation, Paul invoked the image of a new American age dedicated to "the triumph of right, . . . and the development of a new spirit, a new motive power in American life":

> We find an unparalleled opportunity for reconstructing our entire national life and moulding it in accordance with the purpose and ideals of a new age. Customs and traditions which blocked the path of knowledge have been uprooted, and the nation in place of its moral aimlessness has braced itself to the pursuit of a great national end. We can expect a greater openness of mind, a greater willingness to try new lines of advancement, a greater desire to do right things, and to serve social ends.

It will be the purpose of this new spirit to cherish and strengthen the heritage of freedom; to give fuller expression to the principle upon which our national life is built.

More and more has the value of the individual been brought home to us. The value of each citizen is very closely related to the conception of the nation as a living unit. But unity is impossible without freedom, and freedom presupposes a reverence for the individual and a recognition of the claims of human personality to full development. It is therefore the task of this new spirit to make national unity a reality, at whatever sacrifice, and to provide full opportunities for the development of everyone, both as a living personality and as a member of a community upon which social responsibilities devolve.

This universal human spirit eschewed race on behalf of individual and community values; it appealed for unity based on common interest instead of challenging injustice to a minority. Paul underscored his point by painting World War I in far different colors than the prevalent jingoistic ones:

We must realize that this has been a conflict, not only immense in area and volume, but profound and complex in issues. It is not now a question of what nations shall survive, but what institutions shall survive. It is not a question of who is the strongest but of what form [i.e., way] of life is the strongest. Willingly have the sons of America sacrificed their lives upon the altar of a great and common cause; that through us that larger and more altruistic form of life might retain a place in the world. We must not betray their trust. In the words of Lincoln, "We must take increased devotion to that cause for which they gave the last full measure of devotion. These dead must not have died in vain."

With seamless logic, Paul called forth from history the slaves' emancipation, the Confederacy's destruction, and the as-yet unfulfilled declaration that "all men are created equal." Thus, he left no doubt about what kind of freedom he was talking about:

We of this less favored race realize that our future lies chiefly in our own hands. On ourselves alone will depend the preservation of our liberties and the transmission of them in their integrity to those who will come after us. And we are struggling on, attempting to show that knowledge can be obtained under difficulties; that poverty may give place to affluence; that obscurity is not an absolute bar to distinction, and that a way is open to welfare and happiness to all who will follow the way with resolution and wisdom; that neither the old-time slavery nor continued prejudice need extinguish self-respect, crush manly ambition, or paralyze effort; that no power outside of himself can prevent a man from sustaining an honorable character and a useful relation to his day and generation. We know that neither institutions nor friends can make a race stand unless it has strength in its own foundation; that races like individuals must stand or fall by their own merit; that to fully succeed they must practice their virtues of self-reliance, self-respect, industry, perseverance and economy.

This powerful statement of self-determination in the face of all obstacles, even including slavery, challenged the foundations of American racism. Paul called upon whites to live up to their own principles. But he did so from a position of complete moral equality:

In order for us to successfully do all these things it is necessary that you of the favored race catch a new vision and exemplify in your actions this new American spirit. A fraternity must be established in which success and achievement are recognized, and those deserving receive the respect, honor and dignity due them.

We too have a part in this new American Idealism. We too have felt the great thrill of what it means to sacrifice for other than the material. We revere our honored ones as belonging to the martyrs who died, not for personal gain, but for adherence to moral principles, principles which through the baptism of their blood reached a fruitage otherwise impossible, giving as they did a broader conception to our national life.

May I not appeal to you who also revere their memory to join us in continuing to fight for the great principles for which they contended, until in all sections of this fair land there will be equal opportunities for all, and character shall be the standard of excellence; until men by constructive work aim toward Solon's definition of the ideal government—where an injury to the meanest citizen is an insult to the whole Constitution; and until black and white shall clasp friendly hands in the consciousness of the fact that we are brethren and that God is the father of us all.[28]

The overwhelmingly white gathering received Paul's daring speech with rapt attention. They had witnessed a superlative performer with a message bearing the imprint of W. E. B. DuBois's radicalism; a tone suffused with Booker T. Washington's moderation; a nuanced eloquence, at times thundering, but also gentle and contemplative, reminiscent of Frederick Douglass. In Paul's unique voice, there was the ring of a prophet-in-waiting. Many would later assert that no commencement orator in the history of Rutgers College had received such long applause.[29]

II
DESTINY AND DECISION

(1919–1926)

(Above) The *Plantation Revue* cast, the Plantation Club, Harlem, 1921. Paul is at the extreme left; Florence Mills is in the center. *From the personal collection of Paul Robeson, Jr.*

(Below) Paul and Eslanda Robeson, circa 1925. *From the personal collection of Paul Robeson, Jr.*

3

ESSIE

(1919–1921)

In the summer of 1919, Paul pressed on with his promise to his father that he would obtain his law degree in four years, even though he would have to make the journey without "Pop" by his side. Coach Sanford and several influential Rutgers alumni helped him obtain a scholarship to New York University Law School. It seemed that his future was settled.[1] But it wasn't.

Paul expected to capitalize on his fine academic record and football prestige as he began the 1919 fall term at NYU Law School. But he felt out of place in NYU's bohemian environs. Though living with a black family in the Brooklyn community known as Bedford-Stuyvesant, he was constantly drawn to Harlem.

From a tiny two-block enclave in 1900, black Harlem exploded into a thriving, self-contained cultural mecca. Its population would grow from 14,000 in 1914 to 175,000 by 1925. The interaction of blacks from all parts of the United States, the West Indies, and even Africa nurtured a highly race-conscious, sophisticated intelligentsia that was unprecedented in American history.[2]

Paul, despite having to admit a mistake, quit NYU in midterm and looked for a way to get into Columbia Law School. The quiet, studious atmosphere of the Morningside Heights campus, combined with its proximity to Harlem, was ideal for him. Once again, Coach Sanford came to his aid. Through a Wall Street contact of Sanford's, he was able to enroll at Columbia Law School in the spring term of 1920. He lost his scholarship but didn't seem to mind.

At ease and independent, Paul shared an apartment on West 135th Street, across from the Harlem YWCA, with James Lightfoot, a friend

and fledgling bandleader who was frequently on the road. Coach Sanford helped him to get some support from wealthy Rutgers alumni
to tide him over. Paul had decided not to tap the most lucrative
source of income available—professional football—because he felt it
would be too great a distraction. That decision deprived him of up
to $500 a game and forced him to rely on odd jobs.[3] He worked part-
time as an assistant to Fritz Pollard, who was coaching the Lincoln
University football team; he tutored college students; and he organized small concerts and speaking engagements for himself.

Because of his musical talents and intellectual bent, Paul reveled
in the excitement of the unfolding Harlem Renaissance. He gravitated toward gatherings in the homes of poet-writer-lyricist James
Weldon Johnson and his brother, the musician-arranger J. Rosamond
Johnson. Many poets and writers were there too, whom Paul grew
to know well. W. E. B. DuBois, who had an aloof, barely approach-
able manner, would drop in on occasion, and Paul was in awe of his
erudition.

Politics intrigued Paul, but he had no interest in becoming politically engaged. In Harlem, he found many groups vying for members. The Communist Party, then relatively insensitive to the
concerns of blacks, was marginal to Harlem's political and cultural
life, and would remain so for the rest of the 1920s. The nationalist
movement led by Jamaican Marcus Garvey, who preached black separatism and mass emigration back to Africa, was on the rise. Garvey
forged blacks' bitterness over the postwar betrayal of their hopes into
the Universal Negro Improvement Association, an organization with
hundreds of thousands of dues-paying members nationwide, mostly
in northern cities. However, Paul considered the nationalist goal
of separatism with its back-to-Africa theme contrary to his own
interests.

An avid reader with a facility for rapidly processing massive
amounts of information, Paul followed Harlem's political controver-
sies in the leading black magazines of the time: the NAACP's *Crisis*,
edited by DuBois; *Opportunity*, published by the National Urban
League and edited by Charles S. Johnson, literary mentor to a broad
group of aspiring young black writers; and *The Messenger*, edited by
socialist and labor organizer A. Philip Randolph. DuBois and James
Weldon Johnson, simultaneously the leader of both the new black
literary movement and the NAACP, exerted the greatest influence on

Paul's thinking through their commitment to intellectual achievement and the idea that artistic recognition was temporarily the most effective means of advancing the civil rights cause. Paul soon learned that this group represented the black cultural establishment along with liberal white sponsors. He was befriended by an outstanding young member of this circle—the twenty-nine-year-old poet-writer Claude McKay—whose fiery assaults on American racism he found compelling.

Moving in the crowd associated with *Crisis* and *Opportunity* magazines, Paul cautiously entered the heated political debates. At the Johnsons' gatherings, he was a good listener and a brief talker, asking insightful questions without seeming to challenge. And even though he could not yet compete intellectually with the formidable group, everyone was attentive when he sang. Sometimes Rosamond Johnson accompanied him; often he sang a capella.[4]

Paul worked consistently on his singing. As a result, his repertoire expanded, and his delivery became more polished. Although his voice was still far from the disciplined instrument of a professional concert artist, the short programs he had mastered earned him frequent appearances at church fund-raisers, fraternity and sorority affairs, YMCA and YWCA cultural events, NAACP dinners and meetings, and Columbia Law School social affairs, as well as private parties.

He found a willing and able accompanist in May Chinn, a medical student at Columbia University who was a good pianist with a well-developed musical sense. She also possessed rudimentary arranging and transposing skills on which Paul relied to adapt certain songs to his own style. Their repertoire consisted of current popular hits and the favorite spirituals of the black elite. These spirituals were modernized versions created by composer Harry T. Burleigh and made famous on the formal concert stage by tenor Roland Hayes. The pure original spirituals arranged by Rosamond Johnson were far more to Paul's liking, but his middle-class black audiences found them embarrassingly crude. So he quickly dropped them from his repertoire. However, he kept working on them privately.[5]

Meanwhile, he courted Gerry Neale. He visited her often—first at Rutgers, during her term at summer school there, then at Howard University in Washington, D.C., as well as at her home in Freehold, New Jersey. He gave her one of the cherished gold footballs he had won at Rutgers, but she shied away from his talk of an engagement. Fifty-seven years later, at Paul's wake in 1976, Gerry told me that she had loved him deeply but could not commit herself to the kind of life she felt he was destined to lead. "Even that far back I understood that he was a man of destiny and that he would belong to the world, rather than to his family," she recalled. "He was wonderful to be with, and yet I couldn't live with a man like that, nor could I really love him in the fullest sense."

But Paul needed loyal comradeship. Rudolph ("Bud") Fisher, a Phi Beta Kappa from Brown University, became his close friend when both were working summers in Rhode Island. Bud was dating Paul's accompanist, May Chinn, and Paul was dating May's roommate, Frances Quiett. But soon a young woman who was one of May's best friends would eclipse Bud, May, and Frances in Paul's personal world.

Eslanda Cardozo Goode—"Essie" to her friends—was beautiful, intelligent, and vivacious. Paul had barely arrived in New York when they met. Essie recalled: "Paul was making his way down Seventh Avenue [in Harlem] one glorious summer afternoon in 1919 with a pretty girl on his arm; he was greeting friends and admirers along the way with his wide engaging smile." Essie stopped to chat with the girl on Paul's arm, who was a childhood friend, but took careful note of his looks and behavior.[6]

She undoubtedly noticed his ill-fitting clothes. His notoriously unstylish clothing wasn't due to diffidence but stemmed from his difficulty in finding reasonably priced clothes that fit his large body. He didn't relish shopping—the whole process was tedious for him—and though he always looked presentable, he was a far cry from an elegant sartorial figure.

Paul and Essie encountered each other frequently that summer and fall at parties, dances, tennis matches, and in the dining room of the YWCA, where most of their friends ate regularly. At first, they seemed to have little in common. Her light olive complexion and five-foot-four-inch height contrasted with his dark color and massive size. She was mature and settled at age twenty-four, three years older than Paul. She held the position of head histological chemist in the Surgical Pathological Laboratory of Presbyterian Hospital—the first black person to hold such a high position there—and was planning ultimately to become a physician.

Boldly assertive, a "go-getter" and a risk taker, Essie was popular among her peers—both male and female. But she had to work at maintaining her popularity, while Paul, with his contrasting quiet manner, made and kept friends effortlessly. He appreciated her quick mind and her self-assured style, as well as her failure to be bowled over by his charm.

Essie belonged to the Cardozo family, a well-known Washington, D.C., black family descended from black slaves and wealthy Spanish Jews expelled from Spain in the late seventeenth century. Her grandfather, Francis Lewis Cardozo, had served as the first black treasurer of South Carolina during Reconstruction. Her mother, Eslanda Cardozo Goode, was a handsome woman with an aristocratic bearing who was light skinned enough to pass for white. Mrs. Goode, as most people called her, had married John Goode, a dark-skinned young man from Chicago who became a law clerk in the War Department by winning first place among 500 candidates in a competitive examination. Later he completed his study of law at Howard University in the evenings.

Black Washington society accepted John Goode only with reservations because of his dark color, but Eslanda had the support of her parents and was able to ignore community prejudices. She and John had three children: John Jr., Francis ("Frank"), and Essie. John and Frank were dark like their father, whereas Essie's complexion was almost as light as her mother's. John was of medium height and build with a taciturn, serious manner. He was mechanically inclined—always tinkering with machines, anything from watches to automobiles. Frank was big: six feet two inches tall, weighing 230 pounds, and radiating an easygoing charm. His knack of being able to do fairly well at anything he tried prevented him from settling down to a serious career, but he was always fun to be around.

Essie's father died when she was four years old, leaving the family with little savings; her mother responded to this crisis by teaching herself beauty culture and building up a thriving beauty care business that catered to top-level white society women as well as to wealthy blacks. Although Mrs. Goode never became rich, the family lived well by the standards of their times, and money was available for the children's education.

During her childhood, Essie would tag along with her darker-skinned older brothers, and she soon learned to keep up with them in their games. This tomboy experience carried into her adulthood in the form of a certain toughness that belied her arresting femininity and elegance. She also developed a strong identification as a black woman. Unlike her mother, she kept the light-skinned black elite at arm's length. Her closest friends were darker skinned, as were the men she dated.

Essie turned out to be the Goode family scholar. She finished high school at sixteen and won a four-year scholarship to the University of Illinois, ranking third in a state-sponsored competitive examination. There she majored in chemistry, transferring to Columbia for her senior year.

In 1920, both Essie and Paul attended summer school at Columbia—Paul for law courses and Essie for a course in preparation for Columbia Medical School in the fall. Their casual exchanges gradually blossomed into a full-blown romance. Although Essie's personality was strikingly different from Paul's, what they shared in common was more compelling. He was a motherless son, she a fatherless daughter. They were both scholars, and both harbored strong ambitions. And though both were outwardly gregarious, both were youngest children who shared intimacy with difficulty. While he continued to hope that he would marry Gerry Neale, Paul began seeing far less of her. On her part, Essie rarely dated her previous steady boyfriend, Grant Lucas, a quiet, young resident physician. As the summer progressed, Paul became aware that Essie had decided to put off going to medical school until the following year so that she could devote more of her time to their relationship. He knew she was risking more for him than he for her, but he was wary of her powerful will.

During the summer, Paul's friend Dora Cole Norman pulled him in an unexpected direction. As the producer of the 1920 version of *Simon the Cyrenian*, which was staged by the Amateur Players at the Harlem YMCA, Dora begged Paul to play the lead role. She was fascinated by his magnificent bass speaking voice, as well as by his natural presence, and since he lived practically across the street, she constantly intercepted him to press her case. He accepted the offer partly under the sheer weight of her persistence but also because he was intrigued by the challenge.

The play, written by white playwright Ridgely Torrence, broke with theatrical stereotypes of black characters. It told the story of an African who carried Christ's cross to Golgotha. One of a trilogy of one-act plays on black subjects produced on Broadway in the spring of 1917, it featured a predominantly black cast. Charles Gilpin, arguably the finest black actor of his time and the founder of the Lafayette Players, a black company based in Harlem, was the first to play the title role. Though some viewed Torrence's trilogy as the first step toward a national black theater, there were as yet no plays written by blacks.

Kenneth Macgowan and Robert Edmond Jones, two founders of the Provincetown Players, a successful experimental theater group whose Greenwich Village address belied its Massachusetts name, saw Paul's opening night performance. They congratulated him after the show and invited him to audition for them. But he went home and returned to law school the next day as if nothing special had happened.

When the Provincetown Players then called on Charles Gilpin to play the lead role in their production of Eugene O'Neill's *The Emperor Jones*, they found Gilpin running an elevator in Macy's department store. He achieved a major breakthrough for African-Americans in the arts by making the role famous on Broadway. A year later, *The New Republic* would rank him with "the greatest artists of the American stage."[7]

That fall, Paul drifted further away from the theater. It was as if he had put the stage behind him. He and his friend Fritz Pollard were invited to join the Akron Pros during the 1920 season. At $500 or more a game, Paul accepted without hesitation. The Akron Pros won the championship title, crushing the powerful Buffalo All-Americans, the Canton Bulldogs, and the Decatur Staleys. Undefeated in thirteen games, Akron held all of their opponents scoreless. Paul played defense from his left-end position and was a spectacular pass receiver on offense.[8]

After football season ended, Paul took Essie to parties and dances, and spent long evenings talking to her about his law studies, about her hopes for a career in medical research, about people and politics. Although he was ambivalent about their relationship, the more time he spent with her, the more involved they became. He hadn't given up his hope of marrying Gerry Neale, whom he still saw occasionally, but Essie seemed to be in his blood.

Early in 1921, Paul asked older brother Ben his opinion of Essie. Ben warned Paul that he didn't think she was the right woman for him. Unlike Gerry Neale, whom Ben and sister Marian knew and liked, Essie had aristocratic ways. Her manner could sometimes be abrasive. Ben also felt she was too ambitious. This was strong stuff coming from the tolerant and gentle Ben Robeson. Years later, Essie would come upon a letter Ben had written to Paul expressing these reservations. She never forgave Ben.[9]

Opposition to the relationship came from the Goode side too. When Essie asked her mother what she thought of Paul Robeson as a possible son-in-law, Mrs. Goode, who had seen quite a bit of her daughter's companion, commented that his skin was far too dark and that he was not settled or established enough to take care of her. Besides, she added, he lacked the ambition and drive required for big-time success.

Months passed as Paul avoided the worrisome thought of marrying Essie despite her obvious desire for marriage. He also avoided the law. Schoolmates at Columbia Law School recall that his main preoccupation was his singing. U.S. Supreme Court Justice William O. Douglas recalled that "He was very sociable. He wasn't on the Law Review; he was deep into his music." Paul's grades reflected his preoccupation—he earned mostly Cs.[10]

In the early spring of 1921, Paul's conflict came to a head. Alarmed at signs of a possible pregnancy, Essie had gone to see a doctor friend whom she had met through her job at Presbyterian Hospital. He confirmed her suspicion. Determined not to make Paul feel obligated to her, Essie decided not to tell him that she was carrying his child. Instead, with the help of May Chinn, she found a doctor who would perform an abortion. After the procedure, the doctor gave Essie the unexpected news that an abortion had been necessary in any case. He told her she had a condition that was benign in itself, yet would put her at unacceptable risk if she gave birth. His advice was that she should never have a child.[11]

It was characteristic of Essie to have made a critical personal decision without consulting anyone; now, having recovered fully, she wrestled with the problem of what to tell Paul. Fearing that Paul wouldn't want to marry a woman who couldn't give him a child, and dreading his anger at her having an abortion without telling him, she delayed the day of reckoning. Only a month later did she tell him the whole truth.

Her fears were confirmed. Paul was both shocked and angry. But his reasons were different than she had imagined. Himself a motherless child, he felt that having a child was sacred, and abortion seemed sacrilegious. He also shouldered a huge burden of responsibility mixed with guilt. At first he refused to believe the story, and it took Essie some time to convince him that it was true. When it had all sunk in, he backed away from her. Essie was mature and smart enough not to pursue him. She waited patiently as he went back to dating other women, and she returned to dating Grant Lucas, who was on his way to becoming a prominent Harlem physician.

Underneath his calm exterior, Paul was in turmoil. The strength of his overriding need for a wife who would be both reliable friend and caregiver pulled him toward Essie. Yet he also craved a sisterly, emotionally open soul mate, and the spiritual solace he sought was not something Essie, the practical scientist, could provide. Finally, after much hesitation, Paul went to see Gerry at her home. There in New Jersey in August 1921, they talked for a long time. At last, she looked him straight in the eye and gently told him that she could not live her life in his shadow. Her firm, almost motherly advice was that he should marry Essie, who was both willing and emotionally equipped to put his career and needs ahead of her own personal ambitions. In the end, he gave up and returned to New York. He made his decision quickly.[12]

When Paul rang the bell of Essie's apartment early one morning a few days later, he was composed and quietly confident. He asked her to marry him. He found Essie startled but not entirely surprised; she had been waiting for him. Paul appealed to her adventurous spirit. She was confident that she could make him a king, and then she would be queen. At the same time, he appealed to her deep-seated caregiving instincts. She would give him a secure home and be his shield.

As she recalled eight years later, re-creating her perception of the moment in the third person:

> There he stood, a little shy, holding his ground, definitely asking her again to marry him that day. It wasn't a dream, it was a marvelous reality. She asked him to come in and wait until she could make herself presentable; then she dashed about breathlessly, thoroughly excited inside but clinging to some sort of external calm. When she joined him in the living room a little later, she asked him what it was all about. He said he had been thinking of her for the last month or so—about how much he liked her and what a great pal she was. But when she started going out with someone else, he suddenly realized that he was very much in love with her and could not bear the idea of her giving anyone else most of her time and attention. He thought if she cared enough for him they could just go and be married and then always be together.
>
> This sounded like a fairy tale to her, and once more she felt that she was dreaming after all. Anyway, the practical Essie decided then and there that if it was a dream she might as well make it a good one. With a wildly beating heart, she calmly told him she thought it was an excellent idea. They decided to eat breakfast somewhere and talk over the problem of how one got married in New York.[13]

They decided to get married immediately and to keep the marriage secret for at least several months, since they knew both of their families would be opposed. This meant they couldn't go to City Hall for the ceremony, because all licenses obtained there were announced in the papers the next day. Avoiding City Hall, they headed for Greenwich, Connecticut, the usual destination of elopers, with an astonished Hattie Bolling, one of Essie's oldest and dearest friends, as a witness.

When they arrived, they were disappointed to learn of a required five-day waiting period in the state. So they started back to New York City in disappointment, but on the way they realized they could get married in New York State without waiting. They got off the streetcar in the village of Port Chester, New York, just over the Connecticut state line, where the marriage was performed by the town clerk on August 17, 1921.

Back in Harlem on the same day, Paul continued to live with bandleader Jimmy Lightfoot, and Essie shared an apartment with her close friend Minnie Sumner, a dress designer. On many evenings, Paul would go over to have dinner with Essie, Minnie, and Minnie's steady boyfriend, William Patterson, a law student. After dinner, the four of them would clear the table and settle down contentedly to play whist (a card game similar to bridge).

In September some major decisions had to be made. Paul resisted the idea of Essie working to support both of them. He felt it was his responsibility to leave law school and go to work. After many arguments, they finally arrived at a compromise. Paul would continue law school, but he would play another season with the Akron Pros; Essie would keep her job. They agreed to announce their marriage in December in Philadelphia, when Paul's Alpha Phi Alpha fraternity and Essie's Delta Sigma Theta sorority convened.

Paul departed on weekends to play football, establishing a relationship that was more like a courtship than a marriage. When they announced their marriage, Mrs. Goode was vacationing in Bermuda, so Essie sent her a long wire and a follow-up letter. The response was unsupportive, so Essie ordered the announcements in her mother's name and sent them out. Traveling to Philadelphia, Paul gave Ben and Marian the news. They didn't have the heart to oppose him, but they didn't give their blessings. He returned to New York a bit dejected but certain he would prove them wrong.

By this time, Essie had found their first home—an oversized front room on the top floor of a private house at 321 West 138th Street in central Harlem. They furnished it themselves, partly with wedding presents and partly with purchases on the installment plan. At one end of the room they put a mahogany bed, dressing table, and chest of drawers; at the other end a handsome gray Sloane rug with a deep black border, large comfortable chairs, bookcases, a mahogany gate-leg table, and soft lamps. They lived in that single room for two years, and they received their visitors "as though it were a drawing room of a palace."[14]

Paul was supremely happy being cared for by Essie. She took his measurements and shopped for his clothes in men's stores that stocked a good selection of extra-large clothing of all kinds. When people told him he was growing handsomer, he would come home laughing about it and tell Essie that it was because his clothes fit him perfectly for the first time in his life. However, Paul often found himself maddeningly out of sync with Essie. She would get up at seven-thirty in the morning and kiss him good-bye. He rose to begin his day at noon and was still wide awake at midnight, eager for conversation or reading law. She pressed Paul to change. But he would walk around in a daze if he got up at eight and by noon would be fast asleep again, lying across the bed fully dressed. Outwardly passive but unyielding, Paul began to consider himself fortunate that their hours overlapped so rarely.[15]

4

A TASTE OF THEATER

(1922)

In March 1922, Paul explained once again to Dora Cole Norman that her plan for him to appear as the main black character in another play was out of the question. Her relentless prodding two years earlier had brought about Paul's successful acting debut in *Simon the Cyrenian* at the Harlem YWCA, so she was not easily dissuaded. The new play, titled *Taboo*, was the first work of Mary Hoyt Wiborg, a wealthy white socialite. Kenneth Macgowan of the Provincetown Players, who had been so impressed by Paul's performance in *Simon*, was strongly recommending him for the role. And Dora, though she admitted that the meandering tale on a Louisiana plantation didn't amount to much, insisted he take the part.

Dora argued that Paul was being given a golden opportunity to test his acting skills. The director was Augustin Duncan, the brother of Isadora, the famous dancer. He had excellent connections with the New York theatrical establishment. Charles Gilpin had promised to coach the cast, and the well-known English actress Margaret Wycherly, who had just completed a stint with the Provincetown Players, would star opposite Paul. But he would have none of it. Determined to get his law degree out of the way as soon as possible, he decided to stay on course.

Inclined to experiment, Essie saw things differently. She became keenly interested in Dora's idea. Eager to see how Paul would do in the role, she urged him to take the part. She suggested that he give up his part-time job as a postal clerk and defer his studies to summer school. It was such a sensible, appealing plan that he could hardly object. Essie's idea would free him from the tedium of postal work

55

and classes. Finally convinced that he had little to lose, Paul accepted Dora's proposal.

For the next several weeks, Paul threw himself enthusiastically into rehearsals. His virtually photographic memory made learning lines easy. Duncan was impressed with his dramatic abilities. More important, Essie thought he was grand. Encouraged in her growing belief that the theater might well be Paul's road to success, she took it upon herself to become his expert adviser. She began going to the theater often. When she saw an exceptionally fine performance, she would return to it and study the elements and techniques that made the acting outstanding. She read drama criticism voraciously and absorbed the general criteria for excellence.

As Essie observed Paul in rehearsal, she reflected on the reasons why he had resisted thinking of himself as an actor. Later she wrote:

> He didn't want to be an actor, but how high could he go in his [law] profession? This was America and he was a Negro; therefore he wouldn't get far. If he put his foot on the bottom rung of the ladder of the theater, he could climb to the top; if he started up the ladder of the law, his utmost progress would be half-way up. I set my heart and mind more and more surely on a dramatic career for him, [but] I proceeded with the utmost caution. Paul was a member of a conservative family, and had rather conservative ideas. It never occurred to him that acting is a serious profession. I began taking him to the good plays, and he became very much interested.[1]

For Paul to see the possibility of his future on the stage, Essie would need not only to show him the way but also to make it possible. With rising confidence in her vision, she developed a strategy and presented it to Paul. It was both simple and compelling. She would keep her job at the pathology lab in order for Paul to pursue a career on stage without having to work elsewhere. She was offering to give up her hopes for a career in medicine. Paul was not happy about this proposal, but she would not budge.

When *Taboo* opened its trial run in late April, most critics gave it lukewarm or even cold reviews: they called it "diffuse" and objected to its "obscure" plot.[2] By contrast, Paul's reviews were generally favorable. He was given credit for a powerful stage presence and a magnificent speaking voice. Only the *New York Times* drama critic,

Alexander Woollcott, dismissed his acting ability with the tart comment that he belonged almost anywhere but in the theater.[3]

After opening night, Margaret Wycherly and Augustin Duncan both urged Paul to pursue a theater career. Essie was winning the day, even as Paul continued to think of acting as a sideline. As he later wrote about his apprehensions:

> I knew little of what I was doing, but I was urged to go ahead and try. So I found myself in rehearsal. What was most important at that time was that I got about $75 a week, which a law clerk didn't get for quite some time. And I remember the first night after I'd played the role. I came back to the Law School, and Dean [Harlan] Stone, who later became Chief Justice of the Supreme Court, was standing in the door. He looked at me, and he said: "Robeson, what have you been doing?" And he had some newspapers in his hand, and I was rather frightened. I said to myself: "Well, I guess this is it." The Dean says: "Well, I read some nice things about you here—they say you're a very fine actor." I said: "Let me see, Dean"; I hadn't seen the papers, and I—well—I was fairly famous.[4]

The theater stayed on his mind. The play ran briefly, then closed in time for Paul to prepare for and pass his second-year law examinations. Restlessly, he and Essie continued going to the theater together often, discussing the performances and studying how actors and actresses built up their characters. Then they would analyze the reviews together. Paul favored internalizing a character and conveying the essence directly, without intermediate associations. He became interested in acting techniques. The prospect of returning to the theater was beginning to have some intrinsic attraction in addition to being a convenient source of income.

It was quite by accident that he got his next chance in the theater almost immediately. Late one Saturday night in May 1922, Paul was standing on the corner of Seventh Avenue and 135th Street in Harlem, talking to his cronies, when along came Harold Browning. Harold was a young singer and the leader of a quartet called the Four Harmony Kings, then singing in the landmark musical revue *Shuffle Along*, which had become a runaway hit at the David Belasco Theater on Broadway. The all-black cast featured the glorious Florence Mills. The comedians in blackface, "mammy songs," and skits were not far from minstrelsy, but the tunes and performances were irresistible.

Harold was bewailing the fact that the bass singer of the quartet had suddenly left that night for Chicago, which meant that unless they could find another bass by Monday, the Harmony Kings would have to drop out of the show.

Paul stepped up eagerly and said, "Brother, you're looking at your bass right here!" Harold was a little annoyed that his serious problem was being taken so lightly and said, "This means my bread and butter."

"And mine," Paul remembered answering with a smile. No one took him seriously. Finally, out of sheer desperation, Harold took him home to try out a few notes. He was astonished to find that Paul could sing quite clearly three tones lower and many notes higher than his former bass singer, and that his voice was rich and beautiful.

Paul struggled through the rehearsal: he had never sung in a quartet before, and it was hard for him to refrain from singing the melody line carried by the baritone. He also liked the legitimate theater better than vaudeville. But he persisted, and he appeared the next night in *Shuffle Along* as a Harmony King.

Dressed in a parody of the height of fashion, the Harmony Kings walked smartly onto the stage through a small door on the right, jauntily swinging their canes. The three veterans had been so excited as they coached their new bass that they had bombarded him with advice and instructions. They told him repeatedly that he must bend low when going through the door to the stage so that his hat wouldn't be knocked off. Paul, being the tallest, came out last.

He did bend low, as he had been instructed, and saved his hat, but the others had forgotten to tell him there was a small board at the bottom of the doorway over which he must step. Preoccupied with his hat, his cane, and his new responsibility, Paul tripped over the board, nearly fell, and lurched onto the stage. He stumbled in with such force that Essie, sitting in the audience, closed her eyes in horror. When she opened her eyes a moment later, Paul was standing there smiling and singing lustily: his trained body had recovered itself in a split second. Eubie Blake, who had written the show with Noble Sissle, shook his head in amazement. "That boy will bear watching," he said; "anybody who can nearly fall like that and come up with a million-dollar smile has got *some* personality."[5]

Paul's deeply soulful solo rendition of "Ol' Black Joe" wowed the audiences and caught the attention of a number of theater producers and directors. He stayed with the show for a little over a month. As much as he loathed the humiliating features of the show, *Shuffle Along* was making history as the first musical revue written and performed entirely by African-Americans. Although Paul still clung to his intention to finish law school so that he would have a secure profession, he decided to skip summer law studies.

At the end of June, an opportunity for a serious starring role in a summer production of *Taboo* came his way. Paul took it without hesitating. Mary Hoyt Wiborg had convinced the famous English actress Mrs. Patrick Campbell to play the female lead in a British production for which the play was renamed *Voodoo*. It was to begin its trial run in the English provinces, with an eye toward an eventual London opening. Everyone associated with the New York production said Paul was their choice for the lead role opposite Mrs. Campbell. He could appear in *Voodoo* and still return home in time to begin the fall term at Columbia and play another season of professional football. Bored with his law courses, he welcomed the temporary change of venue. Moreover, *Voodoo* appealed to his interest in acting. As part of an intriguing milieu, performing in front of appreciative audiences, he was beginning to feel a greater sense of purpose than he did in his studies.

He also needed to distance himself from Essie to regain his balance and perspective. The problem was not only that he remained uncomfortable about Essie working—although he did, and they depended on her income; it was the undertow of his unrequited love for Gerry Neale that weighed on his conscience and generated the most tension. Paul dealt with his anxieties by sublimation and concealment. Through constant expressions of deep affection for Essie, he affirmed his dream of a happy marriage and smoothed over the conflict without facing its underlying causes. Essie was unable to recognize, or perhaps admit, that Paul was masking his emotions.[6]

Paul left on the SS *Homeric*, which embarked from New York at the beginning of July. Essie gaily saw him off at the pier. He did not know that she had to strain every nerve to appear carefree. She had told him nothing about an impending surgery she had scheduled, for fear that he would refuse to leave her and thus miss his chance. Adhesions from a previous appendicitis operation had begun to cause serious internal problems and had to be surgically corrected. After waving good-bye to him as though nothing were amiss, she went back to their apartment weighed down by worry. Forty-eight hours later, she checked herself into Columbia Presbyterian Hospital.

Essie hadn't been feeling well for some time, and when she had finally gone to her doctor she had received the alarming news that immediate surgery was required. That night she wrote twenty-one letters to Paul—three happy, loving letters a week, predated for a period of seven weeks and filled with idle chatter, love talk, descriptions of imaginary outings, and enough invented news about real friends of theirs to fill hours of reading time. The next day she turned to Bill Colson, a pleasant, quiet, reliable man, and a friend of Paul's from Columbia—one of the few other black law students there. She gave Bill her letters to Paul along with detailed instructions as to when they should be mailed.[7]

From the ship, Paul wrote to Essie after a bout of homesickness:

> Well, I've had a time of it. Meant to write sooner, but from Wednesday night we've had terrible weather. The boat has just crept along and will not arrive in England until 5 o'clock this evening. Sweet, I've really been ill; refused to eat for a day and a half—goodness, how I wanted my baby. Sweet, you've spoiled me terribly; I feel absolutely helpless without you.
>
> How happy I am that in choosing I chose aright. My sweet helped me to choose, and I'll be grateful to her always. I just sit and think of my wonderful little wife, and I'm just the happiest man on earth when I realize that she loves *me, worships me,* idolizes *ME.* How I love her! And she will think of her darling and help him while he's far away from her?[8]

Despite Paul's persistent longing for Gerry, his expressions of love for Essie were genuine, and his dependence on her was real. By now he knew he could do without Gerry but not without Essie. She was the only one who shared his quest for a career. Essie would help him keep his options open by staying in touch with Harold Browning and the Harmony Kings. "You keep in touch with the boys and the doings of *Shuffle Along.* If things go wrong here, I'll get in touch with them immediately," he wrote.

Without any way of knowing that she was hospitalized, much less that she had suffered serious postoperative complications, he continued: "Write me soon c/o Miss Wiborg," and closed with "Lots and lots of love—goodness, how I miss you!" The letter is signed "Dubby," his abbreviation for "darling hubby."[9]

He landed in Portsmouth on July 9, 1922, and wrote Essie three days later. "You sweet old girl—I found your cable at the theater when I arrived Monday afternoon [July 10]. Gee! Wasn't I happy! No one could be as thoughtful as my little girl." He spoke of the excitement of his arrival. "I'm really here and getting to be a real Englishman," he wrote, "but things are quite different from what I expected to find. We did not open last night. I found Mrs. Campbell busy rehearsing—she is playing here in a play, *Hedda Gabler*, by Ibsen. We rehearse between times. She has cut the play up and has really made my part much better—a very fine, connected part."[10] His hope was that he and Mrs. Campbell could create enough of a dramatic impact to get the play to London, where he felt great opportunity might await him. Meanwhile, he had to concentrate on making a good impression in the provinces:

We go to a summer resort—Blackpool—next week where we expect to open Wednesday or Thursday. Mrs. Campbell has made me one of the directors practically. She can't tell them how to do it, but she is far better than [Augustin] Duncan in knowing what she wants. She's really a wonderful woman and a marvelous actress. One thousand times better than Miss Wycherly.[11]

He also made note of how well he was being treated by the British:

Have a nice bedroom, and here they also give you a sitting room. I don't know what I'm paying, as the lady left it to me what we are to pay. She's new in the game. Very nice. She thinks I'm grand.

When we arrived, we went to London to stay over Sunday night at the Cadogan Square Hotel where Miss Wiborg has a suite of rooms. Gee! She's nice. She came in after we arrived and called for us; we had rooms on the second floor. All the Englishmen were there, you know, and she was with a party of swells. She saw me and rushed up—"Hello Paul" and a hearty handshake. "How are you? What kind of trip—do come up and tell me about it." We came here the next day.[12]

Right away he felt accepted. He began searching for a way to make his stay in London last, and to bring Essie over to join him.

> The play is shaping up fine. The plans are to hit London in August, so we ought to be sharp by then. Of course, after 4 weeks I'll talk *MONEY.* And darling, I do so want you to come over. I must stay somehow. If you could only have one of those darling little houses for a starter, if only for a while, and we could start Paul Jr. on the way here. Gee! I hope I can stay a while. How you'll like it! I'll send for you so you can be in London by the time we arrive. Expect to get paid Saturday and will send you all the money I can. How I long for my little girl.
>
> Always and always—
> Your own
> Dubby[13]

Paul continued to seek Essie's counsel as he struggled with alternatives for which nothing in his life experience had prepared him. His prospects for work other than playing in *Voodoo* or in a possible English run of *Shuffle Along* were vanishingly small: after a series of highly successful tours by black entertainers and black shows, the English market for them had suddenly all but closed down. ("The cry about Negroes making money here is bosh. Things are not as pictured," he wrote to Essie a couple of weeks later.)[14] *Shuffle Along* was being considered for a British production only because of its huge box office in America.

Another choice was to return to the United States more or less immediately and try to make some money with *Shuffle Along*—if the quartet was willing to hold his place by using a temporary bass singer until he could join them. Still another option was to forget about the theater altogether and go back to playing professional football.

He was in an increasingly precarious situation. *Voodoo* opened on July 17 in Blackpool with poor results: the audience was unimpressed, and the reviews were bad to mediocre. Paul's initial optimism about the prospects for the play began to fade rapidly, and his skepticism about the chances for black shows in England was reinforced. However, he continued to try to be hopeful in the face of his anxiety and clung to the steadying lifeline of Essie's love for him. From Black-pool he wrote:

> No chance for the boys here now. They are not paying any money. Their best chance is to come here with *Shuffle Along* and to branch out from there. To be truthful, things are none too rosy. Mrs. Campbell doesn't know her lines too well. But I guess we'll hit. I'm really supposed to knock 'em dead.
>
> I marvel, Darling, at the strength of our love. Always I think and talk of you. I know my Dolly does the same of me. And I am so happy, sweet-heart—happy to be far away and want you more than anything else in the world. I know so well what it is to love and be loved. To love as I've always wanted to, sweet-heart. Yes, we do understand each other very well and always will. Darling, you're so wonderful. Need you, sweet! I need you more than you'll ever know.[15]

From Blackpool the play went to Edinburgh, where it opened on July 27 with great success—the audience was enthusiastic, Paul was the star of the show, and the reviews were generally good. He liked Edinburgh, and all three performances of the play went well, but none of this erased the uncertainty he had recently felt about *Voodoo*'s future:

> Really darling, I don't know what to do. These folks want to go to London but are not sure. Perhaps a week or so will tell. I don't want to send for you and then be out of work. And I can't do any-thing definite as to the boys before that time. What I want most is to give you the trip, but we can't be foolish. If I'm coming right back, we can't do it. And I must have some return fare or a con-tract for the same before I bring you over. Can't take any wild chances. The theatre seems in as bad a state as those in N.Y., or worse. Vaudeville pays better here than the *Legitimate*. Of course, if I sang with the quartette [*sic*], you would see Europe; but we could save hardly anything, and I'd be back to the States jobless except for the quartette. And if they didn't want to come when I did, I'd be out of luck.[16]

Always in the back of his mind he kept the prospect of returning to his studies. "I think that if this does not turn out as well as I ex-pected, I'd better head right back and get down to law. The sooner

I build up, the sooner we'll be on easy street & able to come over," he wrote her from Edinburgh.[17]

But he continued to vacillate and appeal to Essie to help him decide what to do. "I think that the time I spend with the quartette and *Shuffle Along* will be wasted & will hold us back. Of course, if the play goes, I'll stay; but if not, I think I'd better come back. Think it over and write me," he appealed.[18]

In Glasgow, as the play began to take form, Paul's performance won increasing recognition. He wrote Essie:

> It is the consensus of opinion that the most enjoyable feature of the show is my singing. Mrs. Campbell is very unselfish. She's always saying when we take our bows at the final curtain: "Come onto the point; it's your show, not mine." And she says: "Sing a lot and long—more, more; my own friends have told me that the most enjoyable feature of the show is your singing." There is always a perceptible outburst of applause when I appear after the final curtain. You see, Mrs. Campbell takes one bow alone; then I come out. The house stormed in Edinburgh—showed who they were with.[19]

Despite his success, Paul expressed the need for Essie's encouragement and support: "So anxious for you to see me and criticise. Know you can help me—I feel awkward in certain new positions. I want you, and you only, to help me. See you soon, Sweet."[20]

Paul could not support the play by himself. It was dawning on him that in this respect the theater was different from football. Sensing that the tour might not reach London, he shared his misgivings with Essie in a later letter from Glasgow: "The play went very well here but was not the howling success it was in Edinburgh," he wrote. "All I want to do is to hit London. Then all will be well." He signed off with the appeal "We may have to make a very important decision. You'll know what to do. I'll leave it to you. You always know."[21]

His misgivings were well founded. The very next day he sent another letter to Essie, stating that Mrs. Campbell had seen "the handwriting on the wall" and was losing interest in the play. If she left, he calculated that the production would never make it to London. He had to make a decision now, and it tortured him. What he wanted more than anything was for Essie to join him in England, but he knew his prospects there were at best extremely unreliable. "The play is not failing," he wrote a few days later. "Only we 'colored folks' are getting all the glory, & Mrs. Campbell is not the big guy. See. They have said nothing final, but I see the end. So I'm working fast. I leave it to you darling. I want to stay & want you to come."[22]

Arriving in Liverpool on August 7, 1922, Paul wrote Essie asserting his intention to stay, even at the cost of delaying completion of his law studies for a year:

> I've still been thinking, and I want you to come over. I don't want you to miss this chance. It may be a long time before we get another opportunity. I'm sure we'll do allright. And at least you'll get a good rest. Then if we go back to America, you'll feel better to do whatever you want to. After a few months rest here, we can start our little one if you want. September is a good month. That would mean begin in January.
>
> I think I'll see Mrs. Campbell, get some sort of final word, and tell you to get in touch with Harold [Browning] at once. Then we'll sure stay awhile. All England is waiting for *Shuffle Along*. I want you to come over now. Stop thinking, or think my way. It's all I'll hear, you see. All right, Dolly; consider all settled. You're coming.

Then he made his commitment to stay in England firm by cabling Browning that he wouldn't be joining *Shuffle Along* in the United States, and he wrote again to Essie, letting her know that he had gone ahead with the decision in order "to forestall all thinking on your part." He added that Mrs. Campbell "thinks I'm a real artist & off-hand suggested I should make a marvellous Othello. So I'd like to remain over here for a while. I've bought a Shakespeare's works and shall look over any Shakespearean acting I see." Evidently, he had taken Mrs. Campbell's "off-hand" remark about his future potential seriously.[23]

While awaiting the play's opening in Plymouth, Paul went to London, where he stayed with the black singer John Payne, an acquaintance from Harlem. Accompanist and arranger Lawrence Brown, who was at that time working with the famous black tenor Roland Hayes, was also staying with the Paynes, and one evening he and Paul teamed up to entertain the guests at one of their parties. Brown was struck by the beauty of Paul's voice, and Paul was in turn drawn to Brown's authentic arrangements of Negro spirituals. Three years later, these two would reunite in America to make musical history.

Now, however, *Voodoo*'s prospects were fading. As Paul had feared, Mrs. Campbell decided to leave the company sooner than originally planned. Moreover, it appeared that *Shuffle Along* would not be coming to England anytime soon. Paul realized, finally and reluctantly, that it was time to make preparations to return home. He wrote from London on August 17: "I'm coming home—can't stay away. From all events, it looks as though I'll be sailing week after next. No use fooling around. Nothing definite after that."[24]

The next day he wrote again, complaining: "I'm about frantic—3 letters are following me around somewhere. . . . So I've had no letter from Dolly this week. The last one was written July 20 from our 'little love nest.' . . . I read it & others over & over again & hug my picture."[25] Shortly afterward, an urgent cable arrived from Essie telling Paul he should stay another month—long enough to give *Voodoo* every possible chance of surviving, but not long enough to prevent him from starting the fall term at Columbia. Relieved to hear from her, he reluctantly went along with her recommendation. "A month more seems a long while, but I guess I can go it," he replied. "Mrs. Campbell is giving the play up this week & I'm glad. She doesn't know her lines. She just sees no point & has lost interest."[26]

Reaching for a game plan, Paul struck upon a new idea: for Essie to come over and help him salvage the play for a run in London. He had been thinking about how to accomplish this and conveyed his thoughts to Essie, asking her to relay them to Mary Wiborg:

> Listen well: tell Miss Wiborg she can most likely figure on Miss Barbara Gott [a fairly well-known British actress] for "Mammy Dorcas" [a key character in the play], and she'll have to find an "Angy" [another character in the play]. She'll have to put out a little money & get a chorus—a good one. If so, the play has a chance. The audience was fine last night—am sending writeups. Call up Miss Wiborg & read them to her.

He was becoming savvy about business concerns: "See that [Miss Wiborg] pays your passage," he added. "I'll be safe when [she] comes, but I can't trust this bunch here." He closed: "This is a sea-side place—reminds me of Nantucket Pier. Wish you were coming in this week as we had planned . . . we could have walked by the sea at night and looked at our sky."[27]

Essie may have heard a plaintive note in Paul's nostalgia for his unencumbered youth. Finally, she wrote to him from the hospital and told him how ill she had been with a serious case of phlebitis. His response was instantaneous and completely supportive.

Plymouth, England
August 23, 1922

Darling—My own precious little wife,

Received your letters of August 10th and 12th—written from hospital—this morning. You know, I was taken absolutely off-guard. I received your cable the morning of my big day—and your big day, but as you have seen by an earlier letter—I thought you were talking about Minnie [i.e., Paul thought it was Essie's close friend Minnie who was ill].

Well, breakfast was on the table, and very tempting it was too. As I sat down, your letters came from London. Of course, I had to read them first. After reading the first few lines, I hastened through. Darling, I'll never be able to tell you how I felt—I cried and cried as though my heart would break. You know how it is when you've passed through a terrible strain, and when it's all over you break down—I've seen you do it. Well, Sweet, in those few moments I passed through it all.

It is as if I had been at your bedside and saw you come to and go back, and finally safe; I couldn't pull myself together. The lady of the house has a little girl—she came in after I had quieted and hadn't heard me. I told her I was sorry I couldn't eat the breakfast, that my wife had just passed through a terrible experience and just escaped death; and I broke down again. The child (about 14) didn't know just what to do—she tried to comfort me. Her mother came in and tried. I soon pulled together, but I'm not right yet.

I don't know what to say. It's all over, and you're better. Sometimes I think you're too plucky. Sweet, I feel like taking the first boat. If I only could. But you've said remain, and I shall—though really, darling, it's rather against my better judgement. You see, I must really get to business now, and the work with the quartette would mean money. They're not coming here, but the show will go on.

Mrs. Knight [the backer of the play] is sailing Wednesday, and I'll send her to see you. Then you talk to Miss Wiborg, and if you think I should stay, cable again. If not, tell me to come. I have my fare here from Mrs. Campbell. If I can't get 2nd [class accommodations], I'll come 3rd. Anything to get there.

"Please now, some word," he insisted. "I'd hate to stay here, have nothing happen, and then be out with the boys [i.e., miss his chance in *Shuffle Along*]." His closing was full of solicitous concern for her health.

Now Sweet—do be careful. Don't travel until you're ready to. Don't catch cold, etc. Darling, I can't imagine you gone forever. If you go—I feel as though I *must* follow. Our life together has been so happy. Let's have years and years and years.

Goodness—your description of your illness surely sounded as though you were in great danger. Yes, sweet, I hope we may be able to have a child. For your sake most of all—you do love them so. But you remember, sweet—when we married I knew then that perhaps it might not be our lot. No child can ever mean as much as my Dolly. And if there is any danger to be undergone beyond the normal—never; and I'll be happy with my little wife and my brave little girl whom I love to distraction. So we will not worry about that. First comes my wife, and last comes my wife.

Lots and lots of love, Dolly. Your Dubby loves you forever and ever and ever—

A bitter clash between Mrs. Campbell and Miss Wiborg over Mrs. Campbell's premature departure and money sealed the doom of *Voodoo*, which closed abruptly in Plymouth. To make matters worse, by this time Browning could no longer guarantee Paul a stint in *Shuffle Along*. Nevertheless, Paul quickly booked passage home so that he could take care of Essie during the rest of her convalescence. He rushed to her bedside as soon as he arrived in New York twelve days later, and he stayed there continuously except for time out to eat and sleep. She was overjoyed to see him, and she flourished under his loving attention. When he took her home from the hospital after a couple of weeks, she was well on the road to recovery. Then they called on her mother to help take care of her while he turned to the task of looking for work.

———

In September 1922, Paul enrolled for his last term at Columbia. With Fritz Pollard, he jumped from the Akron Pros, for whom they had both starred in 1920 and 1921, to the weaker Milwaukee Badgers, who offered them more money. The gamble paid off. Billed by the media as the greatest defensive end in the history of football, Paul consistently drew large crowds even though the Milwaukee team was mediocre, posting a season record of two wins, four losses, and three ties. But Paul was glad to be back in his element. One of the wins was a spectacular 13–0 victory over the Oorang Indians led by the all-time great All-American Jim Thorpe, in which Paul scored both touchdowns. The first was on an outstanding defensive effort that enabled him to recover a fumble in the end zone, and the second was the result of a great offensive move. According to the newspaper accounts, "Purdy shot a forward pass to Robeson, which the negro [sic] nailed by a great leap and carried over the goal line."[28]

However, the news stories didn't report what happened right after Paul scored that touchdown. The game had been a fairly rough one, with an accumulation of personal animosities, and his second touchdown had put the game beyond the reach of the Oorang Indians. Besides, Paul had made devastatingly hard-hitting tackles and blocks all afternoon. Somehow, his second touchdown had unleashed all the pent-up frustration in his adversaries, and four or five of them had rushed to pile onto him in the end zone. But he was ready for them, and for a brief time the large crowd in the stands witnessed the amazing sight of this giant black man cuffing and tossing men aside as if they were children.

Paul's teammates converged on the scene of battle simultaneously with the rest of the other team, and the general melee that followed was quickly broken up by managers and the police; however, the striking image of Paul tossing men around lingered. By sheer coincidence, two boxing promoters happened to be watching and were waiting for him in the locker room after the game. They offered him a large sum of money to train as a boxer in order to take on the role of a "Great Black Hope" challenger to world heavyweight champion Jack Dempsey.

Paul promptly turned down the offer, but rumors traveled; soon the syndicated columnist Lawrence Perry wrote that Paul Robeson was taking up boxing in order to challenge Jack Dempsey because he could not earn enough in the practice of law. Concerned about his public image at law school, Paul protested to the Rutgers Alumni Office, which requested and got Perry's public retraction of his incorrect report.[29] Alexander Woollcott, the harshest critic of Paul's spring appearance in *Voodoo*, indirectly alluded to the episode in his memoirs:

> I fell to thinking of the first time I met him. That was in 1922, when he came around to see me in a small flat I had in the gashouse district of New York. He was uncertain what he wanted to be, but he was quite sure it wasn't a prize fighter. No, nor a lawyer, either. He would finish the law course because he had started it, but a Negro lawyer's chances are slim, and anyway, he felt he was meant to be something quite different. An actor, perhaps. He might do something with his voice. I think I felt at the time that I had just crossed the path of someone touched by destiny. He was a young man on his way. He did not know where he was going, but I never in my life saw anyone so quietly sure, by some inner knowledge, that he was going somewhere.[30]

By Christmas 1922, Essie was in good health, and Paul had made considerable money during the professional football season. Now he temporarily put all of his energy into his law studies. Insisting on his freedom to follow where opportunity led and easily attracting friends and allies, he had learned the hard lesson that he faced critical choices at every turn. At this juncture, at the age of twenty-four, Paul could plunge into the field of law while acquiring some practical experience and passing the difficult New York bar examination. Or he could pursue theater and defer his study for the bar exam indefinitely. He knew now that he could not pursue both careers. The decision had to be unequivocal.

5

THE PERFORMER TRIUMPHS

(1923–1924)

B y February 1923, Paul had made his choice. He decided to concentrate on seeking a position in a major Wall Street law firm and on preparing for the New York State bar examination. His graduation from Columbia Law School was inauspicious and without ceremony. Two official letters from the registrar had arrived certifying that he had completed the requirements for a bachelor of law degree and that the degree would be granted on February 28. Paul chose to receive it by mail. Meanwhile, he appealed to his football coach at Rutgers, Foster Sanford, who had been instrumental in arranging his acceptance to Columbia Law School, for help once again. Sanford called a Rutgers alumnus and trustee from the class of 1890, Louis W. Stotesbury, who headed a powerful law firm specializing in estates and wills.

Stotesbury invited Paul to come in for an interview and was so impressed with him that he not only hired him on the spot but also assigned him to draft the brief for a phase of the high-profile Gould Will case that the firm was litigating. The case had grown out of a dispute over the estate of prominent financier Stephen Jay Gould. Paul accepted the challenge and fashioned a brief that was used essentially unaltered when the case came to trial. His efficiency and meticulous, thorough work won Stotesbury's strong approval.

Almost everyone else at the firm went out of their way to register their hostility in a variety of small ways. Paul ignored the slights until a stenographer whom he had asked to take down a legal document stepped over his threshold of tolerance. She announced acidly that she never took dictation "from a nigger" and stalked out.

Paul explained the situation to Stotesbury, who listened sympathetically, indicating that he could readily eliminate the worst aspects of Paul's mistreatment by the staff; however, he was frank in addressing the broader and far more intractable racial discrimination that Paul would face in the legal profession. Present and future white clients would not agree to have "a colored man" as their trial lawyer, and many judges would be prejudiced against him because of his race. His career prospects were severely limited in the white law market. But, Stotesbury added, there was one alternative worth consideration. He then made a "franchise" offer: Paul could head a Harlem branch office of the firm. This position would not only be financially rewarding but would also provide a solid base for Paul if he chose to enter Harlem politics.

Paul politely heard Stotesbury out, thanked him for his generous offer, and informed Stotesbury that he was resigning his position. It was inconceivable to Paul that he would enter a profession in which his possibilities would be so limited by racial prejudice. As he told the story later, in one stroke, he abandoned his dream of a law career. He would risk casting his lot with the theater.[1]

Immediately, he had to contend with Essie, who was disappointed in what she viewed as his hasty unilateral decision. She had never intended for him to completely forgo the bar exam. At the same time, she pressed him to seek readily available acting jobs in vaudeville. More black song and dance revues were reaching New Yorkers in the broad wake of *Shuffle Along*. Paul had altogether different ideas. He had no intention of taking the bar exam, since he now had no intention of practicing law. He aspired to a significant role in the legitimate theater, following the direction in which he had embarked with great success during the previous year. He viewed vaudeville and musical comedy as an artistic dead end. However, confrontation was not his style, so he pretended to go along. He even made a desultory stab at studying for the bar exam, but his efforts didn't amount to much.

Reluctantly, Paul sang for a short while in the chorus of the *Plantation Revue*, a vaudeville act at the Plantation nightclub in Harlem. The show starred Florence Mills, one of the greatest Negro artists of that time, and Paul realized that being around Mills was like participating in a master class. But his heart wasn't in it. He yearned for a theatrical medium that was less permeated with crude stereotypes.

Finally, during the summer of 1923, after a great deal of argument, Paul convinced Essie that he should quit performing in nightclubs, give up the idea of rejoining *Shuffle Along*, and focus exclusively on developing a career in the legitimate theater.[2]

He didn't tell her that he had already launched a sustained effort to join the Provincetown Players.

In March 1923, Paul had written to Otto Kahn, a Rutgers trustee and a wealthy banker who was a patron of a number of black artists and a major contributor to the Players. In his letter he requested introductions to the Provincetown playwrights and an interview. He was specifically interested in meeting Eugene O'Neill, who, he suggested, "may possibly have Negro roles." He had also asked Augustin Duncan to write a letter of recommendation to O'Neill on his behalf.

Kahn's reply was polite but perfunctory and not helpful. He said he would keep Paul's request in mind, but he declined to write a letter of recommendation. He added that there was no suitable opportunity for an interview "at present." However, Duncan wrote O'Neill a warm letter of recommendation, which Paul followed up with a letter of his own. In November, Paul received a friendly reply, in which O'Neill invited him to keep in touch by phone or letter. The playwright implied that Paul would receive favorable consideration for a part in a major production.

O'Neill was as good as his word: the next month Paul received a note from Kenneth Macgowan, director of the Provincetown Players, inviting him to read the lead part of Jim Harris in O'Neill's new play, *All God's Chillun Got Wings*. The story of a tragic interracial marriage, *Chillun* was one of the first mainstream American plays to confront this issue head-on. In the play, Jim Harris, an aspiring black law student, rescues Ella Downey, a young white woman who was his childhood playmate and has been abandoned by her husband, from life on the streets. They marry, but Ella's prejudice poisons her feelings for Jim, and she ultimately goes mad. Jim is faithful to the end and refuses to leave her.[3]

Paul's audition almost hypnotized the audience of theater professionals. The part was his for the taking. Sixty years later, Bess Eitingon, a former member of the Players who was present at the reading, recalled that she was captivated not only by his "marvelous, incredible" voice but also by his beautiful build and his graceful movements.[4]

Essie wanted Paul to plunge single-mindedly into rehearsals. She urged him to risk everything on this stunning opportunity. When she finished her plea, Paul rose and, to her surprise and exasperation, said, with barely a hint of a smile at the corners of his mouth, "You're right. I decided to do just that months ago."[5]

O'Neill's contract required that *All God's Chillun Got Wings* be published in *American Mercury* magazine prior to its opening performance. An unforeseen publication delay produced a corresponding delay in the opening of the play, and rehearsals were postponed until early April 1924. To fill the gap, Paul kept up a heady round of parties and professional engagements. In January 1924, he was initiated into the Sigma Tau Sigma chapter of Theta Sigma, a black professional fraternity. He sang at prominent public events—an NAACP meeting at Abyssinian Baptist Church in Harlem and a YWCA cultural evening in Brooklyn as the main soloist. He and Essie attended a Heywood Broun lecture at the New York Public Library and were invited to an honorary dinner for W. E. B. DuBois in the spring.

At parties and other purely social gatherings, Paul eased forward to sing spontaneously without an accompanist. He could sing any song in his repertoire in several different keys without difficulty. He could also perform with accompanists of modest abilities, recruited on the spot. At parties he sang mostly contemporary popular ballads. It seemed as if Negro spirituals were not in vogue among either the black or white elites. However, when he performed professionally in black churches and at benefits for civil rights organizations such as the NAACP, he liked to sing the familiar songs from his childhood. Spirituals were the core of the program. His accompanists for professional engagements varied but were drawn from among the many skilled music teachers and church choir directors in Harlem. Between these engagements, Paul scheduled fairly regular rehearsals and continuous voice study.

In late March, with the prominent actress Rose McClendon in the title role, Paul played a wayward preacher who is rescued from his congregation by a strong woman in a revival of *Roseanne* presented by the Lafayette Players. The all-black company, which included the now celebrated Charles Gilpin, performed limited runs of the play for one week each at Harlem's Lafayette Theater and the Dunbar in Philadelphia. Spurred by Gilpin's 1920 Broadway success in the lead role of Eugene O'Neill's *The Emperor Jones*, the Lafayette Players had advanced the cause of black theater by putting on other plays written by white playwrights on black subjects.[6]

On April 1, 1924, a review of *Roseanne* in the *Philadelphia Record* noted that "the players seem a good deal more interesting than the play itself. . . . Paul Robeson is a strapping man with a voice that rolls out of him like a vibrant tide. It would be extremely interesting to see what he could do with *Emperor Jones* or the frustrated young negro [*sic*] in *All God's Chillun Got Wings*."

A series of complications delayed the opening of *Chillun* for yet another month. First, Mary Blair, Paul's costar, became ill. Then, after its publication in February, a controversy over the play's theme of an interracial marriage developed: the play was shrilly denounced in the conservative press, and the Ku Klux Klan made threats of violence against both O'Neill and Paul. It was predicted that there would be riots at the opening.

Paul immersed himself in preparing for his role, which would require all of his novice ability. The Provincetown Players decided to deflect attention from the controversy over *Chillun* and the opening delay by reviving *The Emperor Jones* for a week, with Paul playing the lead. Originally made famous by Charles Gilpin, the play was an ideal vehicle for Paul because it offered both complexity and tragic possibilities—in short, a fully realized character. It would require a tour de force even for a seasoned actor to learn two major roles simultaneously.

Brutus Jones is a wily Pullman porter who becomes self-proclaimed emperor of a small Caribbean island after getting into trouble in the United States and escaping from prison by killing a brutal guard. Ultimately, he is the victim of his rebellious subjects who inflict their revenge upon him for his misrule.

To ensure that Paul knew his lines for both parts, Essie began rehearsing with him day and night. She would often surprise him in the course of their everyday activities by suddenly speaking a cue line to see how quickly he could get into character. He would pick up the dialogue from wherever she cued him. She noted on May 4 that at the dress rehearsal for *Jones*, "Paul wasn't as good as he has been. Stiff, nervous, but will work out fine." The next day, she reported that the rehearsal had gone "marvelously" and that Paul was "easy and natural."

On May 6, *The Emperor Jones* opened. Essie attended with her mother and Paul's sister Marian, and reported in her diary, "Paul was superb. Applause and stomping and whistling, deafening after final curtain. [He] got five curtain calls. Performance really fine."[7] She added that O'Neill, his wife, and the director, James Light, were also "thrilled" with Paul's performance.

This time, the reviews heaped praise on both Paul's performance and the play. The *New York Herald Tribune* critic commented that the play was "vitalized by a Negro with power and a full measure of understanding." The *New York Telegram* reported that "Robeson held his audience enthralled. . . . He has a powerful voice that fairly booms, and it is resonant. . . . If [he] had the proper training he would become one of the greatest singers in the world."

The same account quoted Charles Gilpin on Paul's performance. "A hard worker," he said, adding, "He has studied intensively." In the face of all the enthusiastic praise coming from every other quarter, the comment was noticeably cool. By contrast, Paul went out of his way to be deferential to Gilpin's performance in the role.

The reviewer in the *New York Evening Post* compared Paul to Gilpin: "He is a fair rival of Mr. Gilpin in vigor, although the older actor had the advantage of greater experience and gave the effect of a greater subtlety."[8] But under the circumstances, Paul had neither the time nor the opportunity to concentrate on subtlety; the day after the opening of *The Emperor Jones*, he began rehearsing *All God's Chillun*. It was a grueling schedule, but it suited his temperament. He had a deep-seated need to be engaged in something that demanded all of his heart and energy.

A few days into the run, a delegation of the cultural elite of Harlem, including Mr. and Mrs. James Weldon Johnson and the sister of prominent literary editor Jessie Fauset, came to see *Emperor Jones*, and they approved it. On May 12, however, with the play having been up for only four days, Essie reported in her diary that Mary Blair, "quite disturbed" about Paul's success in *Jones*, was forcing an earlier opening for *Chillun* even though she was not feeling well. On May 13, the initial run of *Jones* closed, to "a full house . . . and a very enthusiastic" response,[9] to go into alternate weeks of performance with *Chillun*.

On May 15, *Chillun* opened at last. After the high drama produced by the threats, not a single protester appeared, and the headline of Alexander Woollcott's review in the evening newspaper *The Sun* read: "O'Neill's Play Tranquilly Produced in MacDougal Street." Essie reported that the audience "seemed gripped, moved and tense," and that it was "at any opportunity . . . generous with applause."[10] "Most critics disliked [the] play," she noted, "but all liked Paul's acting. Morning and evening papers fine. Alexander Woollcott again raved about Paul."[11]

Woollcott praised the "noble figure . . . superbly embodied and fully comprehended by Paul Robeson." Robert Welsh of the *New York Telegram and Evening Mail* wrote that the "difficult role" of the Negro husband was "played powerfully and with a convincing simplicity by Paul Robeson." And Heywood Broun commented in *The World* that Paul brought "a genius to the piece" and wondered if he would play Othello some day.[12] Paul sailed from one performance to the next.

More and more, acting had begun to make sense to him. He was discovering the beginnings of a coherent artistic vision. Simultaneously, the media was discovering in him a ready, articulate voice full of candor and informed, frequently controversial ideas about race, culture, and the larger issues of the day. A conversation with Paul invariably made good copy. In an interview with the *New York Herald Tribune* about his "possibilities," and in two articles for the black magazines *The Messenger* and *Opportunity* where he discussed his "hopes" and O'Neill's plays, he set out his defense of O'Neill's black tragic heroes. In part, he was responding to the strong criticism of O'Neill's characterizations on the part of the black press, black nationalists, and many black civil rights leaders.

Paul believed in *Chillun's* Jim Harris and in Brutus Jones in spite of the black stereotypes that still marred them. "If I do become a first-rate actor," he said, "it will do more toward giving people a slant on the so-called Negro problem than any amount of propaganda and argument."

> In "All God's Chillun" we have a play of great strength and beautiful spirit, mocking all petty prejudice, emphasizing the humanness, and, in Mr. O'Neill's words, "the oneness" of mankind. Any number of people have said to me: "I trust that now you will get a truly heroic and noble role, one portraying the finest type of

Negro." I honestly believe that perhaps never will I portray a nobler type than "Jim Harris" or a more heroically tragic figure than "Brutus Jones, Emperor," not excepting "Othello."[13]

This view informed Paul's life and now it informed his work. Subsequently, despite considerable pressure to recant, it would remain his firm belief that there was nothing to be gained in hiding any aspect of African-American life, even the painful and negative parts, from the scrutiny of society:

> The reactions to these two plays among Negroes but point out one of the most serious drawbacks to the development of a true Negro dramatic literature. We are too self-conscious, too afraid of showing all phases of our life—especially those phases which are of greatest dramatic value. The great mass of our group discourage any member who has the courage to fight these petty prejudices. I am still being damned all over the place for playing in *All God's Chillun*. It annoys me very little when I realize that those who object most strenuously know mostly nothing of the play and in any event know little of the theater and have no right to judge a playwright of O'Neill's talents.[14]

W. E. B. DuBois agreed with Paul, but William Pickens, field secretary of the NAACP, objected to the play. Writing in the black press, Pickens declared that:

> The very nature of this play is to create sentiment against mixed schools of white and black, especially in the North where the common school has so far been maintained. It would hardly be allowed in the South, but it is in the North that this play will do "good," from the Ku Klux [Klan] point of view.[15]

Pickens was not alone in contending that the quality of Paul's portrayals was outweighed by the negative stereotypes that were attached to them. Black nationalist leader Marcus Garvey excoriated Paul for playing these roles, and several leading black clergymen, including Reverend Adam Clayton Powell Sr., of the Abyssinian Baptist Church, and Reverend J. W. Brown of the A.M.E. Zion Church (the denomination of Paul's father), also leveled sharp criticisms.

Paul remained steadfast in his view that O'Neill's tragic hero was a transitional figure in popular culture—a first step away from the all-pervasive "Sambo" caricature. For him, this temporary compromise did not conflict with his *ultimate* goal of portraying black characters from a fully black perspective:

> One of the great measures of a people is its culture, its artistic stature. Above all things, we boast that the only true artistic contributions of America are Negro in origin. We boast of the culture of ancient Africa.[16]

> I am sure that there will come Negro playwrights of great power, and I trust I shall have some part in interpreting that most interesting and much needed addition to the drama of America.[17]

O'Neill heartily agreed with the theater's need for works by black playwrights. He urged black artists to:

> Be yourselves! Don't reach out for *our* stuff which *we* call good! Make *your stuff* and *your good!* There ought to be a Negro play written by a Negro that no white could ever have conceived or executed. By this I don't mean greater—because all art is equally great—but *yours, your own*, an expression of what is deep in you, *is* you, *by* you! [emphasis in original][18]

Paul drew on his native experience and unromanticized truth, ignoring the criticisms and letting his performances speak for themselves. He was now convinced that he had found at least part of his calling in the legitimate theater. O'Neill was gratified by the success Paul had brought to his plays, yet he would always remain somewhat ambivalent about Paul's interpretation of the lead roles.

O'Neill's private comments about Paul's performances partially contradicted his fulsome public tribute, in which he credited Paul with "the most complete satisfaction an author can get—that of seeing his creation borne into flesh and blood" and with achieving "complete fidelity to my intent."[19] In an entry in his "Work Diary" after the 1924 opening of *The Emperor Jones*, O'Neill expressed his opinion that Paul was not as good as Charles Gilpin, except in the later scenes. And in an interview given twenty-two years later, he remarked, "I can honestly say that there was only one actor who carried out every notion of a character I had in mind. That actor was Charles Gilpin as the Pullman porter in *The Emperor Jones*."[20]

Yet O'Neill was drawn to Paul's manifest intellectual depth. As he expressed in a 1923 letter:

> Yes, Gilpin is all "ham." So I've corralled another Negro to do it [*The Emperor Jones*]—a young fellow [Robeson] with considerable experience, wonderful presence and voice, full of ambition and a damn fine man personally with real brains—not a "ham"! He'll be bigger than Gilpin was even at the start. No, I don't think Gilpin's color had much—or anything—to do with the "warping" you speak of. He's just a regular actor-brain, that's all. Most white actors, under the same circumstances, would have gone the same route. The point is, none of them would have *dared* go so far.[21]

While O'Neill was attracted by Paul's insightful exploration of the role, he was disconcerted with the way in which Paul shaded the Harlem-street-stereotype side of Brutus Jones. But Paul's performance, which drew on his own knowledge and experience, added a dimension to the role that O'Neill could not have written. For example, he apparently didn't know that Pullman porters were highly educated. Most, including Paul's brother Bill, had college degrees and possessed a far more sophisticated vision than the character Jones as O'Neill had conceived him. Paul minimized the street-smart aspect of Jones. Playing him as intelligent, rather than merely crafty, Paul brought greater realism, as well as greater dimension, to the role. Furthermore, because of the greater dignity Paul created in the first scene, there was a more shattering dramatic effect when Jones subsequently unraveled.

From Paul's point of view, he achieved his most important contribution to the play by *not* following the playwright's intent exactly. Shrewdly, he avoided public acknowledgment of this digression. Thus, from the beginning of Paul's career, a disparity emerged between his realistic, fully conceived analysis of his stage roles and the critics' overall perception of him as merely an "instinctive" or "natural" actor.

O'Neill, to the contrary, never reconciled himself to Paul's interpretation of his heroes, and expressed that view in a September 27, 1931, interview in the *New York Herald Tribune*. His lingering reservations about Paul's performance in *Chillun* were informative:

> Last year in Paris the Kamerny Theater of Moscow presented its production of *All God's Chillun*. O'Neill was enchanted with the

results. For one thing, he found that the actor who blacked up and played his Negro hero in the play about miscegenation captured the quality he was striving for with considerably more comprehension and completeness than even Paul Robeson ever managed, though the role was practically written for him.[22]

Preoccupied with being color-blind, the playwright crafted a naive victim; Paul, the race-conscious actor, portrayed a noble but deeply flawed protagonist.[23] He could not have known that his portrayals of O'Neill's characters were on their way to becoming indelible images of the twentieth century. These images began to redefine the place of black actors in the history of the theater. In Paul's culturally astute interpretations of these roles, he made a breach in the wall holding back both black actors and black playwrights.

Paul continued working earnestly with the Provincetown Players, doing summer stock theater in New Hampshire. In early August 1924, Essie noted her regret at not being able to go to New Hampshire to see Paul perform, "but I can't get away from the hospital, have no money and no clothes. Would love to have gone up."[24] A couple of weeks later, she went on a month's vacation from the lab, writing: "Am sick to death of the Lab, and do hope I won't ever have to go back."[25] On August 18, *All God's Chillun* reopened in New York, and Essie reported, "standing room out to doors, nice reception."[26]

The following week she reported "a most interesting visit" between Paul and Koriansky, the Russian critic and associate of Konstantin Stanislavsky, the Russian actor and director. At the meeting, Koriansky agreed to give Paul regular acting lessons. "[He] says he thinks Paul is a great artist and just needs a little technique," Essie wrote. "This is indeed a marvelous offer. They will go over 'Othello' together, Koriansky suggesting and Paul learning the part. We are stunned by this good fortune."[27] Engaging Koriansky was the first decisive step in Paul's lifelong and ever-deepening relationship to Shakespeare's tragic Moor.

Chillun closed in late September, to a packed house. As Paul had wished, his finances were finally looking sufficiently promising that Essie could leave her hospital job behind. She quietly assumed the role of Paul's manager. In October, she concluded arrangements with

black filmmaker Oscar Micheaux for Paul's first film appearance in
Body and Soul. He was well satisfied with the contract: "3% of gross
income after the first $40,000 the picture brings in; salary $100 per
week for three weeks." This was good pay for those days, and
Micheaux, who had produced his first film in 1919, was proving himself a deft director and scriptwriter, as well.

Body and Soul appealed to Paul because the project required the
degree of cultural knowledge that erupted imaginatively from his
authentic observations as an African-American man. He performed
the two lead male roles—a charming but evil preacher who is also a
seducer, gambler, thief, and killer, and his twin, an upright young
man who is a model of virtue as he courts the heroine. Here was a
daring artistic experiment for the fledgling actor. The fact that the
film was silent deprived Paul of his main asset—his speaking voice.
Moreover, Micheaux's low budget virtually precluded retakes, so for
the most part he had to do everything right the first time. Scenes
involving his two very different roles were sometimes shot in the
same session, so he had to switch screen personalities within minutes.
During the filming, Paul felt steadied by Essie's presence. On the set,
he wrote her a note:

> Studio, Wednesday
> Darling Sweet—
>
> Some day I'll be able to tell you how very deeply I love you. It is
> not easy to talk to you when you are near me. I am so overcome, I
> can only hold you close and want to literally devour you. It's all so
> strange. I can think of nothing and no one except your activities
> and you. I want you to love me and like me deeply and passion-
> ately. What joy to talk to you and rehearse with you and watch the
> workings of your mind. As in "All God's Chillun," so here in the
> picture your help is invaluable. You see everything so clearly, and I
> understand you so quickly. I shall never worry about any future
> play. You, better than anyone, understand any false move or accent
> or tone. You're marvelous. I only hope to be as useful to you when
> you begin [an independent career].
>
> I love you, darling—I must go on the set. It is lovely to know
> you are near and I'll be seeing you before I go to sleep. Will you
> please pat your baby when you come in? Thanks.
>
> Paul

Increasingly viewing himself as an actor, Paul also surveyed a wider world of options as a singer. Late in August, Mrs. Guy Currier, a Boston socialite who had seen Paul perform in *The Emperor Jones* in New Hampshire, wrote that she wanted to present Paul in concert at the Copley Plaza in Boston. "We are delighted with this opportunity and shall certainly take advantage of it," Essie wrote in her diary. In fact, Paul and Essie regarded the performance as an opportunity for luck to land. "We hope the concert will be such a success that Mrs. Currier will suggest a vocal instructor for Paul," Essie continued.[28]

With distinguished composer-arranger Harry T. Burleigh as his musical adviser, Paul had given small concerts throughout most of 1924 with a regular accompanist named Hooper, who was apparently a friend of Burleigh's. A baritone, Burleigh had long enjoyed being in the Manhattan spotlight and could help his protégé gain respect. Noteworthy appearances at the Provincetown Playhouse on June 1 and at Rutgers on December 17 elevated Paul's visibility. Other performances were private recitals given at the homes of wealthy whites on Long Island and on New York City's East Side.[29] The larger significance of Mrs. Currier's invitation was that it would represent Paul's first appearance as a professional concert-hall soloist.

On November 1, 1924, the concert at the Copley Plaza in Boston took place. Paul had prepared, and Burleigh had coached him well. The house was packed, the appreciative audience gave generous applause, and the critics were kind. Paul had confirmed that he had a potential concert career.

However, from Paul's point of view, his performance failed to satisfy. The decidedly classical European concert style, favored by Burleigh and used so successfully by Roland Hayes, didn't suit Paul. Its formal constraints and vocal style inhibited the natural warmth of his delivery and attenuated the unique richness of his tones. He decided to look for a voice coach who understood his unconventional needs, and to seek out an accompanist-arranger who was steeped in the purity of the original slave songs from the South. He continued to work diligently with Hooper, but after that performance he distanced himself from Burleigh.[30]

At this stage, however, it could be said that singing was Paul's sideline, and acting was his main thrust. On December 29, 1924, he signed a contract with theatrical producer Harry Weinberger for a

Broadway appearance in *The Emperor Jones*. Essie was thrilled by his successful professional journey and her major role in promoting it. She was in a celebratory mood. Paul, by contrast, was gratified but unimpressed by his triumphs. The deeper he delved into his art, the more he craved spiritual and emotional sustenance rather than celebration. He needed something more.

Despite his deep attachment to Essie, he once again sought out Gerry Neale, not yet knowing that she had secretly married her steady beau, Harry Bledsoe. Gerry didn't tell Paul that she was married, but she advised him to make a success out of his marriage to Essie.[31] Paul saw Gerry three more times at social events that holiday season. On each of those occasions, Essie took note that "Paul was quite attentive to Gerry, and I'm unhappy about it." This confession was in her journal entry of December 26. On New Year's Day 1925, she noted, "Paul not loyal to me for the first time. He vamped Gerry before my very eyes." But in typical style she did not dwell on her feelings, continuing dutifully, "Beautiful hall. Paul radioed over Station WOR; sang spirituals." It was easy to understand her denial of the stark signs that Paul was unhappy in their relationship. After all, her husband, the unusual law student for whom she had sacrificed her career, had quickly become a star.

6

SEEKER OF GRACE

(1925–1926)

On January 28, 1925, Essie noted in her diary that she had come "to splendid terms" for a British production of *The Emperor Jones*. "I was able to get tentative terms of $300/week, double passage over and back, six weeks guarantee, 5 percent of gross over $1,000; maybe higher percentage. Am dying to sign the contract." Soon afterward the contract was signed for a London opening in September, presented by Sir Alfred Butt, a leading British producer. With their finances no longer stretched to the breaking point, Essie felt they could afford an apartment in a more fashionable West Harlem building at 355 West 145th Street. She supervised the move in her usual go-ahead manner.

She noted that Lawrence Brown, the brilliant accompanist-arranger, was no longer working with Roland Hayes and had come to New York. "Larry . . . and Paul are going to work together daily," she wrote. "I think they will make a very fine combination." Essie zealously struck a practical deal: "Paul and Larry to go 50–50, and each will give me 10 percent as agent."[1]

Many years later, Larry Brown recalled to Marie Seton, Paul's English biographer, how he had bumped into Paul by accident back in 1925 upon returning to the United States when he heard that his father was dying. After the funeral, he went to the flat of friends at 188 West 135th Street, put his luggage down, and decided to take a walk. As he turned the corner, there was Paul Robeson, standing by himself. If Brown had caught any other train, he would have missed Paul. Brown remembered:

By then, Paul was the most popular man in Harlem, with everyone wanting to shake his hand. I went over and said "Hello." Paul asked me what I was doing that night.

I wasn't doing a thing. Paul said he had promised to go down to Greenwich Village and spend the evening with Jimmy Light, the man who had directed him in O'Neill's plays. He asked me to have dinner with him and then go along. He said we might play some songs. He liked the volume of arrangements I had sent him.

He sang "Swing Low Sweet Chariot," then "Every Time I Feel the Spirit," where I joined in as the second voice. It was completely spontaneous. My joining in excited Jimmy Light. He said, "Why don't you fellows give a concert?" That's how it happened![2]

Their first real performance together was in late March in the home of the writer Carl Van Vechten and his wife, actress Fania Marinoff, and it was a sensation. Through Walter White, executive secretary of the NAACP, Paul had met the Van Vechtens, who had introduced him to their inner circle of friends—composer George Gershwin, writer Theodore Dreiser, publishers Alfred and Blanche Knopf, financier Otto Kahn, and dancer Adele Astaire. Van Vechten, a flamboyant white supporter of the new Negro movement, was a key patron and adviser to a broad array of black cultural figures during the Harlem Renaissance.

"Carl was amazed and just begged for more and more songs," Essie wrote. "Carl and Fania just raved about Paul's voice and Larry's rhythm. Larry is really fine. Carl is so interested he is almost jumping up and down. Some very interesting people dropped in to hear Paul sing."[3] Everyone was struck not only by Paul's voice but also by the effect Paul and Larry created as a duo when Larry joined in with a tenor counterpart. But impressing Van Vechten was especially fortuitous, for he was a mover and shaker not only in Harlem but in the white downtown New York art world.

Less than a month later, when Paul and Larry gave their first public concert together, Essie wrote jubilantly:

Sunday, April 19 [1925]. Today is one of the most significant times in our lives. The all-Negro concert by Paul and Larry took place at the Greenwich Village Theatre tonight. The house was sold out yesterday, and at 8:15, when the theatre doors opened, the lobby, sidewalk and vicinity were packed. They sold reserved standing room at 8:30 P.M., and almost exceeded the fire limit. Hundreds were turned away. The audience was very high class. When the boys appeared, there was thunderous applause, lasting three minutes. Then they sang. They were both very nervous, but did very well indeed. After each number, the applause was deafening. The boys got curtain call after call.

The *New York Times* critic raved. The Negro songs, he said, "voiced the sorrows and hopes of a people," and Paul's spirituals had "the ring of the revivalist, they hold in them a world of religious experience; it is this cry from the depths, this universal humanism, that touches the heart."[4]

While the public triumph buoyed Essie, it was a private tribute that moved Paul deeply. One of his Sigma Theta Sigma fraternity brothers confessed in a poignant note that "Frankly, I didn't know that an evening of Spirituals could afford so much pleasure. Unfortunately, I am in the same position with the majority of Northern Negroes educated in these schools. I do not know my own music."[5] From his point of view, the performance was "wonderful, exhilarating, altogether ineffable."

In contrast to Paul's relative silence on purely political issues, he was developing a consistent voice on matters of culture and challenging some precepts of the black intelligentsia. One manifestation of this was his desire to rescue his beloved spirituals from the disdain of both blacks and whites. As an artist, he saw that the Negro spiritual was a beautiful form of folk music, equal or superior in stature to the folk melodies of European culture, and it had become important to him to bring his people's music to its rightful position of respect in the wider world. Within a year, this would become a frequent theme in his interviews:

My own people—many of them—have felt that the old Spirituals were not in keeping with the aspirations of the modern Negro. They feel that white audiences approach the Spirituals in a patronizing spirit. Perhaps this is true, but it is what they take with them from a concert that means most. The distinctive gift the Negro has made to America has not been from the brilliantly successful colored men and women who, after all, have done only what white people are doing. It is from the most humble of our people that the music now recognized as of abiding beauty has emanated.[6]

Paul reasoned that there was something valuable to be gained in getting this music out to a mass audience. "No one can hear these songs as our people sang them and not understand the Negro a little better," he said, adding that:

> I found that on the stage, whether singing or acting, race and color prejudices are forgotten. Art is the one form against which such barriers do not stand. And I think it is through art we are going to come into our own. Young colored people have always in the past been urged to be as good as the white people—the young lawyer is told to be as good as the white lawyer. That's ridiculous. To be as good as anyone else is no high ideal, especially when the models held up to the colored youth are just the white people in general. The art form is the one in which I am myself.[7]

Indeed, Paul always did pursue his artistic career "as himself"; this was his secret weapon. And it was most powerful on the concert stage where he was free from the theater's encumbrances, not the least of which were mediocre or poor scripts.

On May 3, 1925, Paul and Larry staged a second concert at the Greenwich Village Theatre. "House sold out; standing room sold, and concert very well received. The programs are a remarkable success, and it seems we are really launched at last," Essie noted with satisfaction. After the concert in the Village, the three of them rushed up to the Hotel Astor to an Actors Equity dinner. "Many stars performed, but it seems Paul and Larry were one of the biggest hits of the evening," Essie wrote.[8] By abandoning the studied superficiality and modern pretentions of the Jazz Age, Paul and Larry had struck a nerve.

It certainly seemed that Paul was now launched. Essie booked an increasing number of engagements. The first one was for Mrs. Dorr, a Rutgers trustee. She hired them twice. Essie promptly set their minimum fee for private concerts at $100.[9]

Paul was generally indifferent to the trappings of wealth, but his professional life and social life propelled him into glittering company. On May 10, he was seated in the second-row orchestra of the Metropolitan Opera House for the farewell concert by Fyodor Chaliapin, the great Russian bass, and invited backstage to meet him after the concert. "Chaliapin at once . . . recognized Paul, shook hands cordially with him, and patted him on the back and said 'Bravo! I've heard all about you, good luck,'" Essie wrote.[10] Her diary entry for May 11 described a private concert in the Fifth Avenue home of socialite Mrs. W. Murray Crane:

> The guests were crazy about the songs; the boys sang beautifully, and Mrs. Crane was very much pleased. We were all asked into the drawing room and introduced to everybody, had a wonderful supper served to us, and enjoyed ourselves mightily. To complete a perfect evening, Mrs. Crane presented me with a check for $250 and a neat little package of the extra programs for the evening. She is a most delightful woman. I liked her right off—the first time I saw her; she made me think of those old fashioned, wholesome philanthropists—just a big souled, appreciative, attractive and simple personality, and the personification of good taste. I think I like her more for such a short acquaintance than any woman I can remember.

Eugene O'Neill and his wife entertained Paul at their country home, Brook Farm, in Connecticut. O'Neill also went to visit Paul in Harlem and tasted its nonstop tuxedoed nightlife with him, as Essie reported in her diary:

> *Friday, July 10 [1925].* Gene O'Neill and Harold and Bert McGhee came up and spent the evening and night with us. They all arrived at 7 o'clock. We had cocktails and went to dinner at Craigg's [restaurant]. Then we went to the Lincoln [Theater] and saw Johnny Nit dance. Then home and more cocktails, and cooled off. It was a hot night. Paul sang for Gene an hour, and Gene seemed to enjoy it so much. Gene talked a great deal also. Then we dropped in at the Lafayette [Theater] and saw Eddie Rector dance at the midnight show, then went to Small's cabaret. Had a wonderful time there—Gene and I danced quite a bit, and Gene treated orchestra, waiter, et al., to drinks, and was royal. Gene is a regular guy. The men went out for a beer and left Bert and me alone for 1/2 hour, but we had a lovely time. The entertainers were low down—all the wiggly movements, etc. you could imagine—but we enjoyed it. Then, about 5:30 A.M., we walked over to the Vaudeville Comedy Club; but there wasn't much doing, so we didn't go in. We taxied home, stopping at Barden's Wagon en route to get some ice cream.

> Home, and Gene talked by the hour—all about his thoughts on "Jones," on Paul, on London, himself, . . . , etc.; he is simply fascinating. We had a good breakfast, and then all left about 9 A.M. During the evening, Gene told me all about the play he had in mind for Paul: about this lovable gambler, a straight guy, Smith, whom he knew, and his rise and fall. He felt Paul could do the role very well. He also wants to write another play about the "Emperor Jones" leading up to where "Emperor Jones" starts in.

Although O'Neill never got around to writing either of those plays, his high opinion of Paul found repeated expression in Essie's diary.

Paul continued to sing without fee for his friends, becoming a virtual fixture at parties given by Walter White. When the poet Countee Cullen, who was destined to become one of Harlem's literary stars, graduated from NYU, Paul and Larry performed gratis at the reception. Paul's friends from the Provincetown Players' circle—character actor and stage manager "Gig" McGhee and his wife, "Bert," along with writer and critic Heywood Broun and his wife, Ruth—provided splendid company.[11]

Paul felt remarkably at home in this eclectic, urbane group. His relationship with sculptor Antonio ("Tony") Salemme provided a particularly satisfying diversion. After seeing *The Emperor Jones* several times, Salemme convinced Paul to pose for a classic life-size nude sculpture. For hours, as Salemme worked, they discussed the problems of the world.[12]

Paul was unabashed in posing nude for Salemme and for renowned photographer Nickolas Muray. He was the first African-American celebrity to do so. In contrast to the conservatism that was a hallmark of the African-American cultural tradition, he felt he was participating in a worthy artistic venture. No doubt his father, had he been alive, would have considered this to be in extremely bad taste, but Paul was now exploring his identity and feeling free of the constraints imposed by Reverend Robeson. Salemme remembered Paul as "very easy, slow and composed. He was perfectly relaxed—I'd never seen anything like it. And he didn't talk too much. He always talked just enough. . . . Wherever he was, he seemed to belong." Salemme discerned a strong drive for success under Paul's easygoing exterior: "He was very ambitious, but he hid it very well. He never talked about what he wanted to do; he looked almost indifferent. He appeared to be able to catch whatever came. He was, you might say, an athlete in his private life."

Salemme introduced Paul to the best of Greenwich Village's bohemian artists who congregated at his studio loft. Their unfettered lifestyle had made Paul uncomfortable when he had first arrived in New York, but during the years with Salemme, Paul grew to enjoy them. In return, he often took the sculptor up to Harlem. "Paul . . . usually met people on the street who knew him. And he was more than popular. People threw their arms around him. They hugged him," Salemme recalled.

As Paul and Tony became friends, so did Essie and Tony's wife, Betty. What Tony recalled most was the magnetism of Paul's personality. Everyone was drawn to him, especially women. "Paul was very talented, and women really went at him from all directions—all kinds of women." As for Paul's social activism, Tony felt it was still dormant. "There was concern, but it was not active then. I think Paul always knew that he was an important factor in the history of his people, . . . that he was a man of destiny. He didn't talk about it. . . . He knew that whatever he did counted."[13]

Living in this intoxicating milieu was expensive. Despite signs to the contrary, Paul was constantly in debt and borrowing money. Although two sizable business offers came Paul's way, neither seemed suitable. The first was for exclusive management by entertainment agent Howard Kropf for two years, with an option for two more, and a $10,000 cash advance against a 25 percent commission. The $10,000 advance was a huge attraction. He and Essie considered it, but in the end they agreed to turn it down. Paul wanted his freedom to accept or reject deals as they came along, and exclusive management would drastically curtail this capacity.

He also turned down a second offer to costar with Florence Mills and Charles Gilpin in a new play about Harlem street life. The melodrama by known playwright Edward Sheldon, titled *Lulu Belle*, was to be produced by David Belasco, the established theater owner who had put *Shuffle Along* in lights. Although full of the conventional black stereotypes, *Lulu Belle* had the makings of an enormous commercial success. Essie thought Paul should hold his nose and star in the play, making them financially independent for at least a couple of years. Then he would be in a position to move decisively to higher artistic ground. Paul adamantly refused to consider such a compromise. After starring in the O'Neill plays, it seemed absurd to lower his sights and return to singing "coon" songs.

When *Lulu Belle* became a huge hit, Paul's reaction seems to have been philosophical. He had made his choice and there was little to do about it.[14] Finally, in late May, James Pond, a major concert manager, enticed Paul with a one-year contract for a thirteen-city concert tour. "He's a great fellow," Essie wrote of Pond, "and we like him personally besides thinking he has made us a very fine offer. . . . Hansel & Jones also wants Paul." They chose Pond, with whom they were to do business for years to come.[15]

At the end of June, a wealthy patron emerged just in time to keep Paul and Essie afloat financially. Otto Kahn, the same man who two years earlier had brushed off Paul's request for assistance in approaching the Provincetown Players, invited Paul to his Long Island estate one weekend. Essie's diary paints an admiring picture of luxury. As she recalled:

> *Sunday, June 28 [1925].* Mr. Otto Kahn's closed car called for us at 2 P.M. Mr. Kahn had planned to send his private yacht for us, but the weather was very bad. It was a delightful drive down Long Island to Cold Spring Harbor; it took about two hours. Carl [Van Vechten], Donald Angus, Larry, Paul and I made up the party. At the estate, the butler announced us and led us into the drawing room where Mr. and Mrs. Kahn received us. There were several other guests—Lionel Atwill and his wife (quite impossible); a charming Mr. & Mrs. McDonald and their little girl who had a lovely flower-like face; a Baron something or other; an Italian diplomat, Mr. Stroppa Guaglia, whom I liked immensely. Also a pleasant-faced Episcopal clergyman and a charming Englishman. The boys sang beautifully, and the Kahns seemed so pleased. Mr. Kahn agreed to become Paul's patron. He showed me the grounds of his estate, and we had a long talk about Paul's career.

It was a mixed blessing. Kahn's agreement translated into an interest-free loan of $5,000 to be repaid in two years beginning January 1, 1926 ($2,000 the first year and $3,000 the second year) from the entire net proceeds from his concert contract with the Pond management firm. The collateral for the loan was Paul's $5,000 life insurance policy. Unfortunately, the repayment of this loan plagued Paul and Essie for several years. At the time, however, they were enthusiastic and grateful.

In July 1925, riding on the crest of their critical acclaim, Paul and Larry made their first recordings, for Victor Records, in a studio in Camden, New Jersey. In the first session they recorded five songs, but they were nervous and stiff, and later re-recorded them. Paul adapted to the lack of an audience by relaxing more and singing with less volume, achieving the latter by greatly reducing his distance from the microphone. As a result, the repeat session was unusually rewarding. The records soon became hits, selling upward of fifty thousand, catapulting Paul to fame as a leading recording artist and bringing him a number of offers to appear on radio.[16]

Now twenty-seven, Paul seemed to have more reason than ever to feel content, but he felt restless. Something was pushing him to gamble on higher stakes, even as his fame grew. One evening, at the Van Vechtens, the conversation turned to the topic of personal freedom. Paul was a listener, rather than a participant, but he was agitated by a passing remark of Essie's.[17]

Twenty-one years later, when my father shared with me his recollection of that evening, his humiliation and outrage still showed. He told me that Essie, responding to a comment about extramarital sex, declared emphatically that she would "no more let some other woman sleep with Paul than I would let her use my toothbrush." He was stunned by this vulgar comparison, which implied that Essie thought of him as her possession. He expressed no outward reaction. Instead, he made up his mind on the spot to prove to himself that Essie didn't own him, despite his dependence on her as the linchpin holding his whole career together.

It happened by sheer coincidence that as Paul and Essie left the party they met Freda Diamond, a tall, willowy, dark-eyed Russian Jewish beauty in her late teens just as she was stepping out of the elevator with other members of her family. Paul sent Essie on to their next social engagement and returned to the party to talk and dance with Freda for the rest of the evening. Thus began an intimate friendship that was to last twenty-five years.[18]

A couple of weeks later, on August 5, Paul and Essie sailed to England for the London production of *The Emperor Jones*. A couple of days into the voyage they ran into rough weather, and both became quite seasick. Nevertheless, Paul rallied enough to sing at the ship's concert. Despite the fact that he wasn't feeling well, Essie reported in her diary that "he was in wonderful voice and got an ovation from the audience." The next day he was celebrated by all who had heard him. Essie reported that "hundreds" came up to him as he strolled on deck, to shake his hand and thank him for his singing.[19]

Once again, Paul had an opportunity to reflect on how Essie always came through for him. She found a spacious duplex apartment in a pleasant section of Southwest London's Chelsea, where they quietly spent their fourth wedding anniversary on August 17. Summoning a deep compassion for his malaise, she seemed to forgive and forget his transgressions. Late on opening night, she reported to her diary:

> *Thursday, September 10 [1925].* Well, it was a great night. All day Paul and I were just loafing around the house. I played pinochle with him, and chatted to ease him up. I cooked him a lovely dinner which he ate like a lamb, and then we dressed and went down in a taxi. There was such a nervous strain. When Paul was all dressed, I went out front. The house was packed with the most wonderful audience. When Paul stepped out on the stage yawning, there was terrific applause, a real personal triumph before he had done a thing. The first scene went like a breeze and got more laughs than I ever heard before. Paul was magnificent, and the cockney, Stanley, was fine. At the end of the play, Paul took ten curtain calls, some with "Smithers," and was forced to make a speech. People shouted "bravo," etc.

One reviewer wrote, "Mr. Robeson can act with the whole of his magnificent frame"; another lauded "his truly tragic powers"; and a third declared that "Mr. Robeson is a great actor." Essie proudly wrote in her diary that she convinced the theater management to display Paul's name in lights so that it could be seen from blocks away. But despite Paul's personal success, *Jones* did not catch on in London, and it closed on October 17 after only a five-week run.[20]

For the next three months, Paul and Essie made Europe their home. The change from New York lifted their spirits at first, and, as always, the handsome couple fit easily into intellectual company. Emma Goldman, the American anarchist who had recently been expelled from Soviet Russia, invited Paul and Essie to dinner several times. A motherly fifty-six-year-old, Goldman was intellectually curious, passionate, generous, and refreshingly unpretentious. She was captivated by them, and they were fascinated by her. The three of them spent many hours talking, largely about American culture and their impressions of England. Paul and Essie also listened with interest to Goldman's stories from her 1919 to 1921 sojourn in the Soviet Union during its civil war. When they departed for New York, Emma presented Essie with a beautiful antique brooch as a parting gift.[21]

Emma Goldman and the Robesons continued to correspond, remaining close friends throughout the 1920s and 1930s, and providing each other emotional support. The day before Paul opened in the 1925 London production of *The Emperor Jones*, Goldman wrote: "I know you will be great, dear Paul; still I like you to feel that I shall be with you in spirit and that I shall think inspiring thoughts about you. . . . Essie dear, I know how you will feel tomorrow. . . . I will feel with you, and I wish with all my heart that Paul's interpretation of The Emperor should make the cold blooded Englishman realize his greatness." And two months later, when Goldman returned to London from lecturing in the provinces and found a long letter from Paul and Essie awaiting her, she replied: "That was a joy to hear from you at last. It felt so lonely to come back to this cold city and find you away. Your presence brought me close to my life and friends at home."[22]

Paul and Essie were also invited to the home of the daughter of the famous African-American actor Ira Aldridge. In her diary, Essie remarked: "Spent the afternoon with Miss [Amanda] Ira Aldridge—and enjoyed every minute of it. She is the most charming, interesting and lovable woman. She gave us her father's stage earrings that he wore as Othello, and said she hoped Paul would wear them when he played [the role]."[23] Two days prior to their visit, Amanda Aldridge had written Essie a letter just after she had heard Paul sing on the radio:

> How wondrously beautiful Mr. Paul's voice sounded just now. And how absolutely distinct his softest tones in both singing and speaking were. Everyone will be looking eagerly forward to his next

broadcasting. It is a *most beautiful* voice. And altogether his render-
ings were so artistic![24] [emphasis in original]

In Paris, Paul sang his spirituals in the Latin Quarter under the
sponsorship of Sylvia Beach, who owned the Shakespeare and Company bookstore. The list of reporters and guests provides an important clue to the faces in a crowd that included many luminaries from
America's expatriate community. Writers James Joyce and Ernest Hemingway, composer George Antheil, music publisher Robert Schirmer,
and Lewis Gallantier, who headed the International Chamber of
Commerce, were among the brightest lights.[25]

Visiting the home of Henri Matisse, not far from Nevilly, Paul
and Essie were served tea by the painter's widow and daughter. They
viewed Matisse's first painting, his watercolors, his later works, as
well as a LeGarde canvas and some fascinating carved-wood African
art. Then Paul sang, and everyone was in tears at the conclusion of
"Weepin' Mary."[26]

In Villefranche, a picturesque village at the foot of the southern
Alps, Paul and Essie settled down for a vacation stay. There, many
interesting people found their way to them, including the Jamaican
poet-writer Claude McKay, whom Paul knew from the States. Paul
had always been attracted by McKay's overt challenges to white racism
and his advocacy of collective armed resistance to lynch mobs, and
he went out of his way to spend time talking with McKay about race
and radicalism. Essie was not as impressed, confiding to her diary
that she disliked McKay's somewhat crude and arrogant manner.[27]

The English writer Rebecca West also visited the Robesons in
Villefranche on her way home from Italy. As they were all sipping
coffee and liqueurs in the hotel sitting room one night after dinner,
the lights suddenly went out. Paul hushed the murmurs of alarm by
singing in the darkness for a full half hour until the lights came on
again. The hotel proprietor exclaimed: "Never have we heard anything so beautiful; it is like the voice of angels." West recalled Paul
"walking with the dignity of an African king," adding that she was
"thrilled by the realisation that here was somebody with a gift of the
first order, and the wisdom and the patience to develop it to its
utmost magnitude."[28]

———

A cable from Paul's sister, Marian, on November 25, 1925, introduced a shard of reality. Their oldest brother, Bill, had died in Washington, D.C., of tuberculosis; he was only forty-four. A brilliant perpetual student who had never found his purpose in life, Bill had succumbed as much to frustration as to disease. Marian had been with him at the end.

It was Marian who maintained regular contact with all her brothers except Reed, who had apparently decided to disappear permanently from the family. She, Ben, and Paul continued to remain close to each other. She was also the only Robeson who got along well with Essie, often staying with her and Paul when she came through New York on her way Asheville, North Carolina, where Ben was pastoring, or when she came to see Paul perform in New York or New Jersey. Tall, heavyset, with a quiet demeanor and a gentle look, Marian was determined to carve out a career for herself in the teaching profession. Her home was always a welcome retreat for Paul in times of stress, and the thought of "Sis" always brought him a feeling of security.[29]

Paul and Essie returned to New York in December 1925 on the SS *Majestic* to prepare for Paul's thirteen-city concert tour in January and February 1926. Both seemed somewhat dispirited, as if a certain malaise had settled in during their travels.[30] It was time to get back to business.

Despite Paul's hopes, the tour reeled from exhilarating highs to frustrating lows. True, some of the concerts were very successful. In both New York City and Somerville, New Jersey, everyone remembered Paul from his school days. In Somerville he delighted everyone who came backstage to greet him by remembering personal details about his associates and their families. His unaffected and genuinely kind demeanor moved those who met him. Concerts in Indianapolis, Philadelphia, Detroit, and Burlington, Iowa, also went well, as Paul responded to the acclaim not only with inspired singing but with a gracious manner.

But other concerts did not go as smoothly. The train ride to Pittsburgh was so bumpy that it made Paul ill, and when he sang there, the audience was small. He sang well anyway. In Chicago's Orchestra Hall—a huge barn of a place with poor acoustics—Paul "sang

beautifully and showed the full power of his voice" despite the piti-
fully slim crowd. In Milwaukee there had been no advertising, and,
Essie noted, "only our friends came." She complained that "these
small-towners are not our audience. Callow, silly, ignorant posers—
not for us."[31]

Things went from bad to worse. Green Bay, Wisconsin, was a
disaster—a "messy" town and a hostile Hotel Northland at which the
Robesons "finally got rooms after promising to make ourselves as
inconspicuous as possible." The concert was "rotten," Essie commenting that "the poor kooks didn't know what it was all about." Net
receipts were $37.18.[32]

Matters were only marginally better back in the East. The concert at Springfield, Massachusetts, was "only fair," but the reviews
were "wonderful." But the last concert in Providence, Rhode Island
("dull town"), was a flop—"provincial" audience, Paul and Larry
both "dreadful," concert "a mess."[33]

The best that could be said at the end of the tour was that it had
put Paul and Larry squarely on the concert map. Elizabeth Shepley
Sergeant, in her essay "The Man with His Home in a Rock" in the
New Republic of March 3, 1926, defined the spot:

> Paul Robeson is not merely an actor and a singer of Negro Spiri-
> tuals but a symbol. A sort of sublimation of what the Negro may
> be in the Golden Age hangs about him, and imparts to his appear-
> ances an atmosphere of affection and delight that is seldom felt in
> an American audience. [He] is a symbol of the increasing impor-
> tant place of the American Negro on the American stage, that you
> will magnify or minimize according to your prejudices and desires.
> It is earnestly to be hoped that the men like Paul Robeson with his
> evangelical tradition and Lawrence Brown with his Florida verve,
> who are consciously and lovingly working in an unconscious folk
> art, are establishing a "classic" Spiritual tradition that will long live
> in American music. One of the critics, writing of Robeson's first
> concert, suggested that if Chaliapin could be conceived as singing
> Negro folk songs as his own, he would sing them as Paul Robeson
> does. Let us give thanks that we were not born too late to hear this
> Negro Chaliapin render the Spirituals reverently, with wildness and
> awe, like a trusting child of God.

Early in March, Essie prevailed on Paul to take a week's vacation
in Atlantic City, and when he came home he looked well rested.

Then she picked up the check for his concert tour fees from Pond, which did little to defray their debt to Otto Kahn. From a financial perspective, Paul's first concert tour had been sobering. From a vocal perspective, it had taken all his reserves.

Contrary to widespread belief, his voice box was not a particularly strong one, and he was not capable of easily producing the powerful volume required for a large concert hall. Of a March concert in Boston's Symphony Hall, Essie noted that there was a good crowd, but that Paul was "in poor voice." A couple of days later they consulted with Frantz Proshchowsky, who had been recommended by Paul's voice coach from several years earlier. His initial advice was invaluable: "Found him absolutely marvelous," Essie wrote, "and he has done in one lesson and talk more for Paul than I could have imagined. Showed him all his faults and showed him how to correct them and how to sing right. We are so relieved."

The rigors of a professional tour had revealed that Paul was forcing too much and needed to master the finer points of voice control. He also required some help with his breathing technique. Paul met with Proshchowsky daily. "We feel so differently about his voice—we are confident now," Essie wrote in her diary.[34]

Essie's frequent use of the pronoun *we* implied that her day-to-day involvement in Paul's career was mutually agreeable. To the contrary, there seemed to be a struggle going on between the two over business matters. Essie now controlled Paul's finances almost exclusively. In fact, he had agreed that she would handle all their money and give him a weekly allowance. But in April, Paul decided to take the initiative in responding to an offer from Cecil B. DeMille, arguably Hollywood's leading director. DeMille wanted him for the lead role in an as-yet undefined "Negro film," and Paul decided to negotiate the contract himself.

"Paul asked a good salary, and transportation. Hope it turns out," Essie succinctly commented in her diary. Paul showed little concern about the content of the film; he apparently trusted DeMille implicitly. His negotiating skills produced a lucrative deal that he signed on April 21.[35]

At about the same time, rehearsals were scheduled for *Black Boy*, produced by publisher-producer Horace Liveright, in which the lead

role was patterned vaguely after the black former heavyweight boxing champion Jack Johnson. Ironically, Essie had negotiated that
contract and made "the dreadful mistake" of overlapping dates with
Paul's concert bureau. James Pond was furious, but Paul decided to
go ahead with the play anyway. They barely avoided a lawsuit by
consulting attorney Arthur Garfield Hayes, who helped them work
out a difficult compromise.[36]

To Paul's great disappointment, the DeMille film deal collapsed
abruptly within three weeks when plans to film in Hollywood had to
be scrapped because the date for a New York filming conflicted with
Paul's commitment to *Black Boy*.[37] Paul regretted this loss of opportunity keenly, realizing that the role might have catapulted him into
the front ranks of film stardom, irrespective of the film's content. But
frankly, the lost income hurt the most.[38–40]

On August 23, when rehearsals opened for *Black Boy* in Mamaro-
neck, New York, Paul tried to turn his back on distractions, but Fredi
Washington, a talented black actress, had been chosen to play his
white mistress, and he gave in to their mutual attraction. She was
light-skinned enough to "pass" for white and thus eliminated the controversy associated with casting a white actress opposite him. More
significantly, to Paul, she was amazingly beautiful. Despite long sep-
arations, their affair would last for more than twenty years alongside
his relationship to Freda Diamond. Essie was so devastated that she
stopped writing in her diary. It was easier for her to cope if she kept
protective blinders on, and her personal life had become too painful
to record.

Paul and Essie faced a watershed. Their twin illusions of a perfect marriage and a storybook ascent to fame and glory had been
shattered by the realities of a problem-laden personal relationship
and a tough, uneven struggle for success. The "Dubby"/"Dolly" fantasy was over. Their tacit solution—one that never worked satisfac-
torily but persisted somehow for years—was to find a middle ground
between reality and their illusions. Essie tried not to question, or to
dwell upon, Paul's comings and goings, and continued to take care of
him and his career. For his part, Paul tried to preserve the dignity of
their social life by maintaining their unrelenting schedule of activities as a charming couple. With regard to business matters, the status
quo continued: Essie retained her full-time job as manager-agent-
treasurer-accountant, complete with power of attorney.

There were two compelling reasons why they did not consider separation or divorce. First, they both sensed that their teamwork was essential to Paul's success. For both of them, this promise was too attractive to jeopardize by breaking up a winning team. Second, they were emotionally dependent on each other. After her exciting life with Paul, Essie knew she would find others dull by comparison. And Paul needed Essie to take care of him and to devote herself to his career. None of the other women he had been with or might be attracted to were even remotely willing to do this. So Paul and Essie suppressed their dark mood and cultivated their glittering image for the world to see.

Black Boy brought Paul excellent reviews and increasing notoriety. Brooks Atkinson, the *New York Times* critic, wrote on October 7, 1926:

> From all this hugger-mugger Mr. Robeson's performance emerges as a fine-grained, resilient bit of characterization. His huge frame fits him well for the part of a prize fighter, and his full, deep voice has a sustaining beauty. Mr. Robeson's artlessness brings a finer quality to his part than he could achieve in acting by rote, as all his colleagues do in this play. . . . One suspects that he approaches the authors' conception of *Black Boy* more closely than does the play of their own composition.

When the play closed after only a few weeks, Paul turned back to his concerts in earnest, his hope of gaining a permanent foothold in the legitimate theater seeming more remote than he had previously imagined.

The Reverend William Drew Robeson, Paul Robeson's father, in 1878, at age thirty-five. *From the personal collection of Paul Robeson, Jr.*

Maria Louisa Bustill, Paul's mother (seated, right) as a seventeen-year-old, with her sister (standing, left) and her father, Charles Hicks Bustill. Circa 1870. *From the personal collection of Paul Robeson, Jr.*

Maria Louisa, age twenty-five, in 1878 at the time of her marriage. *From the personal collection of Paul Robeson, Jr.*

William Drew at sixty-seven, in 1910. *From the personal collection of Paul Robeson, Jr.*

On the Rutgers College campus, circa 1915. *Courtesy of Rutgers University.*

On the practice field during the 1916 football season. Coach Foster Sanford is kneeling in the right foreground. *From the personal collection of Paul Robeson, Jr.*

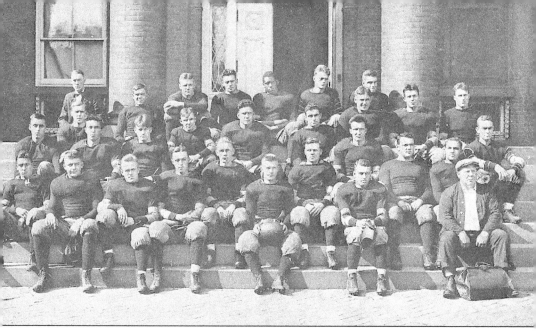

With the Rutgers College 1916 football team (Paul is in the center of the last row).
From the personal collection of Paul Robeson, Jr.

Member of the Rutgers College 1916 track team (Paul is fourth from left in the last row). *Courtesy of Rutgers University.*

Member of the Rutgers College 1916 basketball team (Paul is second from right in the middle row). *From the personal collection of Paul Robeson, Jr.*

Headed toward the goal line at Ebbets Field, Brooklyn. Rutgers defeated the heavily favored Naval Reserve team 14–0. November 24, 1917. *From the personal collection of Paul Robeson, Jr.*

Paul (rear row, third from right) looking over the shoulder of Sadie Shelton in 1917.
Gerry Neale is in the front row, second from right, next to Sadie. *From the personal
collection of Paul Robeson, Jr.*

Paul in ROTC uniform with a friend on the Rutgers College campus, 1918.
From the personal collection of Paul Robeson, Jr.

Member of the Cap and Skull honor society at Rutgers College (1919). *Courtesy of Rutgers University.*

Catcher on the Rutgers College baseball team, 1919. *From the personal collection of Paul Robeson, Jr.*

The Reverend Benjamin C. Robeson, Paul's older brother, dressed in his U.S. Army uniform. Circa 1930s. *Courtesy of Dr. Gregory Robeson Smith.*

Ben Robeson (on the right) with friend, circa 1920s. *Courtesy of Dr. Gregory Robeson Smith.*

Paul's Rutgers College
graduation photograph,
1919. *From the personal
collection of Paul Robeson, Jr.*

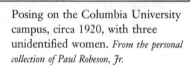

Posing on the Columbia University
campus, circa 1920, with three
unidentified women. *From the personal
collection of Paul Robeson, Jr.*

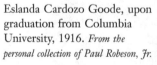

Eslanda Cardozo Goode, upon
graduation from Columbia
University, 1916. *From the
personal collection of Paul Robeson, Jr.*

Paul in 1920, member of the Columbia Law School class of 1923 (Paul is in the fourth row, wearing a bow tie). *Courtesy of Columbia University.*

Playing professional football with the Akron Pros. Circa 1921. *From the personal collection of Paul Robeson, Jr.*

With the St. Christopher Club basketball team for which he played center. Circa 1919. *From the personal collection of Paul Robeson, Jr.*

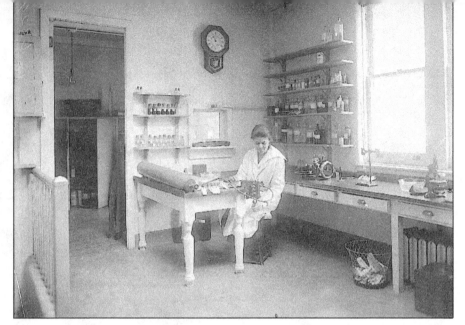

Essie at work as head of the Surgical Pathological Laboratory of Columbia Presbyterian Hospital in New York City. Circa 1921. *From the personal collection of Paul Robeson, Jr.*

With good friends Hattie and Buddy Bolling. Hattie was especially close to Essie. Circa 1921. *From the personal collection of Paul Robeson, Jr.*

1921 portrait by an unknown photographer at about the time of Paul's marriage to Essie.
From the personal collection of Paul Robeson, Jr.

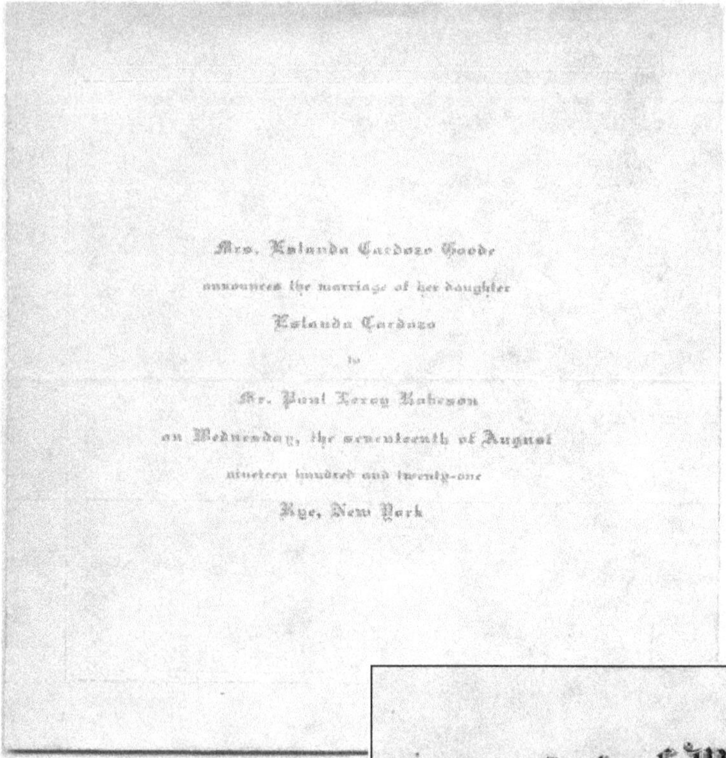

Mrs. Eslanda Cardozo Goode
announces the marriage of her daughter
Eslanda Cardozo
to
Mr. Paul Leroy Robeson
on Wednesday, the seventeenth of August
nineteen hundred and twenty-one
Rye, New York

The wedding announcement that Essie designed and sent out in her mother's name.
From the personal collection of Paul Robeson, Jr.

Certificate of Marriage
THIS IS TO CERTIFY
That on the 17th day of August
in the year of our Lord 1921
Paul L. Robeson
and Eslanda C. Goode
WERE BY ME UNITED IN
MARRIAGE
at Port Chester
according to the laws of New York
Witnesses

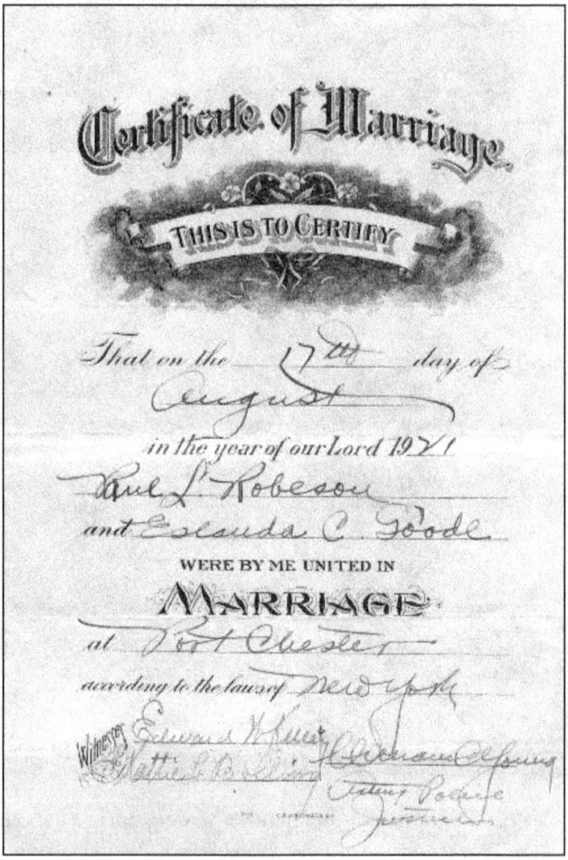

Certificate of Paul's marriage to Essie.
From the personal collection of Paul Robeson, Jr.

Essie's mother, Eslanda
Cardozo Goode, as a
young woman. Circa
1900. *From the personal
collection of Paul Robeson, Jr.*

In *Voodoo* during the 1922
British tour. *From the personal
collection of Paul Robeson, Jr.*

Paul's favorite picture
of Essie, circa 1916.
*From the personal collection
of Paul Robeson, Jr.*

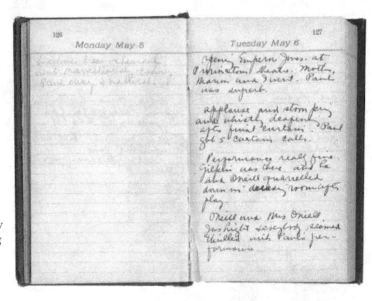

Page from Essie's diary
describing the opening
of *The Emperor Jones.*
*From the personal collection
of Paul Robeson, Jr.*

As Brutus Jones, in the Eugene O'Neill play *The Emperor Jones*, produced by the Provincetown Players, 1924. *Courtesy of the New York Public Library, Lincoln Center Library for the Performing Arts.*

1928 portrait of Essie by
Helen MacGregor, London.
From the personal collection of Paul
Robeson, Jr.

1925 portrait of Paul
by Sasha. *From the*
personal collection of Paul
Robeson, Jr.

With James Light, director of
the Provincetown Players and
Paul's stage mentor. Circa 1925.
*From the personal collection of Paul
Robeson, Jr.*

Lawrence B. Brown, Paul's
accompanist and musical
partner for three decades.
Circa early 1920s. *Courtesy
of the New York Public Library,
Schomburg Center for Research in
Black Culture.*

Antonio Salemme sculpts Paul's likeness, 1926. *From the personal collection of Paul Robeson, Jr.*

Posing as the character Jim Harris in the Eugene O'Neill play *All God's Chillun Got Wings.* Circa 1926. *From the personal collection of Paul Robeson, Jr.*

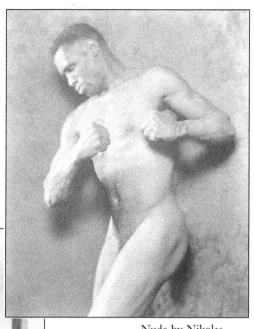

Nude by Nikolas
Muray, 1926. *From the
personal collection of Paul
Robeson, Jr.*

1926 portrait of Paul by Madame
Saint Georges, London. *From the
personal collection of Paul Robeson, Jr.*

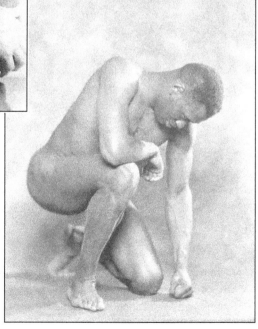

Nude by Nikolas
Muray, 1926. *From the
personal collection of Paul
Robeson, Jr.*

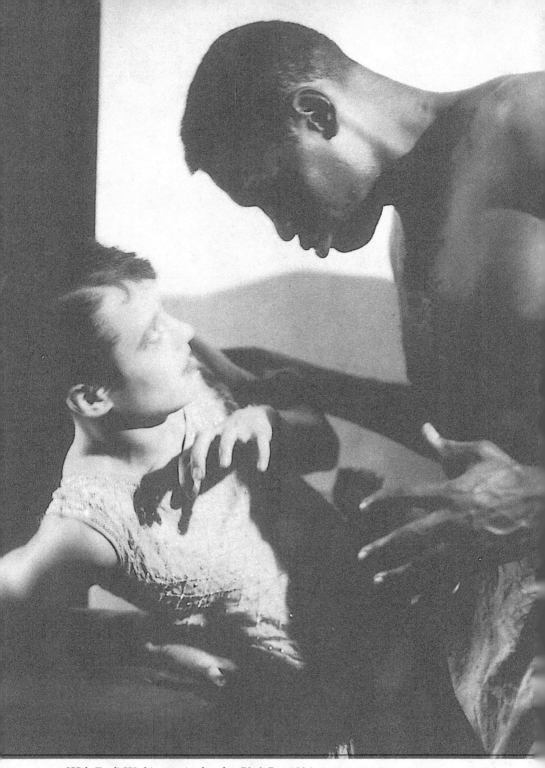

With Fredi Washington in the play *Black Boy*, 1926. *Photograph by Edward Steichen; courtesy of the George Eastman House.*

At the beach in Oak Bluffs, Massachusetts, 1927. *From the personal collection of Paul Robeson, Jr.*

Paul and Essie in Oak Bluffs, 1927. *From the personal collection of Paul Robeson, Jr.*

Larry accompanying Paul in concert, New York, 1927. *From the personal collection of Paul Robeson, Jr.*

Flyer for Paul and Larry's 1927 Paris concert of Negro spirituals. *From the personal collection of Paul Robeson, Jr.*

The original sheet music of "Ol' Man River," 1927. *From the personal collection of Paul Robeson, Jr.*

The changes Paul made in the lyrics of "Ol' Man River" in 1928. *From the personal collection of Paul Robeson, Jr.*

With Larry in Vienna at Beethoven's gravesite, 1929. *From the personal collection of Paul Robeson, Jr.*

Paul and Larry playfully square off in front of Vienna's Reumann Community Building during their 1929 European tour. In his late teens and early twenties, Larry was a top amateur boxer in Florida. *From the personal collection of Paul Robeson, Jr.*

Father and son on
Hampstead Heath,
London, 1929. *From the
personal collection of Paul
Robeson, Jr.*

Flyer promoting Paul's November 10, 1929, Carnegie Hall concert.
From the personal collection of Paul Robeson, Jr.

Paul's 1929 notes written in a pocket notebook: ". . . because everyone isn't important. . . ."
From the personal collection of Paul Robeson, Jr.

In a 1930 letter to Essie, Eugene O'Neill writes, "I sure hope Paul will make them [the English] like his Othello. It is a tough job he is up against." *From the personal collection of Paul Robeson, Jr.*

Paul and Essie during the shooting of the art film *Borderline* in Switzerland, 1930.
From the personal collection of Paul Robeson, Jr.

In Shakespeare's *Othello* at the Savoy Theatre, London, 1930. Act 3, Scene 3: "Farewell! Othello's occupation's gone!"
From the personal collection of Paul Robeson, Jr.

With Peggy Ashcroft. *Othello,*
Act 2, Scene 1: "It gives me
wonder great as my content
to see you here before me."
*From the personal collection of Paul
Robeson, Jr.*

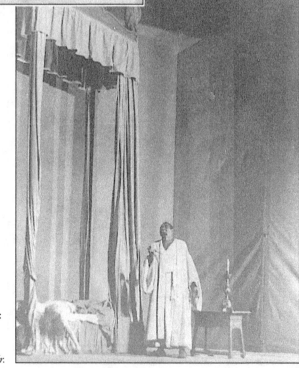

Othello, Act 5, Scene 2:
". . . and smote him—
thus!" *From the personal
collection of Paul Robeson, Jr.*

The plaster casting of Salemme's full-length nude sculpture of Paul. Circa 1930. *From the personal collection of Paul Robeson, Jr.*

Program for the 1931 London production of Eugene O'Neill's play *The Hairy Ape* at the Ambassadors Theatre. Produced and directed by James Light, it was financed through the efforts of Paul's attorney and close friend, Robert Rockmore. *From the personal collection of Paul Robeson, Jr.*

With Yolande Jackson, 1931. *From the personal collection of Paul Robeson, Jr.*

Receiving an honorary master's degree from Rutgers College president Robert Clothier at commencement exercises, June 11, 1932. *Courtesy of Rutgers University.*

Portrait of Paul by Carl Van
Vechten, New York, 1932.
*Courtesy of the Estate of Carl Van
Vechten, Joseph Solomon, Executor.*

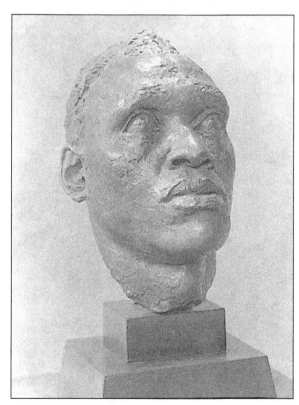

Head of Paul, sculpted
by Jacob Epstein in
1927 in London. *From
the personal collection of Paul
Robeson, Jr.*

Portrait by Edward Steichen, New York, 1932. *From the personal collection of Paul Robeson, Jr.; courtesy of Joanna Steichen.*

III
FROM
PERFORMER
TO ARTIST

(1926–1932)

(*Above*) In the musical *Show Boat* at the Drury Lane Theatre, London, 1928. *From the personal collection of Paul Robeson, Jr.*

(*Middle*) Singing a concert in the Royal Albert Hall, London, 1929. *From the personal collection of Paul Robeson, Jr.*

(*Below*) In *Othello*, with Peggy Ashcroft as Desdemona, at the Savoy Theatre, London, 1930. *From the personal collection of Paul Robeson, Jr.*

7
"OL' MAN RIVER"

(1926–1928)

On January 25, 1927, a large mixed audience packed one of the largest white churches in Kansas City to hear Paul sing. He had gambled everything on going all out for success in the concert field, even though musical theater, radio, and recording might have been more lucrative instead. His first concert tour had won him barely a toehold. Worse still, it had been a resounding financial failure. Yet he was adamant about attempting a second tour in 1927. Paul's friend Walter White had helped him secure a fellowship from the Juilliard Musical Foundation to help underwrite it.

Against Essie's better judgment, she had gone along with his decision in order to avoid further strains on their marriage. She had made this fateful decision quickly, almost casually, yet with a curious reversal of their normal roles. Paul was usually loath to discard a possible option. Essie, normally the simplifier, had urged him to be open-minded about Broadway. In 1926, it had been a moot issue, but in 1927 it became a distinction that would play itself out with considerable drama.[1]

Haunted by his outstanding $5,000 debt to Otto Kahn (Kahn had grudgingly granted a deferment of the $2,000 due on January 1), Paul had considered breaking his vow not to stoop to appearing in musicals. In still another role reversal, Essie had persuaded him with difficulty not to appear in an all-black musical play by Paul Green, *In Abraham's Bosom*, arguing that to do so would set him up for being restricted to "all-Negro" plays. This was one of the few times her theatrical instincts had proved to be wrong, since the play won the Pulitzer Prize for 1927.

137

However, Paul's eye had been on the prize of public acceptance of his distinctive artistry and his people's music. In Kansas City, one of the first stops on his 1927 concert tour, the concert organizer had been Roy Wilkins, the future leader of the NAACP. Wilkins, then a reporter for the weekly black newspaper *The Call*, headed a black group that booked the concert in a large white church and then announced that there would be no segregated seating, contradicting a rule rigidly enforced at all concerts sponsored by white groups.

Paul and Essie were all too familiar with the problem of segregated concert halls and theaters. Essie had recorded their encounter with segregation in a Manhattan theater in her 1926 diary:

> *Tuesday, May 18 [1926].* Jim [Light] got seats for us for "Bride of the Lamb" at the Henry Miller Theater. When I got there, they gave me the seats which were fine orchestra ones. [Essie was light-skinned enough to pass for a Latino or a Southern European.] When Paul came, and we started in, the man at the door took the tickets away from me, took them over to the man in the lobby, who in turn took them over to the box office, dragging us with him. The man looked at Paul and asked him if he "understood." Paul said "No," he didn't. [The] box office man gave us balcony seats instead, and then the lobby man came up to Paul and said: "William, who gave you these seats?" That was too much, so we returned the seats and went out.

Essie had evidently organized their friends to raise hell with the Henry Miller Theater, because nine days later Arthur Hornblow Jr., the managing director, had written a letter to them apologizing. "My dear Mr. Robeson: . . . It is a matter of great personal distress to me that any such thing has happened, and I am sure you must understand it was merely the stupid operation of a general policy. Do forgive us." Apparently this well-meaning white man could not understand that to Paul and Essie the "general policy," rather than just the personal affront, had been the insult.

Contrary to widely held opinion, Paul was unruffled by such incidents and generally ignored them. He often felt embarrassed, and even somewhat guilty, because he was usually treated so much better than the vast majority of his race. He was catered to as a celebrity, while they were treated as second-class citizens. In later life, he made a fuss about these insults only when he felt he could contribute to improving the treatment of all of his people.

The *Kansas City Times* music critic wrote that Paul sang "as God intended him to," and compared him to "Chaliapin in his better days." The reviewer added that "no singer in this reviewer's experience has had such a gift for inflecting the tonality as well as the text."[2] But an intense debate about the concert raged in three successive issues of *The Call*, triggered by a letter to the editor from Mrs. L. J. Bacote, a local music teacher. Articulating the conservative black opinion that spirituals were not really "art," she argued that Paul was "not an artist." His recital, consisting solely of Negro spirituals and folk songs, was, in her view, "humiliating."[3]

Paul's repertoire and performance, however, stayed true to his vision. With the support of Larry Brown's accompaniment, arrangements, programming, and tenor counterpoint, Paul thrived as the tour progressed. They continued until the middle of June, with appearances in Columbus and Dayton, Ohio; Rochester and Ithaca, New York; New York City; and New Brunswick and Princeton, New Jersey. Reviewers consistently applauded Paul's artistic technique ("His mellow baritone seems to have gained in smoothness and control, and had all its old emotional color"[4]) and mastery in the presentation of the spirituals ("Robeson believes that the Negro Spirituals are folk songs that rival those of Russia, Germany, France, and England"[5]). The music critic of the *New York Telegram* wrote: "An unrivalled artist in every sense of the word is Paul Robeson, the great Negro actor-singer-athlete. His broadcast performance, during the Edison Hour over WRNY, was deserving of any music critic's most reserved superlatives."[6] Ironically, at Princeton University, an intensely racist institution during Paul's college days at Rutgers, "The President of Princeton sent Paul a personal note of appreciation, and the students wrote a splendid review of the concert and of his career in the *Daily Princetonian* the next day."[7]

This second concert tour was far more successful, chiefly because of the emerging popularity of Paul's recordings and radio broadcasts.

Thousands of people who listened to his spirituals in the privacy of their own homes found them especially immediate and compelling. Moreover, by trusting his audiences to receive what he offered, Paul had made a start the previous year in establishing the pure spiritual as an accepted concert art form. He was mostly singing Larry Brown's authentic arrangements in the traditional folk style. However, Larry had also modified Harry T. Burleigh's universally accepted, more classically oriented arrangements of such spirituals as "Deep River" and "Balm in Gilead." This apparently caused Burleigh to become upset with Brown, as well as with J. Rosamond Johnson, who, like Larry and Paul, had done much to popularize the authentic spiritual tradition.

Back in 1925, Carl Van Vechten had reported in a letter to Essie on October 9 that

> H. T. Burleigh is in a frightful stew and does not hesitate to show it. Meeting Larry and Rosamond on the street, he abused them roundly, saying that neither of them knew anything about Spirituals or even music itself. . . . He threatened to talk to certain critics and promised them bad notices. "If you knew anything about Brahms and Debussy," he added, "your harmonizations would be far different."

By the end of 1927, Paul and Larry had clearly triumphed over Burleigh. Paul had been listed in the first annual *Who's Who in Colored America*; he was ranked twentieth among concert singers in the United States on the basis of his guaranteed fee of $1,250. (Roland Hayes, the only other ranked black artist, was in tenth place at $3,200, and the number one Irish singer, John McCormack, was at $5,000.) He was also the record holder for the number of times his radio concerts were interrupted for applause by the studio audience.

As the press took to calling Paul "a leader of his race in New York,"[8] he began to comment extensively on his people's distinctive music in his interviews.

> I feel that the music of my race is the happiest medium of expression for what dramatic and vocal skill I possess. In the first place, Negro music is more and more taking its place with the music of

the world. It has its own distinctive message and philosophy. Many critics say it is the only folk music of America. Negro music portrays the hopes of our people who faced the hardships of slavery. They suffered. They fled to God through their songs. They sang to forget their chains and misery. Even in darkness they looked to their songs to work out their destiny and carve their way to the promised land.

There is no expression of hate or revenge in their music. That a race which had suffered and toiled as the Negro had did not express bitterness but expressed love is strong evidence of the influence of Christianity. I am not ashamed of the Spirituals. They represent the soul of my people. White and colored people react alike to the songs. Differences are forgotten and prejudices vanish when mixed audiences meet at the concerts. Humanity is helped and lifted to higher levels.[9]

It was revealing to Paul that his appreciation of the source of Negro spirituals struck a sympathetic chord in the Jewish community. Rabbi Jacob S. Minkin wrote in his syndicated column:

The Hebrew influence has been traced and found in almost all the great poetry of the world, but it was left to Paul Robeson, the colored baritone, to discover the source of the Negro spirituals in the Old Testament. "You'll notice," said Robeson, "that comparatively few of the Negro spirituals are based on the New Testament, most of the inspired songs having been drawn from the literature of the Hebrew Nation."[10]

In working on his development as an artist, Paul was forging his own individual path. "I am trying to get out all that's in *me*," he wrote. "I am not imitating Barrymore, Chaliapin, or anyone else. I am not trying to prove that I can do what the white man does."[11] He was quite aware of his potential and that he had not nearly achieved it:

I set my own standards for myself, and I haven't nearly reached what I want to reach. I always find flaws in my work . . . ; all critics say my voice is great, but I know two years more of experience will make [it] much better. It will have more shade and color. I need more dramatic experience. I need to learn to handle my body better—my hands, etc. . . . I am still studying under a very good voice teacher. The voice means three-fourths of the battle; the singing voice helps the speaking voice.[12]

James Weldon Johnson confirmed the power of Paul's speaking voice, which he heard at its best one evening in the fall of 1927. It happened at a party in the Johnson home where Paul and Clarence Darrow, the legendary lawyer, read aloud to the guests. According to Johnson, Darrow read first, seated "under a lighted lamp, the only one in the room left lighted, reading in measured tones from his book *Farmington*." Paul came next. He read from Johnson's classic poem "God's Trombones." When he finished, Darrow uttered "the words of Agrippa to Saint Paul, 'Almost thou persuadest me to be a Christian.'"[13]

Paul remained uninvolved in the racial politics of the time. The rise of the Ku Klux Klan to a membership of hundreds of thousands nationally and its spread to western and even northern states appeared to hold little personal concern for him. Foreign political developments seemingly escaped his attention altogether, and he made no comment on the rising persecution of immigrants. Marcus Garvey's popular Harlem-based back-to-Africa movement had faded rapidly after Garvey's imprisonment for alleged fraud in 1925, and it all but vanished after his deportation in 1927. Indifferent to the left-wing politics of the time, Paul thought the Marxist ideas of William Patterson, who had married Minnie Sumner, Essie's close friend, were rather quaint. Moreover, the lifestyle that Paul, Essie, and their friends were used to kept them at a distance from mass struggles.

In the summer of 1927, Paul and Essie took a vacation in Oak Bluffs, the elite black enclave on the island of Martha's Vineyard off the coast of Massachusetts. To outsiders and even to their friends, they appeared happy and contented. But appearances were deceiving. Essie had told Paul in April that she was pregnant. Since she had not told him about her recent medical treatment aimed at helping her to conceive, and she had not consulted him about having a child, he was startled. Beneath his calm and sympathetic exterior, he bitterly resented Essie's deception and manipulation.

Beginning in September, Paul urgently sought additional concert work in order to cope with his now growing financial obligations. Despite Essie's advice, however, he declined to pursue the role of "Joe" in the new musical *Show Boat*, with music by Jerome Kern and lyrics by Oscar Hammerstein II. The theme song of the show, "Ol' Man River," had been dedicated to him, but he was not enthusiastic. The opening lines said it all: "Niggers all work on the Mississippi; niggers all work while the white folks play." He dreaded going back to performing stereotypes.

Later, when *Show Boat* became a smash hit on Broadway without him, just as Essie had predicted, Paul must have derived some comfort from a moving send-off note from Langston Hughes: "The great truth and beauty of your art struck me as never before one night this summer down in Georgia when a little group of us played your records for hours there in the very atmosphere from which your songs came."[14]

Finally, toward the end of September, concert impresario Walter Varney offered Paul a concert tour of Europe. Ever since his 1925 trip he had wanted to appear before English audiences again, even though the real money was in the United States. Indeed, Paul knew that if he sought fame and fortune exclusively in Europe, he would lose his American audience, and for this reason he never contemplated any kind of permanent departure from the United States. Instead, he envisioned a multifaceted artistic career on both sides of the Atlantic. Essie's negotiation with Varney was difficult. Word of Paul's dispute with Pond, his previous concert manager, had spread, and Varney drove a hard bargain.

Deeply ambivalent about leaving Essie behind, Paul sailed to Europe on October 15, 1927. After all, she was due to give birth to their first child in three weeks. But there was no turning back. One day out at sea, Paul wrote Essie an affectionate letter:

October 16, On Board the SS *Majestic*

My Darling,

I had a long sleep. Missed breakfast and arose at 10. Feel fine. And lo and behold—I found a lovely letter from my baby. Just what I needed. All happened so swiftly the last few days. But I was so sad the first moments. So hard to leave you, sweet. Seems as though you are me—I feel so lost on here [on the ship]. But you'll come to me soon, and I'll work hard and do you proud. You'll never know how marvelous I think you are. Of course, I love you more than I love my very self. I almost melt away with happiness when I think of the beautiful days we have before us. I love you, darling, with all my soul.

> So many thanks, darling, for all you have done for me— for my career, for your patience and care and devoted love. And know that whatever I achieve shall have been due in great part to your unselfish interest and devotion. Surely it is a kind Providence who could have given a father and a wife such as I have had.

The last sentence was telling: Paul could no more separate from his wife than he could from William Drew. The differences in their temperaments and approach to life made for a rocky road, but Essie's caring for him drove deep into his heart. The strengths of their relationship, particularly the dynamic team they made, compelled his attachment, if not his exclusive devotion or loyalty.

On October 29, Paul and Larry Brown charmed Paris with the first-ever European concert made up entirely of Negro spirituals and folk songs. The stellar audience—including Roland Hayes and jazz singer Alberta Hunter—filled the 1,700 seats at the famous Salle Gaveau concert hall in the Rue de la Boetie, as well as all possible standing room.

Freda Diamond, who happened to be on a vacation trip in Paris alone, vividly remembered Paul's performance. He sang well despite having been in bed with a bad cold for several days before the concert. Larry, who had chosen a lively program, was especially good. The response of both the audience and the critics was ecstatic. Now twenty years old and even more beautiful, Freda braved the backstage crowd to visit Paul in his dressing room after his performance. He was delighted to see her.[15]

News of Paul's triumph was reported widely by the French, English, and American press, and Varney promptly arranged for a second concert. It was an even bigger success than the first. Paul cabled Essie that he was in perfect voice and that everything was "grand."

I was born on November 2, 1927, with the name Paul Robeson, Jr. I was a big baby, a little over eleven pounds, and it was an extremely difficult delivery. More than thirty years later, Freda Diamond told me that my father had expressed no great enthusiasm about my arrival, and that she had urged him, unsuccessfully, to return home immediately.[16] It seems he wondered what to do for two weeks. Then, his mind apparently settled, he wrote Essie two letters that were a mixture of genuine affection, newsy career commentary, and robust attempts to prove his steadfastness. As usual, he found himself anxious to overcome her doubts:

Paris, Saturday, December 10

My Sweet—

It has been a very bad day—dark, gray—and I've been in the house most of it. It became dry and cold this evening, and I went out for a walk and had dinner. I took a bus over to Montmartre and looked at the bright lights. I came back by bus, taking same at a corner where we caught one before. I'm so lonely, honey—so terribly lonely. The only possible way to forget would be to work hard, but I'm not even doing that.

You see, I really have grown, in these two months of separation, to love you with a love that seems unbelievable to me. Nothing matters but you—I don't matter; the world doesn't matter. And I'm so anxious to see you to show you a new love—a new sweetheart, a new husband—just like the old ones but somehow sweeter, kinder, more loving, more considerate. I love you—love you with everything I possess.

How can that boy have a crooked nose; he didn't play football. Or was it the delivery. He sounds grand. Won't I be glad to see him. Haven't really been so excited—I've missed you so much; but I am getting more so all the time. Take good care of him and tell him about papa.

Baby

Paris, Monday, December 12

Sweetheart—

I'm still a little down, and I've been thinking hard. Varney has no more news, so my plans are the same. It looks like the following to me:

I believe that concert work in Europe should have about two months of concentrated work in the spring and early summer. It's almost impossible to stretch a profitable tour over the year. Considering the weather, I wouldn't want to. It's bad here and in London, worse in Madrid, and impossible in Russia. Then the possibility of private work is almost nil, as everybody is away. The south presents the only opportunity, but there the people are looking for other kinds of entertainment.

As for my singing—I'm convinced that in order to attain very substantial success financially I'll need other songs, some in the language of the country or classics that they know. They'll come and rave over our program once or twice, but they don't really get the words; the songs are simple—I do them simply—and they feel that if I can sing so grandly (like Chaliapin), I should do the things he does (Boris Godunoff, etc.). They feel I'm almost wasted upon simple music, no matter how much they enjoy it. So I can't make money doing what I am, I'm sure. I can only attract the concert audience—the most discriminating of it. And there aren't enough places to go to. [Roland] Hayes went to Italy for concerts and lost money. He had to cancel his Russian trip. There is no money here at usual stuff. The only hope is Opera—big splurge and then do all kinds of songs. London offers possibilities, but you know the field there. Would have to be theatre, or Coliseum.

Now, darling, here is what I now firmly believe—just what you have believed all along but what you have been sensible enough to let me find out myself. Before I get so excited about my "*art*," etc., I must be the complete artist. There are so many things I would have done to make us money if I had not been afraid of my "*art*." "Black Boy," Vaudeville, picture houses, pictures, "Show Boat," Hammerstein, etc. Then there are the things I would have done foolishly but for you in the name of art—"Abraham's Bosom," "Porgy"; and it really hasn't been so much "*art*" as thinking what people would say, which of course is silly. So I think I'll turn things over to you. You know how to value me—my dignity, etc.

But we must have money. All the things I hold back from, others do and win. Of course, we won't work too fast and miss the big things; but with our debts and new responsibilities we need *money*, and the money for me is, I believe, in America. I don't mean Europe is a wash-out. But it's for prestige, a nice rest, etc. Europeans will appreciate my art, but the money is home. That's why all the Europeans go there. No matter how much I sing or how successful I am here in concerts, there is no real money.

[Still unaware that she was struggling to recover from a difficult childbirth, he urged her to help him out.] I'm anxious to see what you can do at home as soon as possible. If I can return while things are bad, Varney can have no claim for next year. If I dilly-dally, he'll get just enough to hold me. As things look now, it would be impossible for him to get enough to make your coming possible in the spring. And I just can't stay away from you much

longer than April. But we're so far back now [financially] that it
would be impossible [even] if we sang a lot, and there is nothing in
sight. I'm not pessimistic or homesick, but looking all square in the
face for now & future. After all, there are many things I might do
back home after I get settled. . . . Have a long talk with Miss Armitage [his voice coach], and see about taking all loads off you for a
month or so after my return. If that isn't possible, maybe I can run
around myself. I don't want you to worry and get up too soon to
get things going. You must take plenty of time to get well. . . .

As this letter reflects, Paul was speculating about his chances of
attracting a significant share of the opera audience to his concerts of
spirituals. He wondered if he could win them over by singing a major
group (a "big splurge") of carefully selected operatic numbers at several concerts. Hopefully, once they heard him, they would accept the
integration of only a few operatic numbers into his usual concert
repertoire, since he was well aware that his voice could not sustain a
large number of operatic numbers on a consistent basis.

But he was completely unaware that Essie was desperately ill. Post-
delivery complications had developed into a series of infections and a
severe case of phlebitis. Once again, she had concealed her problems
from her husband, sending him invariably cheery—and deceptive—
letters. Three thousand miles away, Paul remained absorbed in his
own problems. His accompanist, Larry Brown, was one:

I've not spoken to Larry. I will in a few days when I've got [your]
answer to a couple of my last letters.

I trust in you and your judgement wholly from now on. I'm in
Europe only because you knew I wanted to come. Please cable. And
if Larry can't return [to the States], I can make it alone. In fact, that
might be better. I'm a little fed up with having my career handi-
capped by being tied up with that of another person.

Love sweet—always your

Paul[17]

The rapid expansion of Paul's concert repertoire to include European folk songs, classics, and popular ballads had changed the nature
of his collaboration with Larry Brown. In a letter to Essie written

just one day later, Paul considered dropping Larry: "If my career can't be built up and maintained by spirituals, there is no need in having Larry as a load and carrying him, making every move of mine considering him. . . . He considers Varney his choice and can't object if I leave—with you in your present condition."

About a week later an urgent cable arrived from Essie's mother, my Grandma Goode. Against Essie's wishes, it told Paul of her real condition. Consumed with worry and guilt, conflicted by his belief that Essie had unilaterally decided to have a child in order to bind him to a shaky marriage, he booked immediate passage home, leaving his European concert plans—and Larry Brown—suspended in midair. He wrote her from the steamship *Mauretania* on December 25, 1927, as he sailed back:

> If there was a sweet girl in this world, you are it—and such a beautiful spirit. It was so beautiful of you to let me go at the time of your childbirth. I'll never forget that—nor will I ever let you suffer again without my being around to help, if it's only a cold. I love you sweet with all my heart for ever and ever. I feel as though I had never really loved before. Just you wait and see how I shall treasure you and the boy who is part of us.

I was placed in the care of my maternal grandmother, Mrs. Goode, whom Paul, deferentially, still addressed by this name, while my parents devoted almost their entire attention to each other. Grandma Goode was to be my primary caregiver for most of my childhood.

Despite Paul's constant presence and tender care, Essie's recovery was painfully slow, and she remained mostly bedridden for several weeks after his arrival. It would be late March before her health finally returned to normal. Meanwhile, the concert tour remained suspended. In the midst of this uncertainty, a few words from highly influential people served as a balm. A March 5, 1928, note of appreciation from Theodore Dreiser reads: "When I get tired writing, I put on one of your records—Mt. Zion or Witness or Water Boy—and let your sympathetic voice revive my failing spirits."[18]

But praise did not pay the rent. Out of work and in dire financial need in January, Paul had accepted a $500 advance to appear in a cheap New York jazz revue in the fall. In the interim there were no acceptable film roles to be found; they were all crude caricatures. But then a break came: he was offered the chance to replace Jack Carter as Crown in DuBose and Dorothy Heyward's *Porgy*, a role he had previously turned down because of its excessive vocal demands. Now he felt compelled to accept the risk. The $500 weekly salary convinced Paul to go against his better judgment and try it. His misgivings were fully justified as he struggled for six weeks to sing over the orchestra. Fortunately, he was rescued before he ruined his voice when Florenz Ziegfeld offered him the role of Joe in the upcoming London production of *Show Boat*. This time he promptly accepted the part.

Although the London producer, Sir Alfred Butt, feared that Paul's talent would be wasted on such a small part—he sang just one song, "Ol' Man River"—Ziegfeld insisted that he wanted Paul. He won Butt over on the ground that the song would be sung three times, as a recurring theme.

Recovering from her childbirth trauma, Essie eased back into her role as agent/manager. She wrote a letter to Walter Varney, Paul's European concert manager, reassuring him about Paul's availability. And she convinced Paul that Larry's invaluable contribution to rendering the spirituals was essential to Paul's concert career. Then she wrote a warm letter to Larry Brown, asking him to rejoin them in Europe.

In two letters to Larry, Paul shared his plans and his views of the possibilities for a resumption of their previous musical collaboration:

April 10, 1928

Dear Larry—

Well, I'm on this damn ocean again. I arrive in London April 13. Am due to open in "Show Boat" May 3rd. Soon after, I hope, if you are free, we can do a series of recitals and even cover other parts of England and do private work. The part in the play is comparatively easy—just one song—so I'm sure I can do our work on the side with no difficulty. Write me c/o American Express, London, and run over as soon as you can—will you. Love to Zadie,

Paul

Larry's response to this letter has been lost, but apparently he was cautiously open to resuming work with Paul. He had already become almost indispensable to Paul's career, serving as both musical arranger and chief researcher of new songs for his repertoire. Paul now wrote to him, urging him to come work with him again, and offering to guarantee a living for him out of his salary from *Show Boat*:

Grosvenor Hotel
London, S.W. 1

April 19, 1928

Dear Larry—

Was so glad to get your note. I'm so sorry I didn't write from the States—but you know how I am. I was so worried for a while, and so relieved when Essie improved, that I didn't know just where I was, and my plans were so unsettled.

Here are my plans, Larry. I hope we can work them out. I am still where I was last Fall—I want to sing (I went with Porgy only because I had to have some money to keep from starving, and had to get out because my voice would not stand it as I knew it wouldn't).

Now came this shot for "Show Boat"; I sing only one song— "Ol' Man River," but it runs all through the show and I get three good spots for it. I'll get a lot of publicity, and it might make London concerts easy. I reserved my concert rights, and to be fair must give them for Varney. I expect to see him this week-end.

I jumped at the chance to play this in London, because it was the only way to get to Europe and resume our work. I'm sure we can make more now in concert work and private work (after all, we can go to the provinces and sing in Paris too on Sunday) than we could have before.

If we find concerts are not going as we hoped (I'm sure they will), we can talk over some arrangement to cover you. My musical career with you is by all odds paramount, and if I remain in "Show Boat," I'll see that you make as much in concert and privately as we would ordinarily, or I'll guarantee you a livelihood out of my salary—which is only fair. But I took this job only because it brought me back to concerts with you and at the same time will give us something to live on while things are taking shape. You see, I'm only singing in the play and not enough to tire me. It's really made to order.

I am going right to work. There is no reason why we should not give the concert about the end of May or first part of June. Play opens May 3rd. But do come over soon if you can. I'll see about the visa after I see Varney. Anyhow, if you have no definite plans, please make none. I'm here to take up our work and keep it up no matter what happens. Best to you old chappie.

Paul

Never again did Paul consider dropping Larry. When opening night arrived, Paul was more than ready. *Show Boat* became a smash hit that would run for almost a year at the magnificent Drury Lane Theater, and all the reviews hailed Paul's singing of "Ol' Man River" as the best part of the show—"the thing that held it all together."[19] As one critic put it: "Paul Robeson, who proved in Emperor Jones that he could act almost the entire company off the stage, has been given—such are the wasteful methods of musical comedy—a non-speaking part. Yet he dominated the show."[20]

Based on his detailed observations of African-American life and his fruitful exploration of the art of the spirituals, Paul projected "Ol' Man River" as a dignified lament with a hint of tragedy in the midst of a rather trite musical comedy. Marie Seton, Paul's subsequent British biographer, recalled the impact this performance had on her:

Like many other Londoners, I went to see "Show Boat" soon after it opened. [There was] no dramatic build-up for the entrance of this new star, Paul Robeson. The scene shifted from the steamboat to the wharf. Suddenly one realised that Joe the Riverman was Robeson, the silent figure endlessly toting bales of cotton across the stage. [He] filled the whole theater with his presence. Paul Robeson sang about the flowing Mississippi, and the pain of the black man whose life is like the eternal river rolling toward the open vastness of the ocean. The expression on Robeson's face was not that of an actor. The pathos of Robeson's voice called up images of slaves and overseers with whips. How had a man with such a history risen? A most startling quality appeared in Robeson as he accepted the applause. He was visibly touched and yet remote. He seemed to have no greed for applause and he appeared to be a man stripped bare of mannerisms. The story of romance on a show boat plying the Mississippi suddenly moved into the fore-ground and Joe, the son of slaves, went back to toting bales of cotton. I have never forgotten the bend in Robeson's back. It was full of strength, yet it expressed a sorrow which seemed to know no end.[21]

When he recorded "Ol' Man River" with Paul Whiteman's orchestra, Paul reached a mass audience that, as always, arrived at its own interpretations. According to one typical review of the record:

> To anyone who knows the Southern States, Paul Robeson singing "Ol' Man River" will conjure up a quite unforgettable picture. The hot sun beating on coloured folk lolling at their ease, or even stretched out fast asleep, and it takes a negro [sic] to be able to sleep in the full glare of a sub-tropical sun. Somewhere a banjo is heard. Slowly, sleepily, the whole gathering takes up the tune. Someone claps their hands. There is a shuffling of feet. A young buck nigger rouses himself and breaks into a dance; another joins him. Soon, the quay is alive with dancing, gesticulating figures. The player, tired, puts his hand over the strings to still the last throbbing chord. The dancers stop with a jerk. Men and women sink to the ground almost where they stood and once more the quayside sleeps.[22]

The stark contrast between this interpretation and Seton's sensitive description of the "sorrow which seemed to know no end" reflects not only a vast difference in sensitivity to black stereotypes, but also Paul's ability in live performance to overcome these stereotypes with the pure expression of universal emotions.

8

"THE POWER TO CREATE BEAUTY"

(1928–1929)

In May of 1928, Essie joined Paul in London, where they flourished.

[*May 1928*[1]] London! The platform at Waterloo Station; the rush
of a handsome, dark giant all my own—Paul!! . . .

Home! A charming flat in St. Johns Wood facing Regents
Park; the bracing air; the efficient maid. The Royal Drury Lane
Theatre; seeing "Show Boat" for the ninth time, but this time with
Paul as "Joe." The cheering and tremendous applause of the packed
house for his song "Ol' Man River." A cable at the stage door:
"Infant fine, all well. Love, Mother." A feeling of well being.

Paul and Larry give a concert at the Drury Lane and pack that
vast theatre. The audience stomps and cheers approval, and the
press is enthusiastic next day. The Prince of Wales commands them
to sing for him and the King of Spain; the Duke and Duchess of
York request them to sing; Lord Beaverbrook, Baroness Ravensdale, Sir Philip Sassoon do likewise.

Great news!! We are to remain in London for a year or two—
weeks of house-hunting, trying to find the impossible: a house on
high ground to be healthy for small Paul; near enough to the Drury
Lane for large Paul; a garden; central heating, all of which is difficult enough to find separately.

The miracle has happened!!! I was sent to No. 76 Carlton Hill
and found there a fascinating elderly woman—the Countess des
Boulletts. She is an Oxford graduate, has traveled the world, and

153

has lived in Turkey for years when her husband was in the diplomatic service; she had seen Paul in "Show Boat," had heard his concert at the Drury Lane, and was tremendously impressed with him. We talked for hours about Negroes, America, music, the theatre, England. She showed me through the house which is a charming, well built English brick with central heating throughout, all furnished in rich, simple, comfortable taste. I was wild about the place but didn't think I could afford it, and I told her so. She laughed and said, "Oh, never mind the money; if you think it will answer your needs, we'll arrange about that." Then she suggested that I bring Paul over to see the house; if he liked it also, then we could have it. The Countess was delighted to see Paul—they talked for an hour, and then she showed him the house. When we all returned to the garden for tea, she said she had decided to let the house as it stood: silver, linen, and servants—cook, maid, and gardener. There's no use mentioning the price because no one will believe me—it is so absurdly small. We can scarcely believe our luck, but it's all true and real. I [will come back to] London September 21st with small Paul and Mother. And henceforth, until further notice, our address is 76 Carlton Hill, St. Johns Wood, London.[2]

About six months later, Paul and Essie moved to a small mansion, called "One the Chestnuts," in the exclusive Branch Hill neighborhood in Hampstead. But the house in London's St. John's Wood, near Regents Park, had set the tone for their style of living. The large Victorian brick house, on a quiet tree-lined street, had an expansive living room across the back. A hand-cranked Victrola sat on a low table in the corner of the room. Grandma Goode brought me over to London a year later when I was not quite two, and my earliest memories of my father are of his voice pouring out in song from that magical box.

In July, Larry Brown rejoined Paul to perform several matinee concerts at the Drury Lane Theatre—the first time an actor appearing nightly in a musical comedy gave solo concerts in the same theater. The concerts, which consisted entirely of Paul and Larry's usual repertoire of Negro spirituals and secular songs, were greeted enthusiastically. The reviews abounded with praise: "the direct sincerity of the true artist"; "absolutely faultless—perfect and consummate artistry"; "a beautiful, admirably controlled voice, and perfect diction"; "command of vocal color . . . remarkable"; "a bass voice of wonderful compass, but of still more remarkable resonance."[3]

On one occasion, Queen Mary showed up unexpectedly in a box at the Drury Lane, and such a furor developed backstage that Paul was thoroughly nervous and frightened when he faced the audience. He started singing "Ol' Man River" a tone off-key, and when the startled orchestra tried to slow down to help him get back on pitch, he tried to speed up and created a disaster. The queen was quite gracious about it all, and apparently returned without fanfare to hear him in good voice. Essie recalled in her memoir: "He gave some bad performances, but they were never due to carelessness on his part; they were due to colds, exhaustion or nervousness."

After the Drury Lane concerts, things were finally going well financially for Paul. His salary for *Show Boat* was $1,200 a week, and with the additional concerts and private work, his peak weekly earning capacity was about $3,500. But just as he was preparing to start paying back his debt to Otto Kahn, another problem arose. Now he was unable to fulfill his commitment to the New York jazz revue. The producer, Caroline Dudley Reagan, took legal action in both the United States and England to compel his return to appear in her show. Ms. Reagan's lawsuits cost him a temporary suspension by Actors Equity, a lot of bad publicity in the United States, a large financial loss from legal fees, and an out-of-court settlement amounting to $8,000. It was not until 1931, two and a half years later, that Paul was finally able to pay off Kahn's loan.

He continued his performances in *Show Boat* nonetheless, and his popularity soared. The great writers Aldous Huxley, H. G. Wells, and George Bernard Shaw, the composer Roger Quilter, and many others sought his company.

Among his new acquaintances, Paul became friendly with prominent supporters of the Labour Party, and eventually a group of Labour politicians took him to visit their working-class constituencies. Paul also developed the idea of booking concerts in halls frequented by working people at prices they could afford. Thirty years later he wrote that "It was in Britain . . . I learned that the essential character of a nation is determined not by the upper classes but by the common people."

One day during the grim winter of 1929, when unemployment and desperate poverty stalked the British Isles, Paul was on his way to a gala affair when he heard the rich sound of a Welsh miners' choir. He had crossed the path of a group of miners from South Wales who were walking along the street at curbside and singing for money to sustain themselves. One of their signs said they had walked all the way from Wales to petition the government for help. But what Paul instantly seized upon was their spirit and their suffering as human beings.

Without hesitation, he joined the group, walking the streets with them and humming along. When they reached one of the large downtown buildings, Paul climbed the front steps and sang "Ol' Man River," ballads, and spirituals to his new friends. To those who were there, it was a transforming experience as Paul translated their hopes into song. Later, he organized enough contributions to provide them with a ride back home on a freight train that included a carload of food and clothing for the miners of the Rhondda Valley and their families. That year he contributed the proceeds of one of his concerts to the Welsh miners' relief fund and visited the Rhondda Valley in person to sing for the mining communities and talk with the people. This was the beginning of a lifetime of ardent friendship between Paul and the people of South Wales.[4]

When *Show Boat* closed in February 1929, Paul plunged headlong into a world that suddenly could not get enough of him. Essie had already signed him up for the Celebrity Concert Tour that featured the world's top artists. She had also arranged for a test European tour of Vienna, Prague, and Budapest. He studied French and German so that he could sing folk songs in the original tongue and also resumed regular voice lessons. Both tours were triumphs, with the concerts sold out everywhere and Paul consistently in excellent voice. The English audiences in the provinces were at least as enthusiastic as the London ones, and the concerts on the Continent were so popular that extra appearances had to be scheduled. The review in the leading Vienna newspaper *Die Stunde* (April 11, 1929) reported that "They sat enthralled, for they were listening to a wonder." On the same day, the Prague newspaper *Deutsche Zeitung Bohemie* reported that Paul "went far beyond the ordinary concert singer." And in Budapest the review in the newspaper *Pesti Naplo* (April 13, 1929) judged him to be "an extraordinarily cultured singer, technically beyond criticism."

Fresh from his European tour, Paul now scored another major success in a watershed concert at London's Royal Albert Hall, where his performance in front of a packed house placed him in the top rank of concert artists alongside Kreisler, Chaliapin, McCormack, and Paderewski. Nevertheless, American-style racism stalked him even in Europe at the height of his popularity.

In a letter to an acquaintance who was a Labour Member of Parliament, Paul recounted how he and Essie had been barred from the famous Savoy Hotel grill room because American guests there objected to the presence of Negroes. Paul's Labour Party friends made his letter public and raised a furor on both sides of the Atlantic. The English outrage against this treatment rose to such a pitch that the matter was brought to the floor of Parliament, and an investigation of racial discrimination by English hotels was launched. The management of the Savoy was forced to announce that it did not practice racial discrimination, a result that would have been impossible in the United States.[5] By this time, Paul and Essie had already departed for Paul's first American concert tour in three years under the management of the highly respected F. C. Coppicus of the Metropolitan Music Bureau.

When they arrived in New York in late October 1929 to begin a two-month national tour, Paul was thirty-one. The white audiences were curious to see the great new star of the London production of *Show Boat*, America's favorite musical comedy. And black Americans welcomed Paul as their hero who had conquered abroad. They simply ignored both the European correspondents of the black press and the Black Nationalists at home, who harshly criticized him for singing lyrics with the word *nigger* in a show full of stereotypical black characters. Instead, they chose to focus on the fact that they were hearing their own voices in the spirituals he sang. The press reports described Paul as "the king of Harlem." According to one account, "when Paul Robeson . . . comes back to One Hundred and Thirty-Fifth Street, it takes him half an hour to walk a block."[6]

After the time he had spent in Europe, Paul found the return to America exhilarating but unsettling. In his November 8 notes, he confided his concern about the possibilities of his playing the role of Othello on Broadway. He had just signed a contract to appear in a production of the play in London, with the expectation that it would ultimately go to Broadway and tour the United States:

> Went to the theatre to see *Strictly Dishonorable*. Very amusing. Am so upset about American *audience*. Seems so terribly crude—there for entertainment, not because of love of theatre. Very strange feeling for me to be sitting in balcony—I am almost afraid to purchase orchestra seats for fear of insult, when in England my being in a theatre is almost an event. Very curious. I do hate it all so at times. Everything rushes along—not a kind word anywhere. Everyone looking for his own—no sense of peace, calm, freedom as in London. I feel so oppressed and weighted down. I am very alarmed about the chances of *Othello*. Don't see how American audience will accept play. Of course, the liberal group; but mass of theatre goers—never.

His Carnegie Hall debut had been on November 5. He noted in his diary that he now had a "tremendous following" and that the pronouncement of the critics was "no longer of great importance for me, as notices of the 5th were generally *unfavorable*. There you are. Really is exciting."

From the reviews, which on average were excellent, it is at first difficult to understand Paul's disappointment, but close examination of them reveals that he was referring to such criticisms as "the writer begs leave to hope that Mr. Robeson will . . . vary his offerings"; "even though an occasional roughness of tone was noticeable . . ."; "Negro folk music is based on a single pattern, and a very monotonous pattern it soon becomes."[7] Other reviewers complained about "some moments when a conflict in intonation arose as his voice veered slightly sharp" and about his "short range, . . . [and] excessive reserve, . . . together with deficiencies in rhythm and color."[8] Paul disagreed with these evaluations because he felt they stemmed from an underappreciation of black music. On the other hand, his note of triumph reflected his two sold-out Carnegie Hall concerts five days apart, the second of which turned away a thousand people.

For Paul, the reviews had lost their bite. With this greater independence from the power of the critics, he began to explore new ideas and to think about ways to expand his artistic reach:

> Had swell idea this morning and talked it over with Essie: why not series of evenings combining dramatic and musical, Negro and classic. One night—sermon and then spirituals; then scene from *Emperor* [*The Emperor Jones*]; then secular songs and spirituals. Next evening—*All God's Chillun*; then Negro secular group; then classics; then scene from *Othello*, etc. . . . . Shall I consider *musical comedy*, straight theatre, or concerts—not formal concerts after this year, but [an] evening [of] doing what I wish. Now seems feasible— need intimate surroundings: say, good-sized theatre. *Grand idea.*

Though he was fighting a cold, the November 10 concert at Carnegie Hall went well. Paul reported in his diary that he gave "to my mind, the best recital of my career. I sang evenly and with a good variety of mood, color, etc. I did so because I sang the songs and forgot my voice. The audience responded in great style." With this experience, he "completely reversed" his opinion of Carnegie Hall, noting that it had become "like a big drawing room" in which "I had no trouble at all in filling it with my voice." The staff at the hall said that no one had ever filled the place twice in five days, and they raved about Robeson's voice. Laurence Tibbett, the famous lyric tenor, went backstage and told Paul he had never enjoyed a concert so much in all his life. "Everyone was most enthusiastic," Paul noted with satisfaction in his diary.

He wanted to share his joy with Essie, but he was ruefully looking back toward her as he headed away:

> I had to leave Essie, and how I hated to. I wanted to talk to her, and bring her home, and love her and love her—but I had promised to say hello to F. [Freda Diamond] who had come in from Chicago for the concert. She was as beautiful as ever and very glad to see me. We had a nice chat.

There was likely more than a "nice chat," but Paul, even in his diary, was determined to keep up appearances.

In his November 11 diary entry he mentioned a session with Teresa Armitage, his voice coach, who was helping him with a "soft-voice problem" (an occasional difficulty he encountered in projecting his voice). "I see it clearly now," he wrote. "Miss Armitage is really wonderful. She will surely clear it all up in a short while. Then almost the last technical problem will have been solved."

The next day, November 12, he wrote a long entry in which he ruminated about his sense of personal destiny, and his definition of "true art." These matters were all interconnected for him.

Art is art. Can make it question of degree. Schubert song as symphony. Perfection is perfection. Painting of apple as landscape. Piece of Egyptian sculpture as Gothic cathedral.

[There is the] statement that one must be trained to repeat *his* performance at any time—whether he feels so inclined or not. [Supposedly,] that marks true artist. And the allied question. Can I be artist with just Negro songs?

Art is creation, or rather re-creation, of beauty. Artist sees what others omit. He brings it to others.

Take myself as untrained singer—I sing beautifully always in Drawing Room and in some recitals as my first at Greenwich Village and in Chicago. I was as much artist then as now. Repetition has nothing to do with fundamental validity of artistic creation. We must repeat ourselves because of necessity of earning a living.

So repetition is partly economic problem. Suppose I was wealthy—had private concert hall; when I felt good (always sing well then), I called in people who were waiting and ready to come any time.

I had no technique for singing over cold, etc.—I sang when I felt like it. True artist, I should say. I couldn't fill big halls—I would fill small one vocally; no difference if I brought beauty. Simply to fewer people. No need of technique if not professional. Of course, technique might help me grow and widen—expand, but that might not make me *greater* artist. "Water Boy"—*best* record—when I was untrained.

Take C. Franck—just as much artist with one *symphony*. Cervantes with "Don Quixote." Many great artists—only one great work. May not repeat. So "Journey's End." So O'Neill [playwright Eugene O'Neill]—never has developed *smooth technique*. But beauty and truth are there.

Kreisler [famous violinist Fritz Kreisler] plays today—informal and warm. Retires, never plays more. Just as great artist [with] no repetition. Many untutored gypsy violinists more moving than [Yasha] Heifetz. Sheer virtuosity [i.e., Heifetz], intellectually amusing and clever, but not true art.

Then he turned to what his belief in God meant to him. To my knowledge, it is the only time Paul attempted to outline in writing the feelings in the deepest recesses of his soul:

> God doesn't watch over everyone, because everyone isn't important. But perhaps way back He created world to see if from lowest forms of life *God* could emerge. God says to himself: "Where did I come from? How did I get here?" He created several worlds with different forms of life on each. Will see how God can emerge. We have several stages, and on *Earth* man evolves. There may be man or other forms of life on other planets. But on Earth (& Mars, etc.) God is interested in those beings who more closely approach *him*. These God-like people emerge naturally—just like artist creates something more than he knows; so [there are] different God-like people in different epochs. Different *God*-like *qualities*. So many great kings—like *Pharaohs*, Alexander [the Great], Elizabeth, Alfred, Napoleon—could be God-like archangels *thrown* out of heaven.
>
> God is infinite good and infinite evil, since he controls so-called Satan. Satan is other side, so Zeus [the most powerful Greek god] was not always good. But God is good, and thrusts his evil side far away. He recognizes great forces of evil and good as super-human, but he encourages good and sees evil brought to grief. So at one time Christ, Buddha, Confucius, Mohammed, Moses, David, St. Augustine, Luther; so Socrates, Aristotle, Bacon, Shakespeare, Purcell, Rowland. *So founders of Democracy*, etc. Emphasis on different people or classes at different times.
>
> As a reward, he gathers good souls around him to watch others *struggle*—but mass return to inanimate matter or perhaps carry on humdrum life as souls elsewhere; but [I] think—since God [is] interested in finding himself—ordinary mortal [is] of no more consequence than ordinary person in this world. Anyone is born with chance to be God-like—just as any painting [has] chance to be great when artist begins.
>
> So give all a chance, but most fall by the wayside. So if God came to Earth, all would follow—so Christ and *12* [disciples]. So people subconsciously rush to God-like people and hope to get grace from them.

Paul saw himself potentially as one of these godlike people, a giver of grace. Having craved grace from others, he now aspired to give it.

Great artists, Paul concluded, are "blessed with divination of the human soul aspiring toward God." They are inspired by God "in direct contact. Not God in words and precept but in deed. Not sermon on [the] *mount* . . . but Christ *speaking*." As for himself, Paul believed that his life's purpose had been divinely predetermined:

> So by chance have some of this power—have power to create beauty. Have wife as scientist who holds me to truth necessary to create true beauty. So God watches over me and guides me but lets me fight my own battles and hopes I'll win.

The power to create beauty, which he realized he possessed, was in his mind the source of the grace he could offer. Truth, as a measure of right, was beauty's indispensable companion.

Paul's preoccupation with beauty and truth was not accidental. It stemmed from his close ideological kinship with W. E. B. DuBois, who had expressed the same theme in eloquent secular tones in 1926. In an essay titled "Criteria of Negro Art," published in the October 1926 issue of *The Crisis*, DuBois called forth the vitality of the African-American artistic tradition: "We have within us as a race new stirrings; stirrings of the beginning of a new appreciation of joy, of a new desire to create, of a new will to be; as though in this morning of group life we had awakened from some sleep that at once dimly mourns the past and dreams a splendid future."

Then DuBois went on to extol the black younger generation as the bearer of that future: "The Youth that is here today, the Negro Youth, is a different kind of Youth, because in some way it bears this mighty prophecy on its breast, with a new realization of itself, with new determination for all mankind." DuBois then ruminates, as Paul did three years later in his 1929 diary, about the meaning of beauty:

> What has this Beauty to do with the world? What has Beauty to do with Truth and Goodness—with the facts of the world and the right actions of men? "Nothing," the artists rush to answer. They may be right. I am but a humble disciple of art and cannot presume to say. I am one who tells the truth and exposes evil and seeks with Beauty and for Beauty to set the world right. That somehow, somewhere eternal and perfect Beauty sits above [the] Truth and Right I can conceive, but here and now in the world in which I work they are for me unseparated and inseparable.

This vital source of personal strength compelled Paul to sustain himself emotionally through times of personal and professional hardship. He had been grievously hurt on several occasions. He had coped with fear, uncertainty, and disappointment with varying degrees of success. But his abiding faith and unshakable sense of purpose had always kept him emotionally whole. He could be bent, but he could not be broken.

Yet as Paul approached the pinnacle of success at the end of 1929, there was a trace of grandiosity in his speculation about his godlike status. He lived a pampered, aristocratic life, far from the racial humiliations endured daily by even the highest-ranking blacks in the United States. The stock market crash and the beginning of the Great Depression—cataclysmic events that were occurring before his eyes as he triumphed in two successive concerts at Carnegie Hall—were barely in his consciousness.

An occasional high-handedness had emerged in his personality: an incipient feeling of license. Even as Paul embraced his "power to create beauty," he feared to reveal how vulnerable he was. So the aspiring artist clung to the consummate performer's bag of tricks. As his sculptor friend Antonio Salemme would say forty-nine years later, in his personal life Paul chose to remain mostly impersonal.

In 1993, Salemme recounted a telling anecdote to me about this period in Paul's life. It seems that both Paul and Tony were going to be in Paris, and, at Paul's suggestion, they had agreed to meet at a given time under the Eiffel Tower. Tony showed up on time, but Paul didn't show up at all. And he never bothered to contact Salemme after that. Never. Just dropped him. Although Tony, who was celebrating his one-hundredth birthday at the time of our interview, laughed and shrugged when he told me the story, the hurt was still etched in his luminous blue eyes.

Early in 1929, in London, Paul had met Yolande Jackson, a tall, graceful woman in her twenties who was a sometime actress from a conservative, moderately wealthy English family. Her face was the kind usually described as attractive rather than beautiful, but she had a vibrant personality that enchanted Paul. She seems to have been a free spirit—an iconoclastic, adventurous, warm, playful, and demonstrative person who had a quick wit and an irrepressible sense of humor. Like Paul, she also had her reflective, moody side. They were, it would appear, an almost ideal emotional match. However, unlike Paul, she was not dedicated to developing a career and had no serious intellectual interests. Nor did she manifest any desire to take care of Paul. Nevertheless, an instant friendship developed into a love affair that Essie found out about when she accidentally came upon a love letter from Yolande that Paul had carelessly, or coldly, left in the open. This letter jarred Essie onto a high-risk course of publicly exposing some of the tensions in her marriage to Paul.

9

TO FEED HIS SOUL

(1930)

Essie sought to capture the high ground in the event of a divorce. Planning for the worst while hoping for the best, she put her own spin on the nature of her relationship with Paul. Paul knew only that she was writing a book about him. Never confrontational, he distanced himself from it. Paul didn't ask, and Essie didn't tell. Whenever the book did come up, they pretended to have mutual trust.[1]

In January 1930, they embarked as if nothing were the matter on a series of European engagements—Düsseldorf, Prague, Dresden, Brno, Vienna, Bucharest, Turin. Then they returned to England for Paul's annual British tour. Paul thrived, but Essie was less than enthusiastic about some of the cities. In her diary she wrote: "Birmingham!!!—Stupid town. Five concerts. Hanley!!! Stupid town. Five concerts." But the Welsh port town of Cardiff was a different matter. Essie caught the spirit of the place: "Cardiff!!! Saw the famous docks where ships from all over the world come. Welsh people— miners, very poor, but very musical. They sing as they work."[2]

Connected with his audiences, but without the degree of personal identification that he would later feel, Paul was content to head to a picturesque mountain inn in Territet, on the Swiss side of Lake Geneva, to shoot a silent art film called *Borderline*. Paul played the lead and Essie a supporting role in a barely comprehensible story. A black man is living quietly in a small Swiss border town until the arrival of his black girlfriend triggers a dramatic chain of events. Guided rather casually by director-writer-producer Kenneth Macpherson and his wife, Bryher, Paul drew on his performance in Oscar Micheaux's *Body and Soul* six years earlier to make some sense of his character. "Mr. Macpherson buries his intentions in a conglomerate of weird shots . . . , worked out around a dissolute set of unsympathetic characters," wrote one critic. He added that "[The film] stimulates one's natural desire to see and hear Paul Robeson in a first-rate British 'talkie' made for the public."[3]

The experience was more lark than anything else. Paul's mind raced ahead, focusing on the challenging work of rehearsals for Shakespeare's *Othello* in preparation for a May 19 opening. It weighed heavily on his mind that he was on the verge of becoming the first black man to portray Othello on the English stage since Ira Aldridge had done so in the mid-1800s. The preproduction publicity had begun four months before the opening, and public anticipation had grown as Paul was widely interviewed. The announcement that Peggy Ashcroft, a rising young British actress, would play Desdemona had added to the interest on both sides of the Atlantic and raised the controversial issue of interracial marriage. In London, the issue was quickly put to rest by both Ashcroft and most of the press. It was a different story in the United States, where the press generally doubted that the public would accept a black Othello.

On April 15, rehearsals began in earnest for the production mounted by Maurice Browne with his wife, Ellen Van Volkenberg, as director. Paul had agreed to sign up with Browne because Browne had risen from recent obscurity to become one of England's hottest theatrical producers, and because he planned to bring *Othello* to America if the London run proved successful. And two weeks before the opening, Jed Harris, a major American theatrical producer, announced that former American screen star Lillian Gish had tentatively agreed to play Desdemona if he could convince Paul to play the role on Broadway.[4]

The London production got off to a bad start. Maurice Browne, a former actor, insisted on playing the part of Iago, for which he was manifestly unqualified, and his wife, as director, found herself completely out of her depth in her attempts to guide the rehearsals. Essie confided in her diary that "Paul . . . says it looks hopeless. . . . Nellie [Von Volkenberg] doesn't know what it is all about. . . . Poor Paul is lost."[5] Once again, James Light came with his wife, Patti, and worked feverishly with Paul on developing the role. Max Montesole, a fine actor who played the role of Cassio, and Peggy Ashcroft, who played Desdemona, joined them. Working together at the Robeson home, they tried desperately to whip the play into shape. The premiere lifted the shadow of their foreboding.

Most reviews in the major newspapers were glowing. The *Sunday News* claimed: "It is an out and out triumph. . . . He looks magnificent, and his rich, sonorous voice . . . gives an added quality to Shakespeare's words. Never have they been more finely spoken." One representative review appeared in the *Manchester Guardian*, which, though it criticized Paul's "standing in ungainly positions," his lack of movement, and his spacing of the main speeches, went on to say: "The swaying body spoke all the horror of the obsessed mind, and . . . yet kept within the limits of tragedy. It was, to put it as simply as the part was played, large acting, an unusual spectacle in the days of the intimate and united style." The *Spectator* critic noted: "Mr. Robeson is a very remarkable actor. . . . [But] criticism of his performance must admit that he misses the *romantic* aspect of Othello, minimizing such famous passages as 'It is the cause' . . ."

The weekday edition of the *Times* praised Paul almost unreservedly: "Mr. Paul Robeson teaches us anew that Othello on the stage means something more to us than Macbeth, Hamlet, or Lear. . . . Undeniably, Mr. Robeson plays thrillingly upon the nerves and knocks at the heart. His performance is blemished here and there but nowhere seriously flawed."

By contrast, the *Sunday Times* edition leveled the most searing yet insightful criticism of Paul's portrayal:

> He did not trust his powers *as an actor* sufficiently; he certainly did not take the risk, with the result that all that Othello ought to be throughout the first two acts he was not. Mr. Robeson, alas, failed not only to show mastery of the grand style, but also to indicate any idea of its existence! Othello conceives Desdemona's death not as a murder but as a sacrifice, and kills her not out of passion but because her conduct has shaken the world from its propriety. The reason Mr. Robeson failed to be Othello was that he had none of this highly civilized quality.
>
> But Mr. Robeson's performance had, to a quite amazing extent, the qualities of its defects. Though one may not have agreed with the plane, the performance on that plane was entirely consistent. Mr. Robeson has a beautiful voice which he uses clearly and distinctly but not beautifully, or rather not in the way of Shakespearean beauty. Each line, as he delivers it, is a prose line made up of the rhythms and cross-currents of prose. [emphasis mine]

The interesting thing about this review is its clear articulation of the weaknesses in Paul's performance. There is Othello's tentativeness and lack of authority in the first two acts. (The *Time and Tide* reviewer referred to it as his "inferiority complex.") In 1930, Paul had not yet jettisoned the "don't upset white folks" dictum of his boyhood days, thus interfering with his ability to project the regal and commanding posture that Othello should exude from the outset. The pivotal "It is the cause" soliloquy should reveal that Othello considers Desdemona's conduct as grounds for an execution, and that he does not commit a murder out of jealous passion but is meting out carefully considered justice. This is a departure from the traditional portrayal of Othello as entirely consumed by jealous rage, but one that a careful reading of the lines shows to be truer to Shakespeare's text. Paul's inhibitions, however, caused him to focus excessively on Othello's rage.

The anonymous *Sunday Times* critic was one of the few who saw not only where Paul should have tried to go with the role but also why he had failed to get there. In 1930, Paul did not yet possess the confidence needed to deliver the lines with the authority he later found. Because he was too cautious in the attempt, the lines emerged as "prosaic."[6]

On the other hand, Paul's partial success was due to his thorough preparation. Ever since his first trip to England in 1922, he had been reading and studying extensively—the dramatic literature of Shakespeare's time as well as that of his predecessors—"Wyatt and Spenser and other Elizabethans." And he had studied "the work of every other man who [had] ever played Othello, and [had] tried to learn something from each."

As a singer, he appreciated Shakespeare's verse, which "[gave] one a fine opportunity." But his appreciation of the role went well beyond the magnificent language and the "glorious lines." In a newspaper interview he noted:

> It seems to me that Othello's first scene before the Senate is of prime importance. Here was a member of an alien race, facing a highly developed white civilization, knowing exactly where he stood—a great general, but yet in a precarious position because of his race. He stood there, not humble at all, and conscious of his ability. Why should this tragedy of Othello not be his own personal tragedy, as it must be the tragedy of anyone who is, in essence, too great for his station?[7]

On June 8, 1930, the British Broadcasting Company organized a historic radio interview by Paul broadcast to twenty million American listeners over seventy-five stations of the ABC and CBS networks. He spoke of how it felt to play the role of Othello, as well as of his plans to bring the London production of the play to Broadway. Othello "must be of a different race to make the jealousy credible," he said, adding hopefully that "From all I can hear, the present production will come to America. I certainly do want to play *Othello* in the land of my birth."

However, this was not to be at this time. The project was sabotaged by the machinations of Maurice Browne, who, as the producer of the London *Othello*, attempted to dominate the negotiations for the Broadway production.

Ironically, the publicity Paul was soon to receive in the United States stemmed from a sharp racial controversy: the life-size nude bronze statue of him that his friend sculptor Antonio Salemme had recently completed was banned from a 1930 exhibition in Philadelphia. The Philadelphia Art Alliance rejected the statue, stating obliquely that "the colored problem seems to be unusually great in Philadelphia." In view of this attitude, *Othello* might not have received a much better welcome in New York.[8]

In the midst of Paul's success in the London *Othello*, Essie's book about him was finally published. In the flurry of the extensive publicity surrounding it, Paul steeled himself to read it carefully. He was deeply angered by what Essie had written.

She not only harped on his real faults; she invented some. She also took credit for his successes, and disingenuously put her own views into his mouth. And she had written the book in the third person, in an apparent attempt to give it a greater appearance of objectivity. The net effect was a highly slanted account with a patina of credibility that could be penetrated only by a close and informed "insider" reading.[9] For example, the last chapter of the book, titled "Finding Himself," began with a three-way conversation among Essie, Paul, and a mutual friend named Martha Sampson (a pseudonym):

> Essie addressed herself to Martha: "We have argued and disagreed about everything under the sun. Oh, don't worry. I daresay we're better friends than anybody you know; and I'm sure he loves me more than ever, and I know I love him a thousand times more than

when we were first married. He's a blessed confounded, adorable nuisance." "That's just what makes me so mad," said Paul angrily; "she treats me just as though I were a baby or a small child; she refuses to realize that I'm a grown man." He was fuming like a small boy. "Well," said Essie, unperturbed, "perhaps when you grow up I'll treat you as a man."[10]

There was a wide gap between the "Paul" depicted by Essie and his public personification of dignity, discipline, and dedication. Yet Essie expanded the caricature, having herself say to Paul:

"Suppose you tell Martha some of your faults. . . . " "Well" Paul hesitated very boyishly—"she thinks I'm brave and honest and moral, when, as a matter of fact, I'm none of those things."[11]

Three pages of a guilt-ridden litany by Paul followed, punctuated several times by Essie's exonerating counterpoint comments ("But Martha, if he wasn't essentially honest, would these things worry him so?"). Then Martha provided the cue for a discussion of Paul's possible infidelity: "Now let's have your immorality, Paul." The ensuing exchange between Paul, Martha, and Essie revealed the mixture of reality and fantasy to which Essie was clinging in order to negotiate the difficulties in her marriage:

Paul thought a while. "It's very difficult. You see, I don't like to hurt Essie's feelings. But she's so unreasonable and absurd. She keeps raving about [how] she'd never believe I was unfaithful to her, even if the evidence was strong against me." "Are you unfaithful to her?" asked Martha. But Paul refused to commit himself. "If I were to admit I am, what good would it do? She'd never believe it. I wouldn't mind if she wasn't so *sure*."[12]

Essie refused to acknowledge Paul's fierce rejection of her view of marriage as a kind of ownership. Every fiber of Paul's spirit rebelled at this, and his anger fueled his intense desire to destroy this illusion ruthlessly. Essie, however, ended her soliloquy by implying Paul's acceptance of her view:

"I know what you mean about your being unfaithful to me, but you don't know what I mean. You mean that someone may have fascinated you and interested you tremendously, and that you consummated that interest. Let's suppose you did. Would it shock you to learn that I might have suspected as much? Well, darling, if I ever thought there were lapses, I thought of the possible reasons for them, and dismissed them as not lapses at all." Paul's eyes were full of tears, and full of an immense relief.[13]

Paul read this passage as a reflection of what he perceived as emotional obtuseness in Essie, and it stirred his feelings of spiritual deprivation. He became more conscious of an acute need to fill an emptiness in his soul—a void that his calling could not mitigate.[14]

Paul also felt that Essie demeaned that calling by presenting his professional work habits in a contemptuous way in order to amplify her undeniably important role in advancing his career:

> "Laziness, with a capital 'L.' It's the cause of most of your short-comings." Paul was interested, because he was convinced, in spite of all he said, that Essie knew and understood him better than anyone else. "Take your disloyalty to your friends, which is so hard for me to excuse. It's really laziness. Take your work. You never learn the lines of your plays until the last moment." He was tremendously interested. "Do you think I could play Othello now if I worked at it?" "I know you can, silly." "All right, I'll do it." "Attaboy," shouted Essie enthusiastically, placing a resounding kiss on his cheek.[15]

The last exchange, about *Othello*, was especially misleading, since Paul had been meticulously and consistently studying the role for more than five years before he undertook the London production. His hesitations about that production had more to do with his well-placed misgivings about Maurice Browne and less to do with doubts of his own abilities, as suggested in this passage. The reason they had decided to take the role offered by Browne was that in this case Essie's willingness to take risks had outweighed Paul's natural caution.[16]

At the outset of her book she paid extended homage to Paul's elite Bustill ancestry, from which he himself felt alienated, while only briefly mentioning his slave Robeson ancestors, with whom he closely identified. Paul was particularly angered by her substitution of the name "Bustill" for his actual middle name "Leroy."[17]

It was plain to Paul that Essie was writing as much of herself as of him. While she was fiercely loyal to her dark-skinned father, brothers, and husband, and to African-Americans as a people, she categorically rejected the idea of passing for white. More suspicious of whites in general than Paul was, she chose dark-skinned people for her closest friends, both female and male. Yet, contrarily, she identified with the aristocratic culture of the light-skinned black elite, wanted Paul to fit into this world, and resented his embodiment of the black church culture, which she, like many aristocratic light-skinned blacks, considered low class.

The tug-of-war between them, as seen through Essie's eyes, was exposed for all to see. She also took the opportunity to state the case for her right to decide alone what influences would be paramount in my life, greatly exaggerating Paul's lack of fatherly involvement. She quoted him as saying "I don't want you to be disappointed in my lack of interest in the boy. He's a nice baby. But I have no fatherly instincts about him at all." Then she portrayed one of Paul's main concerns about me as an afterthought with which she agreed:

> "Oh, and one more thing about the boy. If we settle permanently here in England as we hope to, I particularly want him to go to America at regular intervals, so he will know his own people. I want him to have *roots*. I feel it will be very important for him."
>
> "Yes, it will be," agreed Essie. "If he's to be an artist in any sense of the word, his racial contacts will be of great value to him. It's great fun to see how he likes coloured people already."[18]

Aside from the fact that here, as elsewhere in the book, Paul's voice sounded more like Essie's than his, Paul's use of the word *roots* spoke volumes contrasted with Essie's use of the word *contacts*. To him, the last paragraph of the final chapter was the most galling moment—a package of negative racial stereotypes of the black male:

> He leaves a trail of friendliness wherever he goes, this Paul Robeson, Negro, who, with his typically Negro qualities—his appearance, his voice, his genial smile, his laziness, his child-like simplicity—is carving his place as a citizen of the world, a place which would most certainly have made his slave father proud.[19]

The immature, petulant Paul depicted in Essie's book was uncomfortably close to the Paul she sometimes saw. But in his own eyes, Paul had grown tremendously over the years, expanding his emotional freedom, his sexuality, his artistry. He had quietly, often secretly, moved on, leaving Essie to guess what was on his mind. In this emotional environment, she became more aggressive, while he grew more detached.

Essie's book was her way of publicly defending what she felt were irrevocable rights as Mrs. Robeson. Paul now read it as an unmistakable warning to him: If you even think of replacing me as Mrs. Paul Robeson, beware of my wrath. You can't even imagine what I will do to you, but here's a little taste of it. This was a provocative way to communicate with a private man whose way of dealing with trouble was to avoid it if possible, but to strike the first blow without warning if conflict was unavoidable. Moreover, Paul was not prone to negotiate, or even to enter into a discussion, under threat. He remained completely silent while he set out to demolish her sense of ownership of him and to free himself from his dependency on her regardless of the cost to their marriage.[20]

Paul's silence on this subject lasted a lifetime, but Essie's public humiliation of him in cold print was beyond his tolerance. Outwardly, Paul would remain his genial self; inwardly, he would never feel the same about Essie.[21]

Naive critics treated the book as an authentic portrait of Paul: "It is a proud wife's account of her husband's success"; "Paul Robeson, when he reads this artless account of himself, should be a happy man"; "It shows us, with friendly gentleness and shining humor, Paul Robeson's career. . . . But chiefly it reveals the whole character, temperament, and imaginative method of the man." One of the more astute reviewers, who called the book "pleasant," came closer to the truth: "I believe there must be more to the story of Paul Robeson as the figure of a man who has experienced a bitter struggle."[22]

Meanwhile, *Othello* ran its course. It stayed at the Savoy for six weeks and then toured briefly in the provinces. Paul, unimpressed by his generally favorable notices, would later dismiss his performance as amateurish. However, he viewed his efforts as a critically important learning experience that confirmed his instincts about how the role should be played and led him to establish permanent standards for his career in the theater. Henceforth he would seek to act only in topnotch productions with the greatest actors to challenge him.

He was proud of his historic achievement as a black actor who successfully portrayed Shakespeare's Moor on the London stage with a white cast for the first time in almost a century. He had the potential as an artist, he felt, to fulfill his dream of advancing the cause of his race through his acting.

Paul and Essie stayed on the move. They heard Toscanini conduct at Albert Hall, attended an exclusive luncheon at Lady Ravensdale's, viewed a cricket match between the English and Australian teams, and had tea at the House of Commons with the top leaders of the Labour Party. In July they entertained Paul's older sister, Marian, who was traveling in Europe with a friend.[23] Publicly, they remained unchanged and charming. When negotiations with Maurice Browne about touring the London production of *Othello* abroad collapsed, Essie arranged for Paul to sign up for concert tours of Britain, the Continent, and the United States for the 1930–1931 season.

I was sent off with Grandma Goode to Territet, Switzerland, the rationale being that the mountain air there was far better for my health than damp, smoky London. We would remain there and in nearby Austria for the next three years.

While Paul was touring, Essie decided on her own to sell the house in Hampstead and to renovate a huge apartment at 19 Buckingham Street in a picturesque small enclave in central London. An entry in her diary, dated simply "August, 1930," refers only in passing to this major step that entailed enormous expense and was to have a critical impact on their future: "Have the perfect flat in Adelphi, just for Paul and me. Am looking forward . . . to being alone with him." Essie meant for Grandma Goode and me to live separately from her and Paul while she concentrated on rebuilding her failing marriage. Paul, who was informed but not consulted about the elaborate living arrangements Essie was preparing, apparently maintained his silence, freeing his mind for the pursuit of ideas that would stimulate his intellect. He felt a strong need to learn and to grow.

In an interview from the period with W. R. Titterton, a leading British columnist and a personal friend, Paul ruminated on his vision of what humanity's goal should be: "to work towards mankind's one big purpose, . . . the great journey . . . towards better and better men and women." His way, Paul said, was "the way of the artist. The talents of an artist, small or great, are God-given. . . . I mean, they've nothing to do with him as a private person. . . . They're just a sacred trust. . . . Having been given, I must give. Man shall not live by bread alone, and what the farmer does I must do; I must feed the people with my songs." Then he went on to avow that he was more dedicated to his art than to his family:

TITTERTON: But suppose your vocation came into conflict with your duty to your family?!

ROBESON: Then my family must suffer.

TITTERTON: That's rather a hard saying.

ROBESON: It is. But it's the truth. An artist gives joy to hundreds of thousands, perhaps to millions. He consoles, he inspires. He must consider his responsibilities to this multitude rather than to those few.

TITTERTON: For whose safety, however, he is *directly* responsible.

ROBESON: He is responsible for his talents and he must not bury them in the earth.[24]

Later on in the interview, Paul returned to this topic from a different angle: "If my wife said to me—'We've made enough money. Let's go away and enjoy life on the Riviera,' or 'I refuse to share you any more with the public,' all I could say would be 'I'm sorry, I've just got to go on!' Believe me, it isn't the money. I don't care two hoots about that. But I can't stop; I daren't stop." This was Paul's public warning to Essie: I'm an artist before anything else. Don't even think of fencing me in.

But Essie's complete immersion in the preparation of an ideal apartment for Paul and herself made her impervious to anything but the most direct challenge. If she did read Paul's comments, she chose to ignore them, even though he had been changing before her very eyes.

Two other points in the Titterton interview—one artistic and one political—leap off the page. They reveal the core of Paul's developing attitude toward the connection—and contradiction—between art and politics:

TITTERTON: Suppose a great cause called you?

ROBESON: I have had my call.

TITTERTON: A friend of mine, a great writer, urged men to fight in the war [World War I]. Later on he felt he must do what he had told other men to do. So he went, and died.

ROBESON: It was a ghastly mistake. Thinking as he did, it was noble of him. All the same, it was a mistake.

TITTERTON: There was his example.

ROBESON: The artist's example is his work.

TITTERTON: Don't you think it will be rather terrible if we make the artists a sheltered class exempt from the ordinary hazards of mankind?

ROBESON: Being a human creature, the artist will often share the common risks; but he ought to be thinking always of his art, as the doctor or the scientist thinks only of his special work. And if that is true of ordinary artists like me, how true it is of the great creative artists like Shakespeare. Do you think Shakespeare ought to have thrown away his life fighting the Spaniards? [during the colonial wars]

TITTERTON: Yes. *(Robeson shrugs his shoulders.)* What about your people?

ROBESON: Do you mean Americans, or men of my colour? Well, I don't think it would ever be my duty to help America to become a predominating nation. As for men of my race, why, certainly. I would do all that I can to help them shed the last rags and tatters of old oppression. But I help them best of all by being an artist. It would be foolish, wrong, of me to be a propagandist and make speeches and write articles about what they call the Colour Question while I can sing.

This attitude is a far cry from Paul's glorification of America's role in World War I expressed in his valedictory address at Rutgers eleven years earlier. At the same time, his commitment to improving the condition of African-Americans remained unwavering. Despite his seeming detachment from the problems his people were facing in America, helping them to "shed the last rags and tatters of old oppression" remained his earnest goal.

Nevertheless, Paul was rejecting political activism, political advocacy, and commitment to a "cause" as suitable modes for an artist.

The artist, he believed, must ultimately be accountable exclusively to himself and to his art; the warrior and the prophet are by definition at odds with the artist. This attitude contradicted DuBois's view that art should serve primarily as a tool for advancing the African-American status.[25]

10

TROUBLED SPIRIT

(1930–1931)

The month of August 1930 was a chaotic time for Essie as she juggled three households. Simultaneously keeping track of Grandma and me in Switzerland and the sale of the Hampstead house, she managed the renovation of the enormous 19 Buckingham Street flat that she was designing for herself and Paul. This was to be their dream apartment, and Essie was consumed with the idea that it was the elixir she needed to restore their marriage. Paul would stay there when he was in town during the brief breaks in his current provincial concert tour.

When the dreaded confrontation with Paul over the publication of her book had not materialized, Essie had put the Yolande affair out of her mind, and busied herself frenetically with preparing the new apartment. She had ignored Paul's warning signal—his studied emotional detachment—by assigning it to one of his familiar moods.

Suddenly, without warning, Essie's carefully constructed emotional world came crashing down. A long entry in her 1930 diary, dated September 1 and devoted to a detailed description of my doings before she took Grandma and me to Switzerland, ends abruptly, numbly: "Found a letter from Peggy Ashcroft at the flat. Exactly like the one from Yolande last year. . . . I dare not think of it 'till I get away from here—my nerves are too far gone."

Essie's rage, pain, humiliation, and feeling of betrayal were deep and intense. Paul's affair with Peggy Ashcroft, a newly married brilliant and beautiful young actress whom Essie had befriended and sponsored for the role of Desdemona opposite Paul in *Othello*, had been conducted under Essie's nose at the same time that Paul was seeing Yolande. The shattering impact of the sudden combined on-slaught of these undeniable facts was too much for Essie to bear. She suffered a nervous breakdown that caused the left side of her face to fall; her three-month recovery period is reflected by the fact that her 1930 diary has only one entry ("October 1930") between September 1 and December 25.

Despite her panic and depression, Essie immediately wrote Paul several letters (which unfortunately have not been preserved), to which she received a prompt reply—one that startled her for its lack of both remorse and commitment. The reply is dated September 9, 1930, and comes bluntly to the point:

> I am very sorry, of course, you read that letter. You will do those things. You evidently don't believe your own creed—that what you don't know won't hurt you. It makes things rather hopeless. It must be quite evident that I'm likely to go on thusly for a long while here and there—perhaps not. I'm certain I don't know, but the past augurs the future. It's my fault for having mail reach me there, but you were not living there as yet, and I felt for the time being it was my apt. It makes matters rather difficult, as I must have a certain amount of privacy in my life. So I see nothing but to leave you the apartment and go to an hotel. I'll keep my front room and come in to see you. I could come over for a couple of weeks before going to America.
>
> I am in a period of transition—where I shall finally finish is of little consequence to me. I would like to get on with my work. To do that I need to be as far as possible absolutely free.

By the time he had received Essie's letters, Paul and Peggy had already decided to end their affair. Peggy's husband, Rupert Hart-Davis, was happy to have her return to him, made no fuss, and Peggy returned to her pre-*Othello* life as if nothing had happened. Paul, on the other hand, had decided to continue his relationship with Yolande Jackson, which explains why his reply to Essie includes a general declaration of his freedom to do whatever he chooses in his private life.

His comments on the flat reflect the problem Essie had saddled them with: they both had to stay at the flat indefinitely, since there was no way financially that they could pay off the already incurred cost of acquiring and renovating the flat, maintaining Grandma and me in Switzerland, *plus* getting another flat for Paul to live in separately from Essie. Consequently, whenever they were in London at the same time, they were trapped together. This would complicate matters considerably, since even as Paul announced his independence from Essie, he surprisingly declared his continuing love for her:

> I'm sure that deep down I love you very much in the way that we could love each other. It could never be wholly complete because we are too different in temperament. We haven't helped each other very much. I feel spiritually starved. You became almost a physical wreck. Something's wrong—maybe my fault, maybe yours—most likely both our faults. There's no need rushing ahead and repeating the same mistakes.
>
> I'd love to come to Switzerland for a short while when I am through and see you, the boy, and mother before going away. If you feel you want the flat—all right. You determine that. But the financial strain must be considered. Love to the boy. Do tell me about him and how he's going along. Of course I'm interested.

None of this went over very well with Essie, but it seems that at this point Paul didn't care much about her feelings. He was temporarily obsessed with demonstrating his independence from her. Even so, his letter was full of ambivalence about the rift between them, and the ending expressed the poignant hope that their relationship could somehow be repaired: "Write me always as you feel. I often feel extremely close to you and want to see you and talk to you and perhaps weep in your bosom. Let's hope it will come out right. Love, Paul."

From Essie's point of view, Paul's behavior was unexplainably outrageous and had spun their well-ordered lives out of control. Her response was her customary one when confronted with a crisis: assume the worst while hoping for the best. Struggling to get herself back on an even keel, she busied herself with the process of settling me and Grandma into our lodgings in Switzerland while pondering what to do about her suddenly disintegrated marriage. Meanwhile, she confided some of her thoughts to her diary.

October, 1930

Pension, Riant Chateau, Territet, Swisse [*sic*].

I was startled to get an answer from him—cold, mean, vindictive. He is all for the protection of Peggy. Paul urges me to stay here, so he can carry on with Peggy, I suppose. It doesn't matter to him that all my clothes are in the flat, all my books, all my work. I came here to stay ten days, and only brought clothes for ten days! Yet if I return to London, he will swear I came to spy on him.

I never expect him to believe that I didn't open that letter to spy. He forgets the most important thing—that he spoke very sweetly over the phone to me from Edinburgh, and that such a letter would be the last thing I would expect to find. As it was, I still feel the shock. Well, none of it matters.

I am surely a jackass if ever there was one. I should have seen the handwriting on the wall. Fancy believing his lies right up till the last. He was a smooth one, though. He must have been lying to me for five years, steadily.[1] Well, I'll never let another man know what goes on in my mind and heart. Paul has told me I refuse to face things, etc. But now I know, and now I shall face things squarely. We will begin from here.

Thus began what from the outside world would deceptively appear to be the bizarre tale of a disintegrating marriage. What actually unfolded, however, was the convoluted but dedicated effort by two complex and conflicted marriage partners to save at least part of a relationship that was vital to both of them.

When Essie resumed her diary writing in late December of 1930, after the family had been temporarily reunited for the holidays and she had seen Paul off for a concert tour of America, she described how, beginning in October and through December 1, she had been in the flat while Paul was touring the provinces. He had come in occasionally on weekends, dividing his time between Yolande and Essie—"Yolande got most of the time," Essie duly noted. "She telephone, telegraphed, and ran him to earth."[2]

On December 1, Paul had come into town and spent six days at the flat with Essie: "We had a marvellous time," she wrote. "We went to the theatres . . . supped with Noel Coward, and had a grand time generally. We became better friends than we have ever been, much, much closer. [Paul] was having such a good time in London that he really did not want to go. Finally, I arranged to dine with Noel Friday evening, and Paul left."[3]

During this period of friendly relations, Essie and Paul came to an amicable agreement to divorce, and Essie accepted Paul's decision to go through with his marriage to Yolande. They spent a very pleasant family Christmas holiday with Grandma and me in Switzerland. "A lovely time together," Essie wrote, "even though Yolande rang him up again . . . on Wednesday and Xmas day."[4]

Faced with the provocation of Yolande's relentless and intrusive pursuit of Paul, even during his Christmas visit with his family, Essie's consent to a divorce proved to be less firm than she had imagined. Her anger boiled over when she and Paul went to Paris for a couple of days, and Yolande tracked them down there. As she confided at the end of her December 27 diary entry, she had undergone a sudden change of heart about the divorce:

> Paul and I left for Paris early Friday morning, December 26, and as soon as we got settled in our hotel, Yolande called him up from London. She knew we were together, and that I was saying good-bye to him forever, but still she pursued. I made up my mind that she will never marry him as long as I live, and am able to prevent it. I changed my mind completely, and decided once and for all, if she can't at least treat me with the courtesy I gave her [when Yolande would call Essie to find Paul], even though I have every right to see him and she none, even though I am turning him over to her, I'll not get a divorce at all. I'll be damned if I will. I'll not divorce him—so there.

Essie appears also to have been pushed to her new resolve in part by a meeting in Paris with Paul's football coach and mentor from Rutgers, Foster Sanford, which she mentioned in the same entry: "Paul thinks the world of him and he of Paul. I knew if [Paul] and I were ever divorced, Sanford and all the men like him would hate [Paul] forever, and that many healthy, friendly doors would be closed to him. Sanford was a symbol, and he helped me finally to make up my mind. I'll sit tight and not move an inch."[5]

Paul, at this stage of his life, was relatively unconcerned about white reaction, but was concerned about black reaction to his involvement with a white woman. Divorcing his black wife who had helped him attain stardom to marry a white woman, he realized, would harm his credibility among his people. He feared that in America his rejection by the black community for having abandoned Essie, combined with white hostility to interracial couples, would leave both him and Yolande virtually isolated.

Nevertheless, Paul feared that if he broke with Yolande, he would inexorably be pulled back into Essie's confining orbit. He needed Yolande as a lover and playmate, and also as a buffer against Essie's control. On the other hand, he needed Essie to take care of him, to continue as a vital partner in advancing his career, and to be a friend and companion. But he could no longer tolerate her attempts to own him. Needing both Essie and Yolande, he could not bring himself to part with either one.

Essie kept vacillating, desperately wanting to keep Paul and angrily wanting to be rid of him. While she needed him and wanted him, she could no longer tolerate his blatant extramarital affairs. Above all, she needed to be Mrs. Paul Robeson.

Essie's last entry in her 1930 diary, dated December 31, poignantly underscores the dilemma she shared with Paul: ". . . I didn't expect to be in Paris, alone. So completely lonely—in spirit, I mean."

On her thirty-fifth birthday—December 15, 1930—she had received a note from Paul: "Happy Birthday. It has been so marvellous and I'm so happy to be spending this day with you. Love, Paul." But Essie's diary entry for that day reads: "Spent [my] birthday eve with Noel Coward at flat, then drank to his health on December 16, that being his birthday." With Paul no longer the center around which her life orbited, Essie was preoccupied with constructing her own, distinct world. She, too, craved her emotional independence after years of a confinement different from Paul's but no less difficult.

On January 27, 1931, Paul wrote Essie a breezy letter from the Grand Rapids, Michigan, stop on his U.S. tour. His concerts were successful, as usual. "Packed Washington Auditorium," he wrote; "only Chaliapin & myself doing that in recent years." He had been denying all rumors of their separation ("Thought it best for you to handle same"), and he wanted to take three months out "to do nothing but learn new songs." The "American scene" was not as trying as it had been the previous year—he and Larry were now able to get into hotels everywhere, but they still had to agree to take meals in their rooms.

In between the small talk, Paul alluded to his dilemma: "I had a talk with Noel Coward. We talked frankly, as he said he knew all the facts. I left my position very clear—I am very anxious to marry [Yolande], etc. He thought that rather inadvisable from career angles, but appears to understand." And in an apparent reference to his assumption that Essie and Noel were lovers, Paul added, "I couldn't gauge him very well. He was non-committal, and rightly so. After all, his business with you is your concern, not mine. He was very nice. We had a long chat. He *is* delightful."

Paul ended his letter with an expression of concern for Essie's health, apparently responding to something she had written to him: "How are you physically, and what had you better do? February is approaching. Do be careful. And you must think of your condition afterward. Wire me & let me know. . . ."

There was ample reason for worry. Essie had discovered she was pregnant. She had apparently told Paul about her decision to have an abortion, and Paul seems to have been offering to help. Only as she departed for New York on March 4 did Essie mention this matter in her diary, and even then only in passing: "I've had a grand week before sailing. . . . I've got to do a 'job,' and I think Dr. West, who did my other one more than ten years ago, is the best bet. And also Presbyterian [Hospital] will be close to hand if anything goes wrong." Judging from Essie's 1931 diary entries for March and early April, she had her abortion a few days after her arrival in New York, and soon appeared to be fully recovered.[6]

Paul had now arrived at a transitional point in his professional life. In addition to his stardom as concert singer, stage actor, recording artist, and radio performer, a film career beckoned. He had to decide how to balance these multiple, sometimes conflicting, identities.

The concert stage, the theater, and the recording studio were the places where he felt he could be true to his calling as an artist. In contrast, radio and film offered the means to reach a truly mass audience and to make the greatest impact on the popular culture. He understood that to be a star in those media he would have to make many distasteful compromises. Not only would he have to accept stereotypical roles but he would descend from the exalted heights he was scaling as an artist back to the more mundane world of the performer. His consolation would be in advancing the cause of his people.[7]

Paul decided to attempt to do it all simultaneously. In preparation, he felt a powerful need to improve his mind, expand his intellectual capacities, and acquire a store of general knowledge about a wide variety of subjects—from science to art, from literature to politics. So he embarked on a period of intensive study that was to last for six years.[8] A February 13, 1930, interview in the *London Evening News* quotes Paul about his music: "Unless I feel a song and its innermost meaning instinctively, I always study the life of the composer, the history of the country, and its background generally." The interviewer added that "Mr. Robeson's room endorsed his words, for the whole of one side of it was stacked with books on all subjects." Once launched into his studies, Paul began to test his ideas in both interviews and articles on a variety of topics:

> I want to find out things for myself, and see the country from where my ancestors came. Anything that can be done to show that the African Negro had some cultural background will help the movement.[9]

> Instead of trying to get away from his folk background, the American Negro should find among his own people the basis of development for his own arts. Some members of my race want to forget how to sing spirituals. They don't like such a play as *The Emperor Jones*, and they probably wouldn't have liked my London *Othello*. There is no good reason for this.[10]

> As to the most important part which the Negro is qualified to play on the American scene, I would define it as "cultural," with emphasis upon the spiritual aspect of that culture. I would much rather see a world striving for deep cultural and spiritual values which acknowledge no narrow national, racial or religious boundaries. Some such impulse might well be given by [my] people upon whom nature has bestowed, and in whom circumstances have developed, great emotional depth and spiritual intuition, comparable indeed to that of another race whose faith was nurtured upon African soil— the ancient Hebrews.[11]

> I found at once that the [Russian] language and the music suit my voice, and I think there is a psychological explanation. There is a kinship between the Russians and the Negroes. They were both serfs, and in the music there is the same note of melancholy touched with mysticism.[12]

Although Paul was deeply immersed in his work and studies, the turmoil in his personal life was more than just a distraction. His letters to Essie often contained passing references to his sadness and loneliness. Despite his desire to be free of her, he missed her. He felt a need for her care. And he wanted to share his intellectual and artistic life with her. Notwithstanding his fascination with Yolande, she was not much of a friend. And it was friendship that meant the most to Paul. Though Yolande kept pursuing him, he still could not bring himself either to marry her or to divorce Essie. For her part, Essie couldn't make up her mind whether to reconcile with him, divorce him, or deny him a divorce.

On other fronts, matters were simpler. Paul distanced himself from the Van Vechtens and their circle of white and black literary and society people who were closer to Essie than to him. He gravitated back to theater and journalistic circles, and to his old Harlem friends. During this period, he became especially close to Robert Rockmore and his wife, Bess, both of whom he had met in 1924 when Bob was backing *All God's Chillun Got Wings*. Rockmore was a brilliant and rising entertainment lawyer, doubling as an agent-manager for selected clients like Paul. A short, compact man with a Lower East Side New York Jewish background, Bob combined a tough exterior with a sympathetic heart and an unimpeachable integrity. He became one of Paul's closest and most trusted friends.

Bob Rockmore signed Paul to appear in a London production of Eugene O'Neill's play *The Hairy Ape* in May 1931. The story was originally written with a white character as the protagonist. It describes the brutalization of a stoker in the hold of a transatlantic liner to the point where he self-destructs by entering the gorilla cage at a zoo. Paul's April arrival in London to play the part followed Essie's return from New York by only a few days. When Essie attended the dress rehearsal of *The Hairy Ape*, she worried about his "using too much voice." At the opening she felt that Paul "was magnificent," but she was still concerned that he would strain his voice. Four days later, Essie was proven right in her concern. The reviews were excellent, but the run of the play ended abruptly when Paul landed in the hospital with a severe case of laryngitis.

After he recovered, Paul saw Essie once in a while under a variety of circumstances, but they were now living separately. On one occasion he came to dinner at the apartment, stayed overnight, and had "a delightful talk about many things" with Essie. Another time he and Larry rehearsed in the apartment, and afterward she cooked dinner for a group of his friends and entertained them. Paul's Russian tutor and his wife were among the guests. Paul was studying Russian intensively while working seriously on expanding his concert repertoire. It became routine for Paul and Larry to show up at the apartment to rehearse and then to have lunch with Essie.[13]

Without changing their official marital status, Paul and Essie remained separated and undecided. Essie's August 19, 1931, diary entry reports that while visiting Grandma Goode and me in Austria she had been "taken suddenly ill" and rushed to the local hospital. Her August 22 entry reveals that she was still there. There is little doubt that the cause of her medical troubles was her botched New York abortion of the previous March. This tends to be confirmed by an August 5, 1931, letter from Paul to the doctor who treated Essie at the Austrian hospital. Apparently, Essie had asked him for such a letter in advance, fearing trouble and knowing that an Austrian doctor would require a letter from her husband before performing any procedure related to an abortion.

Fortunately for Essie, Dr. Lowinger, armed with Paul's letter, performed the procedure—no doubt a D&C—immediately and expertly. The hospital bill, which Paul paid directly, reveals that Essie was hospitalized for six days. The incident affected Paul profoundly. Apparently believing that Essie had become pregnant by a white man (foreigner), he wrote her a long letter dated August 27, 1931. He expressed, as directly as he ever would, his deep anger at her; yet, once again, almost in the same breath, he expressed his love for her:

> After all the trouble, you can't take any further chances. If we decided to go ahead with things sometime, we must be careful & give every possible chance from the first. Which, I am afraid, during the Period of Possibility will have to exclude foreigners (*verstehen sie?*) [*you understand?*]. One can be just so liberal in such important matters.
>
> You're a dear, and I'm really very devoted to you—love you very much in fact, much more than I ever did, & miss you beyond words. I have a lovely picture of you which I've always kept, and I hold onto it.

Though Paul's admonitions to Essie were plain enough, she was certain to misinterpret the emotional ambivalence he expressed. He meant it to convey primarily his anger, moderated by his love. She would focus on the love while ignoring the anger. The result of this miscommunication, combined with their own emotional contradictions, would rupture their tenuous relationship.

I I

GIVER OF GRACE

(1931–1932)

W ithout Essie as his organizer, Paul's life was being reduced to an enervating struggle to get from one engagement to the next. In November 1931, Essie confided to her diary that he was "behaving very, very strangely." He was in bed with influenza at his hotel, refusing to see Essie but willing to talk to her on the phone. His sold-out concert at Albert Hall had to be canceled, along with a concert scheduled in Cambridge. "He is certainly degenerating," Essie noted. "He can't seem to make up his mind what to do about his work, about his life, about me and Yolande. . . . He really will have to settle down and get busy, if he wants to hold his place. Poor fellow—I'm sorry for him."[1]

Three weeks later, Paul returned to their apartment when Essie was out and discovered a long letter she was writing him. She had finally laid out her grievances—her hurt feelings, as well as her criticisms of his faults. According to Essie, he took most of it to heart:

> I gave him breakfast, and we really talked about what was on our minds. We got closer and more friendly than we have been. He says he wants to see me often, and that we have something between us which no one else will ever be able to duplicate. He thinks he wants to marry Yolande, but he isn't sure; but he is sure he wants us always to remain close and friendly. He went to Bournemouth [to sing a concert], and came back and remained till early morning. We had another long talk—I told him all about my book *Black Progress* which I am writing for the screen, and he seemed deeply interested. We had a lovely time, slept together, and enjoyed it enormously. I'm so glad things are pleasant and friendly. Most important of all,

he has found his feet, so far as his work is concerned, and is through with slacking and sliding and muddling through. Thank God for that![2]

In December 1931, Grandma Goode and I arrived from Austria for a visit, and Christmas Day was a genuine family gathering. According to Essie, Paul and I played together happily, and he spent all of his last day with us before sailing for New York. "Paul . . . arrived here at the flat at 7:30 A.M., remained nearly two hours with us . . . while Yolande waited downstairs in her car for him [to take him to the ship]," Essie wrote in her diary.[3] Thus, a friendly standoff was temporarily reached. Paul and Essie agreed to get an uncontested divorce, but not to go their separate ways.

In April, Essie received a long letter from Paul asking her to start proceedings for divorce at once, naming Yolande as corespondent. She cabled him that she would do so, confiding to her diary that she was "glad to have it all over with at last." Her attorney started the process, and by May rumors were flying, including a false one that Essie had filed suit against Lady Louis Mountbatten for alienation of Paul's affections. (Both of them got a laugh out of this, but Lady Mountbatten saw no humor in it and successfully sued the offending newspaper.)[4]

In June, Paul was quoted in the *Chicago Defender*, a major black newspaper, as saying that he wished Essie well in her independent career. As for his possible marriage to a white woman, he declared that "If my action stirs up prejudice, then I am prepared to leave the country and go to Europe."[5] It is doubtful that Paul meant this defiant statement seriously. More likely, it expressed his occasional impatience with his black critics. Meanwhile, with the constant turmoil in his personal life, he sought solace in reflection.

Early in 1932 he gave an interview, again to his friend Titterton, which was published with the title "The God I Believe In Is the Friend of Simple People." Our family reflected a variety of attitudes toward religion. As an adult, Paul attended church rarely. Grandma Goode was a militant atheist, and Essie was an agnostic. I can remember my father leading my mother and me in prayer when I was about five. Yet he never tried to convert others to his way of thinking and rarely discussed his religious creed. Now he spoke out about it publicly.

Paul talked freely and unselfconsciously to Titterton. "I am a black man," he began, "and all black men are religious. Africa has given religion to the world." He had been "thinking about things" in the past five years, he said, adding that he remained "convinced of an omnipotent and loving Providence":

> God is good. And that tells you what we owe to the Hebrews. Before Moses the everlasting powers were malevolent. They had to be placated to save man from destruction. It was left to Christ to give us the idea of love, of mercy, of compassion. That changed everything. What if, from the back of beyond, the hand of God came out, not primarily to punish, but to caress us! That's one side of it. But there is the other. What if malevolence is not merely wrong, but silly! What if gentleness and goodwill are bound to win! How marvellous to hear echoing through the universe: "Blessed are the meek, for they shall inherit the earth." What a shattering blow is that to our heaped battalions with their artillery!

"Well," he continued, "my God is the God that Christ preached. The friend of simple people. A merciful God, and one that loved merciful men." He added his thoughts about the human condition, making it clear that his was an optimistic philosophy: "We are striving, more or less, to become Godlike. Again and again we fall. But in the end, with the help of much that has gone before, we shall attain." Noting that "just now we are very near the brute," he offered the thought that "simple men survive, and they are the ones who know most about the Eternal."

Titterton did not hesitate to challenge the core of Paul's faith, eliciting the following reply:

> But how, you may say, can God be merciful when such terrible things happen? I'm not frightened by that. He created men—by what process, evolutionary or otherwise, I don't know—and allowed them to work their own will. God can't be blamed if man's works are evil. We had proof that the suffering of the Negro had ennobled his soul in the Spirituals which I am so proud to sing. But in America Negroes are going mad in the race for money and power. Their priceless heritage which made them whole is forgotten. They do no worse than the whites around them, you may say.

True! But all the fruit of their old sufferings is wasted. It is a ghastly catastrophe.

The interview ended with Paul's reflection on how he had come to these beliefs:

> How do I know anything about God? I think that most men know. When a man looks into the eyes of his beloved he knows. When a simple man faces the majesty of Nature he knows. And as an artist I have my moments of ecstasy when the thing is plain. But I do not exalt the artist above the common man. The common man feels; we artists have the power of expression—that is the difference. Nevertheless, when I sing my Spirituals, in which is the whole history of my race, it is then, more than at any other time, that I am liable to be caught away, and feel and know, that God exists, and God is love.[6]

This deeply felt religious belief, an important source of Paul's artistic strength, was harder to discern as a principle in his private life. There was a selfish side to him—an aspect of his personality that protected his sense of spiritual freedom and sometimes conflicted with his principled, self-sacrificing behavior.

On May 19, 1932, Paul took his place on stage as Joe in the spring revival of the musical *Show Boat* at New York's Casino Theater. This was the first time an American audience would hear him sing "Ol' Man River" live.

In a letter to Alexander Woollcott, Edna Ferber, the author of the novel *Show Boat* on which the musical was based, described the scene when she attended the opening-night performance. She arrived late at the jammed Casino Theatre just as Paul came on to sing "Ol' Man River." "I never have seen an ovation like that given any figure of the stage, the concert hall, or the opera," she wrote. "It was completely spontaneous, whole-hearted, and thrilling. . . . That audience stood up and howled. They applauded and shouted and stamped. Since then I have seen it exceeded but once, and that was when Robeson, a few minutes later, finished singing 'Ol' Man River.' The show stopped. He sang it again. The show stopped."[7]

Paul was now deluged with lucrative offers. His concerts were sold out in advance. He was getting $1,500 a week in *Show Boat* and $1,500 for a single twenty-minute radio appearance. He appeared on several top radio shows by popular demand during his five-month stint in *Show Boat*.[8]

Throughout this time, Paul was frequently interviewed by the press. He supported the emerging use of the racial designation "Negro" instead of "colored." Yet he had nothing to say about the looming presidential election between the conservative incumbent, Republican Herbert Hoover, and the liberal Democratic challenger, Franklin D. Roosevelt. Black communities across the nation were organizing in support of the legal defense of nine black youths framed on a rape charge and sentenced to death in Scottsboro, Alabama. But Paul remained publicly silent on this issue.[9] By contrast, he was consistently outspoken on cultural issues:

> The Negro or the African must have a pride in himself. He must feel that, in his culture, he has something valuable to be developed but not to be replaced.[10]
>
> We are a race, but not a people. The Negro intelligentsia radically differs from the Georgian Negro worker whose lot, despite emancipation, is almost that of a slave. The dispersion of Negroes over the world has resulted in a natural cleavage within a healthy race. The lead in culture is with the American Negro, the direct descendant of the African ancestors. [He] is totally different from other Negroes. The mingling with American and English culture and spirit is most potent, yet the American Negroes are the most self-conscious of all. The real great man of the Negro race will spring from North America. [He] cannot be begotten but in the land of ancient oppression and revolutionary emancipation. For the Negroes of North America will never perfectly assimilate like their South American brethren.
>
> Have, then, the Negroes produced outstanding personalities? W. E. B. DuBois—I know of no more original journalist in this world. In the theatrical world we have Rose McClendon, Richard Harrison who played God in *Green Pastures*, Frank Wilson. Of scientists I will mention Ernest Just, the biologist; of our novelists, James Weldon Johnson and Claude McKay; our great poet Langston Hughes. All that does not prove much except perhaps that the Negro is capable of the same achievements as the White. His health and vigour in many respects destine him to even greater ones.[11]

The year 1932 was also marked by an event that Paul, at the age of thirty-four, called "the greatest hour of my short life." On June 11, at the commencement exercises of his alma mater, Rutgers University, he proudly received an honorary master of arts degree. The youngest man ever to be so honored by Rutgers, he drew special satisfaction from Rutgers President Robert Clothier's declaration that "Seldom is it given to one man to bring joy to the hearts of his hearers by the arts of singing and acting as it has been given to you, and you have well discharged the trust which that gift implies." He had succeeded at Rutgers "despite cruel race-prejudice," and now he felt that this special recognition would help to give his people "confidence and self-respect." A year later Paul commented that "When I come up against thoughtless colour prejudice or rank brutality, I think of that hour, and do not grow bitter."[12]

On August 2, 1932, Paul wrote to Essie about his current state of mind and the status of his career:

> There is nothing much to say. The show has gone splendidly and I'm really *singing* the *song*. I've put it up a whole tone, which shows how much singing often helps my voice. In the higher key (C) I have much more brilliance—the kind of quality I used to get in "Stan' Still Jordan." The high tones are swell, and the low tones of course gain immeasurably. I sang at the [Lewisohn] Stadium Sunday, July 31st. Marvellous reviews. This country is *really* mine. And strange, I like it again and deeply. After all—this audience understands the Negro in a way impossible for Europeans. Looks as though I'll have to leave, but I am enjoying it all. Financially, of course, I'm still struggling. My salary has been cut almost in half. They will run the show indefinitely. I'll leave end of August. Guess I'm really in love this time. Enjoy sit and moon for the lady [Yolande]. Think I'm knocked cold. Gee—the boy looks grand. I would often love to see you and talk to you. Many problems could bear that common-sense approach of yours. I do remain so *esoteric* at times. Very Russian I guess. Write me. I love your letters. Don't shorten them. Do know I shall do all I can in this settlement business. I want to be fair, but I don't want to be too unreasonable to myself. While working here—swell, but if I must transfer my activities to the continent the [financial] going will be tough. But remar-

riage will change things here. I am still adored in Harlem. They still don't quite understand [that he intended to marry a white woman].

Love—
Always,
Paul

When he wrote to Essie in August, Paul was still in New York playing in *Show Boat*, but was making plans to leave the show and join Yolande in the south of France. In September, he left New York and returned to London.

In October, he wrote to Bob Rockmore:

> For next season please keep *Radio* foremost. I would also like some repertory theatre. I am back in London because it's the only place in the world I'm really happy. I can make records, do concerts, and I have some splendid offers on the Continent. Though I'll need money eventually, I shall worry about my "Soul" for a space. I do *love* London, and at base I do *dislike* New York and America exceedingly. My ultimate plans are to "dig in" here in London & try to get my own theatre.[13]

In the same letter, Paul confided his marital unhappiness to Rockmore, but added:

> [I am] finding solace in pleasures of the mind. Have had one of the greatest treats of my life in my first reading of Carl [*sic*] Marx. Loving it. I am also very happy with Proust and in some of the experiments in higher mathematics which I began to pass the time, but the study of which has led me for the first time to an understanding of physics. I am busy with my songs of course, & Russian is coming along fine.[14]

Then he turned to personal matters:

> The facts are these. Yo [Yolande] and I have decided to call it a day. She has been very hard hit by the last months, and I suppose months of separation have convinced her that a longer one is possible. I am sure she will feel any social ostracism keenly, and I on my part can give up just so much time. My work must occupy much. So I think

it best. She is living in Paris where she has made fine friends. All luck to her. Please go ahead with the divorce & get it over as soon as possible. I talked with Crane [Essie's lawyer]. I want to give Essie a flat sum next year and forget it all. At present will let the old arrangement stand of $100 a week. I'll try to get it down to $75. When I see a big contract ahead I'll have you open negotiations as to final settlement for Essie only. So divorce can go through with settlement still pending.

This part of Paul's letter reflects a fundamental decision already made. Apparently, Paul reserved time, probably during his boat trip to England from the United States, for quiet contemplation. His artistic career and destiny as a public figure, he decided, took precedence over his personal and family life. Based on this decision, he would have to distance himself from *both* Yolande *and* Essie, breaking off his affair with Yolande and divorcing Essie.

Paul wanted to be free of Essie while reducing the financial burden he would have to shoulder if he divorced her. He also asked Rockmore to provide for my future, but expressed no emotional commitment to me: "I'll assume [financial] responsibility for the boy until he is grown. Put something by for him in trust fund or something. But that cannot begin until next spring." Then he appealed to Rockmore to use his power of attorney to get rid of the financial drain that Yolande represented. The contrast to Paul's concern about Essie's $100 a week is stark: "I sent Yo a big sum of money before I left—about $2,500. She had to cover her brother or something. As always—the money disappeared—I don't know where. With your power of attorney, I don't think I have to do anything more about it."[15]

The picture Paul painted of his immediate financial condition was somewhat misleading. Essie soon found out the real story of Paul's earning power from actress Rita Romilly. Rita, an old friend of theirs who had just crossed the Atlantic on the same ship with Paul, came to visit Essie in September and filled her in on all the latest news from the States. Essie's diary entries tell the rest of the story:

September 16, [1932]: Rita arrived in London last night. She had crossed [on the ship *Lafayette* from New York] with Paul. She gave me a great deal of news—that Paul was making $1,500 a week in *Show Boat* at first, then it was cut to $900; that he left when the cast gathered together and begged him to remain [and] the manager

offered more money; [that] on the ship [coming] over he received
wires begging him to sign a radio contract for Maxwell House Coffee Hour for more than $1,500 weekly for twenty minutes once a
week! And he has been beefing about paying me $100 a week and
$500 a quarter! Well, that settles it! He has gone to Paris to join
Yolande, and they are going to the South of France to live for a
year. He sent her $2,000 for their expenses, gave Jim Light $500,
gave Ben, Marian [Robeson] money! He is astounding. I saw Mr.
Crane at once, cancelled the divorce, am suing him now for separate maintenance, and will see him in hell before I divorce him,
unless he gives me my allowance a year in advance *and* a contract
for 20 percent of his gross. I was so angry I couldn't sleep, thinking about it all. The swine!

Ten days later, Essie and Rita went to Paris together, where Essie discovered to her surprise that Paul was there too, this time without
Yolande. She immediately decided to confront him in person:

September 27, [1932]: I saw Paul this morning. He was astonished
to see me, and was very nice. He and Yolande have decided not to
marry after all. He left *Show Boat* and all his great opportunities in
New York in order to come to her. Paul says Yolande got a lot of
pressure put on her in London, so she has called it off. They are
definitely not going to marry, but Paul says he wants to be free anyway. He is in touch with Crane, so he can arrange a definite term
for settlement of all his obligations to me, and to the boy, at one
fell swoop.

He told me that Charles Behan, of Universal [Studios], offered
him a contract for four films, to be done in a year. He said Maxwell
House Coffee offered $60,000 for a year's contract—half an hour,
once a week, to start October 6.

We had a most delightful, pleasant talk, about his work, about
my work, about Russia, and about Yolande, and about America. He
looks fairly well, but depressed, and confused and unhappy.

By October 7, he and Essie were both back in London, and Essie had
already begun to take care of him once again:

October 7 [1932] [London]: Saw Paul at the Great Central [Hotel]—
He is ill with the flu, as usual.

October 8 [1932]: Saw Paul again today, and took him some medicine.

October 23 [1932]: Paul opened at the Palladium [London's most famous variety hall] this afternoon. I have never seen him worse. I think it was because he sang the wrong songs. Anyway, he was terrible. I rushed backstage afterwards, and we talked it over. I begged him to change his program altogether, and suggested new [songs]. Then I talked with Clapham [Paul's music coach and accompanist for variety shows], who played for him, and who was terrible. I suggested the new program to Clapham as well. I was so upset over Paul's performance, I was nervous as a witch. I rushed back to the Palladium for the second performance. Paul had changed his program almost entirely, and was a great success. Paul seemed pleased that I was interested and concerned. [Soon Paul was "well away" with his Palladium shows, eliciting "fine applause" from his audiences.]

October 29 [1932]: Paul rang up this afternoon and asked me over to the hotel for tea. I went, and we had a long talk. He says he would like to stop the proceedings for the divorce, and that we should make another try at it.

My fifth birthday was November 2, and Paul spent most of that week with us. According to my mother, we all had "a grand time" together, and I enjoyed long talks with my father. One of my first and best memories of him comes from this week, when he took me to see *Peter Pan* with Jean Forbes Robertson in the lead role, and softly talked me through the scary parts, holding my hand and helping me deal with my fear of Captain Hook and the crocodile.

Toward the end of November, my father saw all of us off at the London train station when we returned to Switzerland. He remained behind to fulfill concert and radio engagements he had lined up on the continent. By prearrangement, my mother settled Grandma and me in Switzerland, and then went on to meet my father in Holland. There they regained some of the footing they had lost over the previous couple of years, and began once again to work together as a professional team, discussing Paul's career options and concert repertoire.

Paul offered to take Essie on a side trip, and she chose to go to Brussels so that she could visit the famous Congo Museum with its treasures of African art. While they were there, Essie fell ill, and noted in her diary that Paul took care of her and was "very sweet."[16]

By December 2, they were back in London in the flat at 19 Buckingham Street, where Essie described an interlude of domestic contentment:

> *December 2 [1932]:* Home to London. Paul and I arrived at the flat, lit the fires, and had dinner, and soon the place was as cosy and attractive as I had always known it would be. Paul adores it, and we are very happy.

Unfortunately, it proved to be only a brief respite of peace and harmony; on December 6, the harsh realities of Paul's unfinished business intruded with a vengeance:

> *December 6 [1932]:* Had just settled in nicely—Paul happily reading quietly in the drawing room, when he said he'd better go to Paris to see Yolande, as she was burning up the wires, leaving her name at the hotel, etc., and he was afraid she might get reckless and talk; no use having a scandal at this late date. He decided to go over the weekend. So [he] arranged his rehearsal with Clapham for three o'clock, but at three Andy [Paul's longtime valet] came in, looking worried, and they went into a huddle. A few minutes later, Paul said he must catch the 4 P.M. train for Paris, as Yolande had telephoned Andy and said that if Paul wasn't in Paris that night, she would catch a plane over to London. So I helped Paul pack a bag, gave him all my cash, and wished him Godspeed. He made the four o'clock train.

Though Paul's affair with Yolande had been peppered with erratic interludes, he had ceased to be ambivalent. His ultimate rejection of Yolande was complete. There is no record of any direct communication between them after early 1933, despite Yolande's entreaties to Larry Brown and Bob Rockmore to get word through to him. Paul would always speak of her with fondness, but he seems to have decided that, unlike his relationships with Freda Diamond and Fredi Washington, his affair with Yolande was a thing of the past.[17]

The most chaotic chapter in my parents' lives was over, and their reconciliation was to be permanent—not as idyllic as Essie's diary entries make it appear, but nevertheless unbreakable "until death did them part." Essie ceased claiming ownership of Paul, and Paul stopped challenging Essie's status as Mrs. Paul Robeson. The tensions in their marriage would never disappear, but they could now no longer sunder its bonds.

Under the implicit terms of the reconciliation, they could each have affairs, provided they were discreet and did not lead to public notoriety. Essie would retain her advisory status, but control of finances, the final word on contracts, and power of attorney would remain with Bob Rockmore. Essie would never regain control of Paul's affairs. For Paul, the arrangement meant that he was free to be self-absorbed in fulfilling his life's mission with minimal demands from Essie. With this resolution of their conflict, an aura of peace, and especially of purpose, enveloped both of them, finding expression in a note Paul wrote to himself on December 5, 1932:

> Am terribly happy at No. 19 [the London flat]. Henceforth, all my energies will go into my work. Must take advantage of sessions to work with [Clapham], as he has genius for teaching. I love to work out songs in broad outline, and gradually polish. Unquestionably Russian songs are right—most right for me—though I now think I shall be able to sing German songs. I must be practical, and first attend to songs I know.
>
> As for languages: Russian—basic; German [and] French for pictures; Spanish; Dutch (as bridge to German); Hungarian along with Turkish (as bridge to Hebrew); then Swedish. I feel so ambitious. Want to work all day at something—music and languages.

By now he was confident of both his command of the Russian language and his mastery of a significant repertoire of Russian songs, including the main arias from Mussorgsky's opera *Boris Godunov*.

Paul was clear about the road he wished to travel. He would strive to offer his audiences not only an artistic gift but a spiritual one as well. As he had confided to Titterton, "When singing for the Radio, I . . . go close [to the microphone] and sing quite softly to it, as if I were alone with a friend. . . . The folk who listen get that feeling just when I do, as I know from hundreds of letters I have had just afterwards."[18]

IV
TRIBUNE
OF A CULTURE
(1933–1936)

(*Above*) Greeted by Russian filmmaker Sergei Eisenstein in Moscow, 1934. *From the personal collection of Paul Robeson, Jr.*

(*Middle*) As Bosambo in the controversial film *Sanders of the River*, London, 1934. *From the personal collection of Paul Robeson, Jr.*

(*Below*) Paul and Essie with African students in London, 1936. *From the personal collection of Paul Robeson, Jr.*

I 2

FILM AND THE POLITICS
OF CULTURE

(1933–1934)

Now Paul reached for vehicles that were both powerful and familiar. He found them, once again, in the plays of Eugene O'Neill. The inspiration this time was Flora Robson, one of England's top young actresses. She had moved into the apartment across the hall from Paul and Essie at 19 Buckingham Street. Charming, talented, intelligent, and a meticulous practitioner of the acting craft, Flora immediately hit it off with both of them. On January 6, 1933, Essie noted in her diary that she and Paul had talked to Flora about her playing Ella opposite him in *All God's Chillun Got Wings*. Describing Flora as "attractive, . . . sensitive, with a fine sense of humor," Essie added in her diary, "I am sure she and Paul will act together." By the end of February, Flora had agreed to play the role of Ella in a London production of *Chillun*.

Paul intended to use this opportunity to improve his theatrical image from the tragic primitive hero he had created in *The Emperor Jones* and *The Hairy Ape*. Of all of O'Neill's characters, Jim Harris, the failed black law student in *Chillun*, provided the greatest scope for expressing intrinsic dignity, unlike the brutish stoker in *The Hairy Ape* who was, according to one major drama critic, a "symbol of primitive humanity."[1] Nor had Paul been impressed by the *London Times* review, which declared that "We need not hope to see the part . . . played better than Mr. Robeson plays it. Nobody will watch . . . [his] progress . . . from the stokehold . . . to the gorilla's cage . . .

203

without thinking better of the play, or regretting that the play is not better than it is."[2]

Paul sought to reclaim the refined intellectual and spiritual quality he had brought to the character of Jim Harris. His calculation was that in London this play's theme of an interracial marriage would cause far less disturbance than it had in New York seven years earlier.

A search began for a director-producer to stage the production. For the first time they did not call on James Light. Paul felt he needed a director whose view was broader and more refined than that of the Provincetown Players. After Essie had seen a new play directed by Andre Van Gyseghem, a talented young director with leftist political leanings, she showed Paul the program, and they promptly scheduled a meeting with him. The result was a production, starring Paul and Flora Robson, at the Embassy Theatre, a well-known venue for successful experimental plays. Paul was so committed to the effort that he agreed to a salary of only ten pounds ($50) a week. He also wrote a check for a hundred pounds to rescue the production by covering a last-minute demand by O'Neill's agent for advance royalties.[3]

By the time the play opened on March 13, Paul, Flora, and Van Gyseghem had melded into an effective team. The critic of the highly respected magazine *Punch* commented that the production created "that rare illusion of our being rapt away from the theater and absorbed in the agony of imaginary characters that have assumed an intense life. . . . Mr. Paul Robeson played the seemingly subordinate but actually more fundamentally tragic part in this poignant interlude with a passionate intensity which was overwhelming. The audience had positively to pull itself together before it could offer its tribute of stormy applause to these two fine artists."

Chillun ran for two months and closed only because Paul had to leave for the United States to shoot the film version of *The Emperor Jones*. The overall critical response to his portrayal of Jim Harris challenged the persistent notion that he was merely an "instinctive" actor lacking technical ability. Although some critics still felt that he was not yet "a finished actor" or sufficiently "subtle," and that his powers were "still imperfectly controlled," even one of his most severe detractors acknowledged that his performance was "one of immense force and sincerity." The *News-Chronicle*'s E. A. Baughan was the only one who was explicit about this ambivalence: "Flora Robson . . . makes you forget she is acting. Of Paul Robeson, I am never sure if he is acting, but is just himself. Only . . . his voice persuade[s] one that he is an actor of uncommon gifts."[4]

It was this criticism to which Paul paid the most attention. To be a true artist on the legitimate stage, he needed to abandon himself to the character as he did to the song on the concert stage. Instead of *using* the character to send a message, he needed to *become* the character, who would then *personify* the message. With few opportunities for rigorous practice, he would spend another decade learning how to accomplish this in the theater. He could already achieve this state of grace on the concert stage.

On the other hand, he smiled wryly at the *London Sunday Times* review, which ridiculed the notion that Paul's acting skills were inferior to Flora's:

> There has also been the suggestion that Miss Flora Robson plays Mr. Robeson off the stage. Again, insane! In this piece he is as firmly rooted as an oak; indeed, the roots which he gives to Jim Crow are the very essence of the play, upon which the quandary of the white woman can be no more than a decoration, though an agonizing one. The essential tragedy is that of the negro [*sic*], since the burden of inferiority is universal, while the hard case of the white woman . . . is individual, and therefore lesser. If Mr. Robeson's figure can be likened to an oak, then one would repeat what Hazlitt said of the greatest of English tragedians, that his voice is like the soughing of the wind through cedars. His performance is intensely moving: it is, so far as I can judge, flawless.[5]

He knew full well that working with Flora and Van Gyseghem had been an invaluable learning experience. He had acknowledged to both of them that he still had a long way to go on the painful journey from performing actor to theatrical artist. Van Gyseghem would later recall Paul as an unfinished actor. Flora believed that he was an "instinctive" actor. Unfinished he was, but instinctive he wasn't. In fact, the only way he could become more finished was boldly to unleash his carefully controlled and calibrated instinct. Publicly, Paul chose to accept the false "instinctive" label, thus concealing his true deficiency and acquiring an air of mystery.[6]

Rebecca West, after calling the play "one of the most thrilling performances that I have ever seen," paid insightful, even prescient homage to Paul:

> He put all the forces of his vitality behind the conception of Eugene O'Neill, and built a character so vast that in the memory one sees him as larger than life-size. . . . It occurred to me as I watched this amazing evocation that we have gained something as well as lost something by the curious circumstance that one of the greatest theatrical personalities of our time is a Negro. It means that he is physically debarred from playing most of the parts that a great actor tries; but it has in consequence meant that he has acted comparatively rarely. . . . This has enabled him to enjoy more than most artists a sufficiency of leisure, in which he can live quietly the life of imagination, where he can slowly incubate the artistic discoveries which he later embodies in his acting.[7]

Despite Paul's deficiencies, the 1933 London production of *Chillun* marked a turning point in his theater career—the point where he transcended the constraints of Eugene O'Neill's playwriting. For almost all of the London critics agreed that both Paul and Flora had created great characters out of an ordinary play.

On May 10, 1933, Paul and Essie arrived in New York for the filming of *The Emperor Jones*. For some time, Paul had courted the burgeoning "talkie" film industry. The first talkie, *The Jazz Singer*, had been made in 1927, so the medium was still new. But Paul realized its potential for reaching a mass audience of hundreds of thousands, and then millions. Recordings and radio appearances had served this purpose well, along with the single exceptional musical, *Show Boat*. Now the unprecedented medium of the talkie film beckoned, offering the combined advantages of recordings, radio, musicals, and legitimate theater.

Artistic purity and control of the message remained Paul's signatures on the concert stage and in the legitimate theater. But in film, as had been the case with radio and recording, his overall image and the audience were paramount to him. Cultural, racial, and political rectitude was not. He was far from indifferent to the content of his films, and fought tenaciously to improve it. However, he was willing to compromise. Producer John Krimsky and his partner, Gifford Cochran, had, at Paul's request, developed an independent production free of Hollywood interference. It was budgeted at a respectable $250,000, to be released by United Artists. The jungle scenes were shot in Astoria, Queens, because a special clause in Paul's contract precluded filming in the South. The director, Dudley Murphy, was an experienced professional best known for two films on black subjects: *Black and Tan*, with Duke Ellington, and *St. Louis Blues*, with Bessie Smith.

Paul approached his role with full concentration. He worked out consistently with Fritz Pollard, his old friend and football teammate, to get in top physical shape by running, boxing, and tossing a medicine ball. He also helped Pollard get a small part. Upon its release in September 1933, the film became a modest financial success. Artistically, it was hailed both in the United States and abroad. Paul's performance was almost universally praised in the mainstream press as a breakthrough by a black actor as a leading man. The response of the black press was mostly ambivalent, as it had been to the play. Critics praised Paul's acting, but condemned the film's stereotypes.[8] The New York *Amsterdam News* complained bitterly about the repeated use of the word *nigger* (September 27, 1933), and the *Philadelphia Tribune* denounced Robeson's portrayal of "a miserable victim" (November 2, 1933).

But Paul took comfort from the fact that the response of black moviegoers was overwhelmingly positive: they loudly cheered the powerful and at times defiant images he had created. He gently turned aside or ignored most critics of this perceived "opportunism." He also rejected those who urged him to become a true prophet who preached political action. In response, he resorted to either dignified self-criticism or the low-key equivalent of *if this be opportunism, then make the most of it*. Edward Steichen, then arguably America's leading photographer, made twenty-six portraits of Paul in his Emperor Jones costume, etching Paul's image as Brutus Jones in the popular culture. Steichen's favorite photograph from that sitting— the portrait of the brooding black emperor that appeared in the August 1933 issue of *Vanity Fair*—captured the character's vulnerable humanity in his expression of defiance mixed with fear.[9] This identification of Paul Robeson with a tragically flawed but heroic character marked the transition in American film from the dehumanized black "Sambo" caricature to a fully human, though still partly stereotypical, black male image. Fifteen years later, a black London critic called *The Emperor Jones* "a landmark in Negro films" and included it among the most original films of the 1930s.[10]

Sensing Paul's commercial potential, several Hollywood magnates made him offers that he turned down flatly, protesting that Hollywood wanted to portray only "the plantation type of Negro."[11] But he was well satisfied with the result he had achieved by putting *The Emperor Jones* on the screen. He ignored criticism from both the black nationalists and the left. His deeper concern was artistic rather than cultural.

Paul alluded to this matter in one of his first interviews after his return to London: "The film has taught me a lot about myself—revealing many little faults," he said. "My wife did the rest; she found the remedies, and her advice has been invaluable."[12] Paul was referring to his partly successful effort to portray the familiar part of the *Emperor* with greater reliance on instinct—to *become* Brutus Jones in front of the camera without warm-up or continuity. Here Essie was invaluable in her ability to cue him for particular scenes. Her overall advice was also helpful: He shouldn't overdo the evil part of the character. Moderate the meanness and arrogance with vulnerability, fear, and even a touch of underlying compassion.[13]

As soon as Paul arrived back in London, he announced that he was looking for a new story about Africa to film. A few weeks later, he was tentatively invited to appear in *Sanders of the River,* based on a popular adventure story by the famed novelist Edgar Wallace. The two main characters were a British commissioner and the resourceful African chief of a British colony in Africa.

Early in 1933, both Paul and Essie had enrolled in London University—he to study African languages and Chinese, and she to study anthropology with an emphasis on Africa. Asked in 1934 to contribute to a collection of articles by celebrities, titled *What I Want from Life*, he commented:

> I am learning Swahili, Tivi, and other African dialects—which come easily to me *because their rhythm is the same as that employed by the*

American Negro in speaking English. Meanwhile, in my music, my plays, my films, I want to carry always this central idea: to be African. Multitudes of men have died for less worthy ideals; it is even more eminently worth living for.[14] [emphasis mine]

In another piece, he stressed that it was important to him not only to *be* African but also to inspire in his people a pride in their heritage:

It is astonishing and, to me, fascinating to find a flexibility and a subtlety in a language like Swahili, sufficient to convey the teachings of Confucius, for example, and it is my ambition to make an effort to guide the Negro race by means of its own peculiar qualities to a higher degree of perfection along the line of its natural development. It is my first concern to dispel [the] regrettable and abysmal ignorance of the value of its own heritage in the Negro race itself.[15]

Noting the fact that Negroes "for centuries" have been "for better or worse [an] integral part of American life," Paul concluded that there was "no possible chance of Negro millions developing a separate culture." There was no point in a "black culture with no black country." But he did believe that Negroes would "deeply influence" future American culture. The Western Negro "is cut off from his source," he said, but maintained that Africa held the future of the black man. He added that "racial unity must be informed with [the] constant goal that all human life is one in spite of prejudice and narrow opinions."

Paul believed that the non-African culture from which people of African descent could learn the most was the traditional Chinese culture that concerns itself "mainly with the inner development of man." He saw Chinese culture as "most antithetical to Western and closest to African," and emphasized the ideological strength of Chinese philosophy. In a comment that perceived the contradiction between Marx's international vision and the pull of national cultures, he wrote: "It is my belief that even an ideology as fanatical as communism may later disappear into the deeper roots of Chinese philosophy. I cannot see China [becoming] Western, or really accepting [an] ideology [Marxism] based on Western metaphysics."[16]

Finally, Paul pointed out the two ways he saw for the Negro people to deal with being American. Either they could "disappear into the American mass," which seemed to him "spineless and unthinkable," or they could become "a self-respecting, solid racial unit with its spiritual roots back in Africa," which developed its powers to the point where "there [would be] no possible denial of equality." Implicit in this belief was his out-of-hand rejection of "melting pot" assimilation. He did not believe blacks or any other cultural or ethnic group should deny their roots in order to assimilate into the dominant culture. Blacks, he insisted, must be integrated into American society as a recognized, fully equal *group*—not as a reward to the few who were willing to deny their cultural roots in pursuit of the American dream.

Appearing as a speaker at a meeting of the League of Colored Peoples on December 11, 1934, Paul made it clear that his extraordinary personal success in breaking through racial barriers had strengthened, rather than weakened, his resolve to help demolish the barriers themselves. He went on to profess his belief that the future of the African was tied up with the people of the East, not with the West. Then he added: "For myself, I belong to Africa; if I am not there in body, I am there in spirit."[17]

On October 26, 1933, producer Alexander Korda, the brother of the renowned film director Zoltan Korda, wrote an enthusiastic letter to Essie confirming his offer for Paul's appearance in the central role of *Sanders* and promising to send Paul a script. Zoltan Korda had developed the *Sanders* screenplay into an exciting African adventure story set in a genuine African background. He had assembled the cultural tapestry out of 60,000 feet of film and countless recordings during several months of travel through central Africa. Paul signed enthusiastically to play the lead part of Chief Bosambo, the faithful supporter of British Commissioner Sanders. To Paul the film represented indigenous African culture "in a really magnificent way," and the music was excitingly authentic. "The hit of the picture should be a song I sing going down the river in a canoe," he said in an interview.

From the beginning, Paul was fully aware of the negative aspects of the film. Both the original story and the script unabashedly glorified British colonialism and contained many racial stereotypes. Nevertheless, for him, as with *The Emperor Jones*, these drawbacks had been outweighed by the exciting opportunity to portray Africans as real human beings in a new medium that had a broad appeal. Moreover, in a distinct advance beyond *The Emperor Jones, Sanders* would depict genuine African culture and would permit him to play a hero who was entirely a "good guy."[18]

Throughout the summer of 1934, *Sanders* was filmed at Sound City in Shepperton, just outside London. The experience was exhilarating for Paul. Four hundred blacks, mostly Africans, were recruited for the film from all over the British Isles, and he was able not only to practice his African languages but also to learn firsthand about African culture and politics. A group of Nigerians on the set, having listened to the rhythm and tonalities of his English-speaking voice, were convinced that he was descended from their Ibo tribe. He, in turn, felt a natural kinship with their spoken language and their songs, even though he had never studied either. Ultimately, after careful research, Paul decided that the Nigerians were right in their conclusions about his ancestry.[19]

Among Paul's friends on the set as extras or with small parts was Jomo Kenyatta, who was then an anticolonial activist, and later the leader of Kenya's independence movement and her first president. Kenyatta had been one of many Africans in London who urged Paul to take the Bosambo part. Apparently, the British authorities became aware of this association. During a break in the shooting schedule, Paul was discreetly accosted by two agents of British Intelligence who warned him not to try to influence the Africans on the set. The anticolonial movement was subversive, they said.[20]

Images that Americans have of my father's private personality stem almost exclusively from the 1920s, 1940s, and 1950s, when he was either recently out of college or over forty years old. Few, if any, date back to the 1930s, when he was in his thirties living in London.

It was at that time, in 1934 when he was thirty-six, that I formed my first vivid impressions of his appearance and personality. I was seven, and, at my father's insistence, the entire family—he, my mother, my grandmother, and I—were living together in the large London apartment at 19 Buckingham Street. My father, still a relative stranger to me, was at first an intimidating presence. However, since his eyes, voice, and body language were almost always easy to read, I quickly learned how to approach him with a degree of confidence by observing him closely.

Then in top physical condition, he was an impressive sight. Six feet three inches tall, with a large head, immensely broad shoulders, a narrow waist, and a fifty-one-inch chest, he appeared more massive than his trim 230 pounds. Unlike most men of his size, who moved with a lumbering gait, he glided gracefully with a long, smooth, forward stride. When he stood, he was erect and still, as if rooted to the ground, but still relaxed.

His many demeanors, expressively conveyed by his eyes, voice, and body language, created a powerful impression. His welcoming smile, accompanied by the sparkle in his wide-open eyes, was like the emergence of a bright sun. When he frowned with his eyes narrowed, I was reminded of gathering thunderclouds. A compassionate look could ease hurt feelings.

His speaking voice ranged in pitch from a deep velvety bass to a high baritone that sounded like a tenor. It had a seemingly infinite gradation of volume and emotion—from an audible whisper to a rollicking belly laugh to an earsplitting roar. The tone could envelop in a soft caress, probe tentatively, command peremptorily, dismiss contemptuously, or lash angrily. An easy lilt signaled contentment; a rise in pitch and volume denoted annoyance; a hard-edged, quiet rumble with a steady pitch was a sign of anger. Silence, accompanied by moving eyes and an alert body, reflected anxiety.

He taught me games of all kinds, told me stories, and stimulated my intellectual curiosity. I remember him as surprisingly playful for one who appeared on the surface to be so serious.

Several times he took me along with him to the film set of *Sanders of the River*. There I noticed that he carried his near-regal dominance of his surroundings with a natural ease, making himself accessible to everyone. He was a popular superstar who belonged to the outside world, yet behaved like a regular person.

He had retained his agility and quickness, as I found out while being driven to the *Sanders* set outside of London in a limousine one morning. I was sitting on one of the jump seats so that my father could spread out in the back with only my mother sharing the space. We were going eighty miles an hour on the highway when I started to get carsick and tried to open the window next to me. Opening the door by mistake, I found myself half out of the car, hanging on to the door handle. In the blink of an eye, my father's huge right hand shot out and grabbed the back of my jacket, yanking me next to him and slamming the door shut with his left hand, all in one continuous motion. He didn't say a word, and silenced my mother with a gesture when she started to say something. I was left to contemplate what had just happened.

Soon afterward, the shooting of the film ended. Paul and Essie went on a provincial concert tour after arranging to visit the Soviet Union at the end of December. Grandma Goode and I were sent to the United States for a year so that I could become acquainted with the homeland I had left when I was barely more than a year old.

For some time, the talented and boldly experimental Russian film director Sergei Mikhailovich Eisenstein had been wanting to work with Paul. Having come upon the compelling story of Haiti's liberator, Toussaint L'Ouverture, in 1931, he wanted to make Toussaint's story into a film. For Eisenstein, the fact that a black slave organized an army that defeated the troops of Napoléon was proof of African genius.

Sergei had heard much about Paul as both a singer and an actor. A music lover, he had heard some of Paul's radio broadcasts and had obtained a number of Paul's records during a 1932 trip to New York. Intuitively, he felt he should seek Paul out for the lead role in his planned film about Toussaint. He faced a problem, however. His 1931–1932 Mexican film venture, *Qué Viva Mexico!*, had ended in monumental disaster, with his American financial backers withdrawing their support and the Soviet government ordering him home. Personally chastised by Stalin, he had returned to Moscow in disgrace in April 1932. Now still in Soviet filmdom's doghouse, Sergei had no assurance that the cinematic authorities would sanction one of his films.

He turned to his close friend and biographer, English writer Marie Seton, who was also close to Paul and Essie. Marie urged him to write a letter of invitation directly to Paul.[21] Eisenstein wrote to him in English on March 10, 1934:

> My dear Robeson!
>
> I never had an opportunity to meet you, and I was always sorry of it because you are one of the personalities I always liked without having known them personally!

During my trip to Mexico [in 1931–1932] I was planning a big film about the revolutionary movement of the beginning of the XIX*th* century, and I was full of desire to have you work upon it with me. But you know how my Mexican adventure turned out, shattering these plans as well!

Now I am extremely pleased to hear from Marie [Seton] that you get interested in our country and the problems which run around it all over the world. And I am enthusiastic to see you here. As soon as you'll be in this country we will have an opportunity to talk (at last), and we will see if finally we will get to do something together.

I am returning for a while back to the theater this winter, so that it opens both fields of possible activity.

I am immensely pleased to hear that your interests cover a much bigger field than theater and film. So are mine! But what amuses me most is that both of us we are interested in basic English, which I introduced to be learned in our Film University where I am teaching the art of directing.

Hope to see you soon and remain with best regards to your wife and yourself.

Always,
Sincerely yours,

Sergei Eisenstein

Arrangements were soon completed for Paul and Essie to visit Russia at the end of the year. Until that time, Paul turned his main attention to his extensive 1934 concert tour throughout the British Isles. In his spare time, he studied Russian intensively and continued to add to his formal concert repertoire.

To his sophisticated audiences in London and in the large cities, Paul offered a mixture of the spirituals, Russian songs that he had fully mastered, and a few well-known English art songs ("Drink to Me Only with Thine Eyes," for example). His humility regarding his vocal expertise was consciously designed to lower the artistic expectations of his performances and to disarm the critics by cultivating the myth of his limited range, low technical competence, and wholly natural delivery. Those critics who had contempt for the spirituals as black music consistently amplified the myth.

Actually, by the early 1930s, Paul had, by dint of consistent study and hard work, developed a high level of technical skill and a phenomenally fluid phrasing based on the most refined breath control. W. H. Breare, in an article titled "Paul Robeson's Technique," which appeared in the *British Musician and Musical News* (vol. 9, no. 7, July 1933, pp. 156–158), assessed the special qualities of Robeson's vocal technique:

> It is the perfection of production and technique which makes the finished voice of the artist. We hear today plenty of so-called "natural" voices and "natural" singers who are very far from cultivated. But with Paul Robeson it is quite another thing. He has an extraordinary voice, but he knows how to use it so that the tones and phrases pour forth without effort, naturally, [in] the full sense of the term. His tone is always *lyrical*; it flows like a deep river which has not a ripple on its surface. He has a wonderful range. His low tones are full, round, mellow, rich as velvet. His entire scale is perfectly and artistically graded. From these deep tones with their long, slow vibrations there is, in taking an upward passage, a gradual and proportionate ascent. He moves from the lower voice to the middle and upper so gradually and with such perfect proportion that there is never a false element in any tone. His command of the nasal element is so perfect that he might be a tenor in extreme altitudes.
>
> It is that ability to move from one portion of the voice to another which makes his work so beautiful. It is Robeson's knowledge of the office of the breath which enables him to achieve the emotional shades or [an] effect which is as real as life.

Responding to Paul's increased artistic skills and his growing classical repertoire, an increasing number of music critics began speculating about his operatic potential. With Essie's strong support, Paul rejected this possibility. Coincidentally, he resolutely turned his back on two prime opportunities to become America's first black opera star. In a letter dated April 25, 1934, George Gershwin had responded to a letter Essie had written to him, telling him of Paul's interest in his opera, *Porgy and Bess.* "I have had Paul in mind for the part of Porgy which I think suits him admirably," he replied. "I am bearing in mind Paul's voice in writing it, and if there are some things which are out of his range, I am sure I can fix it up." A few months later, an invitation from the Chicago Opera to sing the role of Amonasro in *Aida* offered both fame and fortune.

But Paul turned both offers down—not because he had any doubts that he could break the color barrier in the world of opera but because he knew his voice and delivery technique were not suited to most operatic music. In addition, he was determined to reach a broad popular audience that did not follow opera. Although in future years he would, on occasion, sing individual operatic arias with a full orchestra, these decisions essentially signaled the end to any aspirations he might ever have held for an operatic career.

By contrast, whenever a journalist wanted Paul to talk about his views on popular music, he readily answered the question. He found Tin Pan Alley jazz banal, and he felt its poor attempts to steal Negro rhythms resulted in music that was of only passing interest: "I would much rather get together half a dozen African drummers and listen to them. Their rhythm is so much more complicated. . . . Duke Ellington—with his orchestra, which is really a continuation of the African drum—means a great deal to me." Asked about his reported love of classical music, he replied that although he found Handel too mechanical, he felt that "the religious music of Bach has power and that mystical quality," and "Mozart, like Shakespeare, seems to run the whole gamut of human emotion." However, Mussorgsky's music was for him more "vital," and he was working on the opera *Boris Godunov*. And though he loved classical music, he was highly critical of modern classical music, which he felt had no melodic appeal: "People like Stravinsky and Schoenberg write music which, technically, looks well on paper; in performance it is static, ugly. Modern writers should get back to the melodic appeal of Bach, of Purcell, and of the madrigal school. Music is not literature: it is sound—it should please the ear."[22]

Paul did not agree to appear in concerts during his forthcoming visit to the Soviet Union. He felt unready for that. First, he needed to absorb Russian culture, to immerse himself in the language and music. Only then could he sing to their hearts.

Meanwhile, echoing the attitude of many leaders of the anticolonial movements, Paul did not hesitate to stir controversy by publicly expressing his favorable view of the Soviet Union. In response to an interviewer's question as to whether he expected to encounter any racism in Moscow, he replied: "Oh no. There is absolutely no color prejudice there. One reason is they have so many colored races in the Soviet Union."[23]

Through a growing acquaintance with Ivan Maisky, the Soviet ambassador to England, and from conversations with Emma Goldman and Marie Seton, Paul had become knowledgeable about the Soviet system. Thus, on the eve of his visit to Moscow, he was well informed about both Russian culture and Soviet politics.[24]

The 1934 trip to the Soviet Union aroused a new sense of purpose in Paul. It marked the beginning of his public expression of his private political views. As a result of his African studies, his contacts with Africans in the anticolonial movement, and his five-year association with British socialists, he had already raised his voice on behalf of the struggle to free Africa from colonialism. Now the trip to the Soviet Union, a country viewed as a reliable ally by the anticolonial movement, was a striking symbolic gesture.

Yet he cast his visit as an exclusively cultural one. He was going as an artist, rather than as a political figure. For despite Paul's increasingly strong political beliefs, he felt certain that he was called to play primarily a cultural role on the world stage.[25]

13

TEST RUN:
LONDON—MOSCOW—HOLLYWOOD

(1934–1935)

P aul, Essie, and Marie Seton arrived at the Berlin train station together early on the morning of December 23, 1934. Essie took care of the luggage, leaving Paul and Marie chatting on the nearly deserted station platform. Paul's body tensed suddenly. Brown-shirted storm troopers were arriving from two directions and forming a rough semicircle around them, cutting them off from the other passengers who were gathering on the platform. The only escape route was across the train tracks behind them. As the storm troopers began muttering among themselves, Paul explained to Marie, who knew no German, that they thought she was German. As their epithets became louder and more provocative, Paul told her to stay outwardly calm.

"This is . . . how a lynching begins," he said quietly. "If either of us moves, or shows fear, they'll go further," he continued, occasionally scanning the troopers' ranks with a neutral, unconcerned look. A few minutes later, Essie returned, and soon afterward the train to Moscow pulled in. The three travelers boarded without interference—probably because the storm troopers had concluded that both women were foreigners. Once they were safely on the train, however, a palpable fear lingered in the air. Paul broke the spell: "I never understood what fascism was before. I'll fight it wherever I find it from now on."[1]

It was an enormous relief to reach the customs station on the Soviet border. At the Moscow train station, a delegation headed by Sergei Eisenstein had gathered gaily to welcome them. Eisenstein had also thoughtfully included John Goode, Essie's brother, in the welcoming party. John had come to Moscow a year earlier as a skilled auto mechanic to help reorganize the bus repair system. Essie's other brother, Frank, was also in the Soviet Union, traveling with a circus. He didn't make it to the train station to meet them but showed up at their hotel suite a couple of days later.

The contrast between Paul and Sergei was striking—the giant, quietly reserved, dark-skinned American towering over the short, emotionally noisy, fair-skinned Russian. Yet they had much in common. They were both born in 1898. After his mother had abandoned the family to go to France, Sergei, like Paul, had been brought up by his father. He also shared Paul's dedication to the study of cultures and languages.

Within minutes, they were chatting away in Russian like two long-separated old friends. Occasionally, Paul would laughingly switch to English in order to slow down Sergei's rapid-fire Russian. Sergei accompanied Paul and Essie from the train station to their hotel suite so that he and Paul could continue to talk. He quickly briefed Paul in preparation for two press interviews: the first in Russian with a reporter from the Soviet news agency, Tass, and the second in English with a correspondent from the *Chicago Defender*, an African-American newspaper.[2]

He was frank with Paul, both concerning his own situation and the highly charged Soviet political atmosphere. Sergei was still in political disgrace, barred from making his own films but allowed to teach and consult. He would face severe public criticism at a special Conference of Cinema Workers in January 1935. Political tensions, Sergei said, were high everywhere since the recent murder, on December 1, 1934, of Sergei M. Kirov, the Leningrad Party leader. Kirov had been the most popular political figure in the Soviet Union, and Moscow was still rife with rumors that Stalin had engineered the murder in order to dispose of a potential political rival. In any case, Soviet politics had swung sharply toward a harder line. Sergei advised Paul to confine his public comments to cultural topics and to avoid politics. This only strengthened Paul's own inclination.

A trickier problem, Sergei feared, would arise if Paul were to discuss his spiritual-based repertoire of songs. The government's anti-religious campaign had intensified in recent years, which meant that the overtly religious lyrics that permeated the spirituals were considered to be politically subversive. Several months earlier, a Moscow radio broadcast of Paul's Negro spiritual "Steal Away to Jesus" had triggered an investigation of "anti-Soviet propaganda [by] the class enemy" at the main Moscow radio station. Six prominent radio officials and announcers had been fired, and the chairman of the All-Soviet Broadcasting Committee had published an apology to the Soviet public.[3]

Paul's interview in Russian with the Tass reporter was a model of political caution. He commented exclusively on cultural matters, except for a brief reference to his interest in "the national minority policy of the Soviet Government." And he was careful to stress the fact that the spirituals, though couched in religious language, were essentially songs about a people's struggle for freedom. Then, after mentioning his desire to play *Othello* in Russian, he put in a plug for Sergei. He looked forward to making a film about Haiti's liberator, Toussaint L'Ouverture, with Eisenstein, and also to collaborating with Eisenstein in bringing a production of the American labor play *Stevedore* to Moscow.[4]

By contrast, the *Chicago Defender* interview was noteworthy for Paul's uncharacteristically overt political comments:

> Robeson said that he considers the Soviet theater the most inter-esting in the world. [And] Not only the theater but the whole new social system—new life, new economy, new people. The former Rutgers football star said that he expects to spend much of the rest of his life in Russia, Soviet Asia, Africa, and Soviet China. [He says] the whole future of the Race is tied up with conditions in those parts of the world, especially the Chinese situation, which is much like the situation in Africa. How the national minority problem has been solved there [in Russia] deserves the closest of study, as its solution there offers a model for the solution of the black man's problems.[5]

Here Paul felt he could be openly political because he was address-ing an African-American audience as one of their own. However, ad-dressing an English audience two weeks earlier, he had told a London interviewer: "Political systems rise and fall, but the soul of a people lives on. Therefore I am more interested in cultures than in policies." And while his first visit to the Soviet Union did not significantly alter this priority, it did cause him to overstate his enthusiasm for life in the Soviet Union, Africa, and "Soviet China" when he suggested that he might "spend much of the rest of his life" in those places.[6]

Nonetheless, the two-week stay in Moscow sealed Paul's friendship with the Soviet people. He was an instant success everywhere, conquering everyone with his fluent and purely accented Russian. His singing voice captivated the Russians. Although he sang no concerts during this visit, he happily sang a capella on frequent occasions. Everywhere, people greeted him on the streets, cheered him, and begged him to stay. Essie wrote in a letter to Grandma Goode: "They say that he and Larry will sweep the country. . . . We will always have an entree here."[7]

Paul was profoundly affected by the climate of racial tolerance in the Soviet Union and by the sincere warmth expressed toward him by Russians in every walk of life. "Here, for the first time in my life I walk in full human dignity," he told Sergei. "You cannot imagine what that means to me as a Negro."[8]

One day, as he was walking through a small park past a group of mothers watching over their tots playing in the snow, the children spotted him and rushed toward him with cries of delight. When he spoke to them in Russian, they called him their "black Grandfather Frost" and refused to let him go until their mothers finally freed him. He couldn't get over the fact that the children hadn't been taught to fear black men.[9]

On a visit to the House of the Cinema, Paul enchanted the assembled cinematographers by giving a brief speech in perfect Russian, followed by an a capella rendition from the aria "Prayer and Death," one of the highlights of Boris Godunov. Then, to their delight, he sang many other songs, including "Ol' Man River," which he introduced to them as a song of protest. (His audience dubbed the song simply "Meesseesseeppee," which Russians continue to call it to this day.)[10]

Essie spent considerable time looking after her brothers, John and Frank. She gave them extra money so that they "could get the right things to eat," found them better lodging and paid for it in advance, and bought them expensive winter clothing to protect them from the bitter cold. Every morning, she had one or both of them over for breakfast, feeding them "eggs, meat, vegetables, etc., which are scarce." She and Paul went to visit John at his bus terminal, and Paul sang for the employees there.[11]

Paul had several long talks with John and Frank. Both of them were unequivocal in reporting that there was no race prejudice in the Soviet Union. Frank, who traveled to rural as well as urban areas with the circus, was especially emphatic on this point, announcing that he had decided to become a Soviet citizen and to marry a Russian woman. They confirmed that sharp conflicts had arisen in the previous several years, especially in the countryside. But they were reluctant to go beyond what could be read in the Soviet press, and Paul decided not to probe for further information.[12]

He and Essie went to the theater, the ballet, the opera; they saw various Soviet films with the filmmakers at their side to explain them. Paul went off with Eisenstein and others to pursue his interests in linguistics and the Soviet national minorities, while Essie explored the state of Soviet studies in anthropology, psychology, and medicine. Together they met and partied with the leaders of Moscow's cultural community, with some of its government elite, and with the outstanding members of the small but important group of African-Americans residing in Moscow.[13]

On the day after their arrival, Paul and Essie spent Christmas Eve at a dinner party held in the home of Maxim Litvinov and his charming English wife, Ivy. Litvinov was the Soviet commissar of foreign affairs and the architect of Soviet foreign policy. A short, roly-poly man with an expressive face and round glasses, he had a pleasant, open, cultivated manner and a wide range of intellectual interests. The other guests were outstanding personalities from the cultural and diplomatic world, except for Russia's top military man, Marshal Mikhail Nikolaevich Tukhachevsky, and his deputy. Tukhachevsky was a Civil War hero and arguably one of the greatest military strategists in modern history. A highly educated and cultured man who played the violin well, Tukhachevsky was seated next to Essie at dinner and conversed with her at length in German.

Later on, Tukhachevsky talked with Paul about the inevitability of a war between Nazi Germany and the Soviet Union. According to my father's recollection to me years later, Tukhachevsky was confident that he could build up the Red Army to the point of both defensive and offensive superiority over the Nazi war machine. When Paul asked him how long this would take, Tukhachevsky replied, "three years." Toward the end of the evening, Paul sang a capella for the gathering.[14]

Paul couldn't avoid politics in Moscow, even if he wanted to. Soon after Christmas, he visited his old Harlem friend William Patterson. "Pat" was in Moscow recuperating from tuberculosis. He was also serving as a representative of the U.S. Communist Party. He made it clear to Paul that he was speaking on behalf of both the American and Soviet party leaderships when he strongly advised Paul to return to the United States to "join the struggle" there. According to Pat, "the great fight" was going to be made in America. Paul listened politely and answered noncommittally, but he had no intention of returning home any time soon. He felt no obligation to any political organization.[15]

Nonetheless, he backed the campaign that Pat had mounted to save the lives of the Scottsboro boys—nine black youths falsely accused of raping a white woman in Alabama and sentenced to death. A few days later, he made a public statement strongly supporting the communist leadership of the protest against the frame-up of the Scottsboro boys.[16]

On January 6, 1935, Paul and Essie traveled to Leningrad. The majestic old city with its statues, bridges, and museums spread out before them "rather like a very beautiful, very spacious Paris," Essie wrote in her diary. Paul felt at home. The evening after their arrival, they attended a concert by the African-American contralto Marian Anderson at Philharmonic Hall. According to Essie, "a good crowd, and she sang beautifully. Her voice . . . [has] wide range with deep, rich tones and high, effortless tones; . . . she has a smoothness, polish, finish and ease which is delightful. She is herself beautiful too—tall, very slim, fine carriage, lovely face, and beautiful smile. She is absolutely first class, and a great success." They went backstage after her concert to congratulate her, and apparently spent some time with her socially during their stay in Leningrad.[17]

Paul and Essie returned to London via Finland, Denmark, and Sweden. The Finns more or less ignored Paul, but his records were immensely popular in Stockholm and Copenhagen. Journalists called him "the black Chaliapin," recalled his appearances in *The Emperor Jones* and *Show Boat*, and printed extensive comments by him on *Sanders of the River*, which was soon to be released. One Stockholm newspaper published an extensive interview with him regarding his slave ancestry and his study of African culture, and a major Copenhagen paper announced that he would return in April to sing a concert.[18]

Back in London, Paul's attention was occupied by his opening concert at the Royal Albert Hall and a tour of the British provinces. Paul sang basically the same program everywhere. To the spirituals and popular songs he had added several classical Russian songs, an occasional Hebridean, Finnish, or Hebrew folk song, and several English art songs. However, he refused to include German and French classics in his programs, even though many critics and parts of his audiences, including middle-class and upper-class blacks, had insisted that he should sing the classical concert repertoire including German lieder, like Marian Anderson and Roland Hayes. He replied that they didn't suit his culture, his voice, or his musical preferences.[19]

At last, on April 2, at one of London's biggest and most publicized gala cultural events of the year, *Sanders of the River* premiered. The large Leicester Square Theatre was rewired for top-quality sound at great expense; the proceeds were earmarked to support the Newspaper Press Fund (the favorite charity of Edgar Wallace, the deceased author of *Sanders*), and, with Robeson's presence serving as a major draw, the tickets were sold out in advance. Socialites, including former Queen Victoria Eugenie of Spain, American Ambassador Bingham and his wife, assorted lords, ladies, film stars, bankers, and industrialists, flocked to the opening. When Paul and Essie arrived, the huge crowd of onlookers cheered them and mobbed their car.

However, Paul himself had gone to the opening with decidedly mixed feelings. Having by now decided to become a vocal supporter of the colonial freedom movements in the British colonies, the blatant pro-colonialist propaganda line of *Sanders* was an embarrassment. Although several leaders of the African independence movement (for example, Kenya's Jomo Kenyatta) had urged him to make the film, he knew this would not help him escape sharp criticism from his socialist and communist admirers. His quest for a mass audience had inevitably collided with his growing political commitment and clarity of artistic vision.

Paul suppressed his anxiety and gave a well-received speech to introduce the film. But then, as he watched it unfold in finished form with the retakes added, he slipped out of the theater without a word to Essie and went back to their flat, mortified. He had known the retakes would glorify British colonialism, but their cumulative impact in edited form was far greater than in the separate scenes.

Essie soon noticed he was gone and immediately deduced what had happened. Since the flat was not far from the theater, she caught up with him there, fretfully pacing back and forth. She talked to him earnestly. It was too late now to disavow the film, she said, and he had made it with his eyes wide open. Its positive side remained unaltered, even though the glorification of British colonialism had been magnified by the retakes. Moreover, since the film was certain to be a huge success, his criticisms would be drowned out. Finally (and this was perhaps her most convincing argument), he had better wait for the African reaction, because if he denounced the film and they did not, he would look ridiculous. To underscore this last point, she reminded him that Jomo Kenyatta, who had played a bit part in the film and was then already a prominent figure in the anticolonial movement, had applauded Paul's opening speech and had not left the theater during the showing.

Paul returned to the opening with Essie, slipped back in unnoticed, and when the film was over, went back onstage with his white costar, Leslie Banks, who had played Sanders. As he had done in his introduction of the film, Paul charmed his audience with a brief but convincing speech in which he "confessed" he was far too nervous to sing for them. However, one perceptive critic noted in his review of the event that "Paul Robeson is a charming man, and a wise one to boot," adding, "All evening we had been listening to his wonderful voice, twice as large as life as reproduced by the talkie loud speaker. . . . Wisely enough, [he] decided that to sing on the stage then would only have been to create an anti-climax."[20]

Sanders seemed to be a smash hit from every standpoint, and Paul, who had top billing, benefited enormously. Critics praised both the film and him. It was also a huge commercial success in London, in the provinces, and abroad. The *Times of India* reported "packed houses" in Bombay, where it was held over for a second week, and called it "a triumph." The City of Venice awarded it a cup for best musical accompaniment. And the New York press, although critical of the "romantic portrait of the benevolent white father" and the "absence of punch and conviction," called it an interesting and ambitious work, praised Paul's singing, and welcomed its "pictorial suavity" and "flashes of uncommonly good dramatic suspense."[21]

The next year, the film was awarded the annual gold medal for the best British film of 1935 by the Institute of Amateur Cinematographers. Despite Paul's misgivings, *Sanders* had set up a major British film career for him while opening the door wide for his acceptance by Hollywood as Joe the Riverman in the upcoming production of *Show Boat*. Paul left the contract negotiations for *Show Boat* to Essie and Bob Rockmore, while he sought a touchstone to match his standard of artistic integrity.[22]

Eager to reassert his own values after the *Sanders* opening, Paul attempted to create a people's theater based on the notion that "what the public really wants from the theater are ideas . . . [and] the exploration of deep human problems. I was trained in what one may call the Little Theatre tradition, in circles where it is understood that the theatre is the home of one of the greatest, and perhaps the most comprehensive, of all the arts." He began by joining forces with the Arts Theater Club to present *Basalik*. This play by Peter Garland (a pseudonym for Norma Munro, an American), about an independent-minded African chief, had a three-day trial run in mid-April at the experimental Arts Theater with Paul in the title role. But ponderous dialogue sank the show. Although Paul got fairly good reviews for his performance, he failed to elevate the role beyond the noble-savage level.[23]

Though disappointed with *Basalik*, Paul revived his artistic partnership with Andre Van Gyseghem, who had directed him in the 1933 production of *Chillun* at the Embassy Theatre, to present the play *Stevedore*. Written by American playwrights Paul Peters and George Sklar, *Stevedore* tells the story of black workers who organize against their white bosses and end up facing down a lynch mob. A cast of amateur actors was recruited, and after a month of rehearsals the play opened for a two-week run at the Embassy on May 6, 1935. Paul considered the role to be one of the finest he ever played because it honestly portrayed Negro everyday life. However, the critics once again felt that Paul was better than the play, which got mixed reviews.[24]

During this period, Essie proved once again that her managerial and negotiating skills were out of the ordinary. On April 16, she wrote a letter to her friend, Cecil, at the Gramophone Company Ltd., in which she proposed that "something special be done for Paul." The "something special" was to double the normal royalty rate after the first 50,000 records sold, and by July 6 her negotiations had resulted in a contract containing this provision. Meanwhile, her preliminary negotiations with Universal Pictures for *Show Boat* resulted in agreement on a huge salary, all expenses paid for both Paul and herself, approval of the location (Paul was still refusing to go south of the Mason-Dixon Line), and the promise that he would have no lower than fourth place in the billing. The only provision left unresolved was Paul's demand that he have the right to approve not only the script but his actual filmed takes.[25]

At the end of June, when Paul began his 1935 summer tour of thirteen concerts, he scheduled appearances a week apart to leave time for his studies. Prestigious invitations and honors had no appeal if they interrupted his scholarly pursuits. In London, the Royal Institute of International Affairs invited him to speak on "the future of the negro [*sic*] race"; the British General Press asked him to write six syndicated articles on his views about life, his film work, and his experiences in Europe and America; the National Liberal Club invited him to speak on "the conservation of the true African culture"; and the students of Scotland's Edinburgh University requested permission to nominate him for the rectorship. Paul politely declined all of these requests.[26]

Paul delved into an amalgam of topics, seeking the linkages between them. Believing that language and music reflected the emotional tones of the cultures they represented, he wrote, "Languages . . . are built on sound, accent and rhythm, rather than on anything that can be written down in black and white. . . . The folk songs of almost all peoples are completely emotional. . . . They come easily and naturally to me. . . . For the Negro, art is an expression of what he *feels*. For the European, it is an expression of what he *thinks*. . . . What I want to preserve for the Negro is this thing that he can give to European art—this capacity of feeling." For Paul it was not only the music that was important; his chief concern was with the emotions the music expressed.[27]

This concern led him to explore in depth a variety of languages and their attendant cultures. A November 22, 1935, article in the *Jewish Transcript*, a Seattle newspaper, reported that he was learning Hebrew and liked singing Hebrew songs such as the traditional "Ovinu Malchainu." Having remarked that Russian Jews were among his best friends in London and New York, Paul was quoted as saying, "I think my people can take a lesson from the Jewish people in self-respect and pride in their culture."

However, Paul kept his main focus on African culture and drew upon many sources, including his friend Melville Herskovits, a leading anthropological authority on Africa, with whom he had struck up a friendship in the 1920s at Columbia University. During the 1930s, they corresponded fairly often. A November 11, 1935, letter from Herskovits to Paul was accompanied by a packet of six anthropological publications and a reference list of ten major papers that Herskovits had written on the culture of Africa and of the black diaspora. Paul made good use of those references and many other sources, and nineteen years later his cultural scholarship was fulsomely acknowledged by the British historian Arnold Toynbee:

> A distinguished Negro American singer felt the thrill of making a surprising discovery when he came to realize that the primitive culture of his African ancestors was spiritually akin to all the non-Western higher cultures, and to the pristine higher culture of the Western World itself, in virtue of it having preserved a spiritual integrity which a Late Modern Western secularized culture had deliberately abandoned.

Then Toynbee quoted from a 1935 article Paul had written under the title "Negroes, Don't Ape the Whites":

> I discovered that the African languages—thought to be primitive because monosyllabic—had exactly the same basic structure as Chinese. I found the African way of thinking in symbols was also the way of the great Chinese thinkers. I found that I, who lacked a feeling for the English language later than Shakespeare, met Pushkin, Dostoyevsky, Tolstoy, Lao-tsze, and Confucius on common ground.
>
> With the coming of the Renaissance, Reason and Intellect were placed above Intuition and Feeling. [But] to what end does the West rule the world if all art dies? Jesus, the Easterner, was right. "What shall it profit a man if he gain the whole world and lose his own soul?"[28]

Sharpening his understanding of complex cultural issues, Paul, over a period of several months in 1935, carried on a stimulating debate both in person and by correspondence with Dr. Norman Leys. A British physician who had grown up in the English East African colony of Kenya, Leys had written, among others, a widely read book titled *Kenya*. A committed socialist, he was passionately anti-colonialist and antiracist, and believed strongly in the full human equality of Africans and their right to "political liberty."

However, Leys approached matters exclusively from a rational standpoint, whereas Paul, although he did not reject such an approach, relied heavily on spiritual insight and emotional instinct. Leys based his worldview on the proposition that "distinctive national (or tribal, or racial) traits were undesirable and should not be fostered," that "the family tie" was a handicap, and that "world citizenship means . . . maximizing liberty and variety *inside* every human group." For him, liberty was bound to "diminish or destroy characteristics *peculiar* to the group." In contrast, for Paul the characteristics peculiar to the group were its primary source of strength—the key to cultural growth and to the capacity for interacting positively with other cultures.[29]

Paul wrote a carefully thought-out rebuttal to Leys, and requested that their mutual friend, Marcia de Silva, publish it in an appropriate venue. *Nash's* magazine agreed to publish an interview with de Silva that would contain the essence of Paul's views. In addition, two of his original pieces—"Note on Nationalism" and "Note on Materialism"—would be published in full. But de Silva's piece appeared in such a truncated form that it distorted Paul's intent, and significant amounts of his original texts were cut. The omitted remarks bear reading now, for these notes reveal key aspects of the philosophy that informed Paul's thought from that time on:[30]

> I am not a nationalist. I am more profoundly impressed by the likenesses in cultural forms which seem to me to transcend the boundaries of nationality. Whatever be the Social and Economic content of the culture—Archaic, Clan and Tribal organization; Feudalism, Capitalism, or Socialism—this cultural Form seems to persist, and to be of vital importance to the people concerned.[31] Just as it seems that the social and economic foundation must be broadened to transcend national boundaries if the world is to prosper, so there seems to be a possible synthesis of related cultural forms.
>
>   Africa's geographic location appears to have symbolic significance. She stands between East and West, and in the future must take from both.

> Materialism places the acquisition of property above all else. It creates a varied external life but does little to cause the growth of a

deep "inner life." I refer to the contrast between the inner life of the artist and the external activity of the merchant who is concerned with selling his goods. [In the West] knowledge (and, through knowledge, power over the *external* world) became the measure of all things.

[In the Chinese culture] the problem is not one of knowledge, but of ethics, proceeding from the *will*, not the *intellect*. [This problem] has deeply occupied the African [who], in adapting himself to his environment, has also made great use of the third, old division of the *Human Mind*, the *Emotions*—the domain of feeling.

There is much to be learned from these and other Eastern peoples, especially in the realms of Morality and Feeling, in Ethics, in Art, and in that aspect of pure science which depends upon the intuitive flash as a starting or integrating point of departure.

On September 20, 1935, Carl Laemmle, Jr., the producer of the upcoming film *Show Boat*, sent a cable to the London office of Universal Pictures offering Paul transportation from New York to California and back to London; the right to do recordings, concerts, and radio appearances in his spare time; and a guarantee that he would not have to go to the South for filming. However, Laemmle rejected Paul's demand to approve his takes, stating that no one—not even Greta Garbo—had this privilege. A couple of days later, a telephone call from Laemmle to Paul sealed the agreement on Laemmle's terms with the added proviso that Paul would be released in time to begin his English winter concert tour on January 19, 1936.

On September 25, with the contract signed, Paul and Essie headed to the States. To friends who saw them, they seemed exceptionally well. "[Paul] is extraordinarily happy these days," Essie wrote to her mother, "and it seems permanent. We get on marvellously, and I'm very happy, too."

Since the shooting of Paul's *Show Boat* scenes and the recording of the songs was not to start until November 18, Paul, finding that his popularity in America was undiminished despite a three-year absence, made the most of the intervening time. He rehearsed his songs with Larry Brown intensively to keep his voice in top condition, scheduled a concert mini-tour (two New York concerts, followed by appearances in Montreal, Chicago, Milwaukee, Portland, and Seattle) to maintain his performing edge, and appeared on the

General Motors Concert Series broadcast from coast to coast. The enthusiastic response to his radio concert reflected his popularity as a recording artist—his record sales at least matched those in England, which were now well over a hundred thousand annually.[32]

In New York, he and Essie stayed with their oldest friends, Hattie and Buddy Bolling, in the heart of Harlem on 135th Street at the corner of Seventh Avenue. They enjoyed socializing with their old Harlem crowd again, and Paul engaged in some damage control of his image in interviews with selected members of the black press. Criticism of his screen roles, first in *Sanders* and now in *Show Boat*, and the rumor that he was going to star as Uncle Tom, though false, couldn't have surfaced at a worse time from the standpoint of his reputation among both African-Americans and leftists.

Paul realized that the criticism of *Sanders* required a swift, sophisticated defense. The highly respected black journalist Ted Poston provided Paul with the opportunity at dockside on his arrival from England. He challenged the criticism coming from the left directly, and addressed criticism from the African-American community more obliquely. "To expect the Negro artist to reject every role with which he is not ideologically in agreement . . . is to expect [him] under our present scheme of things to give up his work entirely," Paul said, "unless, of course, he is to confine himself solely to the Left theatre. Under such an arrangement, I might as well give up my singing, my concert work, everything. To say that I had no right to appear in *Sanders of the River* is to say I shouldn't have appeared in *Emperor Jones*—that I shouldn't accept the role in *Show Boat*."

Having dismissed the arguments of the left on artistic grounds, Paul approached *Sanders* from the popular black point of view as a useful, if flawed, means to an end. He added the explanation that "the . . . film . . . was not originally planned as an empire-building epic . . . ; the imperialist angle was placed in the plot during the last five days of shooting." Moreover, the success of *Sanders* had led to an invitation for him to appear as King Christophe of Haiti in a subsequent Korda film, and he stressed the wonderful opportunity that this offer represented. ("Could you imagine a Black King being treated seriously in Hollywood?") With these words, he reached out to his primary black supporters.

However, Paul chose not to reveal at that time his hope that *Show Boat* would ultimately give him the opportunity in Hollywood that *Sanders of the River* had created for him in England. For it was his long-run plan to succeed in *Show Boat*, and then to turn his back on Hollywood. He hoped to build his film career on progressively more meaningful films in England, and finally retackle Hollywood from a position of greater strength.

At the end of the interview, Paul turned back to addressing his growing left constituency. Poston reported that he "was lavish in his praise of the Soviet Union, and reiterated his statement that only there could a Negro artist feel free." Poston also noted that Paul momentarily turned from the interview to say farewell in Russian to a group of Soviet technicians who had crossed the Atlantic with him en route to the Ford plant in Detroit. His parting shot to Poston was that he had turned down an offer to appear in the talkie remake of *The Green Pastures*, which was to be filmed soon in Hollywood with blackface comedian Al Jolson playing "De Lawd."[33]

Before going to Hollywood, Paul came to see me and Grandma Goode at the small country house just outside of Pittsfield, Massachusetts, where we had been staying since the early spring of 1935. We had been living in North America for eighteen months—first in New York's Greenwich Village, then in Montreal, Canada, and finally in the Berkshire Mountains of western Massachusetts. What Paul found when he arrived troubled him. Nearly eight years old, depressed and angry, I was tired of being away from my parents, tired of Grandma's inflexible tutelage, sick of being confined to an exclusively white environment, and enraged at the unrelenting racism we encountered in the United States. (The stay in Canada had been a great relief.) I had walked out of the local public school in Pittsfield before the end of the spring term, been expelled from a private summer camp for fighting, and was now refusing to go back to school. Grandma was at her wits' end.

Nothing in my father's boyhood resembled mine. By now, I had already traveled to England, Yugoslavia, Austria, Switzerland, the United States, and Canada; learned to speak fluent German and to play the piano; received sufficient instruction from innumerable tutors to acquire a wide variety of athletic skills (swimming, soccer, tennis, horseback riding, softball, skiing, figure skating, and ice hockey); become an avid reader in both English and German; and advanced two years beyond my age in standard schoolwork. But I had lived most of the previous five years away from my parents as a black rich kid in an almost entirely white environment. My father could easily see that I was in sore need of being surrounded by my own people.

The day after he arrived, he encouraged me to take him for a long walk along the paths in the surrounding woods, which had become my haven. Gradually, he got me to talk about how I felt, and once I started in earnest, he listened without interrupting. Only when I paused did he ask an occasional question. When I finished, we walked a bit in silence until we reached a small clearing, where he stopped and stared for a while at a large tree across from us, silent, his hands in his overcoat pockets. There was something entirely reassuring about his demeanor. He looked down at me with a serious but kindly look and said in his soft, deep voice, "When you come back to London next spring, you will live with Mama and me, and Grandma will live separately from us. I promise you."

That was all. He didn't expect a response, and it didn't occur to me to give him one. We walked back to the house in silence, enjoying the sights and sounds of the woods together.

A few days later, Paul was back on the road. His concerts of spirituals and folk songs were as well received in the United States and Canada as they had been in the English provinces, with critics, for the most part, accepting his limited repertoire on its own terms. By the time he arrived in Hollywood, he was in excellent voice, and Essie wrote to her friend Hattie Bolling:

> Well, the first recordings are "in the box," as they say here, and perfect, and that much is off our minds. We spent all of Sunday doing "Ol' Man River," with the orchestra, with the chorus, with and without everything you can imagine. Paul was in marvellous voice. When he had finished singing the song the second time, the members of the orchestra put down their instruments and applauded! They tell me it never happened before. James Whale [the director] is really good; he knows just what he wants and how to get it. [He] seems to want, at least with Paul, just what we want. I think the film is going to be good, and I think it will be largely Whale's fault. Jerome Kern was out here yesterday, and we had a nice talk. He and Hammerstein have something new in mind for Paul, and we'll talk it all over at Kern's home one night next week.[34]

———

In *Show Boat*, Paul revolutionized the technique of "synching" a separately recorded sound track with the visual track. He astonished the Universal sound engineers by adamantly insisting on singing from a point less than two feet from the microphone, rather than from the standard ten-foot distance, a technique he had developed in his radio broadcasts and in recording the *Sanders* sound track. Then he proceeded to sing in intimate fashion, instead of at full volume. Through the use of this method, he was able to keep his voice projection so even and unstrained that when he had sung one song twenty-five times for the recording machine, it was found that he had sung it every time exactly the same in measure and phrasing. In addition, since he went over all the action in each scene with Whale before singing in the microphone room, he was able to act out the scene mentally, complete with timing of the action, while he was singing. Then, as he acted, he sang mentally. When the sound and picture were combined, it was found that he had synchronized perfectly.

Paul's singing and acting performances during the shooting of his *Show Boat* scenes created such a stir in Hollywood that he was now deluged with film offers. Some Hollywood magnates, unaccustomed to having anyone turn them down, were taken by surprise when he declined their offers. When he told one studio head that he had to go back to England to begin a concert tour at London's Albert Hall, the man turned to a subordinate with the comment: "Where's that? We'll *buy* the Albert Hall!" But despite their tenacity, Paul turned them all down flat. Before risking a Hollywood film again, he was determined to develop his film career in England, where he had a good chance to work with the Korda brothers, or with the famed Hollywood director King Vidor, on a serious black film. He also felt that England, rather than Hollywood, was the place to experiment with comic roles. As he put it, "I am determined to try to express in my future screen parts that grand humor that the Negro possesses."[35]

14

WHITE FILM,
BLACK CULTURE

(1936)

Departing from New York on January 12, 1936, Paul chose, as he had on his arrival, to address issues close to the hearts of his most important American constituencies—blacks and the left. In an interview with the *New York Herald-Tribune*, he predicted "an Africa freed of foreign domination" and ridiculed "the suggestion that the rise of black nationalism might create a menace to white civilization." In his view, there wasn't a sharp division, with one race uniting against another: "the race question isn't of primary importance [on a world scale]."

His message to the left appeared in an interview with black communist leader Benjamin J. Davis, Jr., in which his comments about the Soviet Union mixed exaggeration ("I intend to live there—yes sir, to make my home there. Why, it's the only country in the world where I feel at home") with sober evaluation ("I believe that the Soviet Union is the bulwark of civilization against . . . fascism") and political caution ("In England they call me a 'Communist' because of my views, but I'm certainly not a member of the Communist Party").[1]

In answer to a question about the Stalinist purge of 1934–1935, which followed Kirov's murder, Paul said: "They ought to destroy anybody who seeks to harm that great country." This despite the fact that he harbored grave doubts about internal Soviet politics. Paul's apparently contradictory attitude on this issue—a refusal to criticize the Soviet Union publicly even when outright condemnation was called for—was already hardening at the beginning of 1936 and would

235

remain a fixture thereafter. His reasoning was clear and was shared by many nonwhites in general and many African-Americans in particular: for them the Soviet Union's consistent opposition to racism, colonialism, and fascism far outweighed all other considerations.

Back in England from January through April 1936, Paul once again embarked on a concert tour. Audiences everywhere loved it, but the critics were far more demanding and were sharply divided. The most interesting comment came from Ireland, where "Rathcol," the critic of the *Belfast Telegraph* (February 7, 1936) wrote, "It is sad to see [his art] wasted on the restricted type of music he favors. There is no point in arguing that Mr. Robeson would not be nearly so good in art-songs as he is in the Spirituals. . . . I entirely disagree." By now, Paul himself had altered his previous opinion that he could not do justice to art songs; it all depended on *which* art songs he chose. And he set out to attack this problem seriously as he prepared Russian songs for his tour of the Soviet Union.

In mid-April, at the end of the British tour, he made good on his promise to me the previous fall in America: he brought me to live with him in the Buckingham Street flat. The fact that he spent a lot of time at the flat studying and writing, rehearsing his music, and preparing for his roles meant that for the first time in his life he could see his son often. He took to calling me "Chappie" and wanted me to call him "Pop," as he had called his father. "Chappie" was fine with me, but I wasn't comfortable calling him "Pop," so I called him "Dad," and he accepted it. Essie continued to call me "Pauli" (the German diminutive for "Paul" and a nickname I never liked) to distinguish me from Paul. I called her "Mama," the name she used for Grandma Goode.

Paul's career dominated the household. Even when Paul and Larry Brown went back on tour, Essie was busy with complicated negotiations involving Paul's film career. The tentative plans to make another film about Africa with Zoltan Korda or King Vidor had collapsed over scheduling conflicts with the Soviet concert tour, which Paul refused to cancel or postpone. A proposal by Oscar Hammerstein II that Paul star in a film based on the play *Black Majesty*, a story about Toussaint L'Ouverture of Haiti, which both Eisenstein and Korda had wanted to film, fell by the wayside for the same reason.[2]

Essie managed to negotiate roles for him in three films that were to be made by major film companies and completed before their departure for Moscow in October. This time she made sure that Paul was contractually entitled to script approval (including the shooting scripts) for all three movies throughout the filming process, as well as approval of the takes of his songs. He didn't want another *Sanders*, and these approvals were sufficient to guarantee that neither a director nor an editor could significantly distort the film overall.

However, the main problem continued to be the unavailability of commercially viable film stories based on black characters. In this context, he made a conscious decision to settle for mediocre but commercial stories with a relatively weak social message in order to portray powerful black male images that could deliver a positive cultural message. He had already come to the conclusion that this was possible in England but not in Hollywood. And this was part of the reason he had defended *Sanders* on his return to London in January 1936, even though he had just denounced the film in New York's left-wing press. Additionally, he reasoned that for black audiences the film's affronting pro-colonialist message was outweighed by his positive image—a conclusion that had been thoroughly confirmed by the enthusiastic reception of *Sanders* by both African and African-American audiences.

Yet *Sanders* haunted him. In a January 1936 interview in New York with Benjamin J. Davis, Jr., Paul had given a misleading impression of his attitude toward the film: "I had no idea that it would have such a turn *after* I had acted in it. . . . Moreover, . . . at its premiere . . . I was called to the stage and in protest refused to perform. Since that time I have refused to play in three films offered me by that same producer. . . . I think all the attacks against me and the film were correct." However, a week later in London he told a reporter for the *Evening News* that in the United States the audiences liked *Sanders*, but "the critics got a bit muddled." He was also considering the possibility of making another film with Zoltan Korda, the director of *Sanders*, he added.

Paul remained ambivalent about *Sanders* for many years. Documents notarized by Julius Meltzer, on January 17, 1951, in Springfield, Massachusetts, reveal that Paul did not divest himself of his 5 percent share of the film's gross income until 1951. An interesting letter on audience reaction to *Sanders of the River* in the United States was written to Paul and Essie by Rena M. Vale, who sat in theaters in various parts of Los Angeles County where the film was playing. She wrote:

> I learned that audiences are very responsive to ideas which American producers are afraid to screen. Tennessee would have banned the script of *Sanders*. Although it is likely they accepted the finished product when presented with box-office figures from other states. Why? Because "respectable" white people were shown risking their lives to save a Negro. But the audiences? They "ate it up." Not once, but at least five times in the eight showings of *Sanders* I witnessed, the audience burst into applause.[3]

Paul approached his new film projects with guarded optimism. The first one he contracted for was *Song of Freedom*. Based on a story by Claude Williams and Dorothy Hollaway titled *The Kingdom of Zinga*, it was about a black English dock worker who becomes a famous singer after being discovered by an opera impresario. Learning that he is descended from African royalty, he ultimately returns to his people in Africa. The film was produced through the collaboration of two major film companies: British Lion and Hammer. The well-regarded Elder Wills directed, and original footage for the film was shot in Sierra Leone. Elizabeth Welch, the famous black revue and radio singer-actress, costarred, and the shooting of Paul's scenes began in early April.

The second project, a comedy about a working-class black couple who live near the Marseilles docks and befriend a rich white runaway teenager, was based on a novel titled *Banjo*, by Claude McKay. It was retitled *Big Fella* for the film, and was Paul's first attempt to play a genuine nonstereotypical comedy role. Scheduled to be shot immediately after completion of *Song of Freedom* by the same Hammer–British Lion production team, it again costarred Elizabeth Welch. Both Essie and Larry Brown appeared in small but significant parts.

The third and most ambitious undertaking was a lavish Gaumont–British Picture Corporation production of H. Rider Haggard's adventure novel *King Solomon's Mines*, with Cedric Hardwicke costarring as Allan Quatermain. Paul played an African chief (Umbopa) disguised as a servant. A straight adventure film with no political overtones and minimal stereotypes, it was a bit like *Sanders of the River* without the pro-imperialist slant and with fewer loincloths. Shooting would begin in the early fall.[4]

Meaningful plays tended to be as scarce as good film scripts. So far Paul had not been able to muster enough consistent support to establish an experimental theater group of his own, but he kept looking for promising stories. In March 1936, the Stage Society sponsored two performances of C. L. R. James's play *Toussaint L'Ouverture* at the Westminster Theater, with Paul playing the lead. Despite his strong public identification with the Trotskyist opposition to Stalinism, James, a black scholar of West Indian descent and a famous figure on the left, had become close friends with Paul, who tended to ignore political differences when it came to personal friendship. The warm friendship between James and Paul flourished, and James remained one of his political confidants for the remainder of the 1930s. Decades later, James recalled, "to have spent half an hour in his company or to have ten minutes alone with him was something you remembered for days, and if I had to sum up his personality in one word, or rather two, I would say it was the combination of immense power and great gentleness."[5] Notwithstanding Paul's best efforts and the enthusiastic response of the standing-room-only audiences, James's play, deemed "episodic" and "unevenly written and produced," failed to attract sufficient critical or financial support to continue even for a short run.

At long last, a letter from Lillian Bayliss, manager of the world-renowned theater company The Old Vic, offered a sudden prospect for Paul to break out of the mundane roles that held his talents in check. Bayliss wrote, "You know how we have hoped that you would work with us one day, and I think you, too, would like to do something here. . . . We hope to produce *Othello* immediately after Christmas; Laurence Olivier joins the company then, and will play Iago, and it would be very wonderful if there were any chance of your being able to consider the title role." She added, in closing, "We should all rejoice if you could say yes."

Strikingly, Paul passed up the opportunity. His firm commitment to his Soviet concert tour was one reason. His other reasons for turning down the offer were more private. He did not consider the six-week preparation period sufficient for him to do justice to the role. My guess is that deep down he was not yet certain he could fully master the part. He had not played a complex and demanding role in the theater since the 1933 London production of *Chillun*, and he knew he had not even begun to overcome the evident flaws in that performance. He resolved not to attempt *Othello* until he could aspire to near perfection.[6] Now was not the time.

However, with his trip to Moscow a certainty, he decided not to go to South Africa. For almost a year, Paul had wanted to go, despite the fact that both South African and British authorities had politely but clearly expressed their opposition to such a visit because of his well-publicized anticolonialist views. Paul bided his time, skeptical of efforts by left-wing Britishers, including his friend Norman Leys, to sponsor and manage his trip; if he were to travel to Africa, he preferred to be in the hands of black South Africans from the freedom movement.

As a compromise, Paul asked Essie to refuse the left-wing group's invitation on his behalf, then proposed that Essie should go not only to South Africa but also to British East Africa. Essie agreed, and decided to take me along with her to share this once-in-a-life-time adventure. For the arrangements, Paul turned to Max Yergan, who had worked in South Africa for many years under the sponsorship of the International Committee of the YMCA. He had been the 1933 winner of the NAACP's Spingarn medal for his contribution to improved education for black South Africans, and had been put in touch with Essie and Paul by their old friend, NAACP leader Walter White. Yergan was fully trusted by the underground black leaders. He arranged for my mother and me to stay at the homes of key Africans in the antiapartheid movement and at his own home near Bloemfontein. He subsequently became one of Paul's closest political associates for almost a decade.

Paul made his own public statement on South Africa by singing two songs and narrating the prologue in a documentary film, *My Song Goes Forth*, which was produced in England as a subtle indictment of the apartheid regime. Joseph Best, the producer, accepted his rewrite of the draft prologue, in which racial inequities were exposed more starkly than in the original version, and refused to make any changes when the film was vehemently attacked by supporters of colonialism. Paul was satisfied with the film, and it was generally well received by critics, though the U.S. Communist Party paper, *The Worker*, dismissed it for not being militant enough.[7]

As for Paul's commercial film career, George Campbell, an observant critic writing in *The Bystander*, complained that:

> There is something pathetic about Paul Robeson's career on the screen. Nine out of ten white stars are dwarfs alongside of him. And yet he has never made one first-class movie, and it looks as if he never will. The trouble lies in the unimaginative commercialisation of the screen, and in our fundamentally mischievous attitude towards the whole negro [*sic*] race. If he could just forget he is a negro [*sic*], and make producers forget it too, he would be one of the great actors of the world, instead of a tantalising possibility. *Song of Freedom* has its points, but as art it is sentimental and unreal.

Notwithstanding these important insights, Campbell failed to comprehend that Paul was consciously choosing to assert his blackness, rather than to "forget" it (assuming that was possible), and that his purpose was to impart authenticity to black characters upon whom an unreality had been imposed by even the most well-meaning white producers. This concept seemed beyond the imagination of even the most liberal whites.[8]

The enthusiastic response of the African-American press and the Indian press to *Song of Freedom* was especially gratifying to Paul. The *Times of India* called it "a mighty drama of three continents . . . not only a festival of lovely melody but . . . a thrilling and poignant story." The *Afro-American* set the tone for the black press, calling it "the finest story of colored folks yet brought to the screen." And Paul's friend Langston Hughes wrote him the exhilarating news that Harlem audiences liked his performance.

If *Song of Freedom* was well received, *Show Boat* was an outright triumph. (*Big Fella* and *King Solomon's Mines* were not released until the following year.) English critics hailed it as the best-ever version of the story, and Paul stole the film despite his small part ("The picture would not have been tolerable without Paul Robeson . . . , the real hero of the film," wrote one critic).[9]

In the United States, audience response, both to *Show Boat* and to Paul, was sensational, and positive critical reaction was not far behind: "[Robeson is] perfectly cast," read one typical review, "[and his] singing inspires applause at the conclusion of each song." However, there were a few dissenters. The *California News*, a black newspaper, vehemently attacked Paul's "revolting" portrayal of "a shiftless moron" and accused him of reviving the Uncle Tom stereotype. Most black reviewers, however, liked the film and praised Paul for his "engaging manner . . . [which] seemed to give the picture a curious charm." A piece by Bernice Patton, which appeared on January 10 in the *California Eagle* soon after Paul had completed his work on the film, reported that "Hollywood is marveling over the modest dignity and culture exhibited by Paul Robeson, . . . and a cycle of pictures featuring Colored artists in more respectable roles is the result." Paul himself was satisfied with his work in *Show Boat*: in an interview published in the June 13, 1936, issue of the London *Evening News*, he said that the film meant a lot to him, and that he had enjoyed making it.[10]

By now his appearances in *Emperor Jones, Sanders of the River*, and *Show Boat* had established him as a film star. And after completing his filming of *Big Fella* and *King Solomon's Mines*, he felt that his use of the right to approve scripts and song takes had enabled him to advance to significantly higher artistic ground. *King Solomon's Mines* was important to him both because of its authentic African scenes and because he played a part based on a classic novel. Shot extensively on location in Africa, it featured Paul as an African of royal descent. Moreover, Ben Kubeka, brother-in-law of the regent chief of the Zulus, had a significant part in the film. At the end of the filming, Paul wanted to make a gesture of appreciation to the studio technicians before leaving. Told that they would like to hear him sing, he called Larry Brown, had a grand piano delivered to the set, and sang a concert for his fellow workers.[11]

It was not unusual for Paul to express his genuine concern for people so spontaneously. On one occasion, after a long train trip, he walked the length of the train to thank the train crew personally, shake their hands, and chat.

He also expressed his emotions freely in public. One time, he found himself in historic Canterbury Cathedral as one of the throng of summer visitors. There was no service going on, and he was moving about among the other tourists, taking a great interest in what he saw. Finding himself near the front of the cathedral, he went to the foot of the altar and stood silently there for a while, looking upward with his head thrown back. Then, lost in his own reverie, he began to sing "Were You There When They Crucified My Lord." Like the amazed visitors he seemed transfixed by the fusion of his own spirituality and the majesty of the surroundings.[12]

By the end of 1936, Paul felt more relaxed and secure than ever before. The seeds planted during his 1934 trip through Nazi Berlin to Soviet Moscow, when he had begun to think of himself as a citizen of the world rather than merely an artist who traveled the world, were bearing fruit.[13]

With his impending fall concert tour of the Soviet Union publicly announced, and with extensive publicity attending his decision to send me to school in Russia so that I could experience an environment free of racism, Paul moved decisively toward adopting a public political posture. He identified himself with the cultural left by joining the Executive Committee of the British Trade Union Congress's General Council (along with Margaret Webster, Tyrone Guthrie, Harold Laski, and others) in support of a national campaign to subsidize the Left Theater Group. This organization was to serve the Labour and socialist movement with a permanent repertory theater and a touring company.

Looking ahead, Paul planned to talk with Sergei Eisenstein in Moscow about playing a variety of roles in Russian films, including a Chinese warlord in a Russian version of *Sons*, the sequel to Pearl Buck's *The Good Earth*; the title role in *Othello*; and the lead role in *Black Majesty*, Eisenstein's pet project based on the story of Toussaint L'Ouverture.[14] As he prepared to become more outspoken politically, he also commented on cultural issues more sharply and more often. "I am true to my race," he said in one interview, "but what I give is the common possession of you all. . . . Beneath the accidents of race and culture which define us is the soul of man." And at a luncheon to celebrate the preview of *Song of Freedom*, he chose to answer black nationalist critics who espoused an exclusionary cultural separatism, condemned him for his screen roles, and faulted him for singing Negro spirituals. While expressing a degree of sympathy for their views, Paul voiced his belief in the universality of religious folk music by singing, unaccompanied, a song about the virgin birth as sung by Catholic New Orleans blacks. The song's lyrical language, he said, had a beauty rivaling that achieved by the English medieval poets.[15]

By this time, Paul's conceptualization of the roots and essence of black culture had broadened significantly. His most substantial published article of the 1930s, titled "Primitives," appeared in the August 8, 1936, issue of *The New Statesman and Nation*, a leading British journal:

> The man who thinks in concrete symbols has no abstract conception of such words as "good," "brave," "clever." They are represented in his mind by symbolic pictures. It is not only the African Negro, and so-called primitive people, who think in concrete symbols—all the great civilizations of the East have been built up by people with this type of mind. It is a mentality which has given us giants like Confucius, Mencius and Lao-tze. More than likely it was this kind of thinking that gave us the understanding and wisdom of a person like Jesus Christ. It has, in fact, given us the full flower of all the highest possibilities in man—with the single exception of applied science. That was left to a section of Western man to achieve, and on that he bases his assertion of superiority. The cost of developing the kind of mind by which the discoveries of science were made has been one which threatens the discoverer's very life. The result is that, as Western civilization advances, its members find themselves in the paradoxical position of being more and more in control of their environment, yet more and more at the mercy of it. One recoils from the Western intellectual's idea that, having got himself on the peak overhanging the abyss, he should want to drag all other people up after him into the same precarious position. That, in a sentence, is my case against Western values.

Nine years ahead of the first atomic bomb explosion, and decades ahead of the worldwide movement to preserve the environment, he seemed to foretell that Western culture would bring humankind to a precarious precipice.

In a section of his unpublished 1936 notes, titled "Machine Man; Need Whole Man," he asserted that "the artist in the Western world appreciates fully the emotional intensity and dependence upon spontaneous and intuitive knowledge so characteristic of the African and many Eastern peoples." He included the Russians among these peoples. To him Russia was "a country with no color prejudice . . . in which a Negro can live in terms of complete equality. . . . Russia is one country where he can live as a Russian, as free as is any Russian."

However, Paul did not believe that the Soviet Union could play the role of the black man's liberator. Contending that black people could not be important anywhere in the world "as isolated individuals," he called for them to act unitedly, as "a people [with] a culture of . . . our own." No country, including Russia, would save the black man. He would "save himself." Adding that socialist ideology was not necessarily the answer for blacks, Paul wrote that "even from Russia's viewpoint, to convert 200 million black people to socialism . . . is hopeless. Russia is socialist because they took over a Tsarist state and made it what it is. . . . [However], millions of Negroes are . . . peasants with [an] attachment to land as individual or clan property."[16]

Having a practical side along with his idealistic one, Paul returned to the Soviet Union during the summer of 1936 intent on understanding all of its aspects. Again the guest of Sergei Eisenstein, he visited both urban and rural areas outside Moscow, and talked directly in Russian with ordinary people everywhere without any official escort. Through long private talks with Sergei, he was able to see the Soviet Union partly through Sergei's critical eyes. Sergei had survived his 1935 semibanishment from filmmaking and was now producing a major film about the Russian countryside: *Bezhin Meadow*. Paul frequently accompanied him when he filmed on location.

In their free time, they talked a great deal about languages. Paul had come upon an ingenious use of the Basic English that Sergei used to teach English to his Russian students. Paul's idea was to convert the 840 key words of Basic English—words designed to enable rudimentary conversation on a variety of topics—into universal tools for efficient communication in any language. Having learned these 840 basic words, which stem from universal ideas and practices, in a variety of tongues other than English, Paul could already converse in at least a dozen foreign languages.

Sergei was delighted with this concept. He was even more impressed with Paul's venture into the study of Chinese, in the course of which he had selected what he felt were the 100 most essential Chinese written characters. In turn, he educated Paul in the history of the Chinese theater and initiated him into the teachings of the great Russian philologist Nikolai Y. Marr.[17]

From his conversations with Sergei, as well as from his own observations, Paul came to realize that, despite his optimistic statements about making his home in the Soviet Union, he could never live there permanently. It was a great place to visit, but not a place to stay for more than a couple of months at a time.

He perceived that the Soviet social environment under Stalin was rigid and puritanical. The first public purge trial, which took place in Moscow on August 19–24, 1936, cast a grim shadow over Soviet politics and culture alike. However, Paul would never publicly articulate any of his criticisms and misgivings about Stalin's Russia.[18]

Paul and Essie embarking for New York from England in 1933 for the filming of
The Emperor Jones. From the personal collection of Paul Robeson, Jr.

As Brutus Jones, with Fredi Washington. Still from the film *The Emperor Jones*, New York, 1933. *Courtesy of the British Film Institute.*

Frank Wilson glaring at Paul in *The Emperor Jones*. *From the personal collection of Paul Robeson, Jr.*

Breaking rock and
singing "Water Boy"
in *The Emperor Jones*.
*From the personal collection
of Paul Robeson, Jr.*

Still from *The Emperor Jones*. *From the personal collection of Paul
Robeson, Jr.*

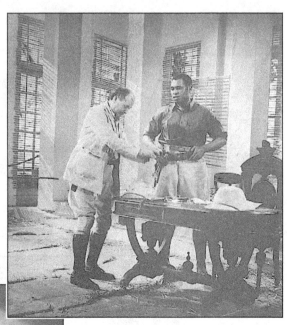

With Dudley Digges
in *The Emperor Jones*.
*From the personal collection
of Paul Robeson, Jr.*

"You has just had an audience wid' de
Emperor Jones," from the film. *From the
personal collection of Paul Robeson, Jr.*

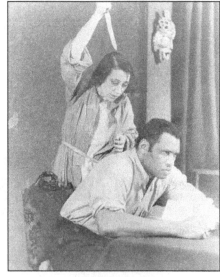

In the 1933 London production
of *All God's Chillun Got Wings*,
with Flora Robson. *From the
personal collection of Paul Robeson, Jr.*

Larry Brown, rehearsing at the piano. Circa 1934. *From the personal collection of Paul Robeson, Jr.*

The Robesons with the group that greeted them in Moscow, December, 1934. Paul is in the center, rear; Essie is second from right, front, holding a large handbag; renowned Soviet film director Sergei Eisenstein is on the extreme right in the rear; Essie's oldest brother, John Goode, is second from left in the front, holding a briefcase; Herbert Marshall, a British student of Eisenstein's and later an associate of Paul's in England, is visible in the rear directly to the left of Paul; Weyland Rudd, a black actor who emigrated to the Soviet Union and was the leader of the small African-American community in Moscow, is fourth from left, just to the right of John Goode; Eisenstein's longtime cameraman, Eduard Tisse, is at the extreme right; Marie Seton's face is visible between Paul and Eisenstein, immediately behind Essie. *From the personal collection of Paul Robeson, Jr.*

John Goode in his twenties. Circa
1914. *From the personal collection of Paul
Robeson, Jr.*

Frank Goode, Essie's second-
oldest brother, in his early
twenties. Circa 1914. *From the
personal collection of Paul Robeson, Jr.*

With Nina Mae McKinney in the film *Sanders of the River*, 1934. *From the personal collection of Paul Robeson, Jr.*

With Jomo Kenyatta, the future leader of the freedom movement in Kenya and independent Kenya's first president, on the set of the film *Sanders of the River*, 1934. *From the personal collection of Paul Robeson, Jr.*

PAUL ROBESON AND HIS RECORDS

RECORDED MUSIC — THE MUSIC YOU SELECT YOURSELF

You can enjoy Robeson's singing whenever you wish from his extensive repertoire of "His Master's Voice" Records. He is, in particular, the acknowledged authority of the Negro Spiritual, of which there are many fine examples in the list overleaf.

EXCLUSIVE TO

"HIS MASTER'S VOICE"

English flyer advertising Paul's recordings. Circa 1930s. *From the personal collection of Paul Robeson, Jr.*

Fifth Ave. PLAYHOUSE

66 FIFTH AVENUE (12th Street)

EXCLUSIVE RE-ISSUE ENGAGEMENT
BEGINNING
MONDAY
FEB. 3

PAUL
ROBESON
in EUGENE O'NEILL'S
amazing story of
Emperor
JONES
with DUDLEY DIGGES

Flyer advertising the film *The Emperor Jones* in the United States pictures Paul and Eugene O'Neill. Circa 1934. *From the personal collection of Paul Robeson, Jr.*

1933 portrait of Paul as Emperor Jones, by Edward Steichen. *Courtesy of the George Eastman House.*

Card advertising a literary luncheon honoring Emma Goldman.
Paul, listed as a participant, appeared. *From the personal collection of
Paul Robeson, Jr.*

Grandma Goode and I, 1935.
Portrait by Carl Van Vechten.
*From the personal collection of Paul
Robeson, Jr.; courtesy of the Estate of
Carl Van Vechten, Joseph Solomon,
Executor.*

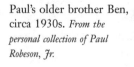

Paul's older brother Ben,
circa 1930s. *From the
personal collection of Paul
Robeson, Jr.*

Relaxing off the set during
the filming of *Show Boat*, 1935.
*From the personal collection of Paul
Robeson, Jr.*

Poster advertising the film
Show Boat, 1936. *From the
personal collection of Paul Robeson, Jr.*

In the play *Stevedore*, London, 1935. *From the personal collection of Paul Robeson, Jr.*

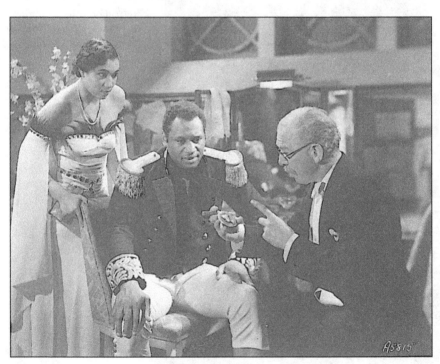

With Elizabeth Welch in the film *Song of Freedom*, London, 1936. *From the personal collection of Paul Robeson, Jr.*

Conferring with Cedric Hardwicke and Anna Lee on the set of the film *King Solomon's Mines*, 1936. *From the personal collection of Paul Robeson, Jr.*

Stills from *King Solomon's Mines*, 1936. *From the personal collection of Paul Robeson, Jr.*

Paul and Essie with Indian students in London, 1936. *From the personal collection of Paul Robeson, Jr.*

On the cover of the *Weekly Illustrated*, London, February 8, 1936. *From the personal collection of Paul Robeson, Jr.*

Larry, Essie, and Paul. London, circa 1938. *From the personal collection of Paul Robeson, Jr.*

Marquee announcing Paul's singing at movie theaters between shows, circa 1938. *From the personal collection of Paul Robeson, Jr.*

With John Oliver Golden
and his daughter, Lillie,
in Kislovodsk, USSR.
July 1937. *From the personal
collection of Paul Robeson, Jr.*

At a VOKS (All-Union Society for
Cultural Exchange) reception in
Moscow. May 1937. I am in the front
center; Tamara Khanum, the famous
Uzbek dancer, is on my left; renowned
pianist Emil Gilels, then a teenager, is
at the extreme right; David Oistrakh,
who was to become one of the world's
greatest violinists, is fourth from right.
From the personal collection of Paul Robeson, Jr.

Photograph of me (front,
second from right) with my
schoolmates in the equivalent
of fifth grade in Moscow's
Model School #25, located
on Pimenovsky Pereulok off
Gorky Street. Circa 1937.
*From the personal collection of Paul
Robeson, Jr.*

Paul with Princess Kouka and two unidentified friends in Marseilles, France, prior to embarking by ship to Egypt to film *Jericho* on location near Cairo in 1937. *From the personal collection of Paul Robeson, Jr.*

With an Egyptian soldier during the filming of *Jericho*. *From the personal collection of Paul Robeson, Jr.*

With *Jericho* costar Henry Wilcoxon (at right) and supporting actor Wallace Ford (at left) near Cairo against the background of the pyramids. *From the personal collection of Paul Robeson, Jr.*

Unjustly condemned to death by court martial, Jericho has executed a daring escape. *From the personal collection of Paul Robeson, Jr.*

Jackson talks his way past his pursuers by pretending to speak French. ("Moi?—Soldat—Anatole France.") *From the personal collection of Paul Robeson, Jr.*

With Princess Kouka and Wallace Ford. Jericho escapes to North Africa with a white sidekick and makes a new life for himself. *From the personal collection of Paul Robeson, Jr.*

264

Still from the film *Big Fella*, 1937. Larry is seated to Paul's left; Essie is standing to his right. *From the personal collection of Paul Robeson, Jr.*

Performing in *Plant in the Sun*, produced by the Unity Theatre Group, London, 1938. Paul is standing in the center. *From the personal collection of Paul Robeson, Jr.*

At a half-barricaded Madrid street, 1938. Paul is in the center at the edge of the barricade; Captain Fernando Castillo, Paul and Essie's escort, is at the right. Note the rifle apertures in the barricade. *From the personal collection of Paul Robeson, Jr.; photograph by Eslanda Robeson.*

With Charlotte Haldane (*right*) and Fernando (*left*) in the streets of Madrid, 1938. *From the personal collection of Paul Robeson, Jr.; photograph by Eslanda Robeson.*

Paul and Fernando at
a Madrid elementary
school, 1938. *From the
personal collection of Paul
Robeson, Jr.; photograph by
Eslanda Robeson.*

Paul (*center*) joins two African-American members of the Abraham Lincoln
Battalion, which consisted of American volunteers fighting in the Interna-
tional Brigade of the Spanish Republican Army. *From the personal collection of
Paul Robeson, Jr.; photograph by Eslanda Robeson.*

At a press conference in Paris soon after returning from Republican Spain. After the press conference, Paul spoke and sang at a huge Paris rally in support of the Republican cause. *From the personal collection of Paul Robeson, Jr.*

Our house (*right*) at 2 St. Albans Villas, Highgate, London. Circa 1938. *From the personal collection of Paul Robeson, Jr.; photograph by Eslanda Robeson.*

Paul and Essie, 1938.
*From the personal collection
of Paul Robeson, Jr.*

At the Soviet children's camp in Folkstone, England, 1938. *From the
personal collection of Paul Robeson, Jr.; photograph by Eslanda Robeson.*

With Max Yergan, London, 1938. *From the personal collection of Paul Robeson, Jr.; photograph by Eslanda Robeson.*

Essie at ease during her August 1938 visit to New York. *From the personal collection of Paul Robeson, Jr.*

In the 1939 U.S. production of the play *The Emperor Jones*. ("You ain't 'sinuatin' I'se a liar is you?") *From the personal collection of Paul Robeson, Jr.*

As a miner in the 1939 film *Proud Valley*. Most of the film was shot on location in the Rhondda Valley of South Wales with local residents playing the majority of the roles. *Courtesy of the British Film Institute.*

Still from the 1939 film *Proud Valley*. Paul singing the Negro spiritual "Deep River" with a choir of miners at the annual Eisteddfodd (a traditional Welsh cultural festival). *From the personal collection of Paul Robeson, Jr.*

With Rachel Thomas, a local Welsh housewife, in the 1939 film *Proud Valley*. *Courtesy of the British Film Institute.*

Returning home on board the USS *Washington*, October 1939. *From the personal collection of Paul Robeson, Jr.*

Freda Diamond and her husband, Alfred Baruch, posing with me in 1939. *From the personal collection of Paul Robeson, Jr.; photograph by Eslanda Robeson.*

Paul (*third from right*) with his brother Ben (*third from left*) and Ben's family (*from the right:* second-oldest daughter Vivian; oldest daughter Marian; youngest daughter Benjamina; wife, Frances; daughter Marian's future husband Bruce Liggins). Circa 1939.
Courtesy of Dr. Gregory Robeson Smith.

Singing with Larry in the well of Harlem's Mother A.M.E. Zion Church. Paul's brother Ben was the pastor. Circa 1939. *Photograph by Morgan Smith; courtesy of the New York Public Library, Schomburg Center for Research in Black Culture.*

V
TO BE A
PROPHET

(1936–1939)

(*Above*) With Princess Kouka of the Sudan in a still from the film *Jericho*. London, 1937. *From the personal collection of Paul Robeson, Jr.*

(*Below*) Singing to Republican troops of the International Brigade during the Spanish Civil War, 1938. The location is a staging area in the Casa Del Campo suburb of Madrid, just behind the front line. *From the personal collection of Paul Robeson, Jr.; photograph by Eslanda Robeson.*

15

RUSSIA'S SUN; STALIN'S SHADOW

(1936–1937)

If Paul was ever seriously concerned about his artistic career in the Soviet Union, he need not have worried. The twelve-concert tour of four major cities (Moscow, Leningrad, Kiev, and Odessa) began in October 1936. In order to align the protest aspect of the traditional religious spirituals with the Soviet emphasis on class struggle, he added a new feature: songs from a newly published volume, *Negro Songs of Protest*. Russian audiences responded positively not only to his singing but also to the image he projected—his size, his blackness, his natural ease and dignity, his fluent command of Russian, his erudition, and his knowledge of classic Russian music, prose, and poetry. Add to this his class consciousness and love of the world's folk music, and he appeared to epitomize the ideal *Soviet* artist.[1]

Sergei Eisenstein wrote in the Soviet press that the concerts had a tremendous impact. He mentioned the "remarkable treasure of Negro folk songs Paul Robeson has brought us." He praised Paul as a cultured and educated musician, and pointed out the refreshing "freedom from concert-stage formality" inherent in his singing style. Eisenstein ended with an appeal that the lyrics of the spirituals be published in Russian translation in Paul's concert programs in order to acquaint the audience with the meaning of the words. And in a subtle reference to the cultural censors who were obstructing such a move because of the religious meaning of the lyrics, Eisenstein commented that "the Bible from the lips of the Negro population is an unusual Bible, . . . ; our concert-goers should be able to evaluate the full power of the new class content in the folk tradition of Negro song." Paul addressed this problem on his own by introducing from the stage the meaning of his spirituals in Russian, stressing the very points Eisenstein had raised in his article.[2]

The American press reported the tour widely, with *Life* magazine featuring a story titled "Robeson in Moscow" and Harlem's *New York Amsterdam News* stressing that his songs of Negro origin had found "a sympathetic audience" in the Soviet Union. Both publications made much of the fact that my father was enrolling me in school in Moscow. *Life* commented: "Slav admiration so touched Robeson that . . . he announced he would send his son Paul Jr. . . . to Soviet schools." According to the *Amsterdam News* story, "The nine-year-old son of Paul Robeson will not grow up in the prejudiced atmosphere of America, . . . [Robeson] announced this week, as he told Russian newspaper reporters of his intention to enroll the lad in a Russian school."[3]

Although I didn't speak a word of Russian, my parents enrolled me in the equivalent of an American fifth-grade class in a "model school" a little over a month after the fall term had begun. Despite its officially public status (all schools in the Soviet Union were public by law), this school was the equivalent of the most exclusive private school in the United States (Stalin's daughter and Foreign Minister Molotov's son attended it along with the children of other high Soviet officials). My classmates went out of their way to be helpful and accepting, and within a month, with an ear for language and after-school tutoring in Russian, I was in every way included as one of the group. Russians of all ages and in all walks of life were friendly to me in a natural and spontaneous fashion.

When Paul and Essie returned from the month-long tour, they were jubilant. All of Paul's concerts had been broadcast live over national radio, as was the custom in the Soviet Union, and he had reached an audience of many millions across the entire nation. Paul asked me endless questions about my experiences, and seemed delighted that I had adjusted to life in Moscow far more quickly than he had expected. I had no clue of my parents' rising concern about the political storm ahead.

When Paul and Essie headed back to London four days later, I thought nothing of it when Uncle John accompanied them, carrying just one suitcase, ostensibly for a short vacation before returning to his job. In fact, Uncle John had no intention of coming back. He had sensed the coming of Stalin's Great Terror of 1937, and had convinced Paul and Essie to get him out of the Soviet Union before it was too late. As a Western foreigner in Moscow, he felt he would be a prime target during a spy scare, so he deliberately left most of his belongings behind so as not to raise suspicion.

Uncle Frank, who lived in the nearby city of Gorky, which was closed to foreigners, decided to stay and take his chances as a Soviet citizen. Fortunately, he survived the successive waves of Soviet internal repression unscathed.

Uncle John's situation was not Paul's only security concern. Earlier, he had met with Eugene Dennis, a top leader of the U.S. Communist Party, who had spent a good deal of time in the Soviet Union and was familiar with its top leadership. Dennis was worried. He urged Paul to publicize my school attendance in the Soviet Union vigorously, explaining that this would greatly reduce the possibility that I would be held hostage—a practice that was then fairly common where foreign communists were concerned. Paul took the warning seriously enough to begin talking constantly in public about my experiences in the Soviet Union.[4]

Eager to make one more film on an African theme, which this time would be entirely free of the negative features of his previous roles, Paul relied once more on Essie to negotiate a contract for him with Capitol Film Corporation to star in what was arguably to be his best film—*Jericho*. Paul would play the part of Jericho Jackson, an African-American soldier in World War I. While rescuing dozens of men trapped when a U.S. troop ship is torpedoed off the coast of Algeria, Jackson accidentally kills an interfering sergeant and is unfairly sentenced to death. He escapes and ultimately becomes the leader of a desert tribe. Nowhere was there a great white father or a black tragic victim—just a triumphant black hero. In a landmark departure from the norm, the African-American soldier was to be portrayed as a brave, resourceful, self-sacrificing, honest, intelligent, and independent human being rather than as a cowardly incompetent. Paul also thought the script had some wonderful nonstereotypical humor.[5]

Capitol sent a film crew to the Sahara to film the background shots and convinced the beautiful daughter of a Sudanese sheik to play the female lead. Discovered by producer Walter Futter and director Thornton Freeland while they were in the Sudan in search of locations, Princess Kouka successfully resorted to a fast in order to convince her father to let her act in the film.

A letter from Essie to a friend conveyed her buoyant mood:

> We will live in Cairo, and work 5–10 miles out in the desert. Then back to London mid-February to June.
> I am a film actress now!! I had a nice part in the last film [*Big Fella*]—I was the proprietress of a cafe on the [Marseilles] waterfront, & spoke some French & wore false hair a la Pompadour! My screen name is Eslanda Cardozo. Ahem!! I have a part in this next film. I am the wife of a Tuareg chief, and wear lovely Arab clothes. Paul was *very pleased* with my work, and so was the Director.[6]

In contrast to earlier disappointments, this time Paul was able to exert a decisive measure of script control—to the point of causing parts of the film to be rewritten. He changed the ending significantly—from the black hero's tragic death to his triumphal and happy retention of his position as a wise and strong leader. And, in a reversal of traditional roles, the comic foil to the black protagonist's dignity was provided by a white Man Friday (played by Wallace Ford). Perhaps for the first time in his film career, Paul was enjoying himself.

Preparing for his first direct contact with the African continent, Paul eagerly gathered information and impressions. He had even learned a little Arabic and studied Egyptian history. To his delight, he found that he was well known and universally welcome in Cairo because the film *Show Boat* had played there. Since Egypt was then under indirect colonial rule, enjoying autonomy in all local matters—unlike the rest of Africa—Paul and Essie were struck by the degree to which "coloured folks are the bosses in such an enormously rich country." They were also fascinated by the fact that the color spectrum, as well as the accompanying stratification into a light-skinned aristocracy and dark-skinned working and poor classes, was similar to that among African-Americans.[7]

One day, Paul's costar, Henry Wilcoxon, an amateur archeologist, hired an Egyptian guide to show them the Temple of Gizeh, the famous pyramid in the desert just outside Cairo. It had already been a glorious day when they found themselves in the inner tomb situated in the center of the pyramid. In the midst of their conversation, Wilcoxon abruptly fell silent as Paul's rich speaking voice echoed through the chamber. Paul hummed a triad of notes. A moment later he stepped to the center point of the chamber and sang, in the original German, the aria "O Isis and Osiris" from Mozart's folk opera *The Magic Flute*.

The stones of the chamber vibrated sympathetically to create the equivalent of an immense high-fidelity speaker, producing a pure sound of overwhelming beauty and strength that held them under its spell. Too overcome to speak and bathed in tears, they emerged into the Egyptian sunset and rode back to Cairo in silence. The universality of ancient African culture had reached across millennia through the synthesis of Egyptian engineering, the genius of the most creative German composer, and the interpretive artistry of a great African-American singer.[8]

When *Jericho* was released in the fall of 1937, lukewarm reviews made much of the artificial way in which Paul's songs were used. The more serious criticism leveled at the film was that it was merely an "average" sort of story, rather than a "grand" one. But for Paul it was an immense and satisfying achievement. He had finally made significant progress in his quest to portray an epic (rather than tragic) black hero.

In the past he had won praise for playing heroic or sympathetic roles, but had drawn harsh criticism for portraying negative characters even though they are an integral part of real life. In an interview with a film magazine he complained that this created "a fantastic situation" for an artist, because it curtailed his ability to interpret the full range of human character. "But," he added, "it's one of those things you can't fight against, and a few years ago I decided I would devote myself in every way I could to the Negroes. Today I am more than resigned to losing my individual status as an artist; I am happy and proud to be of some little use to my people." Although roles like those in *Sanders of the River* and *Show Boat* were necessary at the time he did them, they were not to be repeated. "I'm sick and tired of caricatures. . . . I know where I'm going. Each picture progresses toward my ultimate goal. Hollywood wouldn't do anything but *Show Boat* for me, . . . [but it] proved me to be of star value and is responsible for my present role . . . in *Jericho*. I refused a fortune for *Uncle Tom's Cabin* after that, and if I did another *Show Boat* I would deserve any amount of criticism."[9]

These public remarks signaled a fundamental change in his approach to his artistic career. They reflected his decision to use his artistry as a political weapon. It is in this context that he was limiting himself to the portrayal of positive characters only. Unreservedly taking a position expounded by W. E. B. DuBois eleven years earlier, Paul moved decisively toward using the beauty of his art to advance his truth. Instead of using beauty exclusively to give grace, he would enlist beauty in the service of right.[10]

During the filming of *Jericho*, Paul had concluded that he preferred performing in film, rather than on the concert stage or in the theater, because the cinema had become "the modern medium for entertainment" and he could be "perfectly natural" on camera. Moreover, he was keenly aware that his voice in the cinema was not only better than on recordings but also better than "in real life." Even though the English lagged behind America in cinematic technology and the production of grand spectacles, why not "concentrate upon things which Hollywood cannot do," he remarked.[11]

But the reality proved problematic. A few months after returning to London from Egypt and surveying his prospects in British commercial film and theater, Paul decided to abandon both those ambitions and renounced them both, at least temporarily. Asserting that they would not allow him to "portray the life" or to "express the living interests, hopes and aspirations" of his people, he announced his intention to start anew because "personal success is not enough." And he acted upon this intention by helping to found the Unity Theatre, a workers' theater sponsored and built by the British trade union movement as a working-class cultural institution in the St. Pancras district of northwest London. By October 1937, Paul had agreed to play without fee in a production staged by the new theater. "I have no room for the Uncle Tom's Cabin type of Negro play," he said; "it must be a play of struggle."[12]

When Paul reached this watershed, he was ready to declare his political positions. In America, he backed President Franklin D.

Roosevelt's New Deal against the conservative opposition. In 1937, when Roosevelt attempted to create a more liberal Supreme Court, which would have overturned the anti-Reconstruction rulings underlying the viciously racist political system of the South, the conservative backlash unleashed a surge of antiblack violence in the South and murderous assaults on the industrial union movement in the North. On Memorial Day in Chicago, police killed ten people and wounded thirty when they fired into a peaceful crowd of hundreds of steelworkers who were picketing with their families.[13]

In the rest of the world, Hitler's Nazis had begun their military aggression by marching unopposed into the Rhineland. Mussolini's fascist Italy was committing atrocities in its attempt to conquer Ethiopia, while fascist Japan was ravaging China with a murderous invasion that was slaughtering tens of thousands of civilians. In Spain, Francisco Franco, a rebel fascist general, was being aided openly by Hitler and Mussolini in his civil war against the democratically elected Republican government, which had been abandoned by England, France, and the United States. Only the Soviet Union supported the Spanish Republic and was calling for a worldwide antifascist "United Front."

Freedom movements in the European colonies of Africa and Asia faced fierce repression, with many top leaders in prison or in exile. The eloquent voices of Gandhi and Nehru in India, as well the compelling appeals of freedom movement leaders from the length and breadth of the African continent, were eliciting ever greater international support as the Soviet Union threw its considerable weight behind the anticolonialist cause.

It was in this environment that Paul made his irrevocable decision to become overtly political and to redirect his professional film and theater careers. For him, the issues of race, poverty (class), and war were inseparably linked, and he became an ally of the movement that he felt was most effective and consistent in its actions on these issues: the communist-led left.

In addition, the basic tenets of Marx's philosophy—control of the economy by the workforce rather than by the employers; production for need and use rather than for maximum profit; popular (direct) parliamentary democracy instead of liberal (indirect) republican democracy—attracted Paul.

By 1937, Paul believed strongly that the cause of African-American freedom could achieve significant advances only in the context of a broader struggle for democracy and only in times of severe national crises that aligned the interests of a large proportion of white Americans with the civil rights priorities of African-Americans. He dismissed out of hand the idea that a majority of whites would ever change their behavior as a result of appeals to their conscience, or give up their unfairly appropriated racial privileges unless forced to do so. Racism, he believed, was so deeply entrenched in white America that only structural systemic change, combined with federal compulsion on a vast scale, could end U.S. segregation and discrimination. Paul also understood that the colonial peoples of the world could not become free unless they forced their oppressors to grant freedom. In a July 1937 interview, he summed up his attitude succinctly:

> Events in Abyssinia, Spain and China have led me beyond the racial problem to the world problem of which it is a part—the problem of defending democracy against the onslaught of Fascism. Democracy should be widening, but instead a drive is being made to subjugate not only my group but all oppressed groups throughout the world.

The *New York Herald-Tribune* of January 12, 1936, had reported his comment that "The African states will be free some day. It may come about through partial withdrawal of European power, or there may be a sudden overturn." And the May 10, 1936, issue of New York's *Sunday Worker* quoted Paul's utter lack of faith in the American system on matters of race: "If other young Negroes got the chance, they'd outstrip me a thousand times. But how can they with this damned system of discrimination plugging up every hole of opportunity? And then after they get it, they can't get any recognition for what they really achieve."[14]

Paul read extensively, delving further into cultures and languages in the context of political philosophies and world geopolitics. He read the works of Marx and Engels in German, and those of Lenin and Stalin in Russian. He held discussions with leaders of the British Labour Party (among them Stafford Cripps and Clement Attlee) and the British Communist Party (Harry Pollitt, for example). Ivan Maisky, the sociable and charming Soviet ambassador to London who was personally acquainted with the top Soviet leaders, including Stalin, provided him with accurate interpretations of Soviet domestic and foreign policies. C. L. R. James offered a critical but surprisingly objective view of the Soviet Union from his anti-Stalinist perspective.

Emerging from this period of reflection and study, Paul began to appear frequently and consistently at meetings and rallies supporting anticolonialist and antifascist causes. He became especially active in aiding the fight of Republican Spain against General Franco's fascist rebellion. In April, he sang a benefit concert at the Victoria Palace to aid the women and children of Republican Spain. In May, he gave $1,500 to the U.S.-based International Committee on African Affairs, which was soon renamed the Council on African Affairs, with Paul as its chairman. (For many years, it would serve as the main American organization dedicated to freeing Africa from colonialism.)[15]

A few days later, Paul returned to the Soviet Union with Essie for four months in Kislovodsk, a favorite summer resort. He relished this picturesque old North Caucasus town situated between the Black Sea and the Caspian Sea at the foothills of the Caucasus Mountains. It was a crossroads for Russians, Cossacks, Ukrainians, and Caucasus peoples, and served as a vacation mecca for the elite of all the Soviet Republics.

Without my having to ask, he insisted that I stay with him and Essie. Pleasantly surprised at my broad command of Russian and my familiarity with Soviet culture, he spent a lot of time with me, taking me along on many of his excursions and talking to me in Russian almost as much as in English. I was amazed at how popular he had become among ordinary Russians; apparently most of them had heard his records or his radio broadcasts. They constantly greeted him on the street with the patronymic appellation reserved for the most respected public figures—"Pavel Vasil'evich" ("Paul, son of William")—and in public places, such as parks, friendly crowds would quickly surround us. People's wonderment about Paul's facility in Russian was piqued even further by my fluency, as well as by my feel for the vernacular. My father seemed to be quite proud of me, although, as was his custom, he rarely praised me directly.

One day he watched me playing chess with a boy my own age—something that virtually all Russian kids did from early childhood. I had learned the game quickly and played often, becoming pretty good in the ten- to twelve-year age group. My father was a great checkers player and had always loved the game, but he had never taken up chess. Now he became instantly fascinated by it, and the very next day, to my delight, he sat me down to teach him the moves. Three days later, he had acquired two chess books and was already teaching me some things about the strategy of chess openings.

Exceedingly patient and considerate, he was probably repeating with me a part of his relationship with his own father that he deeply cherished.

In public, he was typically accommodating to whatever company he was in, manifesting grace, humor, command, quietness, empathy, cordiality, severity, detachment, playfulness, dignity, anger, and serenity in natural, comfortable, and appropriate ways. He would generally go out of his way to please others, pretending to be comfortable even if he wasn't. To the public, he was wondrously accessible. Yet in private—among close friends and family—one would usually have to accommodate him in order to elicit the same positive behavior.

When asked, Paul expressed an emphatically positive attitude toward everything Soviet. He let it be known, once again, that he hoped to make films in Russian that were based on the plays *Othello* and *Stevedore*, and revealed that he had recently refused a Hollywood offer to play a part in the pro-slavery film spectacular *Gone With the Wind*. He hailed the members of the Soviet polar expedition who had just conquered the North Pole, adding that he was acquainted with the Negro explorer Matthew Henson who had accompanied Admiral Peary on his 1909 polar expedition and had been the first to reach the pole.[16]

But after a short while, Paul pressed me to tell him about "everything" I had been experiencing, and I had quite a bit to tell, even though it was only through the eyes of a ten-year-old. His invariably casual manner enabled him to elicit a great deal of information without alarming me.

My schoolmates all came from sophisticated political families with a high level of education, so they all read widely, including the verbatim records of the purge trials printed in the daily papers. Moreover, a lot of information filtered down to them from their parents' guarded conversations and the many rumors making the rounds of Moscow political circles. My best friend, Misha, who was from a middle-level diplomatic and military family with connections to the highest Soviet echelons of power, knew children who had contact with the families of leading purge victims. Occasionally, he shared his information and anxieties with me because I was good at keeping secrets. Through this, combined with my own readings and observations, I gave my father some fragmentary insights into the unfolding Soviet tragedy.

Stalin's "Great Purge" of 1937 had reached a peak by that time. The first purge in the summer of 1936 had been of prominent former "opposition" leaders. Consequently, though even the members of Stalin's own faction hadn't really believed the frame-up charges of espionage against their old intraparty adversaries, they weren't willing to risk their political standing with Stalin by insisting on fair trials. Besides, they felt safe because they were Stalin's own people.

Even when the defendants in the first trial were convicted without any credible evidence except their own confessions, and were then shot immediately without any right of appeal, most loyal Stalinists were not worried. After all, they reasoned, there had been no widespread application of the death penalty, which had been formally legalized in 1934 after Kirov's assassination. Throughout 1936, despite the fierce antisubversive campaign following the 1936 trial, the total number of executions was 1,116—not an abnormal number in those days for a population of 159 million. There had been years during Paul's lifetime when the number of African-Americans killed by white mobs exceeded this number—for example, during the "Red Summer" of 1919.[17]

The second purge trial was quite different. Held on January 23–30, 1937, and titled "The Case of the Anti-Soviet Trotskyite Centre," it framed relatively minor opposition figures on charges of espionage on behalf of Nazi Germany in order to sell the idea that the *current* leadership of the party and government had been infiltrated by spies and saboteurs. "Enemies of the People" were said to be hiding everywhere in places of high authority, which meant that loyal Stalinists were the most vulnerable targets. They felt utterly helpless, and all they could do was quietly try to save themselves. The consequences also differed dramatically. In 1989, Soviet historian Roy Medvedev estimated that the number of *official* executions in 1937 reached 353,680.[18]

My classmates mirrored the fear expressed by their parents and loyally repeated the official line: "These are difficult times in which our country is under threat, and innocent people have to be sacrificed in destroying our internal enemies." No one I knew questioned this refrain, including those who lost innocent family members. One classmate lost his father, for whom the secret police came in the middle of the night. My friend Misha's favorite uncle, a colonel-general in the Red Army and a Civil War hero, simply vanished, later to be denounced as an "enemy of the people." Misha's family was lucky to survive when they insisted on his innocence.

There were other things, too, of which I had become aware. Misha wouldn't speak indoors about anything connected with the purge—he would insist on going outdoors because of his fear of eavesdropping devices. Public buildings, including sports arenas and stadiums, had concealed doors to holding chambers where the secret police could detain people off the street. And occasionally there would be a fallout of ash from the atmosphere, which Misha told me came from the crematoria in the cellars of prisons where the firing squads were working overtime. By an ironic coincidence, this human ash was drifting down around Misha and me while we were watching the triumphant parade in honor of the returning heroes of the successful Soviet North Pole expedition.

On June 11, 1937, all Soviet newspapers carried the sensational announcement that Mikhail Tukhachevsky, the Soviet Union's top military figure, along with seven other top generals, had been arrested on the charge of spying for Nazi Germany, secretly tried, and hastily executed. None of my friends or acquaintances believed the charge, but, on the other hand, none of them had heard of anyone who had dared raise a question. This event, more than any other, shocked the nation into an awareness that what was later to be called the "Great Terror" had begun.

My father warned me not to question what was happening and to accept things as they were. When I asked him whether the executions were justified, he replied that, as foreigners, it was not for us to judge—only the Russians themselves could decide. This was all he was willing to say about the subject.

One day we went to visit filmmaker Sergei Eisenstein at his ranch-style country house where he had his own makeshift studio and was working on his film ideas. A short, stocky, fine-featured man, he was a striking figure with his large bald-pated head surrounded by a shock of hair, his almost perpetual smile, and his gently questioning look. Simultaneously erudite and gracefully cosmopolitan in his manner, he contrasted sharply with most of his Soviet colleagues. Although he was under intense political pressure at that time—production of his current film about the controversial issue of collectivization in the countryside, *Bezhin Meadow*, had recently been suspended, and he had been denounced for "bourgeois-influenced formalism"—he seemed outwardly at ease and even joked that in his "semiretirement" he couldn't contribute much help to Paul's efforts to make Soviet films. Paul laughed, and the conversation moved on.

After a while, some of Eisenstein's associates, including several young actors, came in from a film shoot on the grounds, and I went off with them because my father made it clear that he wanted to talk privately with Eisenstein. It turned out that they had been shooting some scenes from a revision of the recently banned film *Bezhin Meadow*, which Eisenstein had renamed *Pavel Morozov* to provide at least some cover for what could easily be viewed as insubordination.

Later on during the visit, I caught a glimpse of Dad and Eisenstein walking the grounds—Dad with his hands characteristically clasped behind his back and listening intently, Eisenstein bobbing his head and waving his hands. I was sure that they were talking about the purge and its implications—many of Eisentein's friends and acquaintances in the higher echelons of the party had vanished, and the fields of film, theater, and music were reeling from devastating censorship.[19]

At the end of June, the Spanish Civil War reached a critical stage as Franco's fascist army intensified its efforts to overthrow the democratically elected Republican government. Nazi Germany and fascist Italy sent massive arms aid and thousands of regular army and air force personnel to bolster Franco. Thousands of left-wing volunteers from all over Europe, along with many Americans and Canadians, answered the Spanish Republic's call for help and were supported by arms shipments, military advisers, and air force pilots from the Soviet Union. The governments of England, France, and the United States maintained a hypocritical neutrality, embargoing arms shipments and volunteers to both sides.

Paul went to a Moscow studio and recorded a message to be broadcast by radio to a giant rally in support of Republican Spain, which was to be held at London's Royal Albert Hall on June 24. But when the Nazis threatened to jam the broadcast, and the Albert Hall management refused to receive it from Moscow, he decided to fly to London to appear at the rally in person. In an extensive interview with a British correspondent from the *Manchester Guardian*, he said that his recorded speech and songs would be broadcast worldwide. Then, having interrupted the family vacation in the Caucasus, he was going to London to sing in person at Albert Hall. He concluded with a fairly extended discourse on his decision to educate me in the Soviet Union so that I could escape American racism.

The Albert Hall appearance on June 24, 1937, was historic. The combined effect of his personal appearance and his broadcast heard by millions worldwide gave an enormous boost to the beleaguered Spanish Republic. A flood of money poured onto the collection table on the stage from the audience of over six thousand. In less than twenty minutes, $8,000 was collected, including $5 from the Unemployed Art Center in South Wales, $2.50 a month from Edmonton tramwaymen, $50 from an American, $325 from the Artists International, $125 from a group of Russians, $25 from a Dutchman, $5 from a Pole, $25 from an Italian "without the permission of Mussolini," $1.25 from a Spanish refugee, $5 from reporters at the press table, and a matchbox containing $2.54 in change—all the donor had. (These amounts meant far more than the figures make it appear, since a dollar then was worth something like 30 or more of today's dollars.)

Paul's speech went beyond a commitment to defend the Spanish Republic against the onslaught of fascism. In words that are often quoted, he defined his understanding of the artist's responsibility to humanity:

The challenge must be taken up. Fascism fights to destroy the culture which society has created; created through pain and suffering, through desperate toil, but with unconquerable will and lofty vision. Progressive and democratic mankind fight not alone to save this cultural heritage accumulated through the ages, but also fight today to prevent a war of unimaginable atrocity from engulfing the world.

The artist must elect to fight for freedom or slavery. I have made my choice. I had no alternative. The history of the capitalist era is characterized by the degradation of my people: despoiled of their lands, their culture destroyed, they are in every country save one [the Soviet Union] denied equal protection of the law, and deprived of their rightful place in respect of their fellows.

Not through blind faith or coercion, but conscious of my course, I take my place with you. I stand with you in unalterable support of the Government of Spain, duly and regularly chosen by its lawful sons and daughters.

Then, as Paul sang his signature song, "Ol' Man River," he changed the lyrics at the end: "I gets weary and sick of tryin'; I'm tired of livin' and scared of dyin'" became "I keeps laughin' instead of cryin'; I must keep fightin' until I'm dyin'."[20] The impact on the audience was electric. Here was the prophet in full cry.

Bright and culturally sophisticated people fueled Paul's passion with information and insight. Ignaty Kazakov, a leading Soviet physician, stood out among these friends. A gregarious but gentle man who was full of laughter, he taught me how to play billiards. He was also an avid reader and enjoyed having long talks with Paul about Shakespeare and ancient Greek philosophy.

John Oliver Golden, the dean of the African-American expatriates to the Soviet Union, contributed to Paul's growing sense of clarity. He was an agriculturist who had made his first trip to Russia in 1925 and had returned permanently in 1927. Paul and Golden, a powerfully built brown-skinned man of medium height with a smooth round face and a quiet demeanor, almost always saw each other privately, except for a couple of times when Paul took me along to meet the Golden family. Golden informed Paul about how the Soviet system worked for the darker-skinned peoples of Russia, and Paul updated Golden on African-American affairs. Years later he told me that when I wasn't around, they also talked about the purge (Golden guessed that there would be another one the next year) and how best to protect me and Grandma in Moscow, as well as Uncle Frank in Gorky. Regarding Frank, who, Golden said, was absolutely right to stay out of Moscow, the advice was that only Essie, who was basically nonpolitical, should go to see him, since Paul had too many currently "controversial" friends such as Eisenstein.[21]

In August 1937, not long before the end of our summer vacation in Kislovodsk, Paul had noticed that Kazakov had left suddenly for Moscow without saying goodbye. So when Paul and Essie stopped in Moscow for a few days on their way home to London, Paul asked his close friend, Sergei Eisenstein, how to inquire privately about Kazakov. Sergei informed Paul of a Moscow rumor that Kazakov had been arrested, and advised him to leave the entire subject of the purges alone.

Deciding to take a risk in an attempt to help Kazakov, Paul made a formal request to see him through official channels. To his surprise, Kazakov called him, and Paul invited him to lunch at the Hotel Metropole. On his arrival, Paul found Kazakov seated between two "translators." Their appearance and body language, even more than their fractured English, proclaimed their identity as plainclothes police. Without missing a beat, Paul, ignoring the two escorts, greeted Kazakov in Russian, sat down, and picked up their last conversation where they had left off. For about two hours they chatted in Russian over a leisurely lunch. The escorts remained silent and stonefaced, but busily gorged themselves. After all, it was at Robeson's expense.

Kazakov and Paul pulled off this grim charade as if it were a normal meeting and conversation between old friends. Only their eyes conveyed messages to each other that came from an emotional realm far different than their gregarious demeanors. Finally, Kazakov, without being prompted by his accompanying "translators," looked at his watch, and told Paul that it was time for him to go back to work in his "medical institute." They rose, and as they parted in the traditional Russian style—with a bear hug and a kiss on both cheeks—Kazakov whispered in Paul's ear: "Spasibo" (thank you).

Casting a backward glance as he left the hotel dining room, Paul caught a glimpse of his friend's broad shoulders pathetically slumped. He realized then that Kazakov was deprived of hope.[22]

Paul returned to London for a whirlwind of political activity. Essie, partly because of her Cardozo Jewish ancestry on her mother's side, became in her own way strongly committed to the fight against fascism. Paul found her an indispensable aide, sometime speechwriter, political secretary, and occasional spokesperson. He sang and spoke at benefits to support Chinese resistance to the ruthless Japanese war of occupation, and continued his nonstop efforts on behalf of Republican Spain. His speeches linked the worldwide colonial freedom struggles to the antifascist resistance, and the songs included favorites of the Chinese and Spanish Republican freedom fighters. He also appeared at several events celebrating the twentieth anniversary of the founding of the Soviet Union.

He became engrossed in the trade union–based Unity Theatre Group, performing the lead role in a production of *Plant in the Sun*. This play, written by American playwright Ben Bengal and directed by Herbert Marshall, an Englishman who had met Paul in Moscow in 1934, told the story of a sit-down strike in an American city. The realistic characters so attracted Paul that he turned down a lucrative offer to star in a major Basil Dean production of *The Sun Never Sets* at the Drury Lane Theatre. Sir Stafford Cripps, a leading Labour Party politician, wrote Paul that "it is a splendid gesture of solidarity with the workers, and I know how deeply it will be appreciated throughout the country."[23]

Paul's popularity in the United States remained high even though he skipped his annual concert tour in 1936 and 1937. The mass sales of his recordings continued as before; his films drew well, especially in black communities, and his status as a leading black role model remained undiminished.[24] Five of Paul's films—*Show Boat, Song of Freedom, King Solomon's Mines, Big Fella*, and *Jericho*—were playing worldwide during 1937, attracting moderate to large audiences despite mixed reviews. His recordings, including the songs from his films, were selling in large numbers throughout the international market, and his radio broadcasts reached huge audiences, eliciting unprecedented responses from admirers.

His political priorities were becoming increasingly urgent. The position of Republican Spain became more desperate as the massive military aid to Franco's fascist army from Hitler and Mussolini was not matched by the Soviet Union. England, France, and the United States not only refused to help the Republicans but maintained an embargo against aid to them. Fascism was on the rise in France, and pro-fascist sentiment had already made significant inroads in England and the United States.

Paul realized that there would be no letup of the purge in the Soviet Union. His friend Ivan Maisky, the Soviet ambassador to England, hinted that still a third purge would probably occur in 1938. By the early fall of 1937, worried that war in Europe might trap Grandma and me in the Soviet Union, Paul considered whether it was time to bring us home. In late September, he decided that we would return to London, ostensibly for a brief Christmas visit. I was not told that my Moscow sojourn was over. In October, he made another decision to go to Spain to sing in person for the Republican troops and for the population in government-held territory.

16

SPAIN'S RAMPARTS:
"THE ARTIST MUST ELECT"

(1938)

Underestimating the powerful symbolic impact that Paul's personal appearance in Spain would have worldwide, Essie held to the pragmatic view that it was absurd for him to risk his life in the war zone when he was effective in mobilizing support from afar. Her opposition was bolstered by two unusually attractive opportunities. A British publisher, having heard Paul speak at the historic Albert Hall rally in support of Republican Spain, had asked him to write a short book on civilization, Spain, and the Negro. And from New York, Carl Van Vechten had written that, in the progressive cultural atmosphere created by President Roosevelt's New Deal, a Robeson production of Shakespeare's *Othello* "would be a great success" in the winter of 1937–1938.[1] However, once Paul made his decision, he would not budge. Finally, Essie undertook the task of preparing for the trip with characteristic energy.

The Spanish ambassador to London, who was a personal friend, readily provided the necessary documents for them to enter Spanish Republican territory, although getting permission from the U.S. Department of State to validate their passports for travel to Spain became a sticking point. Initially the American consul in London informed Paul that Washington had refused permission for the trip. A week later, after intense lobbying by the Spanish ambassador in Washington, the American consul in London wrote Paul that the State Department had reversed its decision in his case but not in Essie's. It took another two weeks before the consul stamped both of their passports "valid for travel in Spain."[2]

On January 21, 1938, Paul and Essie headed off to Paris, the starting point for their journey to Spain. Essie's diary tells the story:

Monday, January 24 [1938]: A fascinating Captain Castillo is our special escort and guide, along with a beautiful Buick car. We took the coast road to Valencia at dusk in a heavy mist. Our soldier driver (Pepe) was marvellous, tearing along the road, up mountains, around hairpin turns, along the sea, at an average of 55 miles an hour. After a five hour drive, we reached an inn where we had supper and spent a comfortable night. Our Captain's name is Fernando Castillo; he is Andalusian and one of eleven living children, with five brothers at the front. Handsome and charming, he speaks fluent English and has a wonderful sense of humor. Our soldier driver, Pepe, is thirty-five and escaped from a Moroccan prison.

Tuesday, January 25 [1938]: Off at 10 AM for the sea resort town of Benicasim. As we left, we were told that bombs had fallen all around the inn recently, but nothing had been hit. Reached Benicasim, now a hospital base for the front line, at noon in bright sunlight after driving past orange and tangerine groves with trees whose leaves are a rich shining green color. Then palms, red earth, and gleaming white villas on the sea front. The roads were thronged with soldiers, wounded and convalescent. As our car came to a standstill, we saw a young Negro soldier who looked at Paul and stopped dead. He was astonished when we stopped the car and Paul went up and spoke to him. He said he had recognized Paul at once, but could not believe his eyes. Many white English, American and Canadian soldiers immediately surrounded Paul and began talking all at once. All had read about him, many had seen his films, and one Canadian soldier from Toronto had heard him sing in Massey Hall. Several other Negro soldiers from Chicago and other cities soon joined us.[3]

Paul sang at the big meeting place where the cultural programs are carried out and where many could congregate. He had to sing without accompaniment, and the soldiers crowded around, wildly enthusiastic. Then he sang in a hospital where many seriously wounded were lying, right in the central ward. And again in another hospital. All asked for "Ol' Man River."[4]

From Benicasim on to Valencia, a large, prosperous coastal city. Heard that Barcelona was bombed four times today, with great loss of life. The first raid was almost immediately after we left! Lunch at the Victoria Hotel, and then straight inland to Albacete which is the base camp for the front line. This is where the headquarters of the International Brigade is located. On the way we saw evidences of bombing—some houses gutted right through from roof to cellar, roads torn up, trees uprooted. It is strange, but so far we are missing all the air raids; we seem to carry peace and quiet along with us.

Approaching all towns and villages, we are stopped by heavily armed militia who examine the Captain's papers and look well into the car. It is also very difficult to get petrol [gasoline]—we must take our Government order to the local authorities. Our petrol is supplied by the military, but every village and town is governed jointly by civil and military Governors, so that neither can run away with power and authority. We finally arrive at Albacete about ten at night. The town and the hotel are dark, as an alarm has been sounded.

Wednesday, January 26 [1938]: Up early in our so-called Grand Hotel, and off to Tarazona, the training camp for the International Brigade. Saw lots of Negro comrades—from Oklahoma, Baltimore, St. Louis. The officers arranged a meeting in the church into which the entire Brigade crowded. But before they filed in, they passed in review in the square for us. First the commander spoke briefly and was cheered when he told the men they are to go up to the front line tomorrow!!!

Then Charlotte [Haldane, wife of a leading British biologist and secretary of the International Brigade Dependents' Aid Fund] gave a simple and moving speech, first in Spanish, then in English, about the support work being done around the world. She brought personal greetings and gifts of cigarettes. It was a beautiful speech, and the men applauded her vociferously.

Paul sang, the men shouting for the songs they wanted: "Water Boy," "Ol' Man River," "Lonesome Road," "Fatherland." The men stomped and applauded each song, and continued to shout requests. All wanted "Together All"—the Canoe Song from *Sanders of the River.* Altogether it was a huge success, and Paul loved doing it. Afterwards we had twenty minutes with the men—gave unlimited autographs and took messages for their families.

Finally off to Madrid. Approached the city about 8 PM in pitch darkness, and passed a bit of road at a crawl with headlights out. It is a stretch within range of the Fascist artillery and is shelled regularly. Great holes in the road, recently repaired, told the story. No women allowed to enter Madrid now; no children either. All are being evacuated. We could pass only because we had special visas and passes.

Finally tramways and Madrid proper. All is quiet. The Captain says the city has been bombed or shelled daily since 1936, and that the people now take it for granted. There are no sirens or alarms. He said he has stood in the streets of Madrid, opposite the telephone building, and seen the populace bet on which windows would be broken by the raiding planes.

Everywhere one sees holes in the streets and in the sidewalks. We heard the official communique at 11:15 PM on the radio. Valencia was bombed today just after we left: 125 were killed and 500 wounded. The actual front line, where fighting is now in progress in University City, is only a mile and a half away!

Paul sang at the table after supper, quite informally, and the Captain knew all his records—"Snowball," "St. Louis Blues," "Lazybones," etc., and sang them all through with Paul, to the vast enjoyment of all.

Thursday, January 27 [1938]: Madrid—windows of hotels, stores, houses stripped with broad heavy paper to prevent them from shattering during shelling and bombing. There was some firing during the night, and we could hear the guns occasionally. Many outside facades are damaged, and at the Palace of the Premier, where we had breakfast, the windows are sandbagged and barricades are built up with openings left for guns and periscopes. We went up to the observation tower with a panoramic view of the front-line trenches, and through periscopes we saw soldiers walking around behind the trenches.

Suddenly a shell whizzed by and hit a big white building on the right, exploding with a flash and a cloud of dust. Then a shell hit the bridge beyond the North Station. Our guns replied, followed by a bit of machine-gun fire, and all was quiet again. Afterwards we went down to the staff room on the lower floor, where a young lieutenant took up his guitar and played us some Flamenco songs as other soldiers and officers gathered around and sang with him. Paul sang "Encantadora Maria" for them in Spanish, and they loved it.

We drove out toward the section of Madrid where the famous street fighting had occurred early in the war—through barricaded streets, some entirely blocked so there was no entrance and some with a center opening. We had to leave the car long before we reached this area, because we were within sight range of the Fascist guns. Often there was firing while we were there, but the people seemed unconcerned and went on about their business.

Back for lunch at the Premier's Palace, and a press conference for Paul and Charlotte [Haldane]. Then we went shopping for Flamenco records and visited a hospital for the wounded from the Madrid front. All during the afternoon, we heard artillery and machine-gun fire, but by now we are used to it.

We went to the theater, from 6 to 8 PM, to see a traditional play in a beautiful old building packed with an enthusiastic working class audience. Many children, even babies, were there, because the bombing prevents parents from leaving children at home.

Then out into the dark streets and back to the Palace Hotel for a rest. At 10 PM Paul broadcast from the Madrid Central Radio Station and was heard throughout Spain. He sang the last verse of "Fatherland" in Spanish, to the delight of the Spanish people. A Spanish opera singer and a fine Spanish violinist were also on the program, which went very well.[5]

Friday, January 28 [1938]: In the evening, Paul broadcast for the "English Hour," and then again for the "American Hour." He had to sing unaccompanied, because the constant bombing of the building had ruined the piano.

Saturday, January 29 [1938]: Went to the Barracks, where Paul sang and spoke to the soldiers out on the parade ground for more than an hour. The motion picture people filmed him with the troops from every possible angle. He sang "Joshua," "Singin' With a Sword in My Hand," "Ol' Man River," "Fatherland" in Spanish, etc. Then a quick lunch and off from Madrid back to Valencia. It was rather sad saying farewell to Madrid. We have come to love it.

We went across grassy plains for a while, then up the magnificent Castilla Plateau—a great stretch of half-barren, half-green terrain as high up as 3,000 feet in some places. Through Tarancon, a big city which is a base for troops, hospitals and supplies, as well as a junction.

Saw great holes left by bombs, houses in ruins, and the charred remains of a bombed petrol store. Finally, by ordinary road to Valencia, arriving about 10 PM after a six-hour drive. The mood is sad. The officials are haggard from the strain of recent bombings in which many of their friends were killed.

Monday, January 31 [1928]: Interviews and more interviews; then lunch with the Minors and Earl Browder [top leader of U.S. Communist Party] who has just arrived from Toulouse [France]. He is a quiet middle-aged man, very sympathetic and interesting. We had a talk over lunch, and afterwards over coffee in the lounge. Then we set off for the French border.

Fernando, in civilian dress, accompanied us, and a British Lieutenant named Conrad Kaye, armed and in full uniform, was our official escort. We found Kaye most interesting. Fernando had told us that the Spanish people loved him as a Spaniard. He had been working very hard the day before, helping in the rescue of the victims of the bombardment.

As we drove along, he told us the story of Oliver Law, a Negro and a former U.S. Army corporal from Chicago, who had risen through the ranks of the Lincoln Battalion to become Commander. Many officers and men considered him to be the best battalion commander in Spain. He was seriously wounded while leading repeated advances in a battle at Brunete. Kaye himself carried him from the battlefield, but Law was mortally wounded by a sniper's bullet while he lay on a stretcher.[6]

At the town of Figueras, Fernando inquired at army headquarters about his brother, Captain Pablo Castillo, and got directions to his home. We doused the headlights and drove around the city till we found the right house. Fernando ran upstairs, and returned in a few minutes with Pablo, a tall, handsome officer.

We set off for the border, all talking at once. After Pablo joined us, he rolled down the window every time we were stopped by the militia and said simply: "They are with me." The militia saluted smartly and passed us on. Fernando explained that Pablo was the commander of all the militia in this area.

And so we arrive at the border. Fond farewell embraces are exchanged, and we are all regretful of our separation. We hope and believe it is only a temporary parting, and that we will all be together again, soon, in a happy victorious Government Spain.

However, the antifascist coalition in Spain and around the world was rapidly weakening. On March 7, 1936, Hitler's army marched unopposed into the Rhineland, a demilitarized buffer zone between France and Germany. U.S. Secretary of State Cordell Hull did not protest, and FDR went fishing. The French and British protested, but made no military move. On May 1, 1937, FDR signed the 1937

Neutrality Act imposing an arms embargo on both sides in the Spanish Civil War and banning loans to either side. In 1938, U.S. public opinion preferred fascism to communism by 31 percent to 22 percent; 47 percent had "no opinion."

Confronted with the bold military aggression by Nazi Germany, Fascist Italy, and Imperial Japan; preoccupied with the rise of growing pro-fascist movements in France, England, and the United States; disillusioned by the appeasement policies of their own governments; and divided by Stalin's purges in the Soviet Union, the left in Europe and the United States was splintering. In foreboding notes to himself, written immediately after his return from Spain, Paul revealed his disappointment: "We are certainly not doing nearly enough. . . . This is OUR STRUGGLE, and if we allow Republican Spain to suffer needlessly, we will ourselves suffer as deeply." Although he was aware of it, he made no mention, even to himself, of the growing Soviet disengagement from the Spanish Civil War.[7]

Throughout 1938, Paul sang and spoke repeatedly on behalf of the Spanish Republican cause—at a huge Paris rally; at a London meeting of over two thousand; in Scotland at the Glasgow City Hall to raise money for a food ship; in Wales at a national memorial meeting to honor the Welshmen of the International Brigade killed in Spain.[8] However, even though tens of thousands of Soviet citizens were volunteering to fight for the Spanish Republic, Stalin cut off Soviet aid.

The government forces, facing overwhelmingly superior fascist military power and weakened by the division between pro-communists and noncommunists, slowly began to crumble. On April 14, 1938, the fascists reached the Mediterranean coast south of Valencia, cutting Republican Spain in two. In July, the Republican army launched what was to be its last counteroffensive on the Ebro front, but by the end of November, Republican forces were in full retreat and the International Brigades had been withdrawn from Spain. It was clear that fascism had won the first major battle of the Second World War.[9]

Paul watched the grim chain of events with mounting frustration. His friends, Soviet Ambassador Maisky and Spanish Ambassador Azcarate, as well as his own independent analysis of international events, revealed alarming international undercurrents. Hitler's unchecked military aggression in Europe (on March 11, 1938, his troops "annexed"

Austria, and by late May he was threatening Czechoslovakia), combined with the U.S.-backed British and French policy of unabashedly
appeasing Hitler, had caused a fundamental shift in Stalin's foreign
policy. Although Stalin continued active negotiations with England
and France toward the formation of an antifascist coalition, he began
moving toward negotiation with Hitler. The abandonment of Czechoslovakia to Nazi Germany by the Munich pact of September 30,
1938, led to more urgent Soviet–Nazi negotiations.[10]

In February 1938, the strategic Spanish city of Teruel fell to the fascists, and Essie, worried about Uncle Frank's fate if a major European war should break out, made a quick trip to the Soviet Union to
see him. In Moscow, on the way to Gorky to see Frank (as before,
he was fearful of visiting Moscow), she tried to see Dr. Kazakov, our
good friend from Kislovodsk days. She was deeply worried to learn
that he had been one of the first to be arrested in the latest purge.

Uncle Frank was still determined to take his chances in the
Soviet Union; he wanted no part of a return to the United States. So
Essie, now more disturbed than before, returned without him. The
Nazis had confiscated her passport as she traveled by train across
Germany, and she was forced to return via Scandinavia. The Span-
ish stamps, rather than the Soviet ones, had caused the trouble.

Upon Essie's return to London, Paul told her about his decision
not to send me back to Moscow, and she readily agreed. Paul had
prevailed upon Soviet Ambassador Maisky to allow me to be enrolled
in the Soviet school for the children of the Soviet diplomatic corps
in London. It proved to be a smaller version of the school I had
attended in Moscow, so I was happily settled in and had many
friends. But I fully expected to return to Moscow in September, so I
would have to be told eventually. In the meantime, my parents said
nothing about a change of plans.[11]

Paul wanted to enlist William Patterson's help to protect Frank.
The specifics of that endeavor would have to wait until the charges
against Kazakov were made public, since it was Kazakov's friendship
with Paul and Essie that posed the greatest danger to Frank.

On March 2–13, Stalin's third purge trial, billed as "The Case of
the Anti-Soviet Bloc of Rights and Trotskyites," unfolded in Mos-

cow. This time the accused were well-known top leaders of the party and major figures in their professions.[12]

Since I had read the verbatim reports of the previous two purge trials while I was in Moscow, it was natural for me to read the verbatim testimony of this third one. I was stunned when Dr. Ignaty Kazakov's name popped out at me; I *knew* him, and I knew he couldn't possibly be guilty of the crimes he was accused of, which included the poisoning of leading Soviet public figures he had treated. I was thus prompted to read the proceedings carefully, and, even with the limitations of an eleven-year-old, I found them full of inconsistencies, contradictions, and transparent lies.

The proceedings as a whole were too unbelievable to be accepted, especially in the safe and open atmosphere of London. The Soviet diplomatic families were safely removed from the nightmare of the purge, so it was definitely not a topic of conversation at school. The feeling I got was that the less said the better, so I kept my thoughts to myself at school. But at home I was troubled by the total lack of comment on the matter by my parents.

The experience was disturbing but not devastating—I reacted very much like my schoolmates did, and I retained a shred of hope that somehow a reasonable explanation of the trial would be forthcoming. I also decided to wait patiently for my father to provide such reassurance.

The trial was open and was marked by the full confessions of all of the accused. On March 13, eighteen of the twenty-one accused, including Dr. Kazakov, were sentenced to death without the right of appeal and were shot immediately. The other three were sentenced to long prison terms.

One day, I finally worked up the courage to ask my father about Stalin's latest purge. The gist of my question, which had been triggered by an incident in school, was whether something major had gone wrong under Stalin's rule. A schoolmate had been distraught because her family was being called home to Moscow, and she was terrified that her parents might be purged.

Paul clearly didn't want to deal with the subject, but I pressed on, refusing to be put off. At last, he bristled, then dismissed my question peremptorily. I refused to back off and yelled something like "We all *knew* he was innocent, and you never said a word." Without looking at me, he commanded me to keep quiet, his voice a barely audible low rumble. I was about to confront him again, when he suddenly looked up. The look in his eyes—an intense rage mixed with hurt—stopped me cold. I got up and left.

A few days later, I asked him about the purges in a neutral, nonconfrontational way. He responded readily and quietly, as if our previous clash had never occurred. He acknowledged that "terrible" things had been done, and that innocent people had been "sacrificed to punish the guilty." But the Soviet Union felt it was already in a situation that was to them "the equivalent of war." They felt they could not tolerate any kind of dissent. Sometimes, he added, great injustices may be inflicted on the minority when the majority is in the pursuit of a great and just cause.

Meanwhile, practical concerns had overshadowed discussion. Kazakov's execution had left Uncle Frank, who had forfeited his American citizenship to become a Soviet citizen, vulnerable to arrest and even execution: his sister and brother-in-law had been close friends of an executed "spy" and "murderer," and in Stalinist Russia that was more than enough cause for suspicion. So my father felt it was time to carry out his plan of enlisting Patterson's help. This had to be done without any reference to Frank. It was decided that my mother should be the one to write to Patterson. In her letters, she supported the purge to the hilt, and denounced Kazakov. Referring to her "scare" over Kazakov's use of "this marvelous clinic of his" for poisoning, she expressed satisfaction with his punishment.[13]

Paul and Essie were justified in their fears for Uncle Frank. Uncle John's timely departure had saved him from arrest and probable execution. In 1991, author and publisher Adam Hochschild sent me a copy of a 1938 Soviet secret police file he had obtained on a visit to Moscow, in which Arthur Talent, a twenty-five-year-old art student from whom John had rented a room, falsely denounced John as a British spy. Talent had been arrested in January 1938 solely because he had emigrated from the United States with his parents in the 1920s.

Terrified of his interrogators, Talent denounced everyone he could think of, including John, whose other "crime" was that he spoke German. A February 19, 1938, decree ordered the arrest of "John Goode" and the prosecution of a separate case against him on the charge of espionage under "Article 58, Section 6" of the Soviet criminal code—a prosecution that promised almost certain conviction and execution. Despite Talent's desperate cooperation with his interrogators, a May 23, 1938, decree ordered his execution by firing squad; the order was carried out on June 7, 1938. Fortunately for John, he had departed in 1937 and was home in New York.

Twenty years later, on January 17, 1958, the KGB officially closed Talent's case, #477468, with the conclusion that he and all those he had denounced were entirely innocent of all espionage charges made against them. The witnesses who testified for the prosecution had all perjured themselves; the interrogators and investigators had proceeded illegally, and it was recommended that those surviving be prosecuted.

Given the intensely charged political atmosphere, a letter arriving in April 1938 from a friend in New York jarred Paul and Essie. Kurt Shafer, of the American Committee of International Relief Association for Victims of Nazism, was worried. He wrote that he had information regarding my "stay in Russia." Noting that he had heard about my departure from the Soviet Union, he implied that I should not return: "As I was . . . the first to suggest Pauli's education in Russia, I felt some responsibility in this regard. I think differently now on this question, and I am glad that you reconsider [sic] your attitude. I am telling you this strictly privately and confidentially. It is a pity because the idea of bringing Paul up in Russia was originally a good one, but according to reliable information—circumstances have changed." Although Paul had already decided I should not return, the letter from Shafer prompted him to tell me about his decision. Any anxiety he may have had about my response was misplaced.

Essie had decided that we needed to move to new living quarters. She had always wanted a home with a big garden in a quiet neighborhood near a big park. And she had found her dream house. It was a modern, comfortably designed three-story structure with large front and back gardens in the modestly fashionable Highgate section of London at the northeast corner of Hampstead Heath. But, unlike the Buckingham Street apartment, which was ideal for both of my parents, the house was designed primarily for Essie. Paul went along with this priority, at least outwardly, in good spirit. After a decade in the huge apartment at 19 Buckingham Street, right in the center of London, our move to 2 St. Albans Villas, Highgate Road, next to the huge green expanse of the Heath, meant a major adjustment in lifestyle for Paul.

Never much of an outdoors person, he had loved the old apartment, with its huge rooms and high ceilings, located in the center of the city. He could shut himself off in the oversized parlor with its grand piano to rehearse with Larry, to listen to records, or to study. In our new house, with its smaller rooms and vertical structure, he wasn't nearly as comfortable in such pursuits. And since a grand piano couldn't be accommodated, he could only tinker on a small upright. His rehearsals were now held elsewhere.

Yet, compared to previous years, I saw my father much more often. Approaching the age of eleven, I had more in common with him, especially where Russian and chess were concerned. I found some contemporary Russian songs for him—songs that we sang in the Soviet school—and my chess game had become good enough to make it interesting for him to play me. What I remember most about those games is his attitude. He derived far more pleasure from an instructive game than from winning—so much so that he instituted the practice of granting each other a second chance on obvious blunders. To him, it didn't make sense to spoil a good game with a foolish move. And he considerately made enough foolish moves to even out our take-backs.

Although Paul spent less time in the house than he had in the apartment, the house offered him significant positives: Grandma Goode had to live elsewhere, and the house was a great place for entertaining friends and having guests, which Paul loved to do. One day Marian Anderson spent an afternoon. In the course of her visit, she offered high praise of President Roosevelt and his New Deal. She also talked about how enthusiastic her reception had been in South America, and urged Paul to sing there.[14] Max Yergan, visiting from the States, spent several days with us, talking about the United States and world affairs, and especially about Africa. Max was an erudite, handsome, elegant man with a smooth manner, whom Paul found to be especially astute politically. They apparently agreed to form some kind of long-term political partnership.[15]

Perhaps Paul's most interesting visitor was a top leader of the Indian National Congress, Pandit Jawaharlal Nehru, recently released from a British jail. Paul and Essie had met him at an India League reception through one of the many Indians whom they had befriended in London. Nehru was a slightly built man of medium height. Despite his soft voice and quietly gentle manner, he had an arresting presence. Even in repose, he was a commanding figure.

One evening, to Nehru's amazement, Paul recited some classic Hindu poetry in the original Hindi to demonstrate the similarity in rhythm and intonation between Hindu and African-American speech patterns. Then they went on to discuss how Nehru thought India might be governed when independence was won and he was prime minister. That evening marked the beginning of a lasting friendship between the Nehru and Robeson families. When Paul spoke and sang at a subsequent mass meeting welcoming Nehru back to London from a trip to Republican Spain, he said:

> We in Black America and other parts of the world have closely watched the Indian struggle and have been conscious of its importance for us. The struggle for an enlightened and progressive European Democracy and the Colonial struggle for Democratic Freedom are interdependent and inseparable. The emergence of leaders like Nehru give the lie to tales of a backward people, of a decayed culture. We peoples of long oppression must remember [that] we must not be talked out of our heritage. I am certain that under the leadership of men such as Nehru the people of India will undoubtedly remain in the front rank of the progressive human forces of our time.[16]

Early in June, Paul's longtime concert manager, Harold Holt, wrote him a letter complaining about an announcement that he was to sing in support of the labor movement at a large London stadium with tickets priced at threepence (six cents):

> Whilst I have no right, or inclination, to prevent you from helping labour or any other movement that you desire, it is my duty, as your representative, to point out that your value as an artist is bound to be very adversely affected by this sort of thing. In view of the fact that it is your desire to be booked in and around London at your usual fee, you must, of course, realise that the possibility of booking you under these conditions is becoming increasingly difficult.

Paul's response was to sing on the stage between film showings three times a day in London's largest cinema houses, where people could hear him perform six songs and an encore for sixpence (twelve and a half cents) or a shilling (twenty-five cents). He also sang a series of concerts in large halls with a six-shilling ($1.50) top ticket price. Thousands of people who couldn't remotely afford the usual price of even the cheapest concert ticket—pensioners, low-paid workers, people on welfare, and even the truly impoverished—were able to hear him sing and to experience something they never forgot. One night, after one of his appearances at a movie theater, an old lady walking with a cane thanked him for the opportunity to hear him in person rather than only on recordings. The shilling she could afford to pay was just enough for her admission plus her round-trip bus fare.[17]

Despite Holt's anxiety, Paul's concert career flourished as never before. He began his 1938 Celebrity Concert tour with a triumphant sold-out performance at the Royal Albert Hall, one reviewer noting that he had "a voice, in texture like rich velvet, fluent alike in delicacy and breadth, used with telling sentiment rooted in sincerity." Then he took the provinces by storm. In Eastbourne's huge Winter Garden, the audience occupied "every seat" and "every inch of standing room," and accorded an ovation to "whatever he sang." In Haverfordwest's County Theatre, he "gripped an audience . . . [with] a depth of feeling and vivid imagination that perhaps no other living singer can equal."

In the seaside resort city of Torquay, traffic in the area was held up for an hour as men and women clambered onto the running board of Paul's car after it was caught in the traffic jam near the pavilion. When he got out of the car to walk the rest of the way, a surging, cheering mass of people carried him into the concert hall. His appearance on stage evoked such an enthusiastic response that for several minutes he could not begin to sing. Hundreds stood outside on the street where his voice could still be heard. Police had to clear hundreds from the pavilion roof garden, and when the concert ended it was with great difficulty that he and Larry were able to leave for their hotel.[18]

Paul drew more people to Glasgow's Exhibition Hall than any artist in the history of the hall, the line outside stretching for a quarter of a mile. After the concert, he continued to reach out to the people around him, recognizing their Scotch national consciousness. Hearing a piper playing the melody of "The Road to the Isles" during a tour of a Glasgow park the day after the concert, he "spontaneously broke into the tune and sang it to the end. Quite unaccompanied, he followed it with his Gaelic rendering of 'Eriskay Love Lilt.'"

The audiences included not only the traditional concert-goers but also many of Paul's film, theater, radio, and recording fans. Mindful of this fact, he expanded his repertoire, adding new folk songs and the most popular numbers from his films and recordings. Critical purists continued to complain that Robeson concerts did not meet the requirements of the classic concert tradition. Once again, Paul ignored this criticism; he kept looking for new ways to sing in person to the working class and poor who were unable to attend concert hall performances.

At the same time, he stepped up his political appearances. Without criticizing the Soviet Union publicly, Paul simply acted in a manner opposite to the shift in Soviet foreign policy. As Soviet spokesmen began to sound less antifascist, he was sounding more antifascist. He focused his attacks on the British policy of appeasement, and urged stronger support of Republican Spain by the left.

Paul also began to place still greater emphasis on the freedom struggles of the world's colored peoples. In London, at the Meeting for Jamaica on July 17, 1938, he hailed the West Indian people's struggle "for their democratic rights, for better conditions, for life itself," adding that "Tonight, I am appealing for . . . my own flesh and blood." In October, he sent a message to the people of China, "who are so heroically defending the liberties of *all* progressive humanity. In the words of [your] national anthem—'one in heart, one in mind; our goal we shall find.'"

When I interviewed C. L. R. James in London almost three decades later, James recalled long conversations with Paul in 1938 about politics and culture. With the antifascist movement in full retreat worldwide, Paul was trying to figure out where he could continue his fight against fascism most effectively. In contrast, James, a West Indian, was focused on the fight against British and French colonialism.

They ultimately agreed that the United States was the best place for Paul to function, because there he could link the fight against fascism to the black freedom struggle. James remained in London, where he could link the anticolonial struggle to the antifascist movement. These discussions reminded Paul of William Patterson's admonition to him in Moscow four years earlier. Pat had advised him to return to the United States where the "decisive struggle" lay. At that time, he had rejected Pat's advice; now it made a lot more sense.

James felt that Paul was a powerful symbol of "the worldwide unity of progressive humanity" against both fascism and colonialism. And he thought that Paul could exert a "tremendous impact" on societies in many parts of the world.[19] If Paul had harbored any doubts, they had probably been dispelled by a January 1938 letter he had received from an old friend, Ralph Bunche. Having borrowed Essie's Kodak eight-millimeter movie camera, Bunche was retracing her steps during her African trip two years previously:

> I've been knocking around in South Africa, [and] ran across many people who are still impressed by Essie's visit, especially the fellows at the Bantu Center in Joburg [Johannesburg]. Paul, you surely are an idol of the Bantu; when one mentions American Negroes they all chorus "Paul Robeson and Joe Louis"—the more sophisticated may also add Jesse Owens and Duke [Ellington]. The rumor still persists that you are coming down to the Union [of South Africa] soon; if you do, the black folk will mob you with enthusiasm.[20]

Paul never did get to South Africa, but his legend continued to grow among its long-suffering black majority. Decades later, Nelson Mandela and his comrades, imprisoned on the barren rock called Robben Island, would draw inspiration from listening to his recordings.

In the fall of 1938, on September 29–30, the pro-fascist British and French governments signed the infamous Munich Agreement, capitulating to the demands of German dictator Adolf Hitler. Czechoslovakia was abandoned, leaving it at Hitler's mercy. The road to central and Eastern Europe was opened to future Nazi invasion. Hitler's complete personal domination of German politics was assured. Stalin lost hope of forging an anti-Nazi alliance with Britain and France, and initiated intensive secret efforts to negotiate a nonaggression pact with Hitler. Six weeks later, on the night of November 10–11, the Nazis launched a nationwide pogrom against German Jews. According to understated official Nazi figures, thousands of Jewish homes and shops were looted and destroyed. More than two hundred synagogues were set on fire, and close to a hundred were burned to the ground. Twenty thousand Jews were arrested, and almost a hundred were killed or seriously injured. Referred to as *Kristallnacht* ("the night of broken glass"), this pogrom was the forerunner of the Holocaust to come.[21]

For Paul, the combination of Munich and Kristallnacht amounted to handwriting on the wall. He felt a general European war with an uncertain lineup and unpredictable consequences was now inevitable. It would come sooner, rather than later. Anticipating that he would have to pull up stakes in London and head home to the United States, he pondered the question of how to ensure his successful reentry into America's highly competitive cultural environment after a long absence. The answer, he decided, lay in his concert career. As had been the case a year earlier when he decided to go to Spain, he kept his own counsel.[22]

17

A HOME IN THAT ROCK

(1938–1939)

In unstable and pro-fascist Western Europe in 1938, there was little that Paul could do directly to influence British politics. Thus, he continued his efforts to find film and theater roles that could be used to send a political message. Spurred on by his vision of returning home, however, he moved with even greater urgency to consolidate his artistic leadership in the field of formal concerts.

All of Paul's singing engagements, with no exceptions, would be routed through concert manager Harold Holt, while his political appearances would be limited to speaking engagements, except for an occasional song or two sung a capella. Benefit *concerts*, as distinct from appearances at meetings, would be arranged in the standard manner like any other professional concert. Paul held scrupulously to his rule of refraining from political statements during a professional concert, although he did include in his repertoire songs from Republican Spain, from the German antifascist resistance, and from the Soviet Union. He also added Negro songs of protest to the spirituals, which had always been the mainstay of his concerts. He sang them without comment, except for brief words to identify the source and subject of the song. In his view, the audience had come to hear him sing, rather than to air his political views; those he would present outside the venue of the concert stage.

His occasional practice of singing half concerts between shows at major cinema houses had to be given up, as it had begun to undermine opportunities for professional engagements. However, he was able to continue singing a limited number of concerts throughout England to packed audiences in large arenas with a top ticket price of six shillings ($1.50). These appearances, along with his recordings of popular songs and the recorded sound tracks of his films, maintained his popularity among the general British public at an unprecedented high.[1] With his concert career providing a secure financial base, he could set his sights on his dream of making serious films and creating stage roles with a political message.

Throughout 1938, Paul tried to generate the production of an independent picture based on the story of Oliver Law, the black commander whose story Paul and Essie heard during their visit to Spain.[2]

Paul could find no takers for the Oliver Law story. In press interviews he bitterly criticized the commercial film industry. A widely read columnist wrote of his encounter with Paul:

> Paul Robeson is going to fight for the cause of the coloured folk. He feels that in the long road of his success, he's gone too far away from them. He talks of them as "my people." He wants to show that his success has not made him forget them. And there's only one way he feels he can do this.
>
> He will never appear on the stage or screen again unless it is in a character whose portrayal will strengthen the coloured race. "I will never be the caricature of a Negro again," he said. "I don't care what money they offer me."
>
> Here's a man chucking up his career for an ideal which is certain to bring him great unpopularity. He is going to America in the early summer, and it stirred me to hear the proud way he means to face the boos that are certain to come to him. It showed me that if you feel you have right on your side you can face anything.[3]

In other interviews, Paul declared that he had broken with the film industry and henceforth would make only "socially significant" films. In his view, the making of his proposed film about the Spanish Civil War was being prevented by "the same money interests that block every effort to help Spain [and] control the motion picture industry." He added that "the workers in the film studios have the power and they ought to realize it. During one of my films, . . . everybody [was] on the set, lights burning, director waiting: [the] head of the company had just come onto the set with some big financial backer. . . . And what happened? Everything stopped . . . because the electricians had decided it was time to go out and eat."[4]

Paul's efforts to find suitable vehicles in the commercial theater encountered similarly stiff resistance. His contempt for the aloofness of the English theater was reflected in his 1938 article titled "The English Theatre."[5] But first he excoriated artists who thought they were "a race apart" and isolated themselves from ordinary people:

> The theatre is one of the organs of society. It will always be found that the vitality of the theatre is derived directly from the closeness of its connection to the society in which it operates. This premise is an obvious one, yet it is surprising how little it is recognized. Take the general field of art. No matter where you look you will find many painters, poets, dancers, singers, actors and writers convinced that they are a race apart, that their art is a question solely of the individual, that they give their wonderful gifts to the common herd because of the need for the artistic expression of their genius. The falsity of this dictum in the theatre is immediately obvious. Incidentally, it must not be imagined that I have always been immune to such conceptions. In fact, for many years I was influenced by these ideas, and were it not for the personal and racial problems which arose from the fact that I was born a member of an oppressed community in the United States of America, and was continually faced with the social implications of my work, I should perhaps still be confused.
>
> English theatre appears to bear no relation whatsoever to your present society; the English people may have won part of their fight for democracy, but the theatre reflects the social relations of a feudalistic or liberal oligarchic society. The only problems which are presented in the English theatre now are those of a very tiny section of the English community.

Paul went on to praise developments in the U.S. theater world, revealing one of the important reasons underlying his urgent desire to head back home:

> A few years ago a somewhat similar situation existed in America, though there the theatre was never so completely separated from the life around it, and had always had a much more democratic tradition. But the growth of co-operative units did much to influence the direction the theatre has taken, to build up highly trained companies and to present socially realistic plays.

With the New Deal and a government conscious of the needs of the people came a government-aided theatre—the Federal Theatre. The result is a vital growth of a new kind of theatre in some 20 cities of America—a theatre which is gaining the allegiance of the ordinary people. Financially this movement has been successful, particularly with the plays *Haiti* and *One Third of a Nation.* In other words, the solution is already before our eyes.

Paul had enjoyed his volunteer work with the Unity Theatre group as a member of its General Council, serving as acting coach, coproducer, and public advocate. Herbert Marshall, an experienced professional whom he had met in Moscow in 1934 and who had studied for several years with Sergei Eisenstein, was the producer for the group, but the actors were all amateurs who held regular day jobs and rehearsed in the evenings or on weekends. Paul was determined not to allow any of his performances to overshadow the group.

In mid-June 1938, Unity Theatre staged *Plant in the Sun*—a play about a sit-down strike in a U.S. candy factory. It had won first prize in the American New Theater League competition. Paul played one of the central characters, an Irishman. It was the first time he had a "white" role in the theater.[6] The critical response was both respectful and enthusiastic:

> Strike Play Thrills. The highest praise one can give the production is that this giant [Robeson] does not make his fellow-actors seem pigmies by comparison. (*Daily Herald*, June 15, 1938)

> He [Robeson] certainly has much better support . . . than in any film I have seen. (*Daily Worker*, June 16, 1938)

> It is a rattling good play, continuously witty as well as a convincing and quite unsentimental and unexaggerated picture of realities in the struggle of American labor. It is first-class entertainment. The production is expert and the actors so much a team that Paul Robeson is not outstandingly better than other members of the cast. The Unity Theatre has found its feet; we may have here the germ of something as important in our national life as The Old Vic. (*The New Statesman and Nation*, June 25, 1938)[7]

The Times (London), which in its June 15 review dismissed the play as "propaganda," nevertheless conceded that it "gained enormously by digressing frequently from its strict propagandist purpose and allowing character to develop." A letter from a thoughtful reader appeared in *The Times* a month later, criticizing the review:

> I paid a visit to the Unity Theatre to see Paul Robeson in *Plant in the Sun*. A regular theatre-goer for many years, I can hardly remember spending a more interesting evening at a theatre. I found *Plant in the Sun* a first-rate piece of work in almost every respect.[8]

Throughout the two-month run of the play, Paul tried to strengthen Unity Theatre's hold on the public's imagination. On July 14, at the House of Commons, he joined with other actors and celebrities to invite the Members of Parliament to a special July 23 performance of *Plant in the Sun*. Many came, and the standing-room-only audience served as convincing evidence that Unity Theatre had scored a breakthrough.[9]

Feeling too long out of touch with his people in the United States, Paul moved to rebuild his ties with all levels of black life. He joined Marian Anderson, Duke Ellington, and James Weldon Johnson as a vice president of the Negro Actors Guild. He also reassured Claude Barnett, director of the Associated Negro Press, that he had not forsaken the Negro church, was not planning to relinquish his U.S. citizenship, and had no intention of making Russia his home.[10]

To the contrary, he had never stopped viewing his own and his people's future as one. Now he wanted to develop a U.S. black company and tour it in England. In addition, he planned to revive *Othello* in London and tour the United States with it.[11] With this long-range plan in mind, along with the thought that he might be able to duplicate in the United States his successful personal appearances in English movie theaters, Paul suggested to Essie that she make a quick trip to New York. In her brief notes on her July 26–August 3, 1938, stay in New York, she wrote:

> Paul wanted me to sound out the personal appearance proposition for cinema houses in America, so I sailed from Southampton on the *Ile de France* July 20 and returned from New York on the *Normandie* August 3.

I had comprehensive talks with William Morris himself [the founder of the famous theatrical agency], with Coppicus [a leading concert manager], with Bob [Rockmore], [and] with McConnell who cut and rearranged the film *Jericho*, making it an entirely new and fine film, renamed *Dark Sands*.

I saw all the cinema stage shows currently running—Paramount, Radio City, Ray's, etc. I also saw the plays *Haiti* (twice), *Our Town* [Thornton Wilder's classic], *One Third of a Nation*, [and] *Pins and Needles*.

Had visits with Bob and Clara [Rockmore], Corinne Wright [one of her oldest and closest Harlem friends], Ben [Robeson] and Frank [his wife Frances], Richmond Barthe [a well-known black sculptor], [John] Gielgud and Maurice Evans [Broadway stars who Essie had in mind for a possible *Othello* production], Fania [Van Vechten], Kenneth Macpherson [with whom they had made the art film *Borderline* eight years earlier], Jimmy Daniels [a popular black nightclub singer]. Talked by telephone with Marian [Paul's sister in Philadelphia]. Had a real visit with Hattie [Bolling, Essie's old and dear Harlem friend], and Minnie [Patterson]. Saw and liked my [Harlem] flat, and bought bedroom furniture.

She found Harlem at once welcoming and yet quite different from the way it was in 1931:

Harlem was grand. When I first arrived at the dock, I noticed many more Negro customs inspectors than I had ever seen before, and it was good to see them. Outside of the pier, Negro porters, Negro taxi drivers, in much larger proportion than before. Later on I noticed, in shopping, in driving through the park Negroes and whites all mixed up together—grown people, young people, children. During my recent visits, always the groups were isolated. Now they are all mixed up, and look thoroughly natural and casual.

Harlem itself is now more scattered—from 110th Street to 155th Street; from Madison Avenue to St. Nicholas Avenue. Within this wide area there are still many white people living. Indeed, in many large apartment houses the white tenants have refused to move out just because Negro tenants moved in, and are now living side by side with them. This was unheard of in my day.

Downtown, in the soda fountain next to the Paramount cinema, I found a Negro soda clerk; at Daly's Theater, West 63rd Street, all the ushers, the box office cashier, [and] everyone on the

front-of-house staff was colored. In the subway, Negro young people talk, laugh and fraternize with white young people; Negro
cashiers [are] at the change kiosks; Negro motormen [and]
conductors [are] on the trains. In Harlem—Negro clerks in all
the shops, big and small; Negroes working everywhere. I felt . . .
that Harlem was no longer *separate*, as it was in my day. Negroes
are downtown, uptown and all around. They are *mixing*, in actual
fact.

In Essie's view, Paul could quickly become a dominant figure in
America's performing arts world if he chose to return home. Even
Hollywood might offer openings because of its growing left-wing
contingent and its occasional manifestation of a social conscience.
There were indications that Ernest Hemingway might be interested
in writing the script for Paul's Spanish Civil War film about the black
commander Oliver Law.

However, Essie's exploration of the proposal to bring the Federal
Theater's play *Haiti* to London as a vehicle for Paul were not fruitful. She was not impressed by the play, and the company already had
another of its productions (*Golden Boy*) running successfully in London's St. James's Theatre. The idea died a quiet death, and Essie
returned to London with lots of information and ideas, but with no
deals made.

Soon after Essie's return in early August 1938, Paul's latest film,
Dark Sands (formerly *Jericho*), was released in the United States to
mostly favorable reviews. The black press was especially enthusiastic,
putting the film on the "must" list and remarking that, unlike
Emperor Jones, it "lacked [the] touch of American prejudice." Paul
had "redeemed himself." Another reviewer called *Dark Sands* "good
entertainment . . . due largely to exceptional photography and a fascinating story of a colored [*sic*] soldier." Still others hailed the "clever
cinematic treatment" and praised Paul's "magnificent performance in
a picture which abounds with drama."

The white press was less enthusiastic: The *World Telegram* complained that the film didn't "come off as well as it should." The *New
York Times* offered a curt dismissal—"out of respect to Paul Robeson
and his magnificent baritone voice, the less said about *Dark Sands*,
the better." But the net result was a successful run of the film, espe-

cially with black audiences, which further prepared the way for Paul's return.[12]

Throughout the fall of 1938, Paul kept up his campaign on behalf of Republican Spain as the flow of refugees increased before the relentless advance of Franco's legions. By October, Fernando Castillo, their guide-host during their trip to Spain, had managed to get his wife and baby girl safely to France. By the end of November, the last Republican counteroffensive had failed, foreshadowing a military collapse on all fronts. At the end of January 1939, Barcelona fell, and the mass flight of over one hundred thousand civilians and military personnel to France began. Paul spoke and sang across England at large rallies to raise funds for the Food for Republican Spain Campaign, the Memorial Fund for fallen British members of the International Brigade, aid to Spanish refugees, and other similar causes. At Mountain Ash in South Wales, he addressed an audience of close to seven thousand at a meeting honoring the Welshmen who had fought and died in Spain.

Paul and Essie also extended a personal helping hand to Cristobal Ruiz, an accomplished landscape and portrait painter who was the father-in-law of Fernando. They organized a showing of his paintings at a major art gallery, and invited him to stay at their house until he could get on his feet.

On March 27, 1939, Madrid fell, and the Spanish Civil War was over. Then the slaughter began. More than two hundred thousand people were shot in mass executions, and a million were imprisoned. Fernando, followed by two of his older brothers, had already escaped to France; his brother Pablo, whom Paul and Essie had met in Spain, had disappeared into the underground resistance; his mother, his seven sisters, and his sixteen-year-old youngest brother had all been arrested and faced execution, but they ultimately survived years in prison.

On a chilly March evening in 1939, the doorbell rang at dinnertime, and I ran downstairs to see who it was. A pale, emaciated man of medium height with a gentle face stood there with the collar of his threadbare jacket turned up against the evening chill. "You must be Pablito," he said softly; "tell Pablo and Essie that Fernando is here." And he waited at the door.

There was an emotional reunion, and Fernando stayed for several weeks until he got himself situated. It took him ten days just to be able to eat normally. That first night, although our table was laden with food—roast chicken with all the trimmings—Fernando could only manage some soup and bread and some cooked cereal with milk.

Spellbound, we listened to his story of the fighting retreat of the Northern Republican Army to the French border, with the able-bodied men taking regular shifts in desperate rearguard battles to protect the slow march of tens of thousands of civilian families to safety in France. And then came the humiliation of being roughly disarmed by the French border troops and herded into detention camps.

Subsequently, Fernando's two older brothers made it to London along with their families, and my parents helped them to get settled and ultimately to emigrate to Mexico. I met them all, and remember them as a wonderfully vibrant group—full of life and without bitterness. Even though they had lost, they knew they had fought the good fight.

Paul had condemned the "betrayal" of Spain by Britain, France, and America with growing frequency, declaring that "because support was not given, many more Americans, Englishmen and Frenchmen will have to die." In a cable to the Negro People's Committee to Aid Spanish Democracy, of which he was international chairman, he had charged that the democratic countries of the world had "retreated at every step" before the onslaught of fascism, and that "the Colored people of the United States must ever keep in mind that the reactionary forces seeking to smash democracy in Spain are the same forces which would destroy our constitutional rights at home."[13]

But it was not only Spain that had been sacrificed to Hitler by the West. On March 15, 1939, just twelve days before the fall of Madrid, Hitler's troops had marched unopposed into the remainder of Czechoslovakia, and within weeks Nazi Germany was exerting military pressure on Poland. A surge of popular indignation swept across Europe, and in England, Winston Churchill stepped up his opposition to Chamberlain's appeasement of Hitler. It was in this highly charged political atmosphere that Paul and Larry set out on a concert tour of Denmark, Norway, and Sweden at the end of March 1939.

In late January 1939, a letter had arrived from Peter Freuchen, a Danish friend. Freuchen, an arctic explorer who had opened up uncharted areas of Greenland and was a Danish folk hero, proposed a plan whereby Paul would come to Denmark's capital, Copenhagen, to sing a benefit concert for aid to Spanish refugee children. This charitable concert would allow the concert manager of the Scandinavian Music Group to obtain a waiver of the government regulation requiring fees from professional performances to be spent solely in Denmark. A major concert tour consisting of five concerts in Denmark, four in Sweden, and two in Norway (Finland was skipped because of its pro-Nazi government) could then be guaranteed. The left-wing newspaper *Politiken*, the most influential in Denmark, was closely associated with Freuchen and would launch a strong promotional campaign for Paul's Danish concerts, assuring overflow audiences. "Everything is fixed for your arrival . . . , and everything will be settled in no time," Freuchen wrote, urging Paul to "hurry up and answer and say yes."[14]

Paul did just that, and proceeded to rehearse with Larry. By the time they arrived in Copenhagen at the end of March to begin their tour, they had thoroughly prepared a repertoire of spirituals, folk songs, and songs of the antifascist resistance, and Paul was in superb voice. The response of the overflow concert audiences was overwhelming. The Swedes and Norwegians were as enthusiastic as the Danes, with some fans in Sweden kneeling to kiss Paul's hand as if he were their king.

It was not only Paul's music to which the audiences were responding. As one of the most identifiable symbols of the antifascist struggle, he galvanized the house when he sang his anti-Nazi and Spanish Civil War songs. The mere announcement of the song titles and their origins was sufficient to ensure an immense outburst of emotion in response to his renditions. The concerts became political demonstrations without a single speech from Paul.

The artistic and political success of this tour reconfirmed for Paul the centrality of his formal concert career to everything that he wanted to accomplish. Like it or not, he would remain, first and foremost, a concert artist. He could still sing occasionally to the masses in stadiums and large arenas, and his political activism would be accepted by his public. Leaving the theater and the film industry for extended periods could not cripple him artistically, whereas his departure from the world's established concert halls for any length of time would eliminate him as a major force.

Thus, Paul came to realize that, notwithstanding his ever-growing image of himself as a prophet who used his art as a weapon, the general public saw him as an artist with a social conscience. A natural performer, he had no inclination to argue with his audience. He simply functioned selectively, separating his political activism from his professional career. His political constituency saw a great singer with a prophetic quality.[15]

By the time Paul returned from his Scandinavian tour toward the end of April 1939, war clouds were descending rapidly on Europe. With Hitler preparing to march into Poland, Paul felt a Nazi-Soviet deal of some kind was imminent. Now he told Essie he had decided it was time to leave London. She should book passage for the fall on an American ship.[16]

Paul lost no time in paving the way for the pursuit of his career in America. In mid-May, he and Larry arrived in New York for a six-week visit that would include several concerts and a revival of the play *The Emperor Jones*. He would also have plenty of time to visit friends, explore artistic opportunities, and assess the sociopolitical climate.

Essie, in close collaboration with Bob Rockmore, had made thorough advance arrangements for Paul's professional engagements and had also alerted all of their personal friends about his arrival. Paul had regained full trust and confidence in her—so much so that just before his departure for New York he gave her his power of attorney for the first time in a decade.

In New York, Paul set up two home bases where he stayed alternately—one in Harlem with the Bollings on 135th Street, where he and Essie had always stayed, and one in Greenwich Village with Harold ("Gig") and Bettina ("Bert") McGhee, old friends from Paul's 1920s days as a member of the Provincetown Players. He paid a courtesy visit to Essie's mother, who was back in New York after a stay in Canada, spent some time with his brother Ben, visited his sister, Marian, in Philadelphia, and looked up most of his old Harlem friends. But, with the exception of the McGhees, Bob and Clara Rockmore, and Freda Diamond and her husband, Alfred ("Barry")

Baruch, Paul ignored his legion of white friends from the twenties. This caused considerable resentment among many of them, and enraged the Van Vechtens, whom Essie later tried unsuccessfully to placate with a letter from London.[17]

His public image in the United States was of great importance to Paul, and he consciously chose the Negro press as the chief means of shaping it. In extensive interviews, he expounded his approach to the race issue, to the Soviet Union, and to communism: "I won't let people forget I'm a Negro," he began. "If I were Joe Louis, I wouldn't let people forget I'm a Negro either; and if I were Marian Anderson, I would want to be known not as a great singer but as a great Negro singer. It should be the mission of Negro artists to earn respect as Negroes."

He said he wasn't worried about communism or about the influence it might have on me in a Soviet school, although he himself wasn't a communist. He had put me in Soviet schools not because of communism but because "only in Russia is there truly no racial distinction." His point of view was social rather than political, and therefore "what goes on in the upper circles of the [Soviet] Government I don't know or care."[18]

His interviews had the desired effect. Editorial comment in the Negro press highlighted the fact that he placed me in a Soviet school not because he was a communist but because I encountered no racial prejudice there. One editorial, under the headline "Docile No More," remarked that most Negroes weren't seeking communism but "equal opportunities in the world to get educations, earn decent livings and live respectable lives. So far they have been unable to do any of these things in America. . . . What Paul Robeson says is believed by most Negroes and now is the time to act."[19]

Paul also made it a point to appear at several major political events. Two of his appearances were at the request of his old friend Walter White, executive secretary of the NAACP, who had asked him to sing and speak at a June 23 meeting of the Greater New York Fund and to address the opening session of the NAACP's Thirtieth Annual Conference on June 27 in Richmond, Virginia. On June 29, he sang at a Symposium on Spanish Culture in Exile at New York's Roosevelt Hotel.[20]

In a private political vein, Paul cemented his ties with the left through Max Yergan and Harlem Communist Party leader Ben Davis, who was a personal friend dating back to the 1920s. In consultation with them, he decided to place primary emphasis on the African-American freedom struggle rather than on international events. At the same time, he would continue to hammer away at the need to oppose fascism. In a long interview with the *Sunday Worker*, the Communist Party paper, he stressed his decision to return permanently to the United States in order to serve the cause of African-Americans "[as] I resume my work in the theatre and take my place in the musical life of the United States."[21]

The Communist Party was now a significant political and cultural force in Harlem. Unlike the Socialist Party and other leftist groups, the Communist Party of the middle and late 1930s recognized and encouraged the central role of culture and the black church in the African-American freedom struggle. They had ceased to pose class against race, and embraced the principal cultural tenets of W. E. B. DuBois. As a result, they had attracted many black intellectuals of the time, including such writers as Ralph Ellison and Richard Wright. Paul maintained a friendly but arm's-length relationship with the party through his friendships with Ben Davis, William Patterson, and Max Yergan.[22]

From a career point of view, Paul's most pressing concern was to acquire prestigious but loyal concert management. After consulting with Bob Rockmore, he turned aside leading concert impresario Sol Hurok's persistent effort to acquire "first bid" and ultimately signed with Columbia Management Bureau's Fred Schang. Paul became close personal friends with Schang, who would manage him with loyalty and effectiveness for a decade. The relationship with Columbia's concert arm would be especially beneficial, because Paul would later decide to record consistently for Columbia Recording Corporation and to appear preferentially on Columbia Broadcasting System radio programs.[23]

The decision to play in *The Emperor Jones* paid good dividends. It was scheduled for a week's run at the Ridgeway Theatre in White Plains, New York, as the first offering of the Westchester County summer theater season. Paul's opening night performance drew unstinting praise in the reviews: "A magnificently robust characterization, tingling with a splendid vigor and sensitivity"; "Power is in his voice, and strength is in his body. . . . A week is too short a time." In this revival, Paul eliminated the word *nigger* throughout after having announced in several interviews that he intended to do so. As a result, there was no public criticism of his performance in either left-wing or black media.[24] Elated, Paul cabled Essie in London:

> DARLING. EMPEROR GREAT SUCCESS. MARVELLOUS REVIEWS. YOU WERE RIGHT. POSSIBILITIES JOHN HENRY BY ROARK BRADFORD; DENMARK VESEY MUSICAL BY LANGSTON HUGHES, AND DUKE ELLINGTON CONCERTS; NEW YORK SHOWING OF EMPEROR. ALSO, MARGARET WEBSTER WANTS TO DO OTHELLO WITH MAURICE EVANS. CABLE ME.[25]

Essie cabled him two days later, and followed it immediately with a detailed letter:

> Of all the ideas, I think the most interesting one is the proposal of *Othello* with Margaret Webster and Maurice Evans. Evans is good enough to do a fine Iago, and not distinctive enough to worry about overshadowing anybody else. He will therefore know, very sensibly, that the way for him to register most strongly will be to do a fine Iago, and not to flaunt himself personally. Margaret Webster is intelligent, very widely experienced, [and] has the formal background and classical knowledge; so I think [she] could give a fine production. Yet she is not mannered, not ultra, not arty-crafty, nor super-psychological or super-technical; so the production might also come out honest, straightforward, modern and powerful. So.
>
> But of course, a lot depends on the selection of the Desdemona, and this I certainly would be VERY careful about. I can't think of anyone better than Peggy [Ashcroft], for the moment, but am open to reason. Peggy would jump at it, too, I think. Because New York is New York.

In this extraordinarily prescient passage, Essie laid out the general approach that would be used so successfully in mounting the historic Broadway *Othello* four years later with Margaret Webster as the director. Moreover, by unhesitatingly suggesting Peggy Ashcroft, who had almost wrecked Essie's marriage nine years earlier, as the best actress to play Desdemona opposite Paul, Essie was demonstrating her objectivity in making artistic decisions.

The rest of the letter reveals her deep feeling of security as Paul's wife and indispensable partner, and at the same time provides a glimpse into the conflicts and difficulties that were inherent in his approach to his artistic career. For example, at one point she refers to his preference for smaller, more intimate theaters and concert halls, whereas commercial success required larger venues:

> As for a New York showing of the *Emperor*, that depends on many things: How you stand the wear and tear of the voice work. Whether the production is first class. And the size of the theatre, although that isn't so important as it is here, for most of the theatres are modern and well built, and not too spread out.
>
> Concerts again depend on many things, as we have already decided. How are you to inform your audiences in advance of what to expect. The smaller halls. The assisting artist. The travel between engagements. The steam heat, the general weather. Perhaps radio is easier to manage, physically???
>
> Now for the Roark Bradford *John Henry*. I read it, and I have read almost as many versions as I have of [Henri] Christophe and the Haitian scene. But I haven't yet read a version of John Henry which I can honestly see you playing in. It's a fine idea, and the story is epic, but I have never seen the right characterization for you. John Henry is always physically magnificent, but is in the end a dumb beast. I don't think you could do him. I think you could do a dumb, humorous mischievous ne'er do well, but I don't think you could do a serious no-count character. You are now too aware, too definite minded, too militant yourself, and you haven't the technical equipment to go against your set personality and quality. As I have always felt sure you couldn't do a hard character, because your voice is too sympathetic. You couldn't do a small person, because you are too big, inside and out. I am open to reason, and would have to re-read the script before I went against you finally.
>
> I like the Vesey [Denmark Vesey, slave rebel] conception because I feel it IS what you think and feel, and you could therefore go for it in a big way. I think lots could be done to improve the script.
>
> The Langston Hughes–Duke Ellington musical sounds very intriguing, but I think it should be examined carefully as to story and characterization. The collaboration itself is so promising that we mustn't be misled. You've got to have a good strong story, or a strong idea, to make a good play. All of Langston's work so far has been definitely ineffective. I saw his *Mulatto*, and his *Don't You Want to Be Free?*, and felt both of them to be amateur. That won't do for big time. It is quite possible that he might be able to do something light and musical much better. For instance his *Weary Blues* are very fine. So we shall see. But DON'T make any rash promises.[26]

The script for *John Henry* would be improved somewhat, and four months later came the announcement that Paul would play the part on Broadway. Essie agreed to his taking the part: he had to reestablish himself quickly in the American theater, and a musical about a black subject was the only available vehicle. Anything short of an overt "Uncle Tom" role would have to do for the time being, and *John Henry* was, at the least, not bad. Essie's initial misgivings about the Hughes-Ellington project would be borne out, and the subject of the Vesey project—slave rebellion—rendered it commercially unsalable.

Paul returned to London from New York in early July, needing six weeks off for a vacation and a rest cure aimed at getting rid of twenty-five pounds. By mid-August, rejuvenated and in top physical condition, he went to work on two projects that would keep his name and voice constantly before the British public. In a concentrated but relaxed series of recording sessions, he recorded twenty songs that were especially popular with his British audience. At the same time, he also made his first-ever appearance on television, and prepared for his film, tentatively titled *David Goliath*, about a black miner in the Welsh coal fields.[27]

In November 1938, in his search for a satisfactory film project, Paul had joined with his friend Herbert Marshall, producer-director of the Unity Theatre, to create a small independent film company whose first effort was to be a film in which Paul starred as a black man working in a Welsh mine and singing at a Welsh cultural festival. Asserting that he was determined to "depict the Negro as he really is—not the caricature he is always represented to be on the screen," he added that he also hoped to make films in which he portrayed Samuel Coleridge-Taylor, the composer of *Hiawatha*; world boxing champion Joe Louis; and Toussaint L'Ouverture.

As matters developed, film producer Michael Balcon became interested in Herbert Marshall's original story *David Goliath*, about a black stoker who leaves his ship when it docks in Cardiff, Wales. Finding himself penniless, he becomes a hobo, then a miner, befriending a poor Welsh family whose life he shares. Balcon, together with a young film director, Pen Tennyson, who had just made a successful Ealing Studios film, convinced Ealing to make the film, and it was scheduled for production.[28]

On August 23, 1939, as the filming of *David Goliath* was about to begin in the Rhondda mining valley of South Wales, the signing of a Non-Aggression Pact between Nazi Germany and the Soviet Union signaled the start of World War II eight days later. It unleashed a wave of anti-Soviet sentiment throughout Europe and in the United States, placing the left, and Communist parties especially, on the defensive.[29]

Publicly, Paul remained unperturbed, insisting that the pact was a justified Soviet reaction to the British and French betrayal of Spain and their appeasement of Hitler at Munich the previous year. Privately, he feared the immediate outbreak of a major war, but he was determined to complete his Welsh film. Despite the risk, he told Essie to delay our trip until October.

London was already on a wartime footing, although war had not yet broken out. Schools serving children from dangerous (i.e., crowded) districts were being evacuated; barrage balloons ("blimps") to help ward off enemy aircraft were floating everywhere; subway entrances and major buildings were sandbagged and windows were taped to reduce flying glass; air raid shelter signs had appeared on every street, the largest shelters being the deep subway stations; anti-aircraft guns had been mounted on the roofs of high buildings. Essie said it reminded her of wartime Madrid.

Meanwhile, she was scrambling to get everything packed and ready for our trip home, and Paul was filming the interior scenes of the Welsh film at Ealing Studios just outside of London. He had arrived back from Wales exhilarated. While shooting the exterior scenes for the film, he and the rest of the cast had lived in miners' homes with their families, and Paul had descended into a working mine. In a visit to another mine called the Tower Colliery, he sang to the miners and spontaneously suggested that the film be named *The Proud Valley*. The miners roared their assent, and this became the title of the film when it was released.

War came in the middle of the filming. On September 1, 1939, Hitler invaded Poland, and Britain and France declared war on Germany. Reservists were called up; general mobilization began; gasoline was rationed; and gas masks, which everyone was required to carry at all times, were distributed to the entire population. At night, a strict blackout was imposed, and cars had to drive without headlights. The reality of the war suddenly hit home.

All entertainment was temporarily suspended; the BBC broadcast nothing but news over the radio until further notice, and the filming at Ealing stopped for a couple of days. However, it soon resumed, and Essie drove Paul for the thirty-minute trip back and forth to the studio. This exercise became quite a problem when Paul had to work late, since the blackout rules often forced Essie to drive home in almost pitch darkness. Somehow, she always managed.

The filming was finally finished on September 25; on September 28, Paul and Essie saw a rough cut of the film. They were overjoyed at the result. "It is beautiful," Essie wrote in her diary. "[It] moves well, has character, real atmosphere, sincerity, authenticity. . . . Paul is very real, very fine, and fits right into the picture. We think it's going to be first class." It was with a fine sense of accomplishment and closure that, with me in tow, they boarded the USS *Washington* two days later at Southampton for the trip home to New York.

Essie shepherded twenty-four big pieces of luggage on and off the boat train, through customs, and onto the ship. I recall quite a bit of nervousness about how safe our passage would be, despite the fact that we were traveling on a U.S. ship. Just a few weeks earlier, the British ship *Athenia*, carrying many American passengers returning home, was torpedoed off Scotland with the loss of one hundred lives. In port, our ship was blacked out, but at sea it would be brilliantly illuminated, with the American flag on the top deck floodlighted.[30]

The first time we went to the dining room, we were politely requested by the head waiter to eat in our quarters—the ship's policy was not to serve "colored" in the dining room. Without hesitation, Paul calmly marched his family into the middle of the dining area, where we sat at an empty table. After a minor furor, studiously ignored by the other passengers who were all white, we were assigned a reserved table in a far corner of the dining room.

Apparently, word of the incident spread among the crew, because the next day at lunch a delegate from the crew—a young white steward—came to our table and addressed a short speech to Paul. He said that the stewards, engineers, and all other crew members sent Paul greetings and welcomed him on the ship. They knew about his work, and they were proud and happy to have him and his family on board.[31] Paul stood up, shook the steward's hand, and promised to come and visit with the crew during the voyage. About halfway through the trip, the captain invited Paul to sing at the ship's evening concert, but he refused and sang to the crew in their quarters instead.

Paul was in a buoyant mood when the ship sailed into New York Harbor on October 12, 1939. Happy and relieved to be home for good, he and Essie had a bounce to their step when they walked off the gangplank. For Paul it was a moment of transcending clarity and confidence. His return to Harlem as the native son could not have been better timed. He had conquered abroad and had arrived home in the midst of a world crisis to offer leadership to his people.

In over a decade of living in London, Paul had become an artist of stature on the world stage. Through diligent work and study, he had fully developed his formidable gifts. Now he would use them openly and uncompromisingly in the service of his political goal of full and immediate freedom for African-Americans.

This was his first and overriding, though not exclusive, priority. All of his activities, including his artistic life and his political ties, would serve this end. He had already made his point clear to the U.S. press, black and white, during his visit the preceding spring. Now he reiterated it to the press corps, which had gathered dockside to interview him.

Paul told them that, as the son of a slave, he had returned to his Southern black roots. When he was abroad he looked at the world from the point of view of Africa. But at home his outlook was that of a black worker in Mississippi. As for the much-discussed search in Hollywood and on Broadway for roles that he would accept, there was no amount of money that could entice him to play a role that did not advance the cultural stature of his people. For him there would be no more stereotypes of any kind.

No, he said, he was not a communist or a fellow traveler. But yes, the communists were his friends because they were strongly antiracist. Fascism, abroad *and* at home, was *the* enemy, not communism. As a parting shot, he added that it was his task to teach his people how to prevent the "whip hand" of the oppressor from being used against them.[32]

In articles, interviews, and unpublished notes, he expanded on his feelings about his return home:

When I sing back to the people the songs they themselves have created, I can feel a great unity, not only as a person, but as an artist who is one with his audience. This has a lot to do with shaping my attitude toward the struggle of the people of the world. It has made me an anti-fascist, whether the struggle is in Spain, Germany or here. . . .

I feel closer to my country than ever. There is no longer a feeling of lonesome isolation. Instead—peace. I return without fearing prejudice that once bothered me. It does not hurt or anger me now, for I know that people practice cruel bigotry in their ignorance, not maliciously.

Civilization is a social phenomenon, not one of aristocracy and genius. The broad basis of achievement rests on the so-called masses. More and more, the masses are participating in the government of their countries—the French Popular Front, Republican Spain, the New Deal; democracies at their best.

A great distinction is being made between the people of a country and its leaders, between the people and a powerful minority which does the controlling, and in no way truly expresses or represents the feelings of the people.

Some believe that a good minimum is enough for most. Not so. The ultimate goal should be complete equality—the disappearance of the difference between the mental and physical realms because all are educated and strong. There is room for genius, but people can be educated to understand the problems genius poses.[33]

Twelve years earlier, my father had left New York as a star performer with a cultural consciousness. Now he returned as a superstar with an unshakable political commitment to the civil rights struggle. The preacher's son had emerged as a prophet ready to speak truth to power.

His vision was far different from that of America's governing elite. Even as his cooperation with the Roosevelt Administration was growing in the face of the Nazi threat, he was ready and willing to challenge even President Roosevelt himself on behalf of the full citizenship of African-Americans. For as early as 1939, my father perceived that America's future as a viable nation in the modern world depended on securing the civil rights of black Americans.

The personal price he would pay for uncompromisingly adhering to this principled stand despite the risk it posed to his artistic

career was incalculable. The monumental task of simultaneously playing the inherently conflicting roles of artist and prophet loomed
ahead.

But the child of destiny accepted his call, ready to begin his quest
on behalf of the human soul.

Once in a while through all of us there flashes some clairvoyance, some clear idea, of what America really is. We who are dark can see America in a way that white Americans cannot. And seeing our country thus, are we satisfied with its present goals and ideals? . . . There has come to us not only a certain distaste for the tawdry and flamboyant but a vision of what the world could be if it were really a beautiful world. . . . It is that sort of a world we want to create for ourselves and for all America.

W. E. B. DuBois, 1926

NOTES

Preface: Paul Robeson: "I Am Myself"

1. From an open letter by James Baldwin criticizing the one-man play *Paul Robeson*, published in the *Village Voice*, March 27, 1978.

2. From Paul Robeson's unpublished 1936 notes on culture.

3. From Paul Robeson's interview in the *Boston Evening Globe*, March 13, 1926.

PART I. MOTHERLESS CHILD
(1898–1919)

1. The Preacher's Son (1898–1915)

1. Gertrude, the firstborn (1879), and Peter, the third child (1884), both died in infancy.

2. Previous biographers have used 1845 as the date of Reverend Robeson's birth, and that is the birth date given on Paul's birth certificate. However, I have decided to accept Paul's repeated use of the 1843 birth date as correct. In his column in the January 1951 issue of *Freedom* newspaper, titled "The Road to Real Emancipation," he wrote: "My own father . . . was a slave. He was born in 1843 in Eastern North Carolina near Rocky Mount, and escaped in 1858 over the Maryland border to Pennsylvania."

Again, in his handwritten notes for a 1950s greeting he sent to the people of Hungary, Paul began with a short greeting in Hungarian and then spoke of the year 1848—the year workers' revolutions swept Europe, including Hungary: "A century can be momentous in the history of any land. At the turn of *1848*, my beloved father was *a boy of five* and a slave."

And in a January 13, 1929, article Paul wrote for the London *Sunday Sun*, his opening sentence reads: "My father, who was born in 1843, started on his career under great difficulties."

Finally, Dr. Aaron Wells, in a December 20, 1955, medical report, notes under family history that, according to Paul, William Drew died at age seventy-five. Since the date of death was 1918, he would have been born in 1843.

Since Paul also referred to at least two visits that Reverend Robeson made to his parents via the Underground Railroad, it is doubtful that he could have made them

337

after the Civil War broke out in 1860. A birthdate of 1845 would mean that he did not even escape from slavery until 1860. These facts support the 1843 date, despite the appearance of the 1860 escape date in Paul's autobiography *Here I Stand* (Boston: Beacon Press, 1988), p. 6.

3. Various histories of the Civil War and many accounts of Union officers attest to the fact that blacks in Union Army labor battalions, as well as black civilians, frequently volunteered to join the fighting ranks of the Union Army in emergencies. (See, for example, *Autobiography of Oliver O. Howard, Major General, United States Army*, 2 volumes [New York: Baker and Taylor, 1907]; cited by Lloyd L. Brown in *The Young Paul Robeson* [Boulder, CO: Westview Press, 1997].)

4. *Lincoln University Catalogs*, 1870–1876; Pennsylvania newspaper: *Oxford Press*, June 14, 1876, and June 25, 1873.

5. Anna Bustill Smith, "The Bustill Family," *The Journal of Negro History*, 10, no. 4 (October 1925).

6. Conversations with my father.

7. *Princeton Press*, November 10, 1900; February 2 and 16, 1901.

8. The facts about George H. White, including quotes, as well as the observation about the civil rights movement, are from *The Unsteady March*, by Philip A. Klinkner with Rogers M. Smith (Chicago: University of Chicago Press, 1999).

9. Paul Robeson, *Here I Stand* (Boston: Beacon Press, 1988), pp. 12–13. Here and throughout the text, I have dropped ellipses in extended quotes to make the text more readable.

10. Philip S. Foner, *Paul Robeson Speaks* (New York: Citadel Press, 1978), p. 314.

11. Eslanda Goode Robeson, *Paul Robeson, Negro* (London: Victor Gollancz, 1930), pp. 24–25. (My mother relied mainly on the recollections of my father's older sister, Marian.)

12. Robeson, *Here I Stand*, p. 7.

13. From a conversation I had with Uncle Ben in the early 1950s.

14. Robeson, *Here I Stand*, pp. 14–15.

15. 1910 photograph of Paul with the Westfield High School baseball team (courtesy of St. Luke A.M.E. Zion Church in Westfield, NJ).

16, Robeson, *Here I Stand*, pp. 9, 13, 18. Conversations with my father.

17. Ibid., p. 8. Conversations with my father.

18. Ibid., p. 20. Conversations with my father.

19. Ibid., p. 14.

20. Ibid., p. 16.

21. Ibid., p. 16.

22. Conversations with my father. Records of the St. Luke A.M.E. Zion Church, Downer Street, Westfield, NJ. Robeson, *Here I Stand*, p. 17.

23. Now Johnson C. Smith College.

24. Robeson, *Here I Stand*, p. 22. Conversations with my father. Many years later, my father told me that Ben was the best athlete in the family and could have successfully played both professional football and professional baseball at the highest level (he played quarterback in football and shortstop in baseball). Although he chose to do neither, Ben was a fine coach for Paul.

25. Robeson, *Here I Stand*, pp. 12–13. Conversations with my father.

26. Conversations with my father. *Somerset Democrat* (Somerville, NJ), June 30, 1911.

27. Ibid., Appendix, pp. 112–114. "My Brother, Paul," by Rev. Benjamin C. Robeson, 1934. Also, p. 19 [teachers and social events].

28. Ibid., pp. 21–22.

29. Ibid., p. 23.

30. *Sunday Star-Ledger* (Newark, NJ), September 26, 1999. Story by Jim Hague, who named Paul the New Jersey high school defensive player of the century.

31. Conversations with my father.

32. Robeson, *Here I Stand*, pp. 18–19, 24.

33. Ibid., pp. 24–25. An article in my father's college Memory Book, titled "The Dusky Rover," from *Outing* magazine, January 1918, stated that he had achieved the highest score ever made in this statewide Rutgers scholarship competition. It is interesting to speculate how different my father's life might have been had he followed the more conventional route of attending Lincoln University.

34. Ibid., pp. 25–27.

35. Ibid., pp. 22–23. Conversations with my father.

2. In His Glory: Robeson of Rutgers (1915–1919)

1. Conversations with my father, with Mrs. Sadie Davenport (widow of Robert Davenport), and with Bishop J. Clinton Hoggard of the A.M.E. Zion Church (retired).

2. Conversations with my father.

3. Conversations with my father. (Many years later, when Paul told the story of his first Rutgers scrimmage, he exaggerated his injuries by including the broken nose and broken collarbone he had suffered the previous year in his Somerville High School game against Phillipsburg. Had he sustained them as a Rutgers freshman, he would have been out for the season.)

4. Paul Robeson, *Here I Stand* (Boston: Beacon Press, 1988), p. 9.

5. The Southern-born Woodrow Wilson had been elected president in 1912 and expanded segregation in federal office buildings. He had also made it a policy of his administration to reject black applicants for federal jobs, and in 1914 he had refused to condemn lynching. (See Harvard Sitkoff, *A New Deal for Blacks*, vol. 1, *The Depression Decade*. New York: Oxford University Press, 1978.)

6. The swimming coach was often outraged by the racist hostility directed at Paul. When I spoke to the coach's daughter decades later, she recounted a funny anecdote her father had related to her about Paul. Not being able to swim at all (he never did learn how), Paul could not meet the requirement of swimming one pool lap in order to pass gym. Giving up in despair after watching Paul fail each time he tried to stay afloat, the coach finally told him to splash a lot while traversing the length of the pool in any way he could. Since Paul was six feet three and the maximum pool depth was only six feet, Paul passed this test with flying colors.

7. Gerry Neale was Paul's first real love, and although she would not marry him, she always remembered him with great affection. The inscription she wrote in a book she gave him in 1975, fifty-seven years later, reads,

> To Paul:
>
> All to myself I think of you;
> Think of the things we used to do;
> Think of the things we used to say;
> Think of each golden yesterday.
> Sometimes I sigh, and
> Sometimes I smile—
> But I keep each olden, golden while
> All to myself!
>
> Gerry

8. Conversations with my father and with Fritz Pollard.

9. Letter from James D. Carr, June 6, 1919.

10. In those days, African-Americans whose achievements shattered the foundations of racist stereotypes were usually classified by the popular culture as rare individuals whose success in any case was due to an admixture of "white blood."

11. *New York Times*, November 4, 1917.

12. Conversations with my father. *New York Herald Tribune*, November 4, 1917.

13. *New York American*, November 25, 1917.

14. Walter Camp, in *Collier's Weekly*, January 5, 1919.

15. Tom Thorp, college football expert and game official, as quoted in an article in the *New York Sun*, November 10, 1918, after officiating a game between the Rutgers and Naval Transport teams on November 5. (Rutgers defeated the strong Naval Transport eleven by 40 to 0.)

16. Conversation with Geraldine Neale, 1976.

17. Richard P. McCormick, *Rutgers, A Bicentennial History* (Rutgers, NJ: Rutgers University Press, 1966), p. 165.

18. *Sunday Sun* (New York City), January 13, 1929.

19. Ibid.

20. Kidney failure was listed as the cause of Reverend Robeson's death in Dr. Aaron Wells's December 20, 1955, medical summary of Paul's state of health.

21. Conversations with my father.

22. An undated clipping in the Robeson Collections reports that Paul "waxed eloquent on the part the American negro [*sic*] had played in past wars."

23. Conversations with my father.

24. Jimmy Conzelman, a football immortal as both player and coach, played for Great Lakes against Paul in 1918 and later recalled that "Paul Robeson . . . played offensive end, defensive fullback, and occasionally stepped into the backfield to throw a forward pass. Almost single-handed he had this highly-touted Great Lakes team beaten 14–0 with but five minutes of the first half remaining to be played. Robeson took a terrific pummeling because he was in every play. It was only when

some of the old heave-ho washed out of him that we were able to march on to scores in the second half that won the game."

This quotation is from a letter written by Jimmy Conzelman, a great football player and outstanding coach in the professional league, to Bill Corum, sportswriter for the *New York Journal-American*. The letter, inspired by Conzelman's meeting with Paul at New York's Commodore Hotel after Paul had petitioned an assemblage of big-league baseball team owners for the entry of Negroes into big-league baseball, was reprinted in Nat Low's column in the December 7, 1943, issue of the *Daily Worker*.

25. Philip A. Klinkner with Rogers M. Smith, *The Unsteady March* (Chicago: University of Chicago Press, 1999), pp. 114–116. Conversations with my father.

26. Ibid., p. 116.

27. *Sunday Times* (New Brunswick, NJ), June 8, 1930.

28. Paul's valedictory address at the Rutgers commencement ceremony on June 10, 1919. In Philip Foner, *Paul Robeson Speaks* (New York: Citadel Press, 1978), p. 62. Conversations with my father.

29. *Sunday Times* (New Brunswick, NJ), June 8, 1930.

PART II. DESTINY AND DECISION
(1919–1926)

3. Essie (1919–1921)

1. Conversations with my father.

2. Amritjit Singh, in the *Oxford Companion to American Literature* (New York: Oxford University Press, 1997), p. 30.

The reference to a two-block enclave in 1900 is from Eslanda Goode Robeson, *Paul Robeson, Negro* (London: Victor Gollancz, Ltd., 1930), p. 51.

3. Conversations with my father.

4. Conversations with my father.

5. Paul's recollections in his article "An Actor's Wanderings and Hopes," *The Messenger*, October 1924, p. 32. Conversations with my father.

6. Part of the narrative in the remainder of this chapter has been drawn heavily from an unpublished memoir written by my mother in 1929, which is included in my personal Robeson Collections deposited at Howard University's Moorland–Springarn Research Center. Since her story was written in a curiously detached third-person style at a time when tensions in her marriage with my father were building, I have told it mostly in my own narrative voice. I have also added to it and modified it in accordance with conversations I had many years after the recounted events with both of my parents and with friends who were close to them at the time.

7. See Jervis Anderson, *This Was Harlem* (New York: Farrar Straus Giroux, 1981), pp. 111–114. Conversations with my father.

8. Paul competed against the greatest players of the time. Buffalo had Heinie Miller, Elmer Oliphant, and Lou Little; Canton had Jim Thorpe and Decatur had

Paddy Driscoll and Jim Conzelman. The combination of Paul and Fritz Pollard, who was not only a great ball carrier but could also throw passes on the run, was capable of overwhelming most opposing defenses.

9. From Eslanda's unpublished 1929 memoir. Conversations with my father and mother.

10. Justice William O. Douglas, *Go East, Young Man* (New York: Random House, 1974), pp. 138–139.

11. Conversations with my father and mother.

12. Conversations with my father and Gerry Neale.

13. From Eslanda's 1929 memoir.

14. Ibid.

15. Ibid.

4. A Taste of Theater (1922)

1. From my mother's 1929 memoir. (The ellipses have been dropped to facilitate easier reading.)

2. *Life* magazine, April 20, 1922.

3. *New York Times*, April 20, 1922.

4. From a 1958 BBC radio interview with Paul Robeson, London, July 1958. (The ellipses have been dropped to facilitate easier reading.)

5. This account has been taken almost verbatim from my mother's 1929 memoir.

6. Ibid. Conversations with my mother and father.

7. Unfortunately, the correspondence that has survived is one-sided: my mother's letters were not preserved. My father was not a long-term saver: he would carry letters around for several weeks or even months, but then they would disappear. In contrast, my mother was a meticulous archivist who kept most of her correspondence in a permanent file. As a result, for the most part my father's letters to my mother have been preserved, whereas most of her letters to him have been lost. The only firsthand documentation for these months is through my father's eyes as he wrote to my mother about the experiences, joys, and insights, as well as the anxieties and problems, he encountered on his first trip abroad.

8. Letter from Paul Robeson to Eslanda Robeson from the SS *Homeric*, Sunday, July 9, 1922, 8:30 A.M.

9. Letter from Paul Robeson to Eslanda Robeson from the SS *Homeric*, July 9, 1922.

10. Letter from Paul Robeson to Eslanda Robeson from Portsmouth, July 12, 1922.

11. Ibid.

12. Ibid.

13. Ibid.

14. Letter from Paul Robeson to Eslanda Robeson from Edinburgh, July 24, 1922.

15. Letter from Paul Robeson to Eslanda Robeson from Blackpool, July 16, 1922.

16. Ibid.

17. Letter from Paul Robeson to Eslanda Robeson from Edinburgh, July 24, 1922.

18. Ibid.

19. Letter from Paul Robeson to Eslanda Robeson from Kings Theater, Glasgow, August 2, 1922.

20. Ibid.

21. Ibid.

22. Letter from Paul Robeson to Eslanda Robeson from Glasgow, August 6, 1922.

23. Letter from Paul Robeson to Eslanda Robeson from Liverpool, August 10, 1922.

24. Letter from Paul Robeson to Eslanda Robeson from 6 Regents Park Road, London, NW1, August 17, 1922.

25. Letter from Paul Robeson to Eslanda Robeson from London, August 18, 1922.

26. Letter from Paul Robeson to Eslanda Robeson from Plymouth, August 22, 1922.

27. Ibid.

28. The game was played in Milwaukee's Athletic Park on November 19, 1922. The quote is from an undated clipping in the Robeson Collections.

29. *New York Herald Tribune* sportswriter Lawrence Perry wrote a column, reprinted in the January 8, 1923, issue of the *Daily Home News* (New Brunswick, NJ), repeating the false rumors. Perry's public retraction (accompanied by a personal letter of regret to Robeson) was reflected in George Daley's "Sport Talk" column in the January 29, 1923, issue of *The World*, which commented: "Robeson takes a forward place among the best Negro athletes of all time, but his fancy turns to more intellectual pursuits than boxing." There are those who have incorrectly speculated that my father, despite his denials, considered taking up the offer to fight Dempsey. In fact, he had no talent for boxing and knew it. Although he was an all-time great football player, a good basketball player, a passable baseball player, and a fair track performer in the weights and pentathlon, he could neither box nor swim.

30. Alexander Woollcott, *While Rome Burns* (New York: Viking Press, 1934), pp. 122–123.

5. The Performer Triumphs (1923–1924)

1. Conversations with my father. Eslanda's unpublished 1929 memoir.

2. Ibid.

3. February 13 letter from Paul Robeson to Otto Kahn; March 12 letter from Otto Kahn to Paul Robeson; February 23, 1923, letter of recommendation on behalf of Paul Robeson from Augustin Duncan to Eugene O'Neill; November 15, 1923, letter from Eugene O'Neill to Paul Robeson; December 19, 1923, letter from Kenneth McGowan to Paul Robeson.

4. Interview with Bess Eitingon, March 30, 1982, conducted jointly by Martin Duberman and Paul Robeson, Jr.

5. Conversations with my father. Eslanda's unpublished 1929 memoir.

6. *Roseanne* was written by white playwright Nan B. Stevens. There were still no serious straight plays available by black playwrights.

7. Essie also noted that O'Neill and Gilpin quarreled over the fact that Gilpin had created the role on stage and felt that it belonged to him more than to O'Neill. However, it was a private argument: when the press interviewed them both, they swallowed their anger and complimented one another.

8. Reviews, in sequence, all May 7, 1924 (*New York Herald-Tribune; New York Telegram; New York Evening Post*).

9. Essie's diary, May 13, 1924.

10. Ibid., May 15, 1924.

11. Ibid., May 16, 1924.

12. Reviews, in sequence, all May 16, 1924 (*New York Herald-Tribune; New York Telegram; New York Evening Post*).

13. *New York Herald-Tribune*, July 6, 1924 ("propaganda and argument"); *Opportunity*, December 1924, pp. 368–370 (*All God's Chillun*).

14. *Opportunity*, December 1924, pp. 368–370.

15. Undated 1924 clipping from the black press in the Robeson Collections.

16. *The Messenger*, October 1924, p. 32.

17. *Opportunity*, December 1924, pp. 368–370.

18. A. Philip Randolph, "Comments on the Negro Actor," *The Messenger*, July 1925, p. 17. (Referenced in George Hutchinson, *The Harlem Renaissance in Black and White*. Cambridge, MA: Belknap Press of Harvard University Press, 1995, p. 17.)

19. Excerpt from O'Neill's inscription to Robeson on the flyleaf of a copy of the 1925 edition of O'Neill's complete works.

20. S. J. Woolf, "Eugene O'Neill Returns After Twelve Years," *New York Times Magazine*, September 15, 1946. (*Conversations with Eugene O'Neill*, Mark W. Estrin, ed. Jackson: University Press of Mississippi, 1990, p. 167.)

21. O'Neill letter to Michael Gold, May 1923. In *Selected Letters of Eugene O'Neill*, Travis Bogard and Jackson R. Bryer, eds. (New York: Limelight Editions, 1994), p. 177.

22. In *Conversations with Eugene O'Neill*, Mark W. Estrin, ed., p. 114.

23. Still, it was because O'Neill was "color-blind" that he later envisioned Paul playing the white lead role in his favorite play, *Lazarus Laughed*. In an April 27, 1930, letter O'Neill wrote:

> The big question remains though—who could play "Lazarus"? None of the well-known regular actors, I am certain. . . . I have thought of Paul Robeson, especially if he makes a good job of *Othello* which he is to do in London soon. He has the voice for it better than anyone I know, could do the laughter, has magnificent stage presence and can act. Also has brains and would know what the part meant. If only Lazarus was masked and everyone else without masks, the fact of his being a negro [*sic*] would not be too disconcerting.

In *Selected Letters of Eugene O'Neill*, Travis Bogard and Jackson R. Bryer, eds., p. 365.

24. Essie's diary, August 1, 1924.

25. Ibid., August 15, 1924.

26. Ibid., August 18, 1924.

27. Ibid., August 27, 1924.

28. Ibid., August 25, 1924.

29. Ibid., December 17, 1924 (Rutgers); December 6 and December 29 (wealthy whites).

30. Conversations with my father.

31. Conversation with Gerry Neale Bledsoe, 1976.

6. Seeker of Grace (1925–1926)

1. Essie's diary, March 20, 23, 24, 1925.

2. Marie Seton, *Paul Robeson* (London: Dobson Books, Ltd., 1958), pp. 34–35.

3. Essie's diary, March 29, 1925. The "interesting people" included Alfred Knopf, the publisher, and his wife, Blanche.

4. *New York Times*, April 20, 1925.

5. These sentiments are representative of many comments that Paul received at this time from members of the black elite who had a low opinion of Negro spirituals until they heard him sing them. It is noteworthy that Paul created a wider black audience for the spirituals, as well as a mainstream white audience.

6. *Detroit Evening Times*, January 20, 1926.

7. *Boston Evening Globe*, March 13, 1926.

8. Essie's diary, May 3, 1925.

9. Ibid., May 7, 1925.

10. Ibid., May 10, 1925.

11. Ibid., June 10, 1925 (Countee Cullen); March 25 and April 7, 1925 (Walter White); March 21 and 22, 1925 (McGhee: Essie and Bert were both avid basketball fans and witnessed one of the greatest basketball games of all time between the white Celtic team and the black Renaissance team); May 27, 1925 (the Brouns).

12. Ibid., May 14, July 20, and August 3, 1925. Essie and Paul also extended their cultural horizons, attending the famed Yiddish Art Theater on a number of occasions. On February 19, 1925, Essie commented in her diary that the acting was "simply perfect" and the direction "very fine." After seeing a performance of *Peter the Great*, Paul recalled that in London the Yiddish Art Theater was considered to be one of the best theatrical companies ever to perform there.

13. Conversations with Antonio Salemme. The quotes are from his interview with BBC television, which aired on November 26, 1978, as part of a one-hour documentary titled *Paul Robeson*. Salemme created two magnificent bronzes of my father in 1925–1926, and came to know both my father and mother quite well. I met him in 1977, when he was eighty-four years old, and kept in contact with him for sixteen years. The first sculpture, one of Salemme's greatest works, bore the title *Negro Spiritual*. It was a life-size nude with arms and face upraised to the heavens. Philadelphia banned the work in 1930 because it depicted a nude black man, but it was exhibited to great acclaim in the Brooklyn Museum and in Paris's Salon des Tuilleries in 1930–1931. The bronze subsequently disappeared, along with both the

original and duplicate plaster casts. A half century later, in the mid-1980s, Salemme, then in his nineties, undertook the painstaking task of reconstructing in clay a half-size version of the original statue from photographs and from memory. Two years before his death in 1995 at the age of 102, the half-size figure was complete and currently still awaits enlargement to life size.

The second sculpture is a head with a reflective expression. One of the original castings is in my personal collection; two more recent castings are owned respectively by Rutgers University and the Paul Robeson Foundation.

14. Essie's diary, May 4 and June 12, 1925.

15. Ibid., May 25, 1925.

16. Ibid., July 16, 1925.

17. Ibid., July 20, 1925. The party was at actress Rita Romilly's "salon."

18. From part of an extensive 1946 conversation with my father about his personal life.

19. Essie's diary, August 8, 1925. The Republican senator from New Jersey offered to arrange for Paul to sing for President Coolidge. The invitation was indeed later extended, but Paul declined because of Coolidge's conservative position on racial issues.

20. From reviews in the London papers, September 11, 1925: *Daily Mail; Daily Telegraph; Manchester Guardian; Times; Daily Sketch; Daily Mirror; Daily Chronicle; The Star.*

Essie's diary, September 23, 1925 (Paul's name in lights).

21. Essie's diary, October 15, 1925.

22. Letters from Emma Goldman to Paul and Essie.

23. Essie's diary, October 19, 1925. Paul never wore the earrings, but Aldridge remained his model as an actor throughout his career.

24. Letter from Amanda Ira Aldridge to Essie, October 17, 1925.

25. Essie's diary, November 8, 1925. Press reports emphasized his "magnificent voice," "natural dramatic sense," and "simplicity and dignity of manner" (*Paris Tribune*, November 9, 1925; *Latin Quarter Notes*, November 13, 1925).

26. Essie's diary, November 7, 1925.

27. Ibid., December 1 and 3, 1925.

28. In an undated 1925 newspaper clipping of a column by Rebecca West, which I found among my mother's papers.

29. Essie's diary, November 25, 1925 (Bill's death); June 28 and July 18, 1925 (Marian); Paul Robeson, *Here I Stand* (Boston: Beacon Press, 1988), p. 23 (Marian).

30. Essie's diary, December 26 and 28, 1925.

31. Ibid., January 5, 14, 17, 20, 22, 27, and 28, 1926; February 10, 12, and 15, 1926.

32. Ibid., February 13, 1926.

33. Ibid., February 25, 1926.

34. Ibid., March 16 and 17, 1926.

35. Ibid., April 1, 15, and 21, 1926.

36. Ibid., January 26, 1926.

37. Ibid., April 29, 1926.

38. Ibid., May 5, 1926.

39. Ibid., June 13, 1926.

40. Ibid., June 14 and August 17, 1926.

PART III. FROM PERFORMER TO ARTIST
(1926–1932)

7. "Ol' Man River" (1926–1928)

1. Conversations with my mother and father.

2. *Kansas City Times*, January 26, 1927.

3. *The Call* (Kansas City, MO), February 18 and 25 and March 4, 1927.

4. *New York Times*, April 21, 1927.

5. *Daily Princetonian*, April 4, 1927.

6. *New York Telegram*, June 8, 1927.

7. Eslanda's 1929 unpublished memoir and *The Daily Home News* (New Brunswick, NJ), April 28, 1927.

8. Undated 1927 clipping in the Robeson Collection; column by Mildred Lovell.

9. Interview with the YMCA magazine *Association Men*, July 1927.

10. Rabbi Jacob S. Minkin, *The Post* (Worcester, MA), October 22, 1927.

11. *Association Men*, July 1927.

12. Interview in the black newspaper the *Pittsburgh Courier*, January 8, 1927.

13. Paraphrased from Sterling Stuckey, *Slave Culture* (New York: Oxford University Press, 1987), p. 319. Stuckey's reference is to James Weldon Johnson, *Along This Way* (New York: Viking Press, 1933), p. 124.

14. Letter from Langston Hughes to Paul Robeson, October 11, 1927.

15. Conversations with Freda Diamond.

16. Ibid.

17. Letters from Paul Robeson to Eslanda Robeson, December 10 and 12, 1927.

18. Letter from Theodore Dreiser to Paul Robeson, March 5, 1928.

19. *Morning Post* (London), May 14, 1928.

20. *Sunday Graphic* (London), May 6, 1928.

21. Marie Seton, *Paul Robeson* (London: Dobson Books, Ltd., 1958), pp. 43–44.

22. *Yorkshire Herald*, May 4, 1928.

8. "The Power to Create Beauty" (1928–1929)

1. From Eslanda's 1928 unpublished memoir.

2. Unlike New York City, London welcomed black artists and intellectuals into its best neighborhoods; the primary concern of the British elite was class rather than color.

3. *Evening News*; *Daily Sketch*; *The Star*; *Morning Advertiser* (London), July, 4, 1928.

4. In 1985, during one of my visits to South Wales, I went to the Talygarn Miners' Rehabilitation Center, where I met an elderly retired miner who remembered being in the group of miners that my father had joined and sung to in London.

5. Letter from Paul Robeson to Mr. James Marley, M. P., April 1929; *Liverpool Post* and *London Daily Mail*, October 23, 1929; *Evening Standard*, October 24, 1929; *New York Times*, October 25, 1929.

6. *Sacramento, California Union*, June 18, 1929.

7. *Brooklyn Daily Eagle; New York American; Sun* (Lewiston, ME), November 11, 1929.

8. *New York Times; New York Telegram*, November 6, 1929.

9. To Feed His Soul (1930)

1. Conversations with my mother and father.

2. Essie's diary, March 16, 18, and 19, 1930.

3. *Bioscope*, October 25, 1920.

4. *Glasgow News*, January 15, 1930; *New York Telegraph*, May 4, 1930.

5. Essie's diary, April 16, 1930.

6. The quotes are from reviews in the *Sunday News*, May 25, 1930; *Manchester Guardian*, May 20, 1930; *The Spectator*, May 24, 1930; the *Times*, May 20, 1930; the *Sunday Times*, May 25, 1930; *Time and Tide*, May 31, 1930.

7. All of Paul's comments on *Othello* are quoted from published interviews: *The Observer*, February 16, 1930; an unidentified exclusive interview with J. Murray Smith, April 1930; *Evening Standard*, May 20, 1930; *Morning Post*, May 21, 1930; *The Era*, May 21, 1930.

8. Letter from Walter Hancock to Antonio Salemme, May 1930, on behalf of the Executive Committee of the Philadelphia Art Alliance (quoted in the May 23, 1930, issue of the *New York Herald Tribune*). The bronze casting, as well as two plaster molds and the original plaster cast, all mysteriously disappeared, and a genuine artistic masterpiece was lost. For the complete story of this scandal/mystery and its aftermath, see the *Morning Call* (Easton, PA), April 4, 1988, and August 14, 1994.

9. Conversations with my mother and father.

10. Eslanda Goode Robeson, *Paul Robeson, Negro* (London: Victor Gollancz, Ltd., 1930), p. 128.

11. Ibid., pp. 128–129.

12. Ibid., p. 132.

13. Ibid., pp. 133–134.

14. Conversations with my father.

15. Robeson, *Paul Robeson, Negro*, pp. 134–136.

16. Conversations with my father.

17. Robeson, *Paul Robeson, Negro*, p. 23.

18. Ibid., p. 140.

19. Ibid., p. 146. Conversations with my father.

20. Conversations with my mother and father.

21. Conversations with my father.

22. *New York Herald Tribune*, June 26, 1930; *Daily News* (London), May 19, 1930; *Observer*, March 23, 1930 (prepublication review); *New York Evening Post*, June 25, 1930.

23. Essie's diary, June 1, 1930 (Toscanini); June 3, 1930 (Ravensdale); June 5 and 10 and July 7, 1930 (Maurice Browne); June 10, 1930 (House of Commons); June 28 and July 1, 1930 (cricket); July 7, 1930 (Marian); July 29, 1930 (Canterbury).

24. *Daily Herald* (London), July 11, 1930.

25. Steven Watson, *The Harlem Renaissance* (New York: Pantheon Books, 1995), p. 93.

10. Troubled Spirit (1930–1931)

1. Apparently, Essie had become aware of Paul's relationship with Freda Diamond.

2. Essie's diary, December 27, 1930.

3. Ibid.

4. Ibid.

5. Ibid.

6. Essie's diary, April 9 and 15, 1931.

7. Conversations with my father.

8. Ibid.

9. *The Observer* (London), February 16, 1930.

10. *The Advocate* (Portland, OR), March 21, 1931.

11. *The Spectator* (London), August 8, 1931, pp. 177–178 ("Thoughts on the Colour Bar").

12. *Timely Digest* (London), September–October 1931.

13. The quotes and the narrative in the two paragraphs above are from Essie's diary, May 10, 11, and 15, 1931; June 7, July 2 and 30, 1931.

11. Giver of Grace (1931–1932)

1. Essie's diary, November 10, 1931.

2. Ibid., November 29, 1931.

3. Ibid., December 23, 29, and 30, 1931.

4. Ibid., April 8 (divorce) and May 31 (rumors), 1932.

5. *Chicago Defender*, July 2, 1932.

6. *Daily Gleaner* (Jamaica, B.W.I.), January 9, 1932. This naturally sermonlike talk delivered to a friend is reminiscent of Paul's notes in his 1929 diary and encapsulates his spiritual approach to life—an approach that guided and informed his future political thinking.

7. The quote is from an Edna Ferber letter in Alexander Woollcott, *While Rome Burns* (New York: Viking Press, 1934), pp. 125–126.

8. Concerts: *Boston Globe*, January 27, 1932; *Montreal Gazette*, February 29, 1932; *Musical Courier*, August 6, 1931. Radio: *Call Bulletin* (San Francisco), June 11, 1932. Recordings: *Daily Herald* (London), January 3, 1932. England: *Derby Telegraph*,

October 22, 1932. In England he recorded for His Master's Voice, the world's largest recording company.

9. *The Afro-American*, March 12, 1932 (Negro). Conversations with my father (Hoover–Roosevelt election; Scottsboro boys).

10. *Oxford Mail*, September 3, 1932.

11. *Daily Gleaner* (Jamaica, B.W.I.), October 3 and December 17, 1932.

12. *John Bull*, May 13, 1933.

Essie noted in her 1929 memoir that when Paul sang a concert at Rutgers in 1927, the small group of blacks who had attended this concert were huddled together in a segregated corner of the auditorium. Moreover, Dr. McCrannie from Paul's hometown of Somerville informed her that in 1915 he had convinced Rutgers President William Demarest to accept Paul, because Demarest had not wanted a Negro on campus. These pointed reminders of the pervasive and harsh racism that permeated the Rutgers campus during Paul's years there belie the attempts of some historians to cover it up.

13. Undated fall 1932 letter from Paul Robeson to Robert Rockmore. (The letter was postmarked London; therefore it postdated Paul's September return to England.)

14. Ibid.

This passage demonstrates conclusively that Paul educated himself thoroughly in the fine points of Marxist theory well before his first trip to the Soviet Union in 1934. His interest in socialism and communism had been sparked in 1928–1929 by his association with the Welsh miners, George Bernard Shaw, and the leaders of the British Labour Party. However, he concealed his sophistication in this area so that he could more easily justify his chosen focus on his art.

15. Ibid.

16. Essie's diary, November 28, 1932 (Holland); November 30 and December 1, 1932 (Brussels).

17. Letter from Yolande Jackson to Robert Rockmore, April 22, 1950; letter from Yolande Jackson to Lawrence Brown, 1950; letters from Yolande Jackson to Lawrence Brown, July 10, 1949, September 5, 1950, and two undated from 1950 (all in the New York Public Library/Schomburg Lawrence Brown Collection).

18. *Daily Herald*, July 11, 1930.

PART IV. BEARER OF A CULTURE
(1933–1936)

12. Film and the Politics of Culture (1933–1934)

1. *Daily News-Chronicle*, May 12, 1931.

2. *London Times*, May 12, 1931.

3. Marie Seton, *Paul Robeson* (London: Dobson Books, Ltd., 1958), pp. 61–62.

4. *Punch*, March 22, 1933; *The Sketch*, March 22, 1933; *The Spectator*, March 17, 1933; *Daily News-Chronicle*, March 14, 1933.

5. *Sunday Times*, March 19, 1933. (Note the comparison of Robeson to mighty trees—oak and cedar. Recall that Alexander Woollcott compared him to a California redwood tree.)

6. Conversations with my father.

7. *New York American*, April 25, 1933.

8. Examples of reviews in the mainstream press: *New York Times*, September 20, 1933 ("a distinguished offering, resolute and firm, and a compelling portrayal by Paul Robeson"); *New York Sun*, September 20, 1933 ("Mr. Robeson is arresting and powerful"); *Daily News*, September 20, 1933 ("His work is something to marvel at").

9. The full set of Steichen photographs was published six years later in *U.S. Camera Magazine* (vol. 1, no. 6, October 1939) as a photoessay illustrating Steichen's consummate photographic artistry.

10. Conversations with my father. Peter Noble, *The Negro in Films* (London: Knapp, Drewett & Sons, Ltd., p. 58).

11. *Film Weekly*, September 1, 1933.

12. *The Star* (London), August 3, 1933.

13. Conversations with my mother and father.

14. In a collection of articles by celebrities, titled *What I Want from Life*, Edward Cousins, ed. (London: G. Allen & Unwin, Ltd., 1934). (Reprinted in *The Royal Screen Pictorial* [London], April 1935.)

In this article Paul also wrote:

The white man has made a fetish of intellect and worships the God of thought; the Negro feels rather than thinks, experiences emotions directly rather than interprets them by roundabout and devious abstractions, and apprehends the outside world by means of intuitive perception instead of through a carefully built up system of logical analysis. The American and West Indian Negro worships the Christian God in his own particular way and makes him the object of his supreme artistic manifestation which is embodied in the Negro Spiritual. But, what of the African Negro? What is the object of his strong religious sense, and how does his artistic spirit manifest itself? These are the questions I have set myself to answer.

15. "On the Culture of the Negro," *The Spectator*, June 15, 1934.

16. With these comments, Paul partially foretold the peculiarly Chinese underpinnings of Mao's personal deification, his Great Leap Forward, and his Cultural Revolution, which were to take place a quarter of a century later. Moreover, my father's reference to "an ideology as fanatical as Marxism" was, as we shall see later in this chapter, a veiled reference to the public manifestation of Stalin's truly fanatical policies in 1934.

17. *Daily Mirror* (London) and *Daily Telegraph* (London), December 13, 1934.

18. *The Observer*, July 29, 1934. Conversations with my father. It appears also that my father became friends with Zoltan Korda, the director of *Sanders*. Korda's nephew, Michael Korda, writes in his book *Another Life* (New York: Random House, 1999) that "As a child, I had once heard Paul Robeson sing 'Ol' Man River' for my father at home. . . . That for me remains the stump puller of all voices."

19. Conversations with my father.

20. Paul Robeson, *Here I Stand* (Boston: Beacon Press, 1988), p. 35. Conversations with my father.

21. Marie Seton, *Sergei M. Eisenstein* (New York: A. A. Wyn, Inc., 1952), pp. 316–317. Conversations with Marie Seton. *Immoral Memories, An Autobiography by Eisenstein*, translation and introduction by Herbert Marshall (Boston: Houghton Mifflin Company, 1983), p. 192.

22. *Sheffield Telegraph* and *Sheffield Independent*, February 21, 1935; *Sunday Observer* (London), April 28, 1935.

23. Unidentified London newspaper clipping, fall 1934.

24. Conversations with my father.

25. Ibid.

13. Test Run: London–Moscow–Hollywood (1934–1935)

1. Marie Seton, *Paul Robeson* (London: Dobson Books, Ltd., 1958), pp. 81–84. Conversations with my father and mother. Conversations with Marie Seton.

2. Conversations with my father.

3. Conversations with my father. *The Times* (London), January 2, 1935.

4. *Moscow Daily News*, December 24, 1934.

5. *Chicago Defender*, January 12, 1935.

6. *The Star* (London), December 13, 1934.

7. Letter from Essie to her mother, January 5, 1935.

8. Seton, *Paul Robeson*, p. 95.

9. Ibid., pp. 88–89.

10. Ibid., p. 93.

11. Essie's diary, December 29, 1934, and January 5, 1935.

12. Conversations with my father.

13. Essie's diary, December 23, 25, 26, 27, 28, 29, 30, and 31, 1934; January 1, 2, 3, 4, 5, and 6, 1935.

14. Essie's diary, December 24, 1934; Seton, *Robeson*, pp. 89–91. Conversations with my father.

Marshal Tukhachevsky was a close personal and political friend of Kirov's. He and Litvinov were members of a moderate grouping within the top Communist Party leadership who opposed Stalin's hard-line policies in closed deliberations. The people with whom Paul and Essie spent almost all of their time were unmistakably covert supporters of this group, and Paul was soon able to decipher this allegiance in the context of the strident political tone of the Soviet press. Tukhachevsky was executed in 1937 after being framed and falsely condemned by a secret military tribunal.

15. Seton, *Paul Robeson*, p. 91. Conversations with my father.

16. Seton, *Paul Robeson*, p. 92.

17. Essie's diary, January 6, 7, 8, 9, and 10, 1935.

18. *Stockholms-Tidningen*, January 15, 1935 (black Chaliapin); *Berlinske Aften-Avis* (Copenhagen), January 16 and 17, 1935 (*Emperor Jones*; African culture); *Ekstra*

Bladet (Copenhagen), January 15, 1935 *(Show Boat); Politiken* (Copenhagen), January 17, 1935 *(Sanders of the River;* April concert).

19. Interview in the *New York Times,* April 5, 1931 ("I prefer a program entirely made up of spirituals"); *Royal Screen Pictorial* (London), April 1935 ("I learned to speak Russian, since . . . I find myself more in sympathy with that language than with . . . French or German"); interview in the *New York World-Telegram,* August 30, 1933 ("Paul Robeson . . . may soon be singing . . . in Russian, Hebrew or Chinese— but [not] . . . in either French, German or Italian"); interview in the *California Eagle,* December 20, 1935 ("I would have [had] to sing Bach, Beethoven, Schubert and Brahms before I could really be classed with Roland Hayes, Marian Anderson and Jules Bledsoe. But I wasn't interested in the classics particularly. I was interested in folk music.")

For representative reviews of the 1935 winter tour, see the *Nottingham Journal,* February 23, 1935 ("a voice of remarkable beauty, . . . the most sensitive feeling for the subject"); *Newcastle Journal,* February 25, 1935 ("There is individuality in his interpretations, but not a surprising amount of variety; . . . a fine voice"); *Irish News,* February 19, 1935 ("His singing has a personal spell. It holds in it the quintessence of noble sound").

20. The *Daily Mail,* the *Evening News,* the *Evening Standard* (London), and the *Manchester Guardian,* April 3, 1935 (description of premiere). *Daily Mirror* (London), April 5, 1935 (Paul at premiere). Conversations with my father and mother. (The premiere raised a record amount of money for a charitable event of this kind.)

The *Evening News* of April 8, 1935, carried the item about Paul's refusal to sing at the premiere. Many years later, after he had become one of the main worldwide symbols of the colonial independence struggle, he did publicly denounce *Sanders of the River* and his own participation in it. However, to my knowledge, Jomo Kenyatta, leader of Kenya's fight for freedom from British rule and the first president of independent Kenya, never renounced his participation in the ceremonies associated with the premiere.

21. The *Manchester Guardian,* the *Evening Standard* (London), and the Irish Independent, April 3, 1935; *Film Renter,* April 5, 1935; *Empire News,* April 7, 1935; *New English Weekly,* April 11, 1935; *Daily Telegraph* (London), April 8, 1935; *Theatre World,* May 1935 (critics). *Scottish Daily Express,* October 21, 1935; *Birmingham Post,* October 8, 1935; *Jewish Chronicle,* October 13, 1935 (commercial success). *Times of India* (Bombay), May 3, 1935; *Daily Telegraph* (London), November 9, 1935 (Venice cup); *New York Times* and *New York Herald Tribune,* June 27, 1935 (foreign success).

In the first year, *Sanders,* which had cost $500,000 to make, returned $900,000.

22. *Daily Telegraph,* January 2, 1936 (gold medal for best film).

23. *The Era* (London), December 28, 1934 (comments on the nature of the theater). Typical reviews of *Basalik* appeared in the *Daily Telegraph,* April 8, 1935 (the theme was called reminiscent of "the noble savage," and the play was criticized as "unsatisfying in texture"); *The Star,* April 8, 1935 (the play was dismissed as "dull"); *Daily Sketch,* April 7, 1935 (the "thin material [nevertheless] gave Mr. Robeson an opportunity to fascinate us"); *Manchester Guardian,* April 9, 1935 (the play "scarcely suffices as a frame for Mr. Robeson's powers"); *Daily Sketch,* April 8, 1935

("Margaret Webster [who in 1943–1944 was to direct Robeson in his Broadway *Othello*] . . . ran away with the play").

24. For reviews, see the *Evening Standard*, the *Star*, and *The Times*, May 7, 1935; the *Morning Post* and the *Daily News-Chronicle*, May 8, 1935.

25. Letter from Cecil to Eslanda, April 17, 1935; draft contract from Cecil to Eslanda, July 6, 1935.

26. Letter to Paul Robeson from the assistant to the secretary of the Royal Institute of International Affairs, February 21, 1935; letter to Paul Robeson from Allan J. Eidenow, director of the British General Press, April 3, 1935; letter to Paul Robeson from Richard Pennington, librarian and secretary of the National Liberal Club, December 3, 1935; letter to Paul Robeson from James B. Laird and thirteen other Edinburgh University students, May 27, 1935.

27. *Sunday Observer* (London), April 28, 1935 (art and emotion).

28. Arnold Toynbee, *A Study of History*, vol. 8 (Oxford University Press, 1954), pp. 500–501.

29. Letters from Dr. Norman Leys to Paul Robeson, June 11, 13, and 14, 1935. Paul Robeson, "Negroes—Don't Ape the Whites," *Daily Herald* (London), January 5, 1935 (reprinted under the title "I Don't Want to Be White," *Chicago Defender*, January 26, 1935).

In this article, Paul spoke directly to the issue of Negro education:

The Negro will remain sterile until he recognizes his cultural affinity with the East. He must take his technology from the West. But instead of going to the Sorbonne and Oxford, I would like to see Negro students of culture go to Palestine and Peking. I would like to watch the flowering of their inherent qualities under sympathetic influences there. I believe that Negro students who wrestle vainly with Plato would find a spiritual father in Confucius or Lao-tsze. His immense emotional capacity is the Negro's greatest asset. In the West this is at a discount.

30. Letter from Marcia de Silva to Paul Robeson, November 16, 1935; letter from Marcia de Silva published in *Nash's*, January 1936.

31. An example is the Archaic Russian culture, which has persisted through tsarism, socialism, capitalism, and vast changes in national boundaries.

32. Letter from Essie to her mother, February 8, 1935; Paul Robeson record royalty statement for the period 7/1/34–12/31/34 from the Gramophone Company Ltd.

33. *New York Amsterdam News*, October 5, 1935.

34. *The Gazette* (Montreal), October 14, 1935; *Oregon Daily Journal*, November 12, 1935 (critics). Letters from Essie in Pasadena, California, to Hattie Bolling in Harlem, New York, December 12 and 23, 1935.

35. *Sheffield Independent*, January 18, 1936 (Hollywood offers); *Picturegoer Weekly* (London), October 26, 1935 (comedy).

14. White Film, Black Culture (1936)

1. The interview, given during the first week of January 1936, appeared four months later in *Sunday Worker*, May 10, 1936.

2. Letter from Oscar Hammerstein II to Paul Robeson, February 25, 1936.

3. Letter from Rena M. Vale to Paul and Essie Robeson, December 30, 1935.

4. *Film Weekly*, May 23, 1936 (Paul Robeson introduces "The Song of Freedom"). Undated 1936 film contracts between Paul Robeson and Hammer Productions Ltd. (*Song of Freedom* and *Big Fella*; in the Robeson Collections at MSRC). Letter from Gaumont–British Picture Corporation Ltd. to Essie Robeson regarding approval by Paul Robeson of the script for *King Solomon's Mines*, May 22, 1936. (Supporting roles in this latter film were played by Roland Young, John Loder, and Anna Lee.)

5. Program for the March 15 and 16, 1936, performances of *Toussaint L'Ouverture* (in the Robeson Collections at MSRC); *New York Times*, March 16, 1936 (unevenly written and produced); C. L. R. James, "Paul Robeson: Black Star," *Black World*, November 1970 (immense power and great gentleness).

6. Letter from Lillian Bayliss to Paul Robeson, November 13, 1936. Conversations with my father. (He wanted to study the role of *Othello* considerably more before playing it again on the London or Broadway stage. His hope was that one of his steppingstones to that point would be a film version of the play in Russian in the Soviet Union.)

7. Letters from Joseph Best to Paul and Essie Robeson, 1936 and 1944; copy of prologue and film description (in the Robeson Collections at MSRC). *The Worker* (London), April 12, 1937. Typical reviews: *Evening Post* (Aberdeen, Scotland), March 10, 1937 ("[Robeson] introduces the subject . . . so skillfully that he persuades you to the merit of the film before you have actually seen it."); *The Cinema*, March 17, 1937 ("This revelation of the growth of civilisation in Africa is its own tribute to the organising administration of the white man"); *Life and Letters*, summer issue, 1937.

8. *The Era*, August 19, 1936; *Daily Express* and *The Star*, September 18, 1936; *Daily News* (Aberdeen), September 19, 1936; *The Referee* and *Sunday Express*, September 20, 1936; *Daily Mail*, September 21, 1936; *The New Statesman and Nation*, September 26, 1936; *The Bystander*, September 30, 1936.

9. *Times of India*, November 11, 1937; *The Afro-American*, May 27, 1937; letter from Langston Hughes to Essie Robeson (*Song of Freedom*), July 16, 1938. *The Picture Show*, July 11, 1936; *Sunday Pictorial*, June 14, 1936; *The Era*, June 17, 1936; *The Cinema*, June 3, 1936; *Sheffield Independent*, June 12, 1936; *Daily Express*, June 12, 1936; *Sunday Times*, June 14, 1936; *Jewish Chronicle*, June 11, 1936 (all *Show Boat*).

10. *New York Amsterdam News*, June 30, 1936; *California News*, May 8, 1936.

11. *Picture Show*, December 11, 1936; *Natal Witness* (South Africa), December 18, 1936; *Evening News*, November 25, 1936.

12. The train anecdote was told to me at a chance 1997 meeting with Harold Evans, then president of Random House, whose father was a train engineer and the chief of the crew that my father visited. The story about Paul in Canterbury Cathedral appeared in a piece by British radio broadcaster Howard Marshall in *Radio Review*, November 25, 1935.

13. Conversations with my parents. *New York Herald Tribune*, January 10, 1937: "Son of Paul Robeson [in Russia]. . . . His father has decreed a Russian education for him to escape the prejudices he himself faced as a youth."

14. *The Era*, September 16, 1936 (working-class theater); *Edinburgh Evening News*, July 26, 1936; *Evening Standard*, September 19, 1936. Conversations with my father.

15. *Sunday Graphic and Sunday News*, January 19, 1936; *Northern Echo* (Wales), October 29, 1936; *Empire News*, August 20, 1936. (Marcus Garvey's London magazine, *The Black Man*, would later [in its January 1937 issue] accuse Paul of dishonoring the black race.)

16. From Paul Robeson's 1936 notes on culture (the sections titled: "Must Be Proud of Being Negro" and "Huxley").

17. Conversations with my father. Sergei Eisenstein, *Immoral Memoirs*, Herbert Marshall, trans., with Preface and Note by Herbert Marshall (Boston: Houghton Mifflin, 1983).

By this time, my father could converse in elementary fashion in Italian, Spanish, Swahili, Efik, Hebrew, Yiddish, Portuguese, Norwegian, and Gaelic. He was fluent in Russian and at the intermediate level in German and French.

18. Conversations with my parents. *Report of the Court Proceedings in the Case of the Trotskyite–Zinovievite Terrorist Center* (Moscow: People's Commissariat of Justice of the USSR, 1936).

PART V. TO BE A PROPHET
(1936–1939)

15. Russia's Sun; Stalin's Shadow (1936–1937)

1. *Moscow News*, December 30, 1936 (songs of protest). Letter from Essie Robeson to a friend identified only as "Ann," January 3, 1937. Contract between the State Philharmony (USSR) and Paul Robeson, August 13, 1936 (in the Robeson Collections, MSRC).

2. Sergei Eisenstein's review appeared in *Rabochaya Moskva*, December 20, 1936.

3. *New York Amsterdam News*, December 26, 1936; *Life* magazine, January 11, 1936.

4. Frank's daughter, named Eslanda after Essie, ultimately settled in the United States decades later after acquiring dual American and Russian citizenship.

In an ironic twist of fate, Eugene Dennis's son, Tim, was held hostage in the Soviet Union when Dennis was sent on a Comintern mission to China in 1937. In 1959, Khrushchev included Tim in the delegation that accompanied him to the United States so that Tim could attend his father's funeral. However, when Khrushchev personally offered Tim the opportunity to remain permanently in the United States with his family, Tim decided to return to the Soviet Union.

5. *Kinematograph*, September 17, 1936; *Film Pictorial*, October 3, 1936; *Morning Post*, November 23, 1936 (Kouka). Conversations with my parents.

6. Letter from Essie to "Ann," January 1937. The editing of *Jericho* apparently eliminated Essie's part. Larry Brown had a significant role in the first part of the film, which did not involve scenes shot in the desert, and thus did not accompany Essie and Paul to Egypt.

7. Postcard from Essie to Carl and Fania Van Vechten, February 9, 1937. *Film Pictorial*, May 10, 1937; *Film Weekly*, June 3, 1937. Essie also wrote the Van Vech-

tens that Paul was "in fine form . . . , sweeter [and] dearer than ever," and that all was "very well."

8. Henry Wilcoxon told this story during his remarks at the unveiling of my father's star on the "Hollywood Walk" stretch of sidewalk in Los Angeles, California, in 1983.

9. *Daily Worker* (London), October 25, 1937 (average film); *Picturegoer Weekly*, November 20, 1937 (fantastic situation for an artist); *Philadelphia Tribune*, May 20, 1937 (tired of caricatures).

10. W. E. B. DuBois, "Criteria of Negro Art," *The Crisis*, October 1926. DuBois wrote: "I am one who tells the truth and exposes evil and seeks with Beauty and for Beauty to set the world right."

11. *Egyptian Gazette*, February 6, 1937 (preferred film; attracted to British cinema); *Picture Show*, May 15, 1937 (best film).

12. Article by Louise Morgan in an unidentified clipping from a London newspaper, July 7, 1937 (starting anew); *St. Pancras Chronicle*, December 3, 1937 (Unity Theater); *News Chronicle*, October 9, 1937 (playing without fee).

13. Philip A. Klinkner, *The Unsteady March* (Chicago: University of Chicago Press, 1999), pp. 133 and 137 (Roosevelt); Harold Evans, *The American Century* (New York: Knopf, 1998), p. 278.

14. Interview with Louise Morgan in an unidentified clipping from a London newspaper, July 7, 1937 ("Events in Abyssinia . . .").

In a January 1937 radio broadcast from Moscow (see the *Sunday Worker* [New York], February 7, 1937, for the complete text), Robeson spoke of the Spanish Civil War: "Spain . . . can be 'the straw that breaks the fascist camel's back.' . . . It is to their eternal glory that Negroes from America, Africa and the West Indies are to be found fighting in Spain today on the side of the Republican forces, for democracy." He also praised the Soviet Union for its opposition to racism, quoting the 1936 Constitution of the USSR to the effect that:

> The equality of the right of citizens in the USSR, irrespective of their nationality or race, in all fields of economic, state, cultural, social and political life, is an irrevocable law. Any direct or indirect restriction of these rights, or conversely the establishment of direct or indirect privileges for citizens on account of the race or nationality to which they belong, as well as the propagation of racial or national exceptionalism, or hatred and contempt, is punishable by law.

15. Letter from Max Yergan to Paul Robeson, May 25, 1937.

16. Interview with Paul Robeson in *Gazeta Kino* (film industry newspaper; Moscow), June 22, 1937.

17. Roy Medvedev, *Let History Judge* (New York: Columbia University Press, 1989).

18. Ibid., p. 455.

19. Eisenstein was taking a considerable risk in continuing to tinker with the banned film *Bezhin Meadow*. Its subject—collectivization of the peasantry from 1929 to 1933—was arguably the most controversial issue in Soviet society. According to

official demographic data published during the Khrushchev and Gorbachev years, this "revolution from above" that was engineered by Stalin cost up to 10 million lives due to famines and the mass deportation of entire families, including children as young as five, to the most inhospitable regions of Siberia and Soviet Central Asia.

20. In the end, the Albert Hall management allowed the Moscow broadcast (without Robeson, since he was present in person). Although the broadcast "came through badly," it represented a major victory "over the authorities," since it was the first public reception of a radio program from the Soviet Union in England. (Letter to Paul and Essie from Yvonne Kapp, the principal organizer of the meeting, June 25, 1937, in the Robeson Collections at MSRC.)

21. According to Allison Blakely (*Russia and the Negro*, Washington, D.C.: Howard University Press, 1986), Golden organized a group of expatriate African-American agricultural experts from the South to staff an experimental station near Tashkent, the capital of the Uzbek Republic in Soviet Central Asia. The station made a major contribution to the development of the Soviet Union's cotton, sugar-beet, peanut, and other crops. Golden later became a top instructor at the Tashkent Institute of Irrigation and Mechanization, contributing significantly to the modernization of agricultural production in the region. He was elected to the Tashkent Soviet (the equivalent of an American city council) and continued to live in Tashkent until his death in 1940.

22. Conversations with my father.

23. Conversations with my father and mother (summer in Kislovodsk). Invitation from ambassador of Republican Spain, de Azcarate, to a reception in honor of Pablo Casals (support of Spanish Republican cause). Letter of thanks to Paul Robeson from H. T. Lee, leader of the Chinese Students Association and chairman of the National Salvation Committee, November 7, 1937. Paul also made a supportive statement about Edgar Snow's classic *Red Star Over China* for publicity use in response to a letter from publisher Victor Gollancz, September 22, 1937. The first draft of the statement was written by Essie in pencil on the back of the letter: "One is fascinated and deeply moved. And one is also informed. . . . The extraordinary qualities revealed of the leaders of the Long March augur well for the shaping of a new China" (support of Chinese cause). On October 31, 1937, Robeson sang a program of spirituals and Russian songs at a celebration of twenty years of Soviet culture. Letter to Paul Robeson from Stafford Cripps, October 12, 1937 (Unity Theatre). (All from the Robeson Collections at MSRC.)

24. Films: *Show Boat* was still playing in the British provinces with great success during early 1937. *Song of Freedom* received generally good reviews everywhere: "Paul Robeson comes into his own" (*Film Pictorial* [London], March 6, 1937); "Paul Robeson . . . at his best" (*Sunday Times* [Johannesburg, South Africa], February 14, 1937); "Paul Robeson's best film" (*Dundee Courier* [Scotland], February 2, 1937). *Big Fella* was notable for being a different type of Robeson film: "For once he is not typed as the African jungle chief" (*Film Renter* [London], January 2, 1937); "This enjoyable musical drama should not be missed" (*Brighton Standard* [England], December 28, 1937); "As the highlight of the current season's output from British Lion, *Big Fella* is . . . better and bigger . . . than the highly successful *Song of Freedom*" (*Kinematograph* [Long Acre, England], June 10, 1937). As an adventure story,

King Solomon's Mines was popular with audiences despite lukewarm reviews: "A very satisfactory screen version of the Rider Haggard story. . . . The film . . . [is] well worth seeing, despite one or two false touches (*Film Weekly* [London], July 3, 1937); "Stirring cinema adventure" (*Daily News-Chronicle* [London], July 24, 1937); "The style of the film has robbed the narrative of some of its drama. . . . Paul Robeson at times surpasses his best as Umbopa" (*Manchester Guardian* [England], July 22, 1937); "There is something lacking, though the film makes reasonable entertainment" (*The Times* [London], July 26, 1937); "[An] excess of inept songs" (*Pittsburgh Courier* [African-American newspaper], August 14, 1937). *Jericho*, arguably Robeson's best film, which combined African and African-American themes free of stereotypes with an entertaining adventure story, nevertheless received mixed reviews: "Paul Robeson dominates *Jericho* like some great native fortress. . . . A popular blend of unusual incidents rich with excitement, fun and adventure" (*Sunday Times* [London], October 31, 1937); "Mr. Robeson . . . is an actor too good to be thrown away on Jericho who is only a shadow of the man he promised to be at the beginning" (*The Times* [London], November 1, 1937); "A praiseworthy but only moderately successful attempt to provide entertainment off the beaten track. The story opens well but becomes scrappy and unbalanced when its fugitive hero reaches Africa" (*Film Weekly*, October 30, 1937); "The simple tale is enacted with dignity and is free from pomposity. . . . Mr. Robeson . . . appears unusually at home . . . , and the result is therefore one of his most successful pictures" (*Manchester Guardian*, October 30, 1937); "It must be hard to find a suitable Robeson story, but . . . we can rate *Jericho* a good one" (*Star*, October 29, 1937); "It is very powerful melodrama. . . . Paul Robeson . . . gives a performance fully in keeping with his high reputation" (*Picture Show*, September 25, 1937).

During the decade 1927 to 1937, Robeson records were selling worldwide at an average rate of over 200,000 a year.

Role Model: "Robeson Is Model for U.S. Winner in Oratory Contest," *Afro-American*, October 23, 1937.

16. Spain's Ramparts: "The Artist Must Elect" (1938)

1. Letter to Paul from John McMillan of William Heinemann, Ltd., June 25, 1937; letter to Essie from Carl Van Vechten, June 22, 1937; Essie's Spanish diary, titled "We Go to Spain," 1938.

2. Letters to Paul from American Consul James E. Parks, December 21 and 28, 1937. My father's U.S. passport #200 (page 6 carries the stamp and the notation: "This passport is valid for travel in Spain [Dept. cable of Dec. 23, 1937]").

3. During the Spanish Civil War, the U.S. volunteers serving on the government side in the Abraham Lincoln Battalion of the International Brigade were racially integrated—both officers and men. It was the first time in U.S. military history that white and black soldiers fought and died side by side in fully integrated units.

4. Forty-two years later, in 1980, I met a man named Jake Kramer in Buffalo, New York, after a lecture I had given there. He approached me and said that he had been one of the men in the hospital for the seriously wounded when my father came

that day. "I was in a little room . . . [upstairs] all by myself. . . . Suddenly Robeson came up and visited me. He asked me what he could do. I asked him to sing 'Peat Bog Soldiers' [a favorite song of the German antifascists]. He sang it so powerfully it got me out of bed."

5. The broadcast was heard at the battlefronts by both armies over loudspeakers erected at the front lines, and for that brief time the guns of war were stilled. (*Daily Herald* [London], January 24, 1938; *Evening News* [London], January 27, 1938.)

6. Robeson was so impressed by the Oliver Law story that he tried for a year, unsuccessfully, to make a film based on it.

7. Conversations with my father. On May 2, 1936, Mussolini's troops entered Addis Ababa, Ethiopia's capital, and on July 4, the League of Nations formally ended its sanctions against Italy. On July 16, General Franco staged his rebellion against the democratically elected Spanish government, and on July 22, Hitler sent crucial air support to the fascist rebels. (Harold Evans, *The American Century*. New York: Knopf, 1998, p. 282 [Rhineland]; William Shirer, *The Rise and Fall of the Third Reich*. New York: Simon and Schuster, 1959, p. 297.) When Japan occupied Shanghai, Nanking, and many other major Chinese cities in a full-scale invasion, isolationists in the U.S. Congress prevented FDR from imposing sanctions against the Japanese even after Japanese planes had deliberately bombed a U.S. gunboat. (Evans, *The American Century*, p. 167.) During the Spanish Civil War, Mussolini sent Franco 50,000 troops and massive arms shipments; Hitler sent 16,000 troops, including the elite air force Condor Legion, as well hundreds of tanks and artillery pieces. (Evans, *The American Century*, p. 287.) Soviet aid to the government forces was far more modest. This aid decreased in 1937 and all but ceased in 1938. Moreover, mass arrests and executions of the Soviet officers who had taken part in the Spanish Civil War occurred in Stalin's 1937–1938 purges. (Roy Medvedev, *Let History Judge*. New York: Columbia University Press, 1989, p. 724.)

8. *L'Oeuvre* (Paris), February 9, 1938; *The Slough, Eton & Windsor Observer,* July 15, 1938; *Glasgow Herald*, August 19, 1938; *Western Mail* (Cardiff), December 8, 1938.

9. Dolores Ibarruri ("La Pasionaria"), a legendary Republican leader, bade farewell to the surviving International Brigaders on Barcelona's main square on November 1, 1938:

> From all peoples, from all races, you came to us like brothers, like sons of immortal Spain; and in hardest days of the war, when the capital of the Spanish Republic was threatened, it was you . . . who helped save the city. . . . Jarama and Guadalajara, Brunete and Belchite, Levante and the Ebro, in immortal verses sing of the courage, the sacrifice, the daring, the discipline of the men of the International Brigades. . . . Banners of Spain! Salute these many heroes! . . . Mothers! Women! When the years pass by and the wounds of war are staunched, . . . speak to your children. Tell them of these men. . . .
>
> Today many are departing. Thousands remain, shrouded in Spanish earth, profoundly remembered. . . . Political reasons, reasons of state . . . are sending you back, some to your own countries and others to forced exile. You can

go proudly. You are history. You are legend. . . . We shall not forget you; and, when the olive tree of peace is in flower, entwined with the victory laurels of the Republic of Spain—return!

10. Conversations with my father. Shirer, *The Rise and Fall of the Third Reich*, pp. 342, 361, and 414; Medvedev, *Let History Judge*, p. 725.

By this time my father clearly understood that Stalin's purges reflected concealed but fundamental differences within the Soviet Communist Party over both domestic and foreign policy. The internationalists (covert Leninists) supported moderation in domestic policy and a united front with France and England against Nazi Germany. The nationalists (Stalinists) demanded an ultra-hard-line domestic policy and rejected any significant distinction among Germany, England, and France. In the debate over the economy in 1927 to 1929, Bukharin, the main defendant in the 1938 trial, had argued for a negotiated accommodation with the peasantry in opposing Stalin's policy of "eliminating" the kulaks (prosperous peasants) "as a class" with its attendant civil war in the countryside. And at the Seventeenth Party Congress in 1934, Bukharin spoke of an inevitable struggle to the death between the Soviet Union and fascism in successfully opposing Stalin's view that relations with Nazi Germany should be no different from those with other European countries. (The stenographic record of the Congress includes the following remarks by Stalin: "It is not a question of fascism here, if only for the reason that fascism in Italy, for example, has not prevented the U.S.S.R. from establishing the best relations with that country. . . . And if the interests of the U.S.S.R. demand rapprochement with one country or another which is not interested in disturbing the peace, we adopt this course without hesitation.") My father's Soviet circle of friends and acquaintances—for example, Litvinov, Tukhachevsky, Maisky, Eisenstein, Dr. Kazakov et al.—were all internationalists.

11. Conversations with my father and mother. "Robeson, Junior on His [Moscow] School," *News Chronicle* (London), January 25, 1938; "Why I Left My Son in Moscow," Paul Robeson, *Russia Today* (Moscow), February 1938.

12. They were all indicted on charges of conspiring to assassinate Stalin and his closest associates, of spying for Nazi Germany, and of murdering party officials who had apparently died of natural causes. The leading figure in the trial was the popular Nikolai Bukharin, Lenin's favorite and a close friend of Kirov's; another was Genrikh Yagoda, former chief of the secret police.

Almost no one, even among the top leaders of the Soviet Union, knew the complete toll taken by Stalin's 1938 purge, and perhaps the exact number will never be known. Soviet historian Roy Medvedev (*Let History Judge*, p. 455) estimates that at least 200,000 death sentences were meted out in 1938. Khrushchev, in his "Secret Speech" to the 20th Party Congress, revealed that 1,108 of 1,966 delegates to the 17th Party Congress in 1934 ("The Congress of Victors") were arrested and shot on charges of antirevolutionary crimes in 1937–1938. [Nikita S. Khrushchev, *Khrushchev Remembers*, vol. 1 (New York: Little, Brown and Co., 1970), p. 573.]

13. Conversations with my father and mother. Letters from Essie to William Patterson, March 22 and April 5, 1938.

14. Conversations with my father. Publicly, my father "spoke in terms of reverence of her [Anderson's] voice and musicianship" (*Daily Mail* [London], October 29, 1938). Privately, he had the same opinion but was critical of her "cold" delivery.

15. Max Yergan and my father agreed to work together on African issues through the Council on African Affairs, of which my father became chairman. Yergan was its executive director. This organization would serve as my father's political base for over a decade, with Yergan doubling as his personal political aide and speechwriter.

16. I was present that evening when Nehru came to visit us. Paul's speech welcoming Nehru was delivered at a mass rally at London's Kingsway Hall on June 27, 1938.

17. Letter from Harold Holt to Paul, June 10, 1938. *West London Observer,* December 9, 1938 (movie theaters); *East London Advertiser,* December 17, 1938 (concerts with low top price). Conversation with my father.

18. *Sunday Times* (London), April 10, 1938 (Albert Hall); *Eastbourne Gazette,* April 24, 1938; *Western Telegraph,* May 5, 1938 (Haverfordwest); *Daily Mail* (London), August 13, 1938; *The Scotsman,* September 2, 1938, and the *Glasgow Herald,* September 3, 1938 (Glasgow); *Herald and Express* (Torquay), August 22, 1938 (Torquay Pavilion). Commenting on Robeson's Albert Hall concert, the *Jewish Chronicle* of April 8, 1938, praised his rendition of Engel's "Kaddish" in Hebrew: "Magnificent was his interpretation of this eloquent plea."

19. Interview with C. L. R. James, London, April 24, 1985. Concerning the turn in Soviet policy and the purges, Paul and James agreed to disagree. Surprisingly, however, even though James had broken publicly with the Soviet Union and with the British Communist Party, he told me that both at the time and in retrospect he agreed completely with Paul's refusal to criticize Stalinism publicly. Asserting that Paul's situation was different from his, James added, "Times were different then. You were either pro- or anti-Communist. What else was he to do?"

20. Bunche continued:

In a recent letter from Herskovits [Melville Herskovits, the world-famous anthropologist] I was told how you sat on this intellectual snob Nadel—one of [famous, but orthodox] Malinowski's minions. I was surely tickled to hear that—I never ceased looking for an opportunity to jump down his throat myself, but it never was offered.

Following in Essie's footsteps, I will wander about in East Africa until about April and then light out for Java. You might drop me a note in care of Thomas Cook, Mombasa, Kenya—it would be a real treat for me.

21. Shirer, *The Rise and Fall of the Third Reich,* pp. 414–427 and 430–435.

22. Conversations with my father.

17. A Home in That Rock (1938–1939)

1. Conversations with my father and mother.
2. Essie's diary ("We Go to Spain"), 1938.
3. Derek Tangye, *Daily Mirror* (London), March 8, 1938.

4. *Manchester Guardian*, October 14, 1938 (film industry). "Paul Robeson Tells Us Why," *Cine-Technician*, no. 17, September–October 1938, pp. 74–75 (workers in studios).

5. *Russia Today*, January 14, 1938.

6. Draft of Unity Theatre press release, June 1938 (Robeson Collections at MSRC).

7. Other reviews were similar (Robeson Collections at MSRC):

It has a vitality and tension that make it tremendously exciting. (*News Chronicle*, June 15, 1938)

It was melodrama, of course, but with reality in it. Paul Robeson . . . [kept] the balance with his thoroughly capable colleagues. (*Manchester Guardian*, June 16, 1938)

[Paul Robeson's] comrades were able to act on a level with him in an inspiring unity. (*Reynolds News*, June 19, 1938)

Packed with drama, salted with the wit of the worker the world over, with sudden breathless moments of suspense, this is one of the few plays dealing with a specific class that is triumphant. Mr. Robeson . . . plays perfectly, but he never overshadows the others; he gives to them as only a great artist can.

The Group Theatre in America had its first beginnings in workers clubs after the fashion of Unity. It has now become an influential body catering for all sorts of the theatre-going public. There is no reason why Unity in this country should not do as much. (*Weekly Review*, June 23, 1938)

8. Letter from Edmond Terris in *The Times* (London), July 16, 1938.

9. *News Chronicle*, July 15, 1938.

10. *New York Post*, June 3, 1938 (Negro Actors Guild). Paul was prompted to reassure Barnett on these issues by a July 19, 1938, letter to him from Barnett suggesting an interview that would be of interest to Paul's followers in America. Barnett wrote, in part:

This particular urge came about through the visit to the office the other day by the president of a great religious association. He was accompanied by an artist who was preparing a great placard containing the pictures of various celebrities in commemoration of their forthcoming celebration of the 75th anniversary of the freedom of Negroes from slavery.

In the course of the conversation, it was mentioned that your name had been suggested for a place on the placard, but one of the ministers quoted a disparaging comment which he said you had made relative to the Negro church and which he attributed to certain acquired communistic views. It appears that quite an argument developed in the committee, which met in Chicago but was from various parts of the country. For that reason, we have prepared the following questionnaire which we would like to use as the basis for an interview.

Incidentally, the head of this association, the National Baptist Convention, insisted that no man who sang spirituals as you did could do so without loving them or believing in them, and therefore any statement disparaging the church could not represent your real views.

Do you believe the Negro church is filling its mission and living up to its opportunities? Do you appreciate the Negro spirituals? Do you regard them as depressing and catering to certain ideals which whites like to perpetuate? Are you planning to relinquish your American citizenship? Are you planning to become a citizen of Russia? Would you be interested in making Russia your home? Here in America we hear either glowing stories of Russia's success or horrible tales of its failure. Which are true?

11. *Daily Express*, June 9, 1938 (Robeson Collections at MSRC). Conversations with my father.

12. *Washington Afro-American*, August 20, 1938 (black press); *Daily News* (New York) (good entertainment), *Herald Tribune* (New York) (clever cinematic treatment), and *New York Post* (magnificent performance), August 17, 1938, including the *World Telegram* and *New York Times* (Robeson Collections at MSRC).

13. *Sheffield Telegraph and Daily Independent*, March 3, 1939 (betrayal); *People's World* (California), February 25, 1939 (cable to U.S.) (Robeson Collections at MSRC).

14. Letter from Peter Freuchen to Paul and Essie, January 26, 1939 (Robeson Collections at MSRC).

15. Conversations with my father.

16. Ibid.

17. May 11, 1939, power of attorney from Paul Robeson to Eslanda Robeson. *New York Amsterdam News*, May 20, 1939 (Robeson Collections at MSRC). Letter from Essie to the Van Vechtens, July 19, 1939 (Van Vechten Collection at Yale University). Letters from Carl Van Vechten to his wife, Fania, August 2 and 4, 1939 (in *The Letters of Carl Van Vechten*, Bruce Kellner, ed. New Haven, CT: Yale University Press, 1987, pp. 167–168); Letter from Fania to Carl, August 3, 1939 (in the Carl Van Vechten Papers at the New York Public Library, Manuscript Division).

18. Paul's statements that his view was social rather than political, and that he neither knew nor cared what transpired in Soviet leadership circles, was deliberately misleading. He was trying to avoid having to make substantive responses to questions about Stalin's purges. However, his comments about not being a communist were entirely genuine.

19. *New York Amsterdam News*, May 27, 1939 (Robeson Collections at MSRC).

20. Two letters from Walter White to Paul, June 15, 1939; *The Afro-American*, July 22, 1939 (Robeson Collections at MSRC).

21. *Sunday Worker*, June 4, 1939 (Robeson Collections at MSRC).

22. Conversations with my father.

23. Letter from Sol Hurok to Robert Rockmore, May 26, 1939 (Robeson Collections at MSRC).

24. *New York Herald Tribune*, June 20, 1939; *New York Post*, June 20, 1939; *New York World-Telegram*, June 22, 1939; *Sunday Worker*, June 4, 1939 (elimination of the word "nigger") (Robeson Collections at MSRC).

25. Cable from Paul to Essie, June 23, 1939. Denmark Vesey was the legendary leader of an aborted but vast 1822 slave rebellion in Charleston, South Carolina (Robeson Collections at MSRC).

26. Letter from Essie to Paul, June 25, 1939 (Robeson Collections at MSRC).

27. Letter from Walter Legge (Artists' and Recording Manager for His Master's Voice), August 10, 1939. Essie's diary, September 28, 1939. *Radio Times*, August 18, 1939 (television appearance); *Cinema*, August 30, 1939 (Robeson Collections at MSRC). Conversations with my parents.

28. *Manchester Dispatch*, November 1, 1938; *Sheffield Telegraph*, November 1, 1938; *Blackburn Telegraph*, May 27, 1939 (Pen Tennyson and Michael Balcon) (Robeson Collections at MSRC).

29. For the history of the Nazi–Soviet Pact, see William L. Shirer, *The Rise and Fall of the Third Reich* (New York: Simon and Schuster, 1960), pp. 513–544.

30. Essie's diary, September 1–3, 6, 15, 25, 26, 28, and 30, 1939 (Robeson Collections at MSRC).

31. Essie's diary, October 2, 1939 (Robeson Collections at MSRC).

32. *New York Amsterdam News*, October 21, 1939; *Daily Worker*, October 26, 1939. Conversations with my father.

33. *Sunday Worker* (New York), June 4, 1939. Paul Robeson's unpublished 1939 Notes (Robeson Collections at MSRC).

INDEX

Abortion, 50–51, 184, 187

Abraham Lincoln Brigade, *267*

Abyssinian Baptist Church (Harlem), 74, 78

Ackerman, 13, 18

Actors Equity, 155

Africa
anticolonialism, 224, 225, 229, 240, 285, 286
Egypt, *Jericho* (film), 282–283
Ethiopia, 285
film industry, 242
Paul and, 210, 211, 229, 235

African-Americans. *See also* Race relations
culture, 227–228
Essie and, 171–172, 319–320
Harlem Renaissance, 43–45, 86
lynchings, 23, 24, 35, 218, 226, 289
Paul and, 208–210, 243–244, 283–284, 285–286, 318, 325, 326, 331–332
politics, 220, 231
social conservatism of, 90
Soviet Union and, 293
theater, 48–49, 59, 72, 75, 77–79, 138, 143, 157, 166, 316–317

African Methodist Episcopal (A.M.E.) Zion Church, 11, 13, 17, 78

Afro-American (newspaper), 241

Aida (Verdi opera), 216

Akron Pros (football team), 49, 53, 69, *111*

Aldridge, Ira, 95–96, 166

All-American, 30, 35

All God's Chillun Got Wings (O'Neill play), 73–74, 75, 76, 77–78, 80–81, *120*, 186, 203, 204–206, 226, 240, *250*

Alpha Phi Alpha fraternity, 53

American Magazine, xiii

American Mercury (publication), 74

American New Theater League, 317

Amsterdam News (New York newspaper), 207

Anderson, Marian, 223, 224, 308, 318, 325

Angus, Donald, 92

Antheil, George, 96

Anticolonialism
Africa, 224, 225, 229, 240, 285, 286
India, 285, 308–309
Paul and, 311–312

Anti-Semitism, Germany, 313

Armitage, Teresa, 159

Ashcroft, Peggy, *130*, *135*, 166, 178–179, 180–181, 327

Associated Negro Press, 318

Astaire, Adele, 86

Athletics. *See* Football; Rutgers College

Atkinson, Brooks, 101

Attlee, Clement, 286

Atwill, Lionel, 92

Austria, 304

Azcarate, 303

Bach, Johann Sebastian, 216

Back-to-Africa movement, 44, 142

Bacote, Mrs. L. J., 139

Bagg, 14

Balcon, Michael, 329–330

Baldwin, James, xiv

Banjo (McKay), 238

Banks, Leslie, 225

Barnett, Claude, 318

Barthe, Richmond, 319

Baruch, Alfred ("Barry"), *274*, 324–325

Basalik (Garland play), 226

Baughan, E. A., 205

Bayliss, Lillian, 239

Beach, Sylvia, 96

Behan, Charles, 197

Belasco, David, 91

Belfast Telegraph (newspaper), 236

Bengal, Ben, 295

Best, Joseph, 240

Bezhin Meadow (film), 245, 291

Biddle University, 12

Big Fella (film), 238, 242, *265*, 282, 295

Bingham, 224

Birth of a Nation (film), 24

Black and Tan (film), 207

Black Boy (play), 99–100, 101

Black Majesty (film), 243

Black Majesty (play), 236

Black Nationalism, 157, 243

Blair, Mary, 75, 76

Blake, Eubie, 58

Bledsoe, Harry, 84

Body and Soul (film), 82

Bolling, Buddy, *112*, 231, 324

Bolling, Hattie, 52, *112*, 231, 319, 324

Borderline (film), *129*, 165, 319

Boris Godunov (Mussorgsky opera), 203, 216, 221

Bradford, Roark, 328

Breare, W. H., 215

British Musician and Musical Review, 215

British Trade Union Congress, 243

Broun, Heywood, 74, 77, 90

Broun, Ruth, 90

Browder, Earl, 302

Brown, J. W., 78

Brown, Lawrence B., 65, 85–86, 88, 90, 93, 98, *119*, *124*, *126*, 139, 140, 144, 147, 148, 149–151, 154, 187, 199, 221, 230, 236, 238, 242, *251*, *265*, *276*, 322, 323

Browne, Maurice, 166, 169, 171, 174

Browning, Harold, 57, 58, 60, 65

Brown University, 26, 27, 46

Bunche, Ralph, 312

Burleigh, Harry T., 45, 83, 140

Bustill, Charles Hicks (grandfather), *102*

Bustill, Cyrus, 5

Bustill, Joseph, 5

Bustill family, *102*, 171
    reunion of (1918), 33–34
    social standing of, 4–5, 8

Butt, Alfred, 85, 149

The Bystander (newspaper), 241

California Eagle (newspaper), 242

California News (newspaper), 242

The Call (newspaper), 138, 139

Camp, Walter, 30

Campbell, George, 241

Campbell, Mrs. Patrick, 59, 61, 64, 65, 66, 68

Cap and Skull Society (Rutgers College), 35, *108*

Cardozo, Francis Lewis, 47

Carnegie Hall, *128*, 158–159

Carr, James D., 27, 28

Carter, Jack, 148

Castillo, Fernando, *266*, *267*, 298, 302, 321–322

Castillo, Pablo, 302, 321

Celebrity Concert Tour (1929), 156

Chaliapin, Fyodor, 88–89, 139, 141, 146, 157, 183, 223

Chamberlain, Neville, 322

Chicago Defender (newspaper), 190, 219, 220

Chicago riots (1937), 285

China, 294, 311

Chinese language, 245

Chinn, May, 45, 46, 50

Civil rights movement, xiv, 333

Civil War (US), 36

  Birth of a Nation (film), 24

  Bustill family, 5

  Robeson, William Drew (father), 4

Clapham, 198

Clothier, Robert, *132*, 194

Cochran, Gifford, 207

Coleridge-Taylor, Samuel, 329

Colson, Bill, 60

Columbia University, 45, 48, 228

Columbia University Law School, 43, 50, 69, 71

Columbia University Medical School, 48

Commencement speech (1919), Rutgers College, 35–39, 176

Communist Party (UK), 286

Communist Party USA, xiii, 36, 44, 241, 326

  Patterson, 223

  Paul on, 235, 325

  Soviet Union and, 281

  Spanish Civil War, 302

  World War II, 330

Coppicus, F. C., 157, 319

Coward, Noel, 181, 183–184

Crane, 196, 197

Crane, Mrs. W. Murray, 89

Cripps, Stafford, 286, 295

The Crisis (publication), 44, 45, 162

"Criteria of Negro Art" (DuBois), 162

Cullen, Countee, 90

Culture

  African-Americans, 227–228

  language, 227

Cummings family, 20

Currier, Mrs. Guy, 83

Czechoslovakia, 304, 312, 322

Daily Herald (newspaper), 317

Daily Princetonian (newspaper), 139

Daily Worker (newspaper), 317

Daniels, Jimmy, 319

Dark Sands (film), 319, 320

Darrow, Clarence, 142

Darrow, Paul, 142

Davenport, Robert, 26

David Goliath (film), 329, 330

Davis, Benjamin J., Jr., 235, 237, 325–326

Dean, Basil, 295

Delta Sigma Theta sorority, 53

Demarest, William, 27, 31, 36

DeMille, Cecil B., 99, 100

Dempsey, Jack, 69

Denmark, 223, 323

Dennis, Eugene, 281

Denny, Abraham, 9–10
de Silva, Marcia, 229
Diamond, Freda, 93, 100, 144, 159, 274, 324
Die Stunde (Vienna newspaper), 156
Digges, Dudley, 250
Discrimination. See African-Americans; Race relations
Divorce
  agreement to, 181–182, 190
  arrangements of, 196, 197
  Essie contemplates, 165
Don't You Want to Be Free? (Hughes play), 328
Douglas, William O., 50
Douglass, Frederick, 39
Dreiser, Theodore, 86, 148
DuBois, W. E. B., 28, 74, 335
  art and, 78, 162, 177
  influence of, 31, 39, 44, 284, 326
Duncan, Augustin, 55, 56, 57, 73
Duncan, Isadora, 55

Egypt, Jericho (film), 282–283. See also Africa
Eisenstein, Sergei Mikhailovich, 201, 213–214, 218, 219, 220, 222, 236, 243, 245–246, 251, 279–280, 290–291, 294, 317
Eitingon, Bess, 73–74
Ellington, Duke, 207, 216, 318, 328
Ellison, Ralph, 326
The Emperor Jones (film), 206–208, 210, 231, 242, 248, 249, 250, 254, 255, 320, 324
The Emperor Jones (O'Neill play), 49, 75–76, 79, 80, 83, 84, 85, 90, 94, 95, 116, 117, 151, 159, 185, 203, 204, 223, 271, 326–327, 328
Engels, Friedrich, 286
England. See United Kingdom

Ethiopia, 285
Evans, Maurice, 319, 327

Farmington (Darrow), 142
Fascism. See also Politics
  Germany, 218
  Paul and, 292–293, 295–296, 332
  United States, 303
Fauset, Jessie, 76
Fauvam, 27
Ferber, Edna, 192
Film industry
  Africa, 242
  race relations, 207–208, 237, 315–316
  Soviet Union, 243
Finland, 223
Fisher, Rudolph ("Bud"), 46
Football
  Akron Pros, 49, 53
  childhood, 7
  Milwaukee Badgers, 69
  Rutgers career, 21–30, 35
Ford, Wallace, 263, 264, 282
Four Harmony Kings, 57–58, 60
France
  fascism, 295–296, 303, 312
  Germany and, 302
  Spanish Civil War, 291, 322
  World War II, 330
Franco, Francisco, 285, 287, 291, 321
Free African Society, 5
Freedmen's School, 4
Freeland, Thornton, 282
Freuchen, Peter, 323
Futter, Walter, 282

Gallantier, Lewis, 96
Gandhi, Mohandas (Mahatma), 285
Garbo, Greta, 230

Garland, Peter, 226
Garvey, Marcus, 44, 78, 142
General Motors Concert Series, 231
Germany
  fascism, 218, 243
  Munich Agreement (1938), 312
  pogrom in, 313
  Soviet Union and, 222, 289–290, 324, 330
  Spanish Civil War, 291, 292
  World War II, 285, 302–303, 330
Gershwin, George, 86, 215
Gielgud, John, 319
Gilels, Emil, *262*
Gilpin, Charles, 49, 55, 74, 75, 76, 79, 80, 91
Gish, Lillian, 166
God. *See* Religion
Golden, John Oliver, *262*, 293
Golden, Lillie, *262*
Golden Boy (play), 320
Goldman, Emma, 95, 217, *256*
Gone With the Wind (film), 288
Goode, Eslanda Cardozo (mother-in-law), 46, 50, 53, 76, *115*, 148, 154, 174, 178, 180, 182, 187, 190, 198, 213, 221, 232, 233, 236, *256*, 293, 296, 308, 324
Goode, Francis ("Frank," brother-in-law), 47, 219, 221–222, *252*, 281, 293–294, 304, 306, 319
Goode, John, 47
Goode, John, Jr. (brother-in-law), 47, 218–219, 221–222, *251*, *252*, 306–307
The Good Earth (Buck), 243
Gott, Barbara, 66
Gould, Stephen Jay, 71
Great Depression, 163
Great Terror (Soviet Union), 281, 290. *See also* Soviet Union

Green, Paul, 137
Green Pastures (film), 193, 232
Greenwich Village (New York City), 90–91
Griffith, D. W., 24
Guaglia, Stroppa, 92
Guthrie, Tyrone, 243

Haggard, H. Rider, 238
Hairy Ape (O'Neill play), *131*, 186, 203
Haiti, 18, 213, 220, 236
Haiti (play), 317, 319, 320
Haldane, Charlotte, *266*, 299, 301
Haldane, Paul, 299, 301
Hammerstein, Oscar, 143, 233, 236
Handel, George Frideric, 216
Hardwicke, Cedric, 238, *259*
Harlem (New York City)
  Abyssinian Baptist Church, 74, 78
  Essie and, 319–320
  Paul and, 43–45, 85–86, 157, 195, 231
Harlem Renaissance, 43–45, 86
Harmony Kings. *See* Four Harmony Kings
Harris, Jed, 166
Harrison, Richard, 193
Hart-Davis, Rupert, 179
Hayes, Arthur Garfield, 100
Hayes, Roland, 45, 83, 85, 140, 146, 224
Hebrew language, 227
Hedda Gabler (Ibsen), 61
Heifetz, Yasha, 160
Hemingway, Ernest, 96, 320
Henry, Patrick, 13
Henson, Matthew, 288
Herskovits, Melville, 228
Heyward, Dorothy, 149
Heyward, Dubose, 149
Hiawatha (poem), 329

Hitler, Adolph, 24, 285, 295, 302,
    303, 304, 312, 322, 324, 330
Hochschild, Adam, 306
Hollaway, Dorothy, 238
Holt, Harold, 309, 310, 314
Hooper, 83
Hoover, Herbert, 193
Hornblow, Arthur, Jr., 138
Howard University, 45
Howard University College of
    Medicine, 15
Howard University Law School, 47
Hughes, Langston, 143, 193, 241,
    328
Hull, Cordell, 302
Hurok, Sol, 326
Huxley, Aldous, 155

Ibsen, Henrik Johan, 61
Imperial Hotel (Narragansett Pier,
    Rhode Island), 18–19, 26, 28, 34
In Abraham's Bosom (Green play),
    137
India, anticolonialism, 285, 308–309
Intellectual pursuits, of Paul
    Robeson, 185–186, 195, 200,
    208–210, 227–230, 244–245,
    286–287, 293
International Brigade, 277, 299,
    303
Interracial marriage
  Paul and Yolande, 182–183
  theater, 75, 166, 204
Italy
  fascism, 285, 303
  Spanish Civil War, 291

Jackson, Yolande, 132, 163–164, 178,
    179, 181–184, 186, 189, 194,
    195–197, 199
Jamaica, 311
James, C. L. R., 239, 287, 311, 312

Japan
  China and, 294
  fascism, 285, 303
The Jazz Singer (film), 206
Jericho (film), 263, 264, 277,
    281–284, 295, 319
Jewish community
  Hebrew language, 227
  spirituals and, 141
Jewish Transcript (newspaper), 227
John Henry (Bradford play), 328,
    329
Johnson, Charles S., 44
Johnson, J. Rosamond, 44, 45, 140
Johnson, James Weldon, 44, 76, 100,
    142, 193, 318
Jolson, Al, 232
Jones, Robert Edmond, 49
Joyce, James, 96
Julliard Musical Foundation, 137
Just, Ernest, 193

Kahn, Otto, 73, 86, 92, 99, 137,
    155
Kansas City Times (newspaper), 139
Kaye, Conrad, 302
Kazakov, Ignaty, 293, 294, 304, 305,
    306
Kelly, Frank, 22, 23
Kenya, 211
Kenya (Leys), 229
Kenyatta, Jomo, 211, 224, 225, 253
Kern, Jerome, 142, 233
Khanum, Tamara, 262
The Kingdom of Zinga (Williams and
    Hollaway), 238
King Solomon's Mines (film), 238–239,
    242, 259, 295
Kirov, Sergei M., 219, 289
Knight, Mrs., 67
Knopf, Alfred, 86
Knopf, Blanche, 86

Korda, Alexander, 210, 231, 234
Korda, Zoltan, 210, 234, 236, 237
Koriansky, 81
Kouka (Sudanese Princess), *263*, *264*, 277, 282
Kreisler, Fritz, 157, 160
Krimsky, John, 207
Kristallnacht, 313
Kropf, Howard, 91
Kubeka, Ben, 242
Ku Klux Klan, 36, 75, 142. *See also* African-Americans; Race relations

Labour Party (UK), 157, 174, 243, 286, 295
Laemmle, Carl, Jr., 230
Lafayette Players, 49, 74–75
Language
Chinese, 245
culture and, 227
Paul and, 245
Russian language, 185, 203, 219, 220, 221
Laski, Harold, 243
Law, Oliver, 302, 315, 320
League of Colored Peoples, 210
Lee, Anna, *259*
Left Theater Group, 243
Legal profession, racism, 71–72
Lenin, V. I., 286
Leys, Norman, 228–229, 240
Life magazine, 280
Liggins, Bruce, *275*
Light, James, 76, 86, *119*, 166, 197, 204
Light, Patti, 166
Lightfoot, James, 43–44, 52
Lincoln Battalion, 302
Lincoln University, 4, 6, 12, 17, 44
Litvinov, Maxim, 222
Liveright, Horace, 99

London Evening News (newspaper), 185, 237, 242
London Sunday News (newspaper), 167
London Sunday Times (newspaper), 167, 168, 205
London Times (newspaper), 167, 203, 317–318
Louis, Joe, 325, 329
L'Ouverture, Toussaint, 18, 213, 220, 236, 243, 329
Lowinger, 187
Lucas, Grant, 48, 51
Lucas, Inez, 74
*Lulu Bell*e (Sheldon play), 91–92
Lynchings, 23, 24, 35, 218, 226, 289. *See also* African-Americans; Race relations

Macgowan, Kenneth, 49, 55, 73
Macpherson, Bryher, 165
Macpherson, Kenneth, 165–166, 319
The Magic Flute (Mozart opera), 283
Maisky, Ivan, 217, 286, 296, 303
Manchester Guardian (newspaper), 167, 292
Mandela, Nelson, 312
Marinoff, Fania, 86
Marr, Nikolai Y., 245
Marshall, Herbert, 295, 317, 329
Marx, Karl, 195, 209, 285, 286
Mary (queen of England), 155
Matisse, Henri, 96
Maxwell House Coffee Hour account, 197
McClendon, Rose, 74, 193
McConnell, 319
McCormack, John, 140, 157
McDonald, Mr. and Mrs., 92
McGhee, Bettina ("Bert"), 90, 324
McGhee, Harold ("Gig"), 90, 324

McKay, Claude, 45, 96, 193, 238

McKinney, Nina Mae, *253*

Media, myths of, xiii–xiv. *See also* entries under individual newspapers and publications

Medvedev, Roy, 289

Meltzer, Julius, 237

The Messenger (publication), 44, 77

Metropolitan Music Bureau, 157

Micheaux, Oscar, 82, 165–166

Mills, Florence, 57, 72, 91

Milner, Anne, 14

Milwaukee Badgers (football team), 69

Minkin, Jacob S., 141

Montesole, Max, 166

Morris, William, 319

Morton, F. Q., 28

Mountbatten, Lady Louis, 190

Mozart, Wolfgang Amadeus, 216, 283

Mulatto (Hughes play), 328

Munich Agreement (1938), 304, 312

Munro, Norma (Peter Garland), 226

Muray, Nickolas, 90, *121*

Murphy, Dudley, 207

Mussolini, Benito, 285, 295

Mussorgsky, Modest Petrovich, 203, 216

My Song Goes Forth (film), 240–241

Napoleon Bonaparte (e. of France), 213

Narragansett Pier, Rhode Island, 18–19, 26, 28, 34

Nash's (magazine), 229

National Association for the Advancement of Colored People (NAACP), 24, 44, 74, 78, 86, 138, 240, 325

National Theater Hall of Fame, xiii

National Urban League, 44

Neale, Earl ("Greasy"), 29–30

Neale, Geraldine Mamie ("Gerry"), 25–26, 31, 45–46, 48, 50, 60, 84, *107*

Negro Actors Guild, 318

Negro People's Committee to Aid Spanish Democracy, 322

Negro Songs of Protest, 279

Nehru, Pandit Jawaharlal, 285, 308–309

Neutrality Act of 1937, 302–303

New Deal, 285, 297, 308, 317, 333

Newport Naval Reserves (football team), 30

The New Republic (publication), 49, 98

News-Chronicle (newspaper), 205

The New Statesman and Nation (publication), 243, 317

New York American (newspaper), 30

New York Amsterdam News (newspaper), 280

New York Evening Post (newspaper), 76

New York Herald Tribune (newspaper), 76, 77, 80, 235, 286

New York jazz revue, 155

New York Telegram (newspaper), 76, 139

New York Telegram and Evening Mail (newspaper), 77

New York Times (newspaper), 23, 29, 56–57, 87, 101, 320

New York University Law School, 43

Nit, Johnny, 89

Norman, Dora Cole, 48–49, 55, 56

Norway, 323

Oistrakh, David, *262*

"Ol' Black Joe" (song), 59

Olivier, Laurence, 239

"Ol' Man River" (song), 143, 149, 151–152, 153, 155, 156, 192, 221, 233, 293, 298

O'Neill, Eugene, 49, 73, 74, 75, 76, 77, 78, 79–81, 86, 89–90, 92, 128, 160, 203, 204, 206, 254

One Third of a Nation (play), 317, 319

Oorang Indians (football team), 69

Opera, 215–216

Opportunity (publication), 44, 45, 77

Oratory, 18, 33, 35–39, 141–142

Othello (Shakespeare play), 81, 95, 129, 130, 135, 158, 166–169, 171, 173–174, 178, 185, 220, 239–240, 243, 288, 297, 318, 319, 327

Our Town (Wilder play), 319

Paderewski, Ignacy Jan, 157

Patterson, Minnie, 319

Patterson, William, 53, 142, 222–223, 304, 306, 312, 326

Patton, Bernice, 242

Paul Robeson, Negro (E. G. Robeson), 165, 169–173, 178

Pavel Morozov (film), 290

Payne, John, 65

Peary, Robert Edwin, 288

Perry, Lawrence, 69, 70

Pesti Naplo (Budapest newspaper), 156

Peter Pan (play), 198

Peters, Paul, 226

Phi Beta Kappa Honor Society, 30, 35, 46

Philadelphia Art Alliance, 169

Philadelphia Record (newspaper), 75

Philadelphia Tribune (newspaper), 207

Phillips, Wendell, 18

Pickens, William, 78

Pickett, George, 4

Pins and Needles (play), 319

Plantation Revue (vaudeville show), 41, 72

Plant in the Sun (Bengal play), 265, 295, 317–318

Poland, 322, 324, 330

Politics. See also Fascism
    African-Americans, 220, 231
    Paul Robeson and, 30–31, 44, 142, 176–177, 193, 220, 222–223, 232, 243, 284–287, 294–296
    race relations and, 286
    segregation, 36
    South Africa, 240–241
    Soviet Union, 219, 239, 289–290, 293–294

Politiken (newspaper), 323

Pollard, Fritz, 26, 27, 44, 49, 69, 207

Pollitt, Harry, 286

Pond, James, 92, 100, 143

Porgy (play), 149

Porgy and Bess (Gershwin opera), 215

Poston, Ted, 231, 232

Powell, Adam Clayton, Sr., 78

Princeton University, 5, 17, 139

Proshchowsky, Frantz, 99

The Proud Valley (film), 272, 273, 330, 331

Proust, Marcel, 195

Provincetown Players, 49, 55, 73, 75, 81, 90, 92, 204, 324

Pulitzer Prize, 137

Punch (magazine), 204

Purcell, Henry, 216

Qué Viva Mexico! (film), 213

Quiett, Frances, 46

Quilter, Roger, 155

Race relations. See also African-Americans; Lynchings
    college football, 27, 29–30

Race relations (continued)
  commencement speech (1919),
    35–39
  Europe, 157
  film industry, 207–208, 237,
    315–316
  legal profession, 71–72
  lynchings, 23, 24, 35, 218, 226,
    289
  New Deal, 285
  Paul Robeson and, xiii, 10,
    285–286, 331–332
  politics and, 286
  South Africa, 240–241
  Soviet Union, 216–217, 220,
    221–222, 236, 245
  theater, 48–49, 59, 72, 75, 77–79,
    138, 143, 157, 166, 316–317
Race riots (1919), 35–36, 289
Radio concerts, 139, 231, 295
Radio interview (1930), 169
Randolph, A. Philip, 44
Ravensdale, Lady, 174
Reagan, Caroline Dudley, 155
Recordings, 93, 254
Recording technique, 234
Rector, Eddie, 89
Religion
  Paul on, 161–162, 190–192, 244
  Soviet Union, 219–220
Revolutionary War (US), 5
Roberson Plantation (Robersonville,
    North Carolina), 4
Robertson, Jean Forbes, 198
Robeson, Benjamina (niece), 275
Robeson, Benjamin (brother), 3, 7,
    8, 14, 33, 34, 109, 256, 275,
    319, 324
  career of, 17
  education of, 9, 11, 12
  Essie and, 50, 53
  Paul and, xv, 17, 18–19, 22, 97

Robeson, Benjamin (grandfather), 4
Robeson, Eslanda Cardozo ("Essie,"
    née Goode, wife), 41, 46, 58,
    110, 116, 123, 166, 201, 218,
    238, 247, 260, 261, 265, 269,
    270, 332
  Africa visit, 240
  agent/manager role, 81–82, 85, 88,
    99, 100, 143, 149, 156, 174, 200,
    226–227, 237, 281, 324
  biography of Paul by, 165,
    169–173, 178
  career advice from, 55–56, 57, 72,
    73, 91, 92, 137, 203, 208, 215,
    225, 318–319, 320, 327–329
  career of, 46–47, 48, 56, 112
  courtship, 49–50, 51–52
  divorce agreement, 181–182, 190
  divorce arrangements, 196, 197
  divorce contemplated, 165
  emotional crisis, 178–181
  England and, 153–154
  family of, 47–48
  Harlem and, 319–320
  health of, 59–60, 67, 68, 70, 147,
    148, 149, 184, 187, 198
  household management, 178,
    307–308
  intellectual pursuits, 208
  Jericho (film), 282
  Marian Robeson and, 97
  marital relationship, 53–54, 59,
    60, 61, 62–63, 64, 66, 84, 93,
    94, 100–101, 144, 145–147,
    159, 164, 165, 173, 178–179,
    181–183, 186, 187, 189–190,
    198–200, 230, 327–328
  marriage to Paul, 52, 114
  Paul Jr. and, 236
  performance reviews by, 86–87,
    88, 98, 99, 155, 186, 198
  portrait photo, 118

pregnancy of, 50–51, 142, 143, 184
rehearsals with, 75–76
segregation and, 138
separation from Paul, 186–188
social life, 89–90, 92, 95–96
Soviet Union and, 218–223, *251*,
   293–294
Spanish Civil War and, *266*,
   297–302
Robeson, Ezekiel (uncle), Civil
   War, 4
Robeson, Frances (sister-in-law),
   275, 319
Robeson, John Bunyan Reeve
   "Reed" (brother), 3, 33, 34
career of, 12–13
disappearance of, 97
education of, 9
Robeson, Maria Louisa Bustill
   (mother), *102, 103*
death of, 7–8
health of, 3, 7
marriage of, 4
Robeson, Marian (niece), *275*
Robeson, Marian (sister), 3, 33, 76,
   319, 324
education of, 9
Essie and, 50, 53
family role of, 97
Paul and, 15, 174
Robeson, Paul Leroy
affairs of
   Fredi Washington, 100
   Peggy Ashcroft, 163–164, 178,
      180–181
   Yolande Jackson, 163–164, 178,
      179, 181–184, 186, 189, 194,
      195–197, 199
African-Americans and, xiii, 78–79,
   208–210, 243–244, 283–284,
   285–286, 318, 325, 326,
   331–332

Akron Pros (football team), 49, 53,
   69, *111*
All-American, 30, 35
anticolonialism, 311–312
art and destiny, 160
athletics and, 12, 16–17
Ben Robeson (brother) and,
   18–19
Bill Robeson (brother) and, 34
biography of, by Essie, 165,
   169–173, 178
birth of, 3
career concerns, 174–176, 184,
   194–195, 203, 215–217, 234,
   236–237, 239–240, 285,
   309–310, 314–315, 323–324
community and, 10–12, 25
divorce agreement, 181–182,
   190
divorce arrangements, 196, 197
education of, *1*, 9–10, 13–14,
   15, 18
England and, 59, 61–62
Essie courted by, 46, 48, 49–52,
   53–54
father and, 6–7, 8, 9–10, 23–24,
   36
father's death, 32–34
films
   Big Fella, 238, 242, *265*, 282,
      295
   Body and Soul, 82, 165–166
   Borderline, *129*, 165–166, 319
   Dark Sands, 319, 320
   The Emperor Jones, 206–208,
      210, 231, 242, *248, 249, 250,
      254, 255*, 324
   Jericho, *263, 264*, 277, 281–284,
      295, 319
   King Solomon's Mines, 238–239,
      242, *259*
   My Song Goes Forth, 240–241

Robeson, Paul Leroy
  films *(continued)*
    The Proud Valley, 272, *273,* 330,
      331
    Sanders of the River, 201, 208,
      210–213, 224–226, 231, 232,
      234, 237–238, 239, 242, *253,*
      283
    Show Boat, 226, 227, 230,
      231–232, 234, 241–242, *257,*
      282, 283, 284, 295
    Song of Freedom, 238, 241, 243,
      258, 295
  finances of, 81–82, 85, 88, 91,
    92–93, 99, 100, 137, 140,
    142, 148, 149, 155, 179–180,
    193, 194, 196–197, 204,
    226–227, 315
  Harlem and, 43–45, 85–86, 157,
    195, 231
  health of, 189, 197–198
  intellectual pursuits, 185–186, 195,
    200, 208–210, 227–230,
    244–245, 286–287, 293
  law career, 71–72
  law school, 43, 50, 53, 55, 59, 63,
    69, 71, *111*
  London residence, *268*
  marital relationship, 60, 61, 62–63,
    64, 66, 67–68, 84, 93, 94,
    100–101, 144, 145–147, 159,
    165, 173, 179, 181–183, 186,
    187, 189–190, 198–200
  marriage to Essie, 52, *114*
  mother's death, 8
  Neale, Geraldine Mamie ("Gerry")
    and, 25–26, 45–46, 60
  Nehru and, 308–309
  oratory, 18, 33, 35–39, 141–142
  Paul, Jr. describes, 211–213
  personality of, xiv–xv, 15–16, 21,
    23–24, 163, 242–243

  politics, xiii–xiv, 30–31, 142,
    235–236, 239, 243, 284–287,
    292–293, 294–295, 295–296,
    309–310, 311–312, 314, 322,
    325–326, 332–334
  popularity of, 85–86, 88–91,
    95–96, 155, 157, 221, 287, 295
  portrait photos, *113, 121, 133,*
    134, 255
  press conference, *268*
  radio interview (1930), 169
  recordings, 93, *254,* 315, 329
  Reed Robeson (brother) and,
    12–13
  Rutgers College, 20, 24, *105, 107,*
    108, 110
  Rutgers College baseball team,
    108
  Rutgers College basketball team,
    106
  Rutgers College commencement
    speech (1919), 35–39, 176
  Rutgers College football team, *1,*
    21–30, 35, *104, 105, 106*
  Rutgers College honorary degree,
    132, 194
  Rutgers College track team, *105*
  St. Christopher basketball team
    (Harlem), 25, 31, *111*
  Sanford, Foster and, 34, 43,
    44, 71
  sculpture and modeling, 90–91,
    120, 121, 131, 133, 169
  segregation and, 138–139
  separation from Essie, 186–188
  social activism, 91
  son and, 232–233, 287–288, 308
  Soviet purges and, 305–306
  Soviet Union visit (1934–1935),
    216–217, 218–223, *251*
  Soviet Union visit (1937), *262,*
    287–288

Spanish Civil War, *266*, *267*, 291–293, 297–302, 303, 321–322

spirituals and, 8–9, 45, 87–88

television, 329

theater and, 55–59, 62–68

theatrical performances

  All God's Chillun Got Wings (O'Neill play), 73–74, 76, 77–78, 80–81, *120*, 186, 203, 204–206, 226, 240, *250*

  Basalik (Garland play), 226

  Black Boy (play), 99–100, 101, *122*

  The Emperor Jones (O'Neill play), 75–76, 79, 80, 83, 84, 85, 90, 94, 95, *116*, *117*, 151, 159, 185, 203, 204, 223, *271*, 320, 326–327, 328

  Hairy Ape (O'Neill play), *131*, 186, 203

  Othello (Shakespeare play), *129*, *130*, *135*, 166–169, 171, 173–174, 185

  Plantation Revue (vaudeville show), *41*, 72

  Plant in the Sun (Bengal play), *265*, 295, 317–318

  Roseanne (play), 74–75

  Show Boat (musical), *135*, 149, 151–152, 153, 155, 156, 157, 192, 193, 195, 197, 206, 223

  Shuffle Along (musical review), 57–59, 60, 62, 63, 64, 65, 66, 68, 72, 91

  Stevedore (Peters and Sklar play), 220, 226, *258*

  Toussaint L'Ouverture (play), 239

  Voodoo (play), 59, 62, 63, 66, 68, 70, *115*

Titterton interviews, 174–176, 190–192, 200

vocal and concert engagements

  amateur and social, 31–32, 74, 96

England (1928), 154–155

England (1929), *135*, 157

England (1930), 165, 166

England (1935), 223–224

England (1936), 236

England (1937), 292

England (1938), 310–311

Europe (1927), 144

Europe (1929), 156–157

Europe (1930), 165–166

Europe (1935), 227

Europe (1939), 322, 323–324

Larry Brown and, 147–148

Soviet Union (1936), 239, 243, 279–280

US (1924), 83

US (1925), 86–87

US (1926), 97–99, *124*, *125*

US (1927), 138, 139–141

US (1929), *128*, 158–159

US (1931), 183

US (1935), 230–231, 233

voice of, 14, 45, 99, 214–215

wake of (1976), 46

Robeson, Paul, Jr. (son), *127*, *256*, *269*, *274*

Africa visit, 240

birth of, 144–145

childhood of, 232–233, 287–288

divorce arrangement, 196

Paul's feelings for, 172, 198, 211–213, 236, 287–288, 308

Soviet education of, *262*, 280–281, 287, 288–289, 307, 325

Soviet purges and, 304, 305–306

Robeson, Sabra (grandmother), 4

Robeson, Vivian (niece), *275*

Robeson, William Drew (father), 90, *102*, *103*

career of, 3, 5–7, 11, 13

Civil War, 4

death of, 32–34

Robeson, William Drew (father)
  (*continued*)
  education of, 4
  marriage of, 4
  Paul and, 6–7, 8, 9–10, 16, 17,
    23–24, 25, 27, 32, 34, 36
  personality of, 3–4
  racism condemned by, 24
  Reed and, 12–13
Robeson, William Drew, Jr. ("Bill,"
    brother), 3, 7, 12, 14, 33
  death of, 97
  education of, 6, 9, 15
  Paul and, 34
  Princeton University, 5, 17
  race riots of 1919, 35
Robson, Flora, 203, 204, 205, 206,
    250
Rockmore, Bess, 186
Rockmore, Clara, 319, 324
Rockmore, Robert, 186, 195–196, 199,
    200, 226, *275*, 319, 324, 326
Romilly, Rita, 196–197
Roosevelt, Franklin D., 193, 284–285,
    297, 302–303, 308, 333
Roseanne (play), 74–75
Ruiz, Cristobal, 321
Russia. *See* Soviet Union
Russian language, 185, 203, 219,
    220, 221
Rutgers College
  football team, 21–30, 35
  founding of, 20
  honorary degree awarded by,
    132, 194
  scholarship program, 17
Rutgers Glee Club, 28
St. Christopher basketball team
    (Harlem), 25, 31, *111*
St. Louis Blues (film), 207
Salemme, Antonio ("Tony"), 90–91,
    120, *131*, 163, 169

Salemme, Betty, 91
Sampson, Martha, 169
Sanders of the River (film), *201*, 208,
    210–213, 223, 224–226, 231, 232,
    234, 237–238, 239, 242, *253*, 283
Sanford, Foster
  as coach, 21, 22, 23, 24–25, 26, 27,
    28, 29, *104*
  Essie and, 182
  as mentor, 34, 43, 44, 71
Sargeant, Elizabeth Shepley, 98
Savoy Hotel (London), racism, 157
Schang, Fred, 326
Schirmer, Robert, 96
Schoenberg, Arnold, 216
Scottsboro, Alabama case, 193, 223
Segregation, politics, 36. *See also*
    African-Americans; Race
    relations
Seton, Marie, 85, 151, 213, 217,
    218, *251*
Shafer, Kurt, 307
Shakespeare, William, 14, 81, 168,
    216
Shaw, George Bernard, 155
Sheldon, Edward, 91
Shelton, Sadie, *107*
Show Boat (Ferber novel), 192
Show Boat (film), 226, 227, 230,
    231–232, 234, 241–242, *257*,
    282, 283, 284, 295
Show Boat (musical), *135*, 142–143,
    149, 151–152, 153, 155, 156, 157,
    192, 193, 195, 197, 206, 223
Shuffle Along (musical review),
    57–59, 60, 62, 63, 64, 65, 66, 68,
    72, 73, 91
Sigma Tau Sigma fraternity, 74, 87
Simon the Cyrenian (play), 48–49, 55
Sims, 28
Sissle, Noble, 58
Sklar, George, 226

Smith, Bessie, 207
Socialism, 229, 243, 245
Song of Freedom (film), 238, 241, 243, 258, 295
Sons (film), 243
South Africa, 240, 312
Soviet Union, xiii–xiv, 213
  concert tour (1936), 239, 243, 279–280
  criticism of, 246
  film industry, 243
  Germany and, 324, 330
  Goldman, Emma, 95
  Great Terror, 281
  Paul, Jr. and, 280–281
  politics, 239, 286–287
  praise of, 232, 235–236, 245, 288
  purges in, 289–290, 293–294, 296, 303, 304–305
  Spanish Civil War, 285, 291, 295, 303
  visit to (1934–1935), 216–217, 218–223, 243, 251
  visit to (1937), 262, 287–288
  World War II, 304
Spain
  civil war in, 266, 267, 268, 277, 285, 287, 291–293, 295–296, 303, 314
  Paul travels to, 297–302
  refugees from, 321–322
  United States and, 303
Spectator (newspaper), 167
Spenser, Edmund, 168
Spirituals
  Paul and, 8–9, 45, 74, 87–88, 96, 139, 140–141, 148, 236, 243–244
  Soviet Union, 219–220
Stage Society, 239
Stalin, Joseph, 213, 219, 286
  Great Terror, 281
  purges of, 235, 246, 289–290, 303, 304–305
  World War II, 312
Stanislavsky, Konstantin, 81
"Steal Away to Jesus" (song), 220
Steichen, Edward, 134, 207, 255
Stevedore (Peters and Sklar play), 220, 226, 258, 288
Stotesbury, Louis W., 71, 72
Stravinsky, Igor, 216
Strictly Dishonorable (play), 158
Sumner, Minnie, 53
Sunday Worker (newspaper), 286, 326
The Sun Never Sets (play), 295
The Sun (newspaper), 77
Sweden, 223, 323

Taboo (play), 55, 56–57, 59
Talent, Arthur, 306–307
Tass (Soviet news agency), interview with, 219, 220
Television, 329
Tennyson, Pen, 330
Theater
  Paul and, 55–59, 62–68, 226
  race relations, 48–49, 59, 72, 75, 77–79, 138, 143, 157, 166, 316–317
  Soviet Union, 220
Theta Sigma fraternity, 74
Thomas, Rachel, 273
Thorp, Tom, 30
Thorpe, Jim, 69
Tibbett, Laurence, 159
Time and Tide (newspaper), 168
Times. See London Times
Times of India (newspaper), 225, 241
Tin Pan Alley jazz, 216
Titterton, W. R., 174–176, 190–192, 200
Torrence, Ridgely, 49
Toscanini, Arturo, 174

Toussaint L'Ouverture (play), 239
Toynbee, Arnold, 228
Tukhachevsky, Mikhail Nikolaevich,
    222, 290

Uncle Tom's Cabin (film), 284
Underground Railroad, 5
Union of Soviet Socialist Republics.
    See Soviet Union
United Kingdom
    concerts (1928), 154–155
    fascism, 303
    fascism in, 296
    Germany and, 302
    Paul and, 59, 61–62
    Spanish Civil War, 291, 322
    World War II, 304, 312, 330–331
United States
    fascism, 296, 303
    Spanish Civil War, 291, 303, 322
    theater, 316–317
    World War II, 304
United States House of
    Representatives, 6
United States Supreme Court, 6, 285
Unity Theater Group (London),
    284, 295, 317, 318, 329
Universal Negro Improvement
    Association, 44
University of Pennsylvania Medical
    School, 6, 15

Vale, Rena M., 238
Vandeveer, 14
Van Gelder, Robert, 23
Van Gyseghem, Andre, 204, 205,
    226
Vanity Fair (magazine), 207
Van Vechten, Carl, 86, 92, 93, *133*,
    186, 297, 325
Van Vechten, Fania, 319, 325

Van Volkenberg, Ellen, 166
Varney, Walter, 143, 149
Vesey, Denmark, 328, 329
Victoria Eugenie (queen of Spain),
    224
Victor Records, 93
Vidor, King, 234, 236
Voodoo (play), 59, 62, 63, 66, 68,
    70, *115*
Vosseler, 13, 14

Wales (UK), 156, 165, 329–330
Wallace, Edgar, 208, 224
Washington, Booker T., 31, 39
Washington, D. C., race riots in,
    35–36
Washington, Fredi, 100, *122*, *248*
Washington, George, 5
Weary Blues (Hughes play), 328
Webster, Margaret, 243, 327
Weinberger, Harry, 83
Welch, Elizabeth, 238, *258*
Wells, H. G., 155
Welsh, Robert, 77
Welsh miners' relief fund, 156
West, Dr., 184
West, Rebecca, 96, 206
West Indies, 311
West Virginia eleven (football team),
    29–30
Whale, James, 233, 234
What I Want from Life (Cousins),
    208–209
White, George C., 6
White, Walter, 86, 90, 137, 240
Whiteman, Paul, 152
Who's Who in Colored America, 140
Wiborg, Mary Hoyt, 55, 59, 61, 66,
    67, 68
Wilcoxon, Henry, *263*, 283
Wilder, Thornton, 319

Wilkins, Roy, 138

Williams, Claude, 238

Wills, Elder, 238

Wilson, Frank, 193, *248*

Wilson, Woodrow, 5, 24

Witherspoon Church, 5–6

Woolcott, Alexander, 56, 70, 77, 192

The Worker (newspaper), 241

The World (newspaper), 77

World Telegram (newspaper), 320

World War I, 31, 37, 176

World War II

  origins of, 303–304, 312–313, 322

  outbreak of, 330–331

Wright, Corinne, 319

Wright, Richard, 326

Wyatt, Thomas, 168

Wycherly, Margaret, 55, 57, 61

Yergan, Max, 240, *270*, 308, 325, 326

Ziegfeld, Florenz, 149

CPSIA information can be obtained
at www.ICGtesting.com
Printed in the USA
JSHW080158020323
38371JS00002BA/278